£14.00

PLACES OF THE MIND

PLACES OF THE MIND

The Life and Work of
James Thomson ('B.V.')

TOM LEONARD

JONATHAN CAPE
LONDON

First published 1993
© Tom Leonard 1993
Jonathan Cape, 20 Vauxhall Bridge Road, London SW1V 2SA

The publisher acknowledges subsidy
from the Scottish Arts Council
towards the publication of this volume

A CIP catalogue record for this book
is available from the British Library

ISBN 0–224–03118–X

Printed in Great Britain by
Mackays of Chatham PLC, Chatham, Kent

for Eric

who thought well of people

CONTENTS

SWEDENBORG: *The Divine Love and Wisdom*

Everyone who believes that God is a Man can affirm for himself that there are infinite things in God. And because He is a Man He has a body and everything pertaining to a body. Thus He has a face, breast, abdomen, loins and feet, for without these He would not be a Man. And since He has these, He also has eyes, ears, nostrils, a mouth and a tongue; so also the things within a man as the heart and the lungs and the parts which depend on these, all of which taken together, make man to be man. In a created man, these parts are many, and regarded in their connections are innumerable. But in God-Man they are infinite. Nothing whatever is lacking, hence He has infinite perfection . . . The whole heaven consisting of myriads of myriads of angels is, in its universal form, like a man, likewise each society of heaven, be it larger or smaller . . . It cannot be described how many things there are in heaven. And because the Divine makes heaven, it is clearly evident that there are infinite things in Very Man Who is God.

JAMES THOMSON: *(in the margin of his copy of the above)*

We cannot believe in this God-man without a correlative God-woman. The Papists fill up the gap with the Virgin Mary, a sort of Hagar taking the place of the true Sarah. Even the quasi-Pantheistic impersonation of nature (as in Spenser's wonderful Cantos on Mutabilitie) is open identity of the sexes.

SPENSER: *Cantos of Mutabilitie* Canto VII, Verse 5

Then forth issewed (great goddesse) great dame *Nature*,
With goodly port and gracious Maiesty;
Being far greater and more tall of stature
Than any of the gods or powers on hie;
Yet certes by her face and physnomy,
Whether she man or woman inly were,
That could not creature well descry;
For, with a veile that wimpled every where,
Her head and face was hid, that mote to none appeare.

PREFACE AND
ACKNOWLEDGMENTS

THE DEBATE between the behavioural determinist and those who believe in the universal democracy of the individual consciousness, is not of recent development. Some have seen in it the debate between a law-making angry God the Father of the Old Testament, and a loving and forgiving Jesus Christ, of the New. For a person to be born having already inherited the responsibility for making a perfect father so angry, the children must needs have been very bad indeed. But if one was convinced that in essence one was very bad indeed, it might prove difficult to be convinced at the same time that one was worthy in any capacity to be loved. A belief in the redemptive superhumanity of Christ might be founded therefore on the startling proposition that Christ had the capacity to love that which his father had not thought necessarily lovable at all. It was but a step to the silent thought that the triumph of the Son in his Atonement was not to atone for the sins of humanity against the Father, but to atone for the sins of the Father against humanity.

If the Father thought one's body loathsome and worthy of torment, it might be liberating to be assured one should on the contrary love one's self as well as one's neighbour. If one loved one's self, body and all, one might even be able to love one's neighbour, body and all, without feeling too guilty about it, or without thinking there must be something wrong with them if they felt the same way about you. But whilst loving one's own body, one should nonetheless clear one's mind and heart of what was contrary to love: anger or the desire for vengeance. One should forgive the Father, in other words, for hating you so much. This, eighty years before Freud's *Interpretation of Dreams*, was the burden of Shelley's lyric drama *Prometheus Unbound*, in which the tortured Prometheus forgives Jove for torturing him, and thus brings about, through the agency of the god of Necessity – called Demogorgon – the overthrow of Jove from Heaven, and the union of the male Prometheus with the cosmic female creative force, Asia. Prometheus is not actually Jove's son, but has sided with humanity against the angry god. When Prometheus accepts himself in his physical suffering and liberates himself from the desire for vengeance, he becomes of necessity more fit to rule in conjunction with the creative female, than the old god of repression who caused the suffering in the first place.

In the mythology of the German poet Novalis, unity between man and Nature had existed in a past golden age, but the two had become disjunct, and only fundamental change could bring about a reunion. For both Novalis as well as Shelley, the making of poetry could be part of this process. The poet James Thomson on the other hand, who included reference to Novalis and Shelley in his working pseudonym, wrote that making art was essentially a compensatory activity, however great the art that was produced. The pseudonym that Thomson used for most of his writing life was 'B.V.', which was short for 'Bysshe Vanolis': Bysshe as in Percy Bysshe Shelley, Vanolis as an anagram of Novalis, whose work he translated.

Thomson was born in Port Glasgow in 1834, the first son of a dressmaker and a merchant seaman. The mother was a follower of the millennialist preacher Edward Irving, the father someone who only seriously took up with religion after he had been disabled by a stroke. The family moved to London in 1840, and on the terminal illness of Mrs Thomson two years later, the eight-year-old James was placed in a London Scottish asylum. In 1850 he began training as an army schoolmaster, and was employed as such from 1854 until 1862. Thereafter in London he worked as a secretary in the merchant's office of the freethinker Charles Bradlaugh, contributing regular poetry and prose to Bradlaugh's campaigning secularist weekly *National Reformer*. Thomson taught himself French, German and Italian, translated Heine as well as Novalis, and made pioneering translations of Leopardi. In the 1870s he was for a short time abroad in Colorado then was a war correspondent in Spain. He parted company with Bradlaugh in 1875, and from his lodgings in Pimlico then Bloomsbury, earned an uncertain living as a freelance contributor to other ephemeral journals. He corresponded with William Michael Rossetti over Shelley's work, and was a guest both at Rossetti's and at George Meredith's home. In 1880 and 1881 he published in succession two collections of poetry and one of prose. He died in poverty and alcoholism the following year.

Such are the bones of the life on which the following book hopes to put a little flesh, and to tell of James Thomson's work without assuming prior knowledge in the reader. There has been an amount of literary criticism over the years, but it is a century since a new biography of Thomson has been published. One problem has been that he destroyed most of his personal documents as he was approaching his thirty-fifth birthday, when with impending unemployment and with the death of some friends, he was prey to a particular mood of unhappiness in his lodgings. Past intermittent lapses into heavy drinking may have increased his desire for self-disavowal. At any rate he wanted as he put it to 'consume the past', the better to 'face the future come in what guise it may'. It was then he began writing 'The City of Dreadful Night', the great and uncompromising poem which took him four years to finish, and which paradoxically has made his name in European Literature secure.

It is not the intention of the work which follows to proceed either by thesis and demonstration, or to propose causal models of biography. What follows, having been made, can be described as a shape, containing a biography, made slowly in response to the shape of the Art of another. That at any rate is how its author best wishes to describe it. The book began 'officially' as a postgraduate thesis in 1976 at Glasgow University, but has changed out of all recognition since the work done then. It really in any case began some years before that, when the six verses of the opening 'Proem' to James Thomson's 'The City of Dreadful Night' were encountered in Hugh MacDiarmid's anthology *The Golden Treasure of Scottish Poetry*. The energy derived from that occasion has remained the driving source ever since. Though not now written for an academic audience, this book gives sometimes pernickety sources in its notes, for instance in the dating of events taken from the diaries. These are given to save time with fiddly matters for other researchers in the future. The great debt to researchers of the past will be evident enough within.

There are too many people who have helped me with this book for me to remember them all. I will mention a few, and trust that those overlooked will not feel slighted. From the English Literature department of Glasgow University I thank four men: Edwin Morgan, who enabled me to begin the work as a postgraduate student, and was one of my early tutors; Patrick Reilly, who was also a tutor; Marshall Walker (now of Waikato University, New Zealand), who showed daily kindness towards me in the illness that stopped the work in the 1970s; and Philip Hobsbaum, now Professor of English Literature at Glasgow, who always believed I had a book to finish, and who has been of great help in reading through the final manuscript. Needless to say no errors in the following pages are due to these people, and the opinions implicit in the book are my own and not such as with which any of them would necessarily agree.

I thank Hugh McIntyre of Port Glasgow for a helpful correspondence about local history; Timothy Looney of Cahir, Tipperary, for showing me round and sending full details with photographs of the grave of Matilda Weller when he located it after I had gone away; Valerie Shepherd of Nottingham Polytechnic for taking me round Kirby Muxloe and Quorn; Adam MacNaughtan, folksinger and proprietor of 'Adam Books' secondhand bookshop in Glasgow, for loaning me ('for as long as you need it') the very rare complete *Secularist* 1876–1877: I hope a Scottish or at least a British public library buys it from him. And I thank Mrs. A. Enid Leeming and her son Bruce Brodie Leeming, for contacting me and allowing me to consult and quote from the research of Charles Brodie, as described in the appendix.

The work has meant consultation in libraries and record offices in Oxford, Glasgow, Edinburgh, London, Dublin, Cork, Greenock, and Jersey. Respectively in these places the libraries consulted were the Bodleian; the Mitchell and Glasgow University Library; the National Library of Scotland; the British Library, Tower Hamlets Library and the Bishopsgate Institute; the National Library of Ireland and Trinity College Library; Cork University Library and Cork City Library; the Watt Memorial Library; Jersey District Library and the Library of the Society of Jersey. It might be wrong to single out specific libraries or librarians but I do thank especially Steven Tomlinson of the Bodleian Library Oxford, and add that at the Bishopsgate Institute it was very cheering to meet people so evidently committed to the public library service and the sharing of knowledge. Again in London, Nicolas Walter of the Rationalist Press Association in Islington was of great help in giving me photocopies of material which he subsequently donated to the Bodleian Library, but which in photocopy I was able to study at home.

I thank the Scottish Arts Council for a grant in 1984 which enabled me to pick up the book again seriously and to travel in Ireland. The book was brought within sight of its end during a six-months' tenure as writer-in-residence shared between Glasgow University and Strathclyde University from October 1991. I thank the departments of English at both these universities for providing me with a machine of the same make as the one I use at home. Some crucial work was done in both universities, especially – I mean it not too drily – at weekends when nobody was around.

It is appropriate that Jonathan Cape of 20 Vauxhall Bridge Road should be publishing the book. It was at numbers 240 and 230 (both now gone) that Thomson wrote the bulk of 'The City of Dreadful Night'. I thank Cathie Thomson for linking Cape and myself. As regards house style and such matters, I approach prose writing with a prescriptive grammar in one hand and John Clare's words on a banner in the other: 'grammer in learning is like tyranny in government – confound the bitch I'll never be her slave'. The inconsistencies that I hope you will faithfully find in the following pages are, again, my own and not the publisher's. There is the occasional idiomatic or Scottish turn of phrase, as where Thomson and Grant 'went a walk', or where a 'burn' or little river will come down a hill. The word 'read' reiterated towards the end of Chapter Eleven, should be pronounced 'red', which is to say it is the past participle.

Lastly and firstly I thank my wife Sonya. For three-quarters of our twenty-one years together work on this book has been around in one form or another, albeit for some years as just a photograph of Thomson on the wall. This is Sonya's book as well as mine, and I am grateful to her.

Tom Leonard
Glasgow, July 25th, 1992

Part One:
ANGEL

CHAPTER ONE

I N EARLY NINETEENTH-century Scotland the public statement of Christian beliefs known as the Westminster Confession of Faith was
commonly read and learned in schools and homes along with the Shorter
and the Longer Catechisms.[1] Approved by the General Assembly of the
Church of Scotland in 1647, the Confession stated, in Chapter Three,
that 'some men and angels are predestinated unto everlasting life' and
'their number is so certain and definite, that it cannot be either increased
or diminished'. This 'elect unto glory' was chosen by God 'before the
foundation of the world was laid . . . without any foresight of faith or
good works, or perseverance in either of them, or any other thing in
the creature, as conditions, or causes moving him thereunto'.

> Wherefore they who are elected being fallen in Adam, are redeemed
> by Christ; are effectually called unto faith in Christ by his Spirit working
> in due season; are justified, adopted, sanctified, and kept by his power
> through faith unto salvation. Neither are any other redeemed by Christ,
> effectually called, justified, sanctified, and saved, but the elect only.[2]

In 1825 the Parish of Row near Helensburgh in the Firth of Clyde
appointed a new minister, the Rev. John MacLeod Campbell. Campbell
thought many of his parishioners were influenced by their notion of the
Elect to see the Atonement as a kind of limited insurance policy drawn
up for a predetermined number of policy holders: 'instead of resting on
the character of God as revealed in Christ, they looked upon the death of
Christ as so much suffering – the purchase-money of heaven to a certain
number, to whom it infallibly secured heaven.'[3] Christianity became a
kind of distorted selfishness based on fear: 'so long as the individual is
uncertain of being the subject of love to his God, and is still without
any sure hold of his personal safety in the prospect of eternity, it is in
vain to attempt to induce him to serve God under the power of any
purer motive than the desire to win God's love for himself, and so to
secure his own happiness.'[4]

3

What each individual needed, Campbell believed, was to have 'personal assurance' of God's love as something already given and constantly present, not as something to be won or to fear being withdrawn. But such assurance could not be 'unless Christ had died *for all*, and unless the Gospel announced him as *'the gift of God to every human being'*.[5] The Atonement had to be understood as both universal and individually specific; Christ had not died for the generality of 'humanity' nor the exclusiveness of 'the elect'. He had died for each and every specific person alone, in that person's being: the love shown by Christ was presently and constantly available, throughout each person's existence. This forgiveness and love was not a thing to be owned, or achieved, but was a given state of being to be realised and acknowledged. Don't try to do good to win God's love; realise God's love and you will try to do good.

Campbell's preaching stirred up fervour. There were stories of local people on their deathbeds having strange powers and visions of 'a new dawn' in the church.[6] But the greatest stir came about with the publication in 1829 of the memoir of a young woman, Isabella Campbell, who had died of tuberculosis two years earlier in the farmhouse of Fernicarry at the head of the Gareloch.[7] The author of the memoir was a friend of Campbell's, Rev. Robert Story, who as Isabella's minister had often visited Isabella with MacLeod Campbell during Isabella's last illness. The 482-page memoir *Peace in Believing* quickly went through several editions. It told how, after the death of her father and her brother, Isabella had experienced religious doubts until before she died she found 'peace in believing' through 'personal assurance' of salvation. This she had described enthusiastically to her many bedside visitors, and the last moments of her life were described in the memoir like the passing of a beautiful saint: 'she opened her eyes suddenly, and clasping her hands looked upwards with a look of such inconceivable transport as made many present exclaim, "Surely God is here!" . . . Her whole countenance seemed to shine, and all present confessed they had never pictured to themselves an object half so lovely.'[8]

There had been constant prayer meetings round Isabella's deathbed led by her sister Mary. A visitor at the time of Isabella's death was struck by the attitude of Mary and her friends:

I was with them for two or three days after she died, assisting to make their mournings, and truly I thought them most wonderful people. Instead of mourning, Miss Campbell and some of her friends who came to visit her, seemed to be rejoicing in spirit; and I actually heard them say that they thought it ought to be white, instead of black, that Mary should wear for her. Certainly they have no cause to mourn on her account, and it shews their want of selfishness, when they can rejoice in her happiness, instead of mourning their own loss. I was, indeed, sometimes almost ready to think that I had never been amongst real Christians before, and that I myself was only one in name. They can talk with such frequency of their rapturous feelings of joy which they experience, their faith seems to carry them so far, that when speaking of the joys of the heavenly world, one would think that faith is almost swallowed up in sight. When the name of Jesus is mentioned they are filled with rapture of love, and their love to one another seems to burn with fervency; and in a word, they seem to be altogether lifted above the world, and to live only for God.[9]

Mary Campbell herself now became a focus of religious enthusiasm in the region. In becoming this she was helped on her way by another minister friend of Story's who came on preaching tours in the region in 1828 and 1829. This minister was called Edward Irving.

Irving had been an Edinburgh University divinity student at the same time as Story, and when preaching in the Firth of Clyde he stayed in Story's manse at Rosneath. Irving's own Church of Scotland parish was in London and in that city he had early acquired a formidable reputation as an orator. Soon after his arrival in 1823 his sermons had become fashionable with London society, and notable literary figures were amongst those who knew him and who praised his powers of public speaking. De Quincey called him 'by many degrees, the greatest orator of his age',[10] and Coleridge – whom Irving used to visit weekly at his home in Highgate – wrote: 'I hold that Edward Irving possesses more of the spirit and purpose of the first Reformers, that he has more of the Head and the Heart, the Life, the Unction, and the genial power of Martin Luther, than any man now alive.'[11] Some of the society and literary notables became disenchanted with Irving's growing involvement, from 1826, in interpreting the prophetic books of the Bible. But he remained able by his oratory still to attract large if no longer fashionable congregations. The same Greenock publisher who issued in 1829 Storey's *Peace in Believing*, issued that same year a pamphlet by Irving called *The Nature and Use of the Gift of Tongues*.[12] Irving preached that the 'miraculous gifts' of speaking in unknown tongues, miraculous healing, and the ability to prophesy, were phenomena that would be restored to the Church on Christ's Second Coming. This, he told the huge crowds who attended his sermons, was an event soon to take place. The French Revolution could be interpreted as the opening of the Seventh Seal of *Revelation*. The days of the 'latter rain' were at hand: Christ's Second Coming, and the founding of the New Jerusalem, could be expected in about forty years.[13]

Whereas Campbell had preached that Christ is presently available to every person throughout their existence, Irving preached that the Holy Spirit had been presently available to Christ on earth: it was this which had kept Christ's human nature sinless, and this which had enabled Christ to work miracles. This was the power of the Holy Spirit given to the Apostles at Pentecost as a gift to the Church, and only 'the evil heart of unbelief'[14] had caused the power subsequently to disappear. It followed that if the unbelief was to disappear, perhaps the gifts would return. This at any rate was how his words were interpreted by Mary Campbell, who by the end of 1829 was in bed apparently suffering from the same illness which had killed her now locally famous sister.[15] Irving later described how his preaching then affected Mary: 'She came to see what for six or seven years I had been preaching in London, that all the works of Christ were done by the man anointed with the Holy Ghost, and not by the God mixing himself up with the man . . . She straightway argued, if Jesus as a man in my nature spake and thus performed mighty works by the Holy Ghost, which he even promiseth to me, then ought I by the same nature, by the same Spirit, to do likewise "the works which he did, and greater works than these".'[16] On Sunday March 30th 1830 the prayer session round Mary's bed was interrupted:

> When, in the midst of their devotion, the Holy Ghost came with mighty power upon the sick woman as she lay in her weakness, and constrained her to speak at great length, and with superhuman strength, in an unknown tongue, to the astonishment of all who heard, and to her own great edification and enjoyment in God.[17]

The 'gift of tongues' had come to Fernicarry, and within a week it had spread across the Firth of Clyde to Port Glasgow. In that town lived two of Mary's enthusiastic friends, the shipbuilding brothers George and James MacDonald. Former members of Campbell's congregation, they had added Irving's millenialism to their store of beliefs, and had taken to preaching in the open air themselves. But their house was also host to the ubiquitous tuberculosis, and their sister Margaret, like Mary Campbell across the water, was confined to her bed. When news of Mary's speaking in tongues came with the ferry from Rosneath, Margaret MacDonald launched into effusions of her own:

> She said, 'There will be a mighty baptism of the spirit this day,' and then she broke forth in a most marvellous setting forth of the wonderful works of God, and as if her own weakness had been altogether lost in

6

the strength of the Holy Ghost, continued with little or no intermission for two or three hours, in mingled praise, prayer and exhortation. At dinner time James and George came home as usual, whom she then addressed at great length, concluding with a solemn prayer for James that he might *at that time* be endowed with the power of the Holy Ghost. Almost instantly James calmly said, 'I have got it.' He walked to the window and stood silent for a moment or two . . . He then with a step and manner of the most indescribable majesty, walked up to Margaret's bedside and addressed her in those words of the twentieth psalm, 'arise and stand upright'. He repeated the words, took her by the hand, and she arose.[18]

James sent a letter over to Mary Campbell 'commanding her in the name of the Lord to arise'. Mary afterwards described how she felt reading James MacDonald's letter:

As I read every word came home with power, and when I came to the command to arise, it came home with a power which no words can describe; it was felt to be indeed the voice of Christ; it was such a voice as could not be resisted; a mighty power was instantaneously exerted upon me; I felt as if I had been lifted from off the earth, and all my diseases taken from off me at the voice of Christ. I was verily made in a moment to stand upon my feet, leap and walk, sing and rejoice.[19]

Across she came to the MacDonalds' house in Port Glasgow. James and George themselves both shortly began speaking in the tongues during prayers, and within a short period the house had become 'filled with people every day from all parts of England, Scotland, and Ireland'.[20] Not that everyone was impressed. A local minister accused Mary Campbell of being a hysteric who, having burst a blood vessel on her lung, had been pronounced healed and in good health by her doctor two weeks before her supposed 'miraculous cure'.[21] Nor did he find the exhibitions of the 'unknown tongues' any more convincing: 'After a short silence, during which she kept her eyes fixed upwards, she commenced talking in unintelligible *gibberish*, and prayed that Christ would give to some of his members present, the gift of interpretation, that the precious words of the Spirit might not be lost, but that the church might be edified. She continued speaking her *unknown* tongue for a considerable time, but the gift of interpretation was not bestowed; although one young man stood for upwards of half an hour, motionless as a statue; with his eyes fixed intently upon the ceiling, as if he expected to see the Spirit burst through the roof.'[22]

Amongst the believers, the 'tongues' were at first thought to be genuine though unknown earthly languages, a gift from God to enable missionary work to be done abroad without the chore of language-learning.[23] This was Irving's own opinion when word of the Port Glasgow happenings reached him in London. Nor was his friend Coleridge, initially, among the sceptics. A visiting American recorded his reaction to Irving's showing him an account sent him of the Port Glasgow events:

> 'I make no question but that it is the work of the HOLY SPIRIT, and a foretaste of that spiritual power which is to be poured forth on the reviving Church of Scotland . . . Was not the case the same in the apostles' days? Doth not St Paul indicate the fact when he says, "He that speaketh in an unknown tongue, speaketh not unto men but unto GOD, for no man understandeth him; howbeit in his spirit he speaketh mysteries" [see 1 Cor. 14:2]. And is not the whole of St Paul's argument in the 14th Chapter of 1st Corinthians, founded upon the supposition that the saints then spoke in tongues which no man understood? . . . These events,' said he, 'in my opinion, are nothing less than the outpouring of the Spirit, promised in all ages to the Church, and long withheld from the deadness of its faith.'[24]

Irving and his congregation at the National Scotch Church, Regent Square, began to pray for the 'manifestations of the gifts' to be bestowed in London. They did not come quickly, but finally the morning service before a congregation of 2,000 on Sunday October 30th 1831, a witness reported, 'was very unexpectedly interrupted by the well-known voice of one of the sisters, who, finding she was unable to restrain herself, and respecting the regulation of the Church, rushed into the vestry, and gave vent to utterance; whilst another, as I understand, from the same impulse, ran down the side aisle and out of the church, through the principal door. The sudden, doleful, and unintelligible sounds, being heard by all the congregation, produced the utmost confusion'.[25] In succeeding weeks services threatened to become uncontrollable as more and more people, especially women, found themselves 'in the power'. Commonly a loud outburst of incomprehensible speech would be followed by exclamations and exhortations of a Biblically phrased character, taken by others as translation of what had gone before.

There was a problem with all this regarding the owners of Regent Square Church, which was the official place of worship for the Royal Caledonian Asylum, an asylum for the orphaned and indigent children of Scottish servicemen and marines in London but not entitled to parochial relief. The children had a reserved place in the church gallery each week, and the trust deeds owned by the asylum specified that church worship be 'according to the doctrines, forms of worship and mode of discipline of the Established Church of Scotland'.[26] *The Times* was amongst those who repeatedly attacked the goings-on, calling the behaviour 'a disgrace at once to European reason and human civilisation'.[27] It campaigned for the trustees to remove Irving from his pulpit, and on May 2nd 1832 the Presbytery of London ruled that he had 'rendered himself unfit to remain the minister of the National Scotch Church aforesaid, and ought to be removed therefrom in pursuance of the conditions of the trust-deed of the said church.'[28]

About 800 of the Regent Square congregation moved on with Irving, settling after a few months in premises in Newman Street, off Oxford Street.[29] The following year the Church of Scotland – that 'Babylonian confederacy'[30] as Irving now called it – removed him altogether from the Church of Scotland ministry. MacLeod Campbell had already been expelled in 1831. In Irving's opinion the clergy who made up the contemporary Church of Scotland lacked the spiritual integrity of their Reformation forefathers: 'The gifts of the Spirit for the office are not looked for by the Presbyters, but certificates of professors, and petty attainments in literature and science'.[31] The events in Port Glasgow and London had been an attempt to restore the church to the days of its early apostlehood. Welcoming the first news of the miraculous events at Fernicarry and Port Glasgow, Irving wrote: 'I believe that the day of carpenters and fishermen is come again, and the day of masters in arts and doctors in divinity is gone by.'[32]

But the new church which developed round Irving's expelled congregation moved quickly from its Scottish Presbyterian origins. Free of its Scottish context, it was taken over by ex-Anglicans, prosperous founding members of a group with which Irving had been connected in his interpretation of the Prophetic Books since 1826.[33] A whole new church structure was laid down by these ex-Anglicans speaking 'in the power'; and as Irving never claimed to speak so himself, the Holy Spirit had to be obeyed. One of the first effects was to eliminate the practice of inspired declamation from the women in the congregation. The women were put at the bottom of a structure of command in which at the top were 'apostles', then the 'angel' or minister, then presbyters or elders, then deacons. Women could only rise as high as deaconesses for 'the visiting of solitary females', but women speaking in the tongues – the most noticeable feature of the millenarian movement in London and Port Glasgow – were now to be discouraged. That was the job of the 'apostles' at the top. As for the women: 'it was declared that although the Lord would direct His apostles through them, or through infants even, whenever it might please Him to do so, still it was not His will or way, and only to the dishonour of the man so to use them'. It was also 'declared' that if any woman 'has had, or imagines she has had, revelations or spiritual experiences of any kind', interpretation of this should be referred up the structure as far as the apostles if need be, and the reply could be passed back down through the hierarchy; 'and even were its result to be the infliction of some ecclesiastical censure, the sisterly deaconess would be at her side to share and soften it.'[34] In other words the women had to shut up and stop setting the pace, or leave. Many did. The men were in charge now, with Corinthians 1 14:34 – 'let your women keep silence in churches' – as validation. Irving himself remained as minister – technically, as 'angel' – to his congregation in London, though now under the 'apostles' in the rank of decision making and tongues-interpretation.

The new hierarchy did not go down well with the fraternal congregations on the Firth of Clyde, where the MacDonalds had hired a private chapel in Greenock. Neither they nor MacLeod Campbell would have anything to do with the two leading 'apostles' of the new church when they came north to attempt a fusion of forces.[35] However a London-approved church did finally open in Greenock under the care of 'angel' Walter Tait, a former Church of Scotland minister in Edinburgh. The church opened on August 31st 1834, and the *Greenock Telegraph* carried a report:

> On such an occasion it was naturally expected that some of the peculiarities of their form of worship would be manifested; accordingly in a few seconds after Mr Tait entered the pulpit for the forenoon service, Mrs Provan, a very respectable member of the congregation, cried out, in an awfully shrill and vehement voice, 'This is the place! This is the house of God, and the gate of heaven! Enter in ye people, and rejoice!' etc. etc. The sounds were so very unearthly and astounding, that it was only those who were very near her that understood the words. There was, however, no exhibition of the 'unknown tongues'; which we believe will ultimately form no part of their creed.[36]

Then Irving, though now ill, travelled north to Greenock himself. The local newspaper again reported on October 25th, albeit misspelling his name:

> Mr Irvine, the great unknown tongue apostle, arrived at Greenock on Tuesday from Liverpool, via the Glasgow steamer, and has taken up

residence among the disciples in the west for a time. The Rev. gentleman looks tolerably well, although still having the appearance of indisposition about him. It is anticipated that Mr. I. will take part in the worship of the church lately planted at Greenock. This sect are increasing slowly in numbers while the Campbellites, under the auspices of Mr MacDonald, are decreasing by divisions on different points of doctrine. It appears now that Mr Tait by his labours will be able, with the assistance of the London Society, to keep a stronghold for the Irvinites in the west of Scotland. Several of his disciples from the metropolis have visited Greenock since the foundation of the church there, and are zealous in preaching their peculiar tenets on the high-ways and bye-ways.[37]

Irving moved on to Glasgow, from where he wrote a letter expressing guilt at having left behind his congregation with many of whom he evidently retained a special bond: 'Oftentimes I think it is the Lord's gentle hand, breaking that bond by degree between me and my flock, which threatened to grow up into a kind of necessity, and even to pass over into idolatry. O how I love them! how I am thankful to them! how I am laden with their benefits! And I am sure that their love to me is stronger than my love to them, and I do see it is of the great goodness and tenderness of God to take order that such affection should be stayed from passing over into unholiness; and that he hath done us a great favour to put us so far asunder, and for such a time, that we might try our hearts, and prove ourselves that our mutual love is in the Lord.'[38]

One follower of Irving not separated by his return north was a dressmaker from Port Glasgow who married in London in January 1834 and returned later in the year to her native town. The extent of her millenialist enthusiasm was evidenced in a letter written to her future sister-in-law on December 16th 1831, at the height of the controversy in London;

Dear Ann,

I am very happy to hear you are so well and comfortable, as far as visable things are concerned, every blissing should be receved as from the hand of God – I have little to say about myself – but at this time I am wandering about in Sheepskins and goatSkins and in Dens and Caves of the Earth, My dear Ann I am anxious to lay up treasures where moth or rust cannot enter, and at this moment I am called on to forsack all for Christ – and I am happy for he maks me to rejoice in suffering and I believe this is the jerusalem that I am commanded to stay in, till the comforter be sent and we have not waited in vain for the drops are falling but soon there shall be a plentyfull shower for the Lord is coming to water his weary hineratance, oh Ann I cannot tell the life and light that I feel in the midst of trouble – I should be glade to see your face in the flesh, and that you might be a partaker of my joy, do not think I mean not what I say for out of the abundance of the heart the mouth speaketh adeiu   S. Kennedy   burn this scroll it is not fit to be seen by any but you   S Kennedy[39]

But Sarah did not see much of Irving in his new ministry north of the border, for he died on December 7th and was buried in the grounds of Glasgow Cathedral. Two weeks before Irving's death, on Sunday November 23rd, Sarah gave birth to a boy in Port Glasgow. The baby was given his father's name, and the following February James Thomson was baptised.

CHAPTER TWO

S ARAH KENNEDY WAS the daughter of Margaret Lawson, one of Port Glasgow's four midwives.[1] Mrs Kennedy was twice married and widowed.[2] Her first marriage was in 1791 to a George Parker in Edinburgh by whom she had a son John, who became a sailor.[3] Then in 1803 she married Alexander Kennedy in Glasgow,[4] by whom she had already borne Sarah almost five years before. On August 18th 1798 Sarah Kennedy was born in Blantyre 'daughter natural to Alexander Kennedy soldier in Lochaber Regiment and Margaret Lawson College Parish Glasgow'.[5] A sister to Sarah was born and called Margaret after her mother.

Sarah Kennedy's own marriage took place by licence at St Ann's, Limehouse, on January 12th 1834.[6] Her husband James, a merchant seaman eight years younger than herself, was the son of John Thomson and Helen Gow, and born on August 12th 1806 on the estate of Pitnacrea in the parish of Logierait, several miles south of Pitlochry in Perthshire.[7] James had come to Port Glasgow with the rest of his family some time between his second and tenth year. There were twin sisters Helen and Susanna born in Perthshire in 1808,[8] and another sister Mary born in Port Glasgow in 1817.[9] Besides James and the twins plus Mary there was a brother Charles, and the oldest sister, Ann.[10] She was the Ann Thomson to whom Sarah Kennedy addressed her letter in 1831.[11]

John Thomson had worked as a weaver and small farmer in Perthshire. In Port Glasgow he found work in the Custom House,[12] though he remained poor enough to be remembered in the town as having slept some of his children in a trunk on the floor. This anecdote was recounted with relish regarding the 'airs and graces' thought by some townfolk to have later been adopted by one of the children in the trunk, Helen.[13] As Mrs McLarty, Helen in adult years inherited a sailmaking business from her deceased husband and lived in a large house at Clune Park on the edge of the town with her

13

sister Mary – also widowed after her sailor husband was drowned in shipwreck off the coast of Spain – and Ann, who never married.[14]

Sarah's child spent his early years in a town where there was a community of relatives, some of them children who could be his companions. His mother's sister Margaret had married in Port Glasgow only three weeks after Sarah's marriage in London.[15] Margaret had three young daughters within four years,[16] and these sometimes played with the boy James in the street.[17] There were also infant cousins of his Uncle Charles, and a cousin Helen born in the same year as himself to his aunt Helen McLarty.[18] Both the grandfather John Thomson on one side of the family and the grandmother Mrs Kennedy on the other lived in Church Street,[19] a street that ran down to the busy harbour connecting the city of Glasgow with foreign trade. In Church Street at its corner with Princes Street stood the house later claimed as the poet's birthplace.[20] The parish register entry of birth does not give the address, but simply reads 'James Thomson mariner and Sarah Kennedy his spouse had a lawful son born 23rd Nov 1834 Bapt. 28 Feb 1835. Called James.' However the entry was not actually made until May 1848,[21] six months before the boy's fourteenth birthday, and the spelling of the surname in the register is not in fact that used or signed in documents by the parents themselves.

Alone among his family Sarah Kennedy's husband adopted the spelling of the surname 'Thompson' with a 'p', English-fashion. 'James Thompson' is the name and signature on the marriage entry in the parish records of St Ann's Limehouse on January 12th 1834,[22] 'Sarah Thompson' is how Sarah signed herself until her death,[23] and 'James Thompson' is the name entered as first mate on the crew-lists of the 423-ton Greenock trader *Eliza Stewart* in the years 1837 to 1840.[24] That the infant James had a community of relatives during his first years in Port Glasgow is significant in that his merchant seaman father was away from home so much of the time on long voyages. Between June 1837 and September 1840 the *Eliza Stewart* made three voyages to China, the crew being enlisted and discharged each time at London. The first voyage took eleven months, the crew being discharged on May 25th 1838; for the second voyage the crew was re-enlisted less than a month later on June 22nd, and not discharged until June 14th the following year; six weeks later the crew signed up again, and were not discharged at London until September 14th 1840. In other words from before the boy James's third birthday until he was nearly six, he never saw his father except for periods of at most a few weeks every year. He still remembered these visits later as happy occasions, writing that 'father and mother were very happy together when he was at home';[25] his father, he added then, 'may have been a bit gay, in the sense of liking a social song and glass, being, I believe, much better looking and more attractive in company than either of his sons.'[26] Others remembered his father as a man who liked to recite poetry and to sing in company, a cheerful person who 'had a genius for mechanics and was always inventing things'.[27]

The town of Port Glasgow when Thomson was born had a population of about 6,000 people, which is to say about a sixth of the population of neighbouring Greenock – the largest sea-port in Scotland – about a mile west along the shore. Most of the ships entering or leaving Port Glasgow's two harbours traded with Glasgow city or other places on the Clyde; but an average of seven vessels each month arrived from abroad – America, the West Indies, the East Indies, Canada, the Mediterranean. The main import was timber, almost 28,000 tons of it being imported in the year of Thomson's birth. Much of this was stored in large warehouses on the shore front, while other such warehouses held alcohol and refined sugar, both of which were prominent in the trade of the place. The sea dominated local industry, the main manufactures being of rope, sail-cloth and canvas, whilst the town shipyards worked almost exclusively on the construction of the steamboats with which the Firth of Clyde had become internationally associated since Bell's *Comet* of 1812.[28]

The town itself was described by the local minister in 1839 for the forthcoming *Statistical Account in Scotland*: 'In its general appearance the town presents an aspect of neatness and regularity, not often to be met with. The streets are straight, and for the most part cross each other at right angles; while the houses, pretty nearly equal in size, and generally white-washed, give to the whole a light and uniform appearance.' The view from the hill overlooking Port Glasgow and the Firth he thought 'not surpassed in grandeur and loveliness even by the most admired scenes of which England, and perhaps even Europe, can boast.' But there was poverty. A soup kitchen gave out a quart of soup and a roll to each of the poor who had a ticket, and an average of 80 quarts was given out each day except Sunday – when it was shut. The soup kitchen had been launched partly 'to check intemperance among the poor', and intemperance was one thing the minister thought needed checking:

In the year 1790, with a population of 4,000, there were no less than 81 public houses in the town. It is gratifying to be able to state, that in March 1835, and with a population of about 6,000, the number of public houses had been reduced to 70. It would still be more gratifying to be able to add, that the practice of intemperance has diminished in the same proportion. Appearances, however, do not by any means warrant such a conclusion, and seem to indicate, that intemperance never prevailed among the lower classes of society to a wider and more alarming extent than in the present day.

Much of the drinking seems to have been done by the constantly changing dockside population. At any rate the minister, having expressed regret at the widespread drunkenness, wrote also: 'The inhabitants of this place are generally well-informed, diligent in business, and liberal in charity. They may be characterised also as a church-going people.'

In matters religious the 'gift of tongues' had by the time of the minister's report ceased to be a matter of public debate and scandal. George and James MacDonald had both died in 1835, and the MacDonalds' small circle of adherents made no more public noise. One of their followers regretted in a memorial biography that the power of the Holy Spirit had withdrawn locally 'into the retirement of the closet, or the circle of the few who alone have cherished it'.[29] Like the MacDonalds themselves he thought Irving's congregation had been led astray by 'men assuming the apostleship, and, by making the voice of the prophets subordinate to their superior office, gradually suppressing it'.[30] The writer himself though still felt confident of Christ's return sometime around 1844.

That church structured on Irving's congregation had continued its passage away from Presbyterianism. In July 1835 the last of twelve 'apostles' was ordained, and the following year the world was divided into 'tribes' for the purpose of missionary management. England was called 'the tribe of Judah, the seat of apostolic government'; Scotland was thought a bit small to have a tribe on its own:

> Scotland seemed too small, and was therefore combined with Switzerland; inasmuch as both were mountainous countries, and seemed to set forth 'dignified patriotism, though in small nations inhabiting poor countries.' They were taken for the tribe of Benjamin, and were committed to the care of Mr Drummond.[31]

Weekly communion was taken kneeling in the Anglican fashion, tithes were introduced, and by 1840, when it announced itself as the

'Catholic Apostolic Church', its clergy had begun to wear vestments.[32] The Greenock church was described that year as 'a small number of persons designating themselves the Holy Apostolical Congregation, but generally known by the name of Irvingites, on account of their holding the opinions of the late Edward Irving.'[33] For MacLeod Campbell it was a church 'the identity of which with the papacy is daily made more apparent to me'.[34] Mrs Thompson may have worshipped in Greenock, or she may have been one of those whom MacLeod Campbell had in mind when he wrote on Irving's death: 'I do not think that this event will of itself arrest any who have imbibed the system, though it may separate from them any whose bond was the man'.[35] At any rate Sarah Kennedy's bond with the man had been strong, and Irving remained a presence in the home in which James grew up with his mother. He remembered that his mother was not only 'mystically inclined with Edward Irving', having 'followed Irving from the Kirk when he was driven out'; she also kept his portrait on display, and books by Irving on the interpretation of prophecy were sometimes read by the young boy 'for the imagery'.[36]

Mary Campbell definitely stayed loyal to the new hierarchical order; in fact after marrying she lived with her husband as a lay preacher to some of the new sect's wealthy backers in England.[37] Her prosperity did not please the minister of Rosneath, Robert Story, when he noticed her up from England on a visit to the town: 'Look at any seamstress, labouring early and late for a miserable subsistence, and at your present condition, your very servant arrayed in silken attire . . . Where you are I know not, but of this I am persuaded, you are not where Isabella left you.'[38] Mary died in England in 1840, and around this time Sarah and her son James moved south from Port Glasgow to the east end of London.

James had by this time a sister two years younger than himself of whom he was 'very fond'.[39] Then she died, as he later put it, 'of measles caught from me'.[40] This in his opinion deepened a melancholy in his mother that he attributed firstly to the death of her stepbrother John Parker – drowned in shipwreck on the Goodwin Sands off Dover – who had been a favourite with her. But Sarah and the young James in London both had another cause for some unhappiness. Mr Thompson, when he returned from the China voyage with the *Eliza Stewart* in September 1840, was semi-paralysed from a stroke suffered at sea. He was paralysed down his right side, and though he subsequently recovered sufficiently to walk with a dragging motion of his right leg, his right arm never regained its power. Sarah tried to support the family by court dressmaking, a trade learned using money supplied by her mother.[41] But her husband was now unpredictable in his moods and, though there were conflicting accounts from relatives about how he behaved, he was understood by some to have become violent towards her.[42] He settled into what his son described as 'a permanent weakness of mind, not amounting to imbecility, but very, very different I should say, from his former brightness and decision'.[43] He also, in a way hitherto unassociated with him, now after his stroke became earnestly religious, and took his son 'to chapels where the members of the congregation ejaculated groaning responses to the minister's prayer, and to small meetings in a private room where the members detailed their spiritual experiences of the week'.[44]

Though Port Glasgow had its poverty and its poor housing, the East End of London presented poverty and poor housing on a much larger and more intense scale. The district of St Mary's in the parish of St-Georges-in-the-East where the family settled was the subject of a pioneering economic and social analysis in 1844.[45] The parish did not show London poverty at its worst, having been chosen for analysis as 'an example of the *average condition* of the poorer classes of the metropolis,' which meant it was 'a population entirely above the wretched system of sub-letting corners of the same room'. Nonetheless as an averagely poor district it was 'one of those composed of dingy streets, of houses of small dimensions and moderate elevation, very closely packed in ill-ventilated streets and courts, such as are commonly inhabited by the working classes of the east end'. Mary Ann Street, where the Thompsons lived in 1842, was a street of two-storey houses in a warren of streets midway between Commercial Street and Cable Street, not far from St Katherine Docks. It was 100 yards long, 9 yards wide, and described in the 1844 assessment as 'well paved', 'well lit', with 'good' drainage and a 'plentiful' water supply. However, 'good' drains meant 'good and clean surface drains'; and a 'plentiful' supply of water was one that was 'a plentiful supply three times a week' – for two hours at a time. Other streets in the surrounding area were worse off: 'In many parts of St Georges in the East there is no drainage, and the kitchens, in some places, after heavy rains are stated to be several inches under water; which, when it recedes, leaves an accumulation of filth and dirt of the worst description.' However even 'good' surface drains as in Mary Ann Street were not good enough for public health in the absence of a continuous supply of water to clean them. This was recognised at the time:

But even supposing that all the houses had drains, and all the streets sewers, and that they had been properly constructed, so that they had the most approved form, diameter, and fall; still they would be *in great measure* useless, because they could not answer the purpose they were intended for, unless supplied with water; without a sufficient supply of water, to keep up a constant current flowing through the drain, the drain itself becomes positively injurious, generating and diffusing the very poison it was intended to prevent and remove.[46]

The most common male employment in the district was labouring, and a sixth of that was in the nearby docks. In descending order of frequency there were shoemakers, gunsmiths, carpenters, sailors, then a wide variety of trades of all sorts down to 'ginger-beer-seller', 'chair bottomer', and 'house of ill fame'. No details about the latter were entered upon, though the report on St Mary's District where the Thompsons lived, noted 'at least 50' houses of prostitution.[47] Attention was drawn to the problems caused by women's low pay, especially when the women were supporting families on their own: 'we find much greater diversity of age, with very limited means, derived from the narrow range of employments for female hands, especially if unaccompanied by a vigorous frame and habits of bodily exertion. The extent of such employments, as compared with the number of struggling competitors for them, being always limited, their remuneration is low. The relative superiority of men's earnings over those of women, and even more over those of the women and children combined, in the metropolis, as compared with most of the manufacturing districts, is thus very conspicuously shown.'[48] The average rent in the district was 'no less than 3/7d a week' in 1844. A needlewoman could earn about 5s. 9d., though a court dressmaker, as distinct from an ordinary dressmaker, could hope to earn up to 17s.

The work took a terrible toll on women's health, as reports increasingly indicated. 'No slavery is worse than the dressmaker's in London' one woman told a government inspector in 1843.[49] Before the invention and patenting of the sewing machine it was a job which used up young women like Kate on her way to work in Dickens's *Nicholas Nickleby*: 'At this early hour many sickly girls, whose business, like that of the poor worm, is to produce with patient toil the finery that bedecks the thoughtless and the luxurious, traverse our streets, making towards the scene of their daily labour, and catching, as if by stealth, the only gasp of wholesome air and glimpse of sunlight, which cheers their monotonous existence during the long train of hours that make a working day.'[50] Hood's 'Song of the Shirt' became famous in 1843. That was to be the year of Sarah Thompson's death.

Work – work – work
Till the brain begins to swim;
  Work – work – work
Till the eyes are heavy and dim!
Seam, and gusset, and band,
  Band, and gusset, and seam,
Till over the buttons I fall asleep,
  And sew them on in a dream!

Oh Men, with Sisters dear!
  Oh Men, with Mothers and Wives!
It is not the linen you're wearing out,
  But human creatures' lives!
  Stitch – stitch – stitch,
  In poverty, hunger, and dirt,
Sewing at once, with a double thread,
  A Shroud as well as a shirt.

For those trying to do the court dressmaking which paid more, there were the two busy 'seasons', from April till the end of July, and from October until Christmas. But by the end of 1841 Mrs Thompson was in advanced pregnancy, and on the 4th February 1842 she gave birth at 24 Mary Ann Street to another boy, whom she called John Parker Thompson after her late stepbrother.[51] She became ill, and sought help for her family. It was now that her connections with the prosperous Irvingite network came to some use.

Regent Square Church was still the official place of worship for the boys of the Royal Caledonian Asylum in Islington; an asylum 'for the maintenance and education of the children of soldiers sailors & marines, natives of Scotland, who have died or been disabled in the service of their country, and of indigent Scotch parents, resident in London, not entitled to parochial relief.'[52] The Thompsons were now such parents, and application was made to have James taken in. Boys were admitted at the age of eight, and James would reach his eighth birthday on November 23rd that year.

The Caledonian Asylum was a favourite charity of London-Scottish aristocracy and well-to-do. Fundraising balls and dinners were annual events, at which the boys who were the object of the charitable donations would be ceremonially marched round the room before their benefactors. These gala events were an integral part of the court calendar which court dressmakers such as Mrs Thompson would labour to dress. The annual summer fancy dress ball in Willie's Rooms in 1842 was attended, *The Times* reported, by between eight and nine hundred:

> ... a vast number of whom appeared in the rich and picturesque costumes worn at the Queen's Masque. The rooms perhaps never presented a more brilliant assemblage of rank and beauty. The boys of the Caledonian Asylum, attired in Highland kilts of the Royal tartan, preceded by the pipers of His Royal Highness the Duke of Sussex and the Duke of Sutherland, wearing the handsome Scotch mulls recently presented to them by command of Her Majesty, and attended by the officers of the institution, marched round the ball-room as usual, and were most warmly greeted. On returning to the ante-room they were inspected by His Grace the Duke of Wellington, who, in terms of great readiness and condescension, was pleased to express his admiration of their healthful appearance and martial demeanour.[53]

There was competition for the small number of vacancies that became available in the asylum every six months. An application had first to be sponsored by someone already on the list of sub-scribers to asylum funds who had given ten guineas or more as life subscription, or had annually given two guineas in subscription before the sponsorship.[54] The approval of prosperous backers connected with the asylum had therefore first to be obtained. Nor, once so sponsored, was an application guaranteed success. Twice yearly the applications in hand were put to the vote of all the subscribers, the applications with the most votes then being matched with the small number of vacancies available. The Thompsons obtained the sponsorship of James Boyd, late of the Firth of Clyde and now co-director of a sugar-refining company in Breezer's Hill by London Dock.[55] He endorsed the application with statement of circumstances which the Thompsons then had witnessed by a magistrate, as required, at Lambeth Street Police Court Whitechapel on August 16th 1842.[56] The application stated:

> That the parents James Thompson born at Pitnacrea, Perthshire aged 37 years, Sarah Thompson born at Glasgow aged 42 years, reduced to poverty from the Father being incapable to follow his profession as a mariner in which he was actively employed as apprentice, seaman & mate and served in the following ships

CAROLINE	from	Sep 1824	to	Sep 1827
HALYARD		Dec 1827	to	May 1828
LEGUAN		Aug 1828	to	Nov 1828
MOUNT STEWART ELPHINSTONE		Dec 1828	to	Oct 1830

TAMARLANE	Dec 1830	to	Mar 1831
FORTUNE	Apr 1831	to	Jul 1831
HM SHIP SATELITE	Jul 1831	to	May 1832
GANGES	May 1832	to	Sep 1832
NAVARIN	Oct 1832	to	Jan 1834
JEAN	Feb 1835	to	May 1836
MOUNTAINEER	Sep 1836	to	Jan 1837
ELIZA STEWART	Apr 1837	to	Sep 1840

In which latter ship whilst chief officer he had the misfortune to be struck with paralysis which has totally deprived him of the use of his right side and rendered him quite incapable of earning his own subsistence and is dependent on the bounty of his friends and the exertions of his wife. Has two children James Thompson the applicant for admission aged 7 years last November, John Parker Thompson aged six months.

Your petitioner humbly prays, That the said James Thompson may be admitted into the Caledonian Asylum, and that he may continue therein as long as the Directors thereof shall think fit.[57]

Sarah Thompson signed, but her husband, unable to sign because of his paralysis, entered a cross.[58] The application joined another twenty-four, only eight of which were to be successful that December. When the result of the subscribers' votes was declared at the next quarterly meeting the name 'James Thompson' came seventh in the list of eight successfully voted into a place.[59]

Now seriously ill, Sarah on what was her deathbed sent for her sister Margaret to come to London.[60] Though she now had four children including a new baby of her own,[61] Margaret took the infant John Parker Thompson back to Port Glasgow to be brought up with her family. On December 1st 1842, six months before his mother's death in Mary Ann Street,[62] the eight-year-old James Thompson, Registration No. 346,[63] was admitted to the Royal Caledonian Asylum, Islington. On succeeding Sundays he now took his place amongst the ninety asylum boys, 'clad in the Royal Stewart tartan',[64] who sat in the gallery of that same Regent Square Church from which, ten years before, Edward Irving had been expelled.

CHAPTER THREE

IT WAS DURING his stay at the Royal Caledonian Asylum that the spelling of his surname was changed to 'Thomson'. The asylum rule was that a boy was discharged on reaching his fourteenth birthday, and the need to corroborate this date in anticipation seems the likeliest reason why his birth registration should have been entered up in Port Glasgow six months before his fourteenth birthday in 1848. Such retrospective entering when evidence of birth became necessary was not uncommon in the families of dissenters as his parents had been. People outwith the Church of Scotland resented having to pay fees for registration to a church of which they were not members, and before registration was made compulsory many dissenters avoided it.[1] A fragment of a school record of pupils' progress at the asylum shows when 'James Thompson' one month became 'James Thomson' the next.[2] In June 1847 the school roll was enlarged by a 'James Thomson Jnr' who joined the James Thompson and a George Thompson already there. Next month all three were given the surname 'Thomson'. Whether the change came like this from an internal school decision or from one taken by relatives, at any rate James Thomson spelled his surname thus by the time he left. And so in anticipation shall his name be spelled in the rest of this narrative.

The Royal Caledonian Asylum was a Scottish children's oasis in London, first established at Cross Street, Hatton Garden, two years after the end of the Napoleonic Wars in 1817. It had been founded for the benefit of Scottish children in London left bereft from those wars, after a fundraising drive launched by the Highland Society in London under its president the Duke of Kent. The novelist John Galt had been appointed secretary, and he had had a deal to do with the success of the fundraising, '90 titled Scots and 70 others' agreeing to be sponsors.[3] After eleven years the asylum had moved to a spacious site at Copenhagen Fields on the Caledonian Road the year after its official place of worship had moved, with Irving, to Regent Square. The boys wore kilts, and girls – who were admitted after an annexe was opened in 1845 – wore tartan plaids.

The teacher and secretary when Thomson arrived in December 1842 was the Rev. John Lees from Stornoway. Lees had a son the same age as Thomson, and an account of this son's memories of the place at this time can be taken as relevant:

> The Caledonian Asylum . . . was pleasantly situated in the neighbourhood of beautiful Highgate and Camden town. Right in front were the Copenhagen fields and Copenhagen house with large gardens. These gardens with their swings and merry-go-rounds were the favourite Sunday resort of shoals of Cockneys . . . At the back of the Asylum in those days were large brickfields belonging to a man called Polock. These brickfields were diversified by large ponds of water where the clay had been taken out, and swarms of children were often to be seen bathing in these ponds and sporting themselves on their banks. Frequently cases of drowning took place; and the boy received a vivid impression from the fact that as soon as the bodies were recovered they were taken into the Asylum, when hot towels were brought into requisition without effect.[4]

New building was constantly encroaching on the surrounding open spaces, and Pentonville Prison was built within sight nearby in 1842.

A pride in military history was natural in an institution many of whose children were orphans of fathers who had died in battle. There were military stories to be had from one of the asylum's officials: 'One of the functionaries attached to the asylum was an old drill sergeant called Young. He had been through the Peninsular War where he had got a ball in his leg, and his tales of bloody fights found a ready listener'.[5] Another teller of tales was the wife of Rev. Lees, who 'loved to tell the stories of her ancestors'.[6] She had as great-grandfather, Cameron of Lochiel; this may have been of some interest to Thomson as his own mother's great-grandfather was a Kennedy who was surgeon in the same Lochiel's army at Culloden.[7] But whether or not such remote interlockings were ever made known to him, Thomson's days at the Royal Caledonian Asylum were in any case thought cheerful enough by friends for them to tell the poet's first memorialist that his time in Islington constituted 'the happiest period of his existence'.[8] As an environment it was certainly healthier than the East End, and it gave him stability, a secure supply of decent food, shelter, and a large group of fellow-Scottish boys as daily companions.

Some of the boys remained friends with Thomson in later life, notably one called George Duncan, whose brother recalled Thomson at the asylum as 'a fine, clever, high spirited boy, taking the lead among his companions both in the schoolroom and the playground, and thoroughly popular with all who knew him'.[9] Like his father, Thomson showed talent in mathematics and an interest in music, becoming leading clarionet in the school band when one was formed after 1846. There was occasional contact with relatives and previous family friends. More constant was the relationship developed with a Mr and Mrs Gray from Greenock, in whose home in the East End of London he began to spend his holidays. The Grays had been local neighbours in London before Thomson's admission to the asylum; they lived in Well Close, a few streets away from Mary Ann Street.[10] The father William Gray was a plumber who became director of a small plumbing and painting business in Limehouse.[11] There were three infant girls, and the eldest of these, Helen, who was five years Thomson's junior, became his favourite.[12]

The religious teaching at the asylum was established Church of Scotland, but the schoolmaster-minister John Lees was not intolerant of other people's beliefs, if the word of his son can be accepted: 'If there was one virtue more than another that my father possessed, it was the precious one of charity. I have been thought often too tolerant myself, but if I am so it is because I am his son. He never would allow an unkind word to be spoken of those who differed from him, nor would he allow us to do so . . . his favourite theme was that the whole gospel is comprehended in the word *love*.'[13] The Irvingite aspect of Thomson's background would not have been thought peculiar. Many subscribers to the asylum had been attenders at Regent Square during Irving's ministry there, and sympathy for his memory was still expressed by some connected with the asylum's administration. One such was a member of the asylum court, the Rev. John Cumming, who was Church of Scotland minister at Crown Court Church two miles away. Cumming had preached the funeral oration at Irving's funeral in Glasgow in 1834. Though he did not think that the 'gift of tongues' had been inspired or impressive, he still spoke of Irving as having had 'probably the grandest voice I ever heard'.[14] Nor for a boy like Thomson would an Irvingite background have deprived him of early instruction in the central codes of religious belief maintained by the Established Church. Though Irving had rejected the church institution, he had never rejected the Westminster Confession or the Shorter and Longer Catechisms. He had as a detail preferred an earlier Confession of Faith, and had regretted that the Shorter Catechism did not pay more attention to the personal role of Christ in salvation.[15] But of the Longer Catechism he wrote 'As a compendium of Christian morals I know of nothing better.'[16] So Thomson could with equal likelihood have been speaking of his pre-asylum background as of his time in Islington when he later gave a friend 'an amusing account of the sufferings he underwent in committing to memory what is known as the Assembly's Shorter Catechism, and of how he used to lie awake in bed shivering at the thought that he would have to learn another, longer and harder even than that.'[17]

Learning these Catechisms was not an easy matter. The Shorter consists of 107 questions with answers on 'The *chief end*, the *only rule*, and the *great subject* of the Christian religion':

Q.19. *What is the misery of that estate whereinto man fell?*
A. All mankind by their fall lost communion with God, are under his wrath and curse, and so made liable to all the miseries in this life, to death itself, and to the pains of hell for ever.

The Longer Catechism not only has more questions – 196 – but much fuller answers:

Q.113. *What are the sins forbidden in the the third commandment?*
A. The sins forbidden in the third commandment are, the not using of God's name as is required; and the abuse of it in an ignorant, vain, irreverent, profane, superstitious, or wicked mentioning or otherwise using his titles, attributes, ordinances, or works, by blasphemy, perjury, all sinful cursings, oaths, vows, and lots; violating of our oaths and vows, if lawful; and fulfilling them, if of things unlawful; murmuring and quarreling at, curious prying into, and misapplying of God's decrees and providences; misinterpreting, misapplying, or any way perverting the word, or any part of it, to profane jests, curious unprofitable questions, vain janglings, or the maintaining of false doctrines; abusing it, the creatures, or any thing contained under the name of God, to charms, or sinful lusts and practices; the maligning, scorning, reviling, or any wise opposing of God's truth, grace, and ways; making profession of religion in hypocrisy, or for sinister ends; being ashamed of it, or a shame to it, by uncomfortable, unwise, unfruitful, and offensive walking, or backsliding from it.

Each answer to be learned has a quantity of Biblical quotes foot-noted in demonstration of its Biblical authority. Question 19 from the Shorter Catechism cites ten Biblical verses as footnotes; Question 113 from the Longer Catechism cites 158. But learning these Catechisms was part of the ordinary Scottish Protestant culture of the time, and there was nothing remarkable in Thomson's having to do so. However in this Protestant culture there was crisis over a fundamental constitutional division which had effect on the Caledonian Asylum as on all other institutions related to the Church of Scotland. In May 1843, six months after Thomson's arrival at Copenhagen Fields, the Church of Scotland split itself from top to bottom in the conflict that came to be known as the Disruption.

The Act of Union of 1707 had preserved the separation between state and Scottish Church, as against the state's relationship with the Church of England whose bishops sat in Parliament and whose titular head was the crown. But the Patronage Act of 1712 broke the promises to maintain the Scottish separation, in that it gave monarchy and landowner the right to nominate the minister of a Scottish parish church within their domains. The device was an instrument of social control and a repeated source of discontent in parishes whose congregations wished to nominate a minister not of the landowner's choosing. A series of cases from 1833 resulted in a nationwide campaign that took the matter, unsuccessfully, to Court then to Parliament. At the General Assembly of the Church of Scotland in Edinburgh in May 1843, Thomas Chalmers led 470 ministers out of the Assembly to form the Free Church of Scotland. Six of the ten Church of Scotland ministers in London parishes followed suit a month later.[18] Foremost amongst these was Rev. James Hamilton of Regent Square.[19] But the Royal Caledonian Asylum, being under royal patronage, was in no position to side with the seceders. However because of an outstanding debt the trustees were unable to evict Hamilton as they had in the past evicted Irving.[20] Moreover the asylum subscribers and administration were, as representative church members, as split amongst themselves on the matter as the Church was as a whole. Yet for the sake of the children it was best that the Disruption in the Church should cause as little disruption as possible in the Royal Caledonian Asylum. Compromises therefore had to be reached. But some were more inclined to compromise than others.

The nearest church remaining within the established Church of Scotland was John Cumming's at Crown Court, Covent Garden. Cumming had been one of the most vociferous opponents of the anti-patronage campaign, just as Hamilton at Regent Square had been recognised in London as one of its leading supporters. Some believed that Cumming was partly to blame for the great scale of the eventual walkout from the Church, since his published opinion had assured Crown and government in London that they could safely ignore threats that such a walkout might take place. 'I am not satisfied that *any* will secede,' Cumming wrote in his *The Present State of the Church of Scotland*, published just before the Disruption took place.[21] His views had been popular with the President of the board of directors of the Royal Caledonian Asylum, the Duke of Buccleuch. Buccleuch was not only one of the biggest landowners in Europe, he was one who became known for his reluctance to allow the new Free Church ministers to build churches on his land. But the resignation of the asylum's schoolmaster John Lees in the summer of 1844 highlighted the conflict within the asylum's administration, for it raised the problem of the religious status of the teacher who should replace him.

Buccleuch announced, when it came to the appointment of a successor, 'I desire to state distinctly, that neither as president of that institution nor as a subscriber to its funds, will I consent that the connection of the Caledonian Asylum with the Established Church of Scotland shall be severed, or in any way impaired.'[22] A sub-committee tried to recommend that the new schoolmaster merely should be 'an orthodox Presbyterian, and ready to sign the Westminster Confession of Faith'.[23] But this was not enough for Buccleuch or Cumming, and the recommendation was altered to: 'that he must be a member of the Church of Scotland as by law established'.[24] This was approved by the Board, though the vote of 24 to 19 showed the extent of its division rather than its unity. Buccleuch and Cumming carried a further resolution that the children's annual religious examination should remain formally the job of the Presbytery of London – those London ministers who had remained in the Established Church of Scotland. This caused great argument, and one committee member complained that were it carried, the ruling 'would be as much as to tell those who were members of the Free Church that neither their money nor their services were wanted.'[25] The motion was carried, though on the understanding, without a division, that such as James Hamilton of Regent Square would be allowed to attend. After later argument it was agreed that seceding ministers like Hamilton could not only attend but could take part.

It was not a simple matter of the aristocrats and the wealthy backing the Established Church, versus the rest backing the seceders like Hamilton. The Marquis of Breadalbane for instance was amongst the Free Church supporters, and he and others of his opinion continued to be present at public events in connection with the asylum. Breadalbane's pipers were present with those of the Duke of Sutherland, the Duke of Sussex, and the Lord Glenlyon, when at the annual ball in 1845 the asylum boys – including the ten-year-old James Thomson – were marched round the room. On this occasion the boys' 'healthy and cheerful appearance was marked by all observers'.[26] But the interfaction sniping continued. A Free Church member was reported as saying that his party gave more money in support to the children of the asylum than those remaining in the Established Church of Scotland.

An anonymous letter to *The Times* retorted that 'the contributions of seceders who began their existence in 1843 would not buy kilts for the boys or petticoats for the girls of the asylum; or the sums contributed by those who are now seceders were given when they were not quiet, but enthusiastic establishmentarians, who before the unknown tongues broke out in 1830 or the free secession in 1843 treated all Dissenters as unclean persons.'[27]

But still the official place of worship remained Regent Square Church, and still Cumming and Buccleuch were determined that it should now be somewhere else. In 1846 they succeeded in buying a nearby church from a group of Congregationalists, and on January 21st 1847 the Caledonian Church, Holloway, opened its doors. It was under the ministry of the Rev. John Tod Brown, who had resigned his ministry in a Church of Scotland parish in Liverpool. He was persuaded to take charge of the new church in Holloway for three months, and agreed to stay on once his three months were up.[28] He had published a poem the year before in 1846, and its theme may throw some light on why he was thought a good choice for the church of an institution in some party conflict. The poem was called 'The Union of Christians', and it argued in rhyming couplets that dissension amongst Christians must cease if the promised return of Christ on earth was not to be constantly delayed. Tod Brown was no millenialist in the manner of Irving, but he still felt able to invoke the prospect of London becoming the New Jerusalem, should the city mend its sinful ways:

> London! Britannia's glory and disgrace,
> Shouldst thou be ever crowned the Capital of grace. . .
> Ah London! then no Babylon wert thou!
> But nuptial New Jerusalem below,
> Thy husband, Nature's, Revelation's Lord,
> Obey'd with zeal, with ecstasy adored.[29]

During Tod Brown's first year at the new church the record of pupils' progress mentioned at the beginning of this chapter was made. The teacher, R.A. McDougal, noted the performance of each pupil in Religious Instruction, English Reading and Grammar, Writing, Drawing, Arithmetic, and Geography.[30] There was also a column headed 'Conduct'. In January 1847 Thomson's writing was described as 'unsatisfactory' though he was first each week in Arithmetic, and his Conduct was described as 'not amiss'. A month later his writing had become 'good', which was the judgment also on his Conduct and his performance in Religious Instruction. In the ensuing six months that the report was kept on the pupils in this way, his performance in Religious Instruction was rated 'Good' or 'Very Good'; in Writing, 'Fair' and 'Pretty Good'; in Drawing, 'Very Good' and 'Good'. In English Reading and Grammar he came variously between first and fifth in the class; in Geography between first and ninth; in Arithmetic consistently first; and his Conduct was regularly described as 'Exemplary'.

In that year 1847 the school band, in which Thomson now played, made regular public performances, including in May a performance in a Spring Festival at the Star and Garter at Richmond Park.[31] People had to pay for the band's hire, and its setting up had been thought not only good for the musical education of the boys – twenty-five were involved initially – but a way of raising some money while giving the asylum good publicity. Meanwhile in the asylum itself another of the sources of conflict between Established and Seceder was resolved, when a government inspector of schools was found favourable to undertake the annual pupils' examination.[32] This inspector, the Rev. F.C. Cook, made a recommendation that had an important effect on Thomson's future. Cook suggested that two or three boys when due for discharge on their fourteenth birthday should be retained as monitors or pupil teachers.[33] There was much negotiation to get a government grant to cover the additional expense, but Thomson and his friend George Duncan were appointed. In October 1849 – about a year after both had been due to leave the asylum – their salary as monitors was resolved at a court quarterly meeting – 'Thomson and Duncan to have £4 each'.[34]

Thomson was now reading widely, by 1850 'already well versed in many of the masterpieces of Swift, Fielding, Smollett, Sterne, De Foe, De Quincey, and other favourite authors.'[35] As a young child he had been drawn to Walter Scott: 'Our own introduction, at an early age, consisted of the combat between Roderick Dhu and Fitzjames and the battle of Flodden Field in some book or books of selections; together with "Ivanhoe" from a circulating library (paid for by an heroic sacrifice of fruit or sweeties), which we pored over breathless in our play-hours, and took into school up our jacket, getting many a furtive peep into the magic pages when opportunity offered, under shelter of the boy in front of us.'[36] By his fifteenth birthday in November 1849 he had become interested in poetry, his favourite poet around this time being Byron.[37]

Early in 1849 the versifying minister at Holloway Church, Tod Brown, had resigned over money. He complained that 'parties who had started the cause failed to make good their promised payments to me, and I could not see it to be my duty to continue labouring for such scanty remuneration as compelled me to draw on my private resources.'[38] The parties concerned were Cumming and Buccleuch. Cumming had not relinquished his interest in the affairs of the asylum church with the appointment of Tod Brown, and it was Cumming who moved at an asylum court of directors meeting that a request from the office bearers of Holloway Church to have some of the band play at services, be granted.[39] On April 9th 1849 a successor to Tod Brown, Rev. David Magill, took over. Records show that he was appointed 'to officiate as pastor', though 'probably not admitted to the full charge'.[40] He stayed four years, though his salary had to be supplemented by emergency grants from Crown Court Mission Fund.[41] So like Tod Brown he was very much under John Cumming's scrutiny. In fact Cumming can be seen as a relevant factor in Royal Caledonian Asylum administration throughout Thomson's stay there. And by the end of that stay Cumming was not only a known figure in the Caledonian Asylum and the wider world of Church of Scotland politics; he had become as noted a national figure as Edward Irving had once been before him – and for reasons that were not unconnected.

He had a different outlook from the Irving that had preached in Regent Square; whereas Irving's preaching had caused some to assume they could be visited by the power that had visited Christ himself, Cumming preached reverence for hierarchy and the status quo: 'I see in the reverence of rank, the foundation of order and the fruit of Christianity'.[42] The people of England, he thought, were quite a religious group of folk, compared with the foreigners on the Continent. This at least seemed to him to be the message of the 1848 revolutions.[43]

> But why has Old England sat so unmoved upon her throne in the waste of waters? Why have the waves of revolution crouched and slipped away the moment they approached her? . . . It is the living Christianity of our people that is the life blood of our country – it is the grace of God in Old England's heart that is the secret of the fixity and splendour of the crown on the Queen of England's brow. Christianity is the cement of our social system. Our people are so loyal because they are comparatively so religious.

Even the famine in Ireland had only proved how worthy the English were:

> Irish famine only stirred up English generosity, as Irish rebellion has but provoked English forgiveness; and who knows how many Irish hearts refused to be excited, or how many Irish hands refused to lift

one pike against the nation that fed them in famine, and clothed them in nakedness.[44]

History was God at work, and the Word of God in the Bible was literal. Science showed that the earth's age corresponded with 'the Mosaic record'; the study of language showed that Hebrew was the language spoken in Eden.[45] The story of Noah and the Ark was a literal factual report of what had happened one day long ago:

> Infidels have objected to the *account of the ark*, and have asserted that it is quite absurd to suppose that ever there could be a vessel constructed large enough to hold all the creatures that must have been placed in it, together with sufficient food (it may be, six or twelve months) – water for the fishes, corn for the four-footed animals, seeds for the birds, and so on. Now we will take the dimensions of the ark from the record of Moses, and calculate them on the lowest possible scale. There are two definitions given of a cubit – one that it is eighteen inches, or a foot and a half, the other that it is one foot and eight inches; we will take it only at its lowest. Moses states that the ark was 300 cubits long; this would make it about 450 feet long, or about the length of St Paul's Cathedral. The breadth of it he states to be 50 cubits; we have it then 75 feet in breadth. He states it to be 30 cubits high; so that it was 45 feet in height. In other words, it was as long as St Paul's Cathedral, nearly as broad, and about half as high. The tonnage of the ark, according to the calculation of modern carpenters, must have been about 32,000 tons. The largest ship of war – the St Vincent, which is of a size altogether unimagineable to those who have never seen it – is 2,500 tons burden; so that the ark must have been equal to *seventeen first-rate ships of war*, and if armed as such ships are, it would have contained much beyond 18,000 men, and provisions for them for eighteen months. Now Buffon has stated, that all the four-footed animals may be reduced to 250 pairs, and the birds to a smaller number. On calculation, therefore, we shall find, that the ark would have held more than five times the necessary number of creatures, and more than five times the required quantity of food to maintain them for twelve months. Fair and indisputable arithmetic adds testimony to inspiration, and proves that God's word is true.[46]

This was the kind of logic that made R.G. Ingersoll in later days remark that by the Mosaic chronology two sloths from South America would have had to set off for the Ark some years before the world was created.[47] But 'infidels' were the particular focus of Cumming's contempt, be they 'the hoary infidel' Voltaire or the hoariest infidel of them all, the Pope in Rome. Scarcely a sermon went by without a thrust there, as when a YMCA audience was told to ignore the new Greenwich Time and set Protestant watches 'by the sun in the sky which the Greenwich pontiff cannot cover'.[48]

Unlike Irving he did not win a circle of literary admirers. Thackeray thought him a bigot,[49] Tennyson ridiculed him,[50] and George Eliot first came to prominence with a sustained polemical attack on Cumming in the *Westminster Review*.[51] Thomson in later years, while Cumming's notoriety in London maintained itself over two decades, made scornful remarks several times about him in print, including one in which he ridiculed words he remembered hearing from the minister's lips.[52] But Cumming did not merely attract scorn and ridicule: the reason George Eliot chose to show her anger about his teachings was because of their very popularity – a popularity which first manifested itself when from the winter of 1848 Cumming gave, over two winters, a series of sixty lectures on the *Book of Revelation*. The lectures were held on Sunday mornings and evenings in Exeter Hall, Crown Court being closed at the time for enlargement. Like Irving before him, Cumming preached the imminent Second Coming of Christ.[53]

His hearers every Sunday amounted to some 4,000 individuals, including many distinguished and influential personages (amongst whom was Lord John Russell, the then Prime Minister of England), as also individuals of every religious denomination, and many of no denomination at all. Many years afterwards it was stated by himself that 'more deep and enduring impression were then made than during all the previous years of my ministry, and these influences fell more especially on the hearts of young persons.

The lectures were printed and quickly went through several editions. They were based, not on Irving – though obviously Irving had been an influence – but on a millenialist work published in 1844 by the Rev. E.B. Elliott, *Horae Apocalypticae*.[54] The end of the world, Cumming now preached, was due 'in the course of less than twenty years':

If the recent continental convulsions are the first heavings of the last great earthquake, of the seventh vial, – as I think they are, – I may notice the statement in *The Times* of this day, (June 18th, 1848,) that a storm of lightning and tempest has overflowed and torn up Germany a week ago, unparalleled in fury and extent in the memory of man.[55]

The seals, trumpets and vials of *Revelation* were symbols which could be decoded to show how History had been anticipated before it had happened: 'These symbols, as Mr Elliott has shown, are invariably to be explained on the principle of local, historical or national allusion. This, in fact, is the key to all the symbols of Scripture.'[56] The 'hours' and 'days' of the text stood for the real years and multiples of days in the course of real events; by a computation as relentless as his exegesis on the Ark, Cumming concluded that the 'identification of the sixth trumpet with the Turkish invasion and the fall of Constantinople is a great and all but indubitable fact.'[57]

But the 'great and indubitable fact' towards which all these sermons portended, was that in 1867 the earth would be destroyed by fire, when the New Jerusalem would descend and the elect, and they alone, would inherit the earth:

> . . . Christ and his risen saints shall descend from their aerial glory upon the purified earth, called in verse 13, 'the new heavens and the new earth;' and this descended company is here described as 'the Holy City, the New Jerusalem, coming down from God out of heaven, prepared as a bride adorned for her husband.'
> . . . This new Jerusalem coming down out of heaven, is just the sealed ones out of every kindred and tribe and tongue, that is, the 144,000 . . .
> Earth, thus restored, with Jerusalem its sublime capital, may be the greatest school of the universe, – the sublime instructress of other worlds, and thus it may play a part in the future that will cover all the shame of its first aberration.[58]

But the New Jerusalem was not just a body of people. It was a literal city:

> It is plainly a literal city, – a material as well as moral structure, – for risen bodies as well as regenerated spirits; and thus matter as well as mind and conscience will reach its perfection. This city will show what a renovated earth is capable of; what an array of glory, order, harmony, and perfection this chaos shall become at the bidding of Him on whose head are many crowns.
> . . . The very dust shall be of diamond, and the meanest thing where all is magnificent shall be gold. Its soil shall be ever fresh and fragrant as the rose; its sky around like the rainbow, and over it all flowered with stars; and its distant hills shall be for ever alive with light. Darkness shall flee away from it like a doubt before the truth of God, and no night shall draw its sable curtains over earth's head. All space shall be full of Deity, the stars shall be the Scriptures of the sky, and the light of the Sun of

Righteousness the apocalypse of all. All sounds shall be harmony, and all mysteries light . . .

Men from all ranks shall be there. The monarch and mechanic, the prince and the peasant, denuded of all circumstantial differences and distinctions, and glorious in that common righteousness which humbles the heart while it exalts the person of the wearer, shall there see in each other brethren, and wonder where they failed to see it before. Monarchies and republics, schools and universities, sects and parties, shall all present to this city happy citizens, – the fruits of that living Christianity, which so many of them would neither understand, nor patronise, nor thrust out. – Such is our inheritance, incorruptible and undefiled.[59]

The imminent founding of this city should be borne constantly in mind:

Set your affections on this future apocalypse of joy, of beauty, and of happiness. It is revealed, not as a specimen of poetry, or for the gratitude of mere human feelings of delight; but to draw up our hearts to its clear and unclouded sunshine; to enable us to look with comparative indifference on the gilded toys and bright glare of the things of this life, and so to pass as strangers and pilgrims, looking for a city that hath foundations . . .

Tell others of its prospects. Show them the way.[60]

Again and again over those two winters between 1848 and 1850 he exhorted people to prepare for the coming City of God, that City where there would be no darkness, where God would be ever-present, and through which would wend the River of Life.

Make sure of a new heart, and you may safely calculate on an entrance to this city. This is the only indispensable qualification . . . 'Ye must be born again.' Nothing besides is any other than responsibility. This alone is meetness for the inheritance of the saints in light.

. . . Are you in the number of those who alone shall see and enter the New Jerusalem? Are you amongst 'the pure in heart', for they alone shall see God? Are you holy men, have you new hearts, that have been touched, and thereby transformed, by the Spirit of God?

. . . We are upon the eve of a grand response. The spreading anarchy of nations is opening up a clearer and nearer view of that City whose gates are praise, and its walls salvation. It will soon emerge from the chaos in all its predicted beauty – the envy of those that are without, the admiration of those that are within – the rosy eve of departing time – the auspicious twilight of opening eternity.[61]

> Jerusalem, my happy home,
> Name ever dear to me;

When shall my labours have an end,
  In joy, and peace, and thee?

When shall mine eyes thy heaven-built walls
  And pearly gates behold;
Thy bulwark with salvation strong
  And streets of shining gold!

Apostles, martyrs, prophets there
  Around my Saviour stand;
And soon my friends in Christ below,
  Will join the glorious band.

Jerusalem, our happy home,
  Our souls still long for thee;
Then shall our labours have an end,
  When we thy joys shall see.

Part Two:
WARRIOR

CHAPTER FOUR

T HOMSON LEFT THE Caledonian Asylum in August 1850, a few months before his sixteenth birthday.[1] He had wanted to become a clerk in a bank or merchant's office but hadn't the money to support himself during an apprenticeship.[2] He left only to become monitor in another London asylum for orphans and destitute children of servicemen – the Royal Military Asylum, Chelsea. The education of the children in this asylum had recently been reorganised to act as a model for garrison schools throughout the British Army; the asylum was to double as a refuge for the children of servicemen, and as an army teacher-training college. Working as a monitor was the first stage in a new course leading to qualification as Army Schoolmaster. Thomson's friend and fellow monitor in Islington, George Duncan, came with him.

The Royal Military Asylum was divided into an infant school, the small 'normal school' of thirty student teachers, and the main 'model school' of 350 boys.[3] This Model School was under the head-mastership of Mr Walter MacLeod with two assistants, whilst the Normal School was under a Mr Dusautoy.[4] Entrance to the teacher-training course was by competitive examination and interview. There was no religious examination, though there was 'a very scrutinizing examination' of suitability for teaching, with character references and certificates required from the clergyman of an applicant's parish.[5] The course itself could take six years to complete. After up to two years' work as a monitor, the student would be sent to work as assistant to a garrison schoolmaster somewhere in army barracks; on return to Chelsea after perhaps another two years there would be at least a year's further teaching practice in the Model School, then a final term under Mr Dusautoy in the Normal School before the qualifying examinations.[6] Students on the new course included youths who had grown up in the Royal Caledonian or in the Royal Military Asylum itself. There were also soldiers who had taught under the old system but had now applied for the new training; and

39

a number of civilian entrants from other trades. Amongst the first twenty students to take the course were six clerks, three tradesmen, a silk-manufacturer and one described as 'a maker of philosophical instruments'.[7]

Conditions within the Royal Military Asylum only a few years before 1850 show that Thomson was lucky to have spent his childhood from 1842 at Copenhagen Fields rather than at Chelsea. The recent reorganisation at Chelsea had followed a surprise inspection in 1846, when the place had been revealed to be in chaos, the children illiterate 'while not a few wandered about dragging heavy logs which were fastened with chains to their ankles'.[8] Teaching of all subjects had gone on in one large noisy hall with a platform in the middle:

> All the rest was void, except where chairs stood for the accommodation of the masters; and cages for the punishment of the boys. For in addition to the cane, which these sergeant-masters appear to have used very freely, they had at their command four instruments of torture, in the shape of iron cages, each occupying a corner of the room. Observe, that these cages were so constructed, as to render it impossible for the little prisoners to stand upright; who were nevertheless required to turn a heavy handle continually; and whose diligence or otherwise was marked by a process, which, if they did not see it, they never failed to feel.
>
> . . . Four or five groups of boys were gathered round as many sergeant-masters, some bawling out sounds, some repeating the Church catechism at the top of their voices; some conversing, and all shuffling and struggling, amongst themselves.
>
> . . . As to the acquirements of these poor lads, their proficiency proved, on examination, to be exactly such as might have been expected. They had learned nothing. They could not read, they could not write, they could not cipher, they could not spell . . . 'We can't help it, Sir,' said one of the sergeant-schoolmasters, when appealed to on the subject of his school. 'We never learned these things ourselves. How can we pretend to teach them?'[9]

All this was absent from the newly organised structure. The Chaplain-General to the British Army G.R. Gleig had been one of the asylum's surprise visitors in 1846, and his own series of school textbooks, *Gleig's School Series*, were now introduced at Chelsea and throughout the garrison schools. Walter MacLeod the Model School headmaster was also a prolific school text author and his textbooks were also amongst those introduced. McLeod was a progressive educationalist, and there was no prospect under his headmastership of a return to the cruel practices of before. He saw physical education both as an intrinsic part of children's upbringing and a means of reducing the amount of corporal punishment thought proper in most schools of the day:

I have long had a strong conviction that a simple system of drill and gymnastics ought to be introduced into every school in the kingdom . . . Exercise is necessary for the proper development of the bones and muscles, as well as for the health and strength. The best exercise, is that which employs every part of the body, which embraces movements of different kinds, and hence the utility of a system of gymnastic exercises for children . . .

If, instead of punishment, we sent them to run in the playground to breathe the pure air, to engage with the masters in sports which exhilarate the mind, then, as a general rule, it would be found that, on their return to the schoolroom, there would be order, discipline, attention to studies, and healthy moral tone would pervade the school; for the playground is the grand arena where the moral faculties and affections should be cultivated, – where the master should take the place of a parent, and the pupils that of a household, – where heart should be joined to heart by the bonds of affection, and where the highest sympathies of our nature should be called fully and freely into play. Those masters who have never had a playground can hardly suspect the important influence it exercises on the teacher and the taught, both morally, mentally, and physically.[10]

After only a year as a monitor – perhaps from his previous experience as such – Thomson was sent to Ireland to assist Joseph Barnes, schoolmaster in the small town of Ballincollig, five miles south of Cork. Barnes, a soldier-teacher who had retrained at Chelsea and been amongst the first batch of graduates in 1849, was already regarded as an outstanding product of the new system. His school at Ballincollig had become overcrowded with soldiers and their children looking for schooling: hence his need for an assistant.[11] At least children within the barracks now could receive an education. Outside the barracks walls in County Cork itself, only a third of the children got any schooling at all.[12]

The education was frequently Scripture-directed:

The business of the school – we mean of the children's school – opens every morning in barracks at a quarter before nine o'clock with prayer. This may occupy, perhaps, five minutes, after which the *trained* master reads to his scholars, collected together, a portion of Scripture, and explains it in its grammatical and historical bearing; deducing from

41

the whole such a lesson in moral and religious truth as it seems to convey. He touches, in so doing, upon no topic of sectarian controversy. He has been trained to speak as the Scriptures speak, without casting about for inferences which lie beneath the surface. He tells how men were created, – how they fell, – how the work of redemption was prepared and consummated; – and illustrates the moral and religious duties of the present generation, by referring to the virtues and the vices of Scriptural characters. Moreover, he omits no opportunity, – whether he be giving a lesson in history, in geography, or in natural science, – of directing the attention of his scholars to the power, the wisdom, the justice, and the goodness of God; and it is fair to our grown men to state that they receive such allusions, as often as they occur, quite as submissively and thankfully as the children. But beyond this the schoolmaster is strictly forbidden to go. To the clergymen or ministers who have charge of the troops, is committed the care of seeing that the lambs of their respective flocks are fed on such crumbs of polemical doctrine as appear to them necessary for education.[13]

Children were taught in the morning, adults in the afternoon. Most of the time with the latter was spent teaching basic literacy and numeracy. There were extra lessons in the evenings for those adults able to go further and study subjects such as geography, mathematics, algebra, or fortification. In the classroom there was, or at least officially ought to have been, maps of the world, Europe, the countries of the United Kingdom, Palestine; stored for the use of the newly organised schools were pencils, slates, copy books, easels, pens, penholders, rulers, 'Gallon bottles of black ink, in baskets', and pointers. The subjects taught in the morning children's classes besides elementary reading were 'Scripture History; England; Colonies; India; Greece; Rome; France; Arithmetic – Slate and Mental; Geography; Natural History; Object Lessons; Grammar – Dictation and Composition; Writing.'[14] The books set for these subjects were all from *Gleig's Series*. There were also reading books by the Society for the Promotion of Christian Knowledge, and the *First Reading Book* and *Second Reading Book for the Use of Families and Schools* by headmaster Walter MacLeod. His *Second Reading Book* can be seen as indication of how strongly he felt it the teacher's duty to reinforce Christian beliefs in everyday teaching.[15] The book has dramatic passages from Byron, Macaulay, Shakespeare, and Mrs Hemans; but most of the poetry is not only illustrative of scripture but accompanied by notes comparing it with passages in the Bible or Shorter Catechism. Poems are retitled to stress religious significance, with extracts from now forgotten poets such as Milman, Morehead, Pollok, and Kelly – 'I love the sacred book of God!' – on the Incarnation, the Sabbath, the Bible, and the Sabbath morn, respectively. There is Grant's 'For Lent' and Milton's 'Ode on the Morning of Christ's Nativity'; and Knox's versification of Psalm xiv. I is titled by MacLeod 'The Atheist', beginning 'The fool hath said, "There is no God!" ':

> No God! – Who fixed the solid ground
> On pillars strong, that alter not?
> Who spread the curtain'd skies around?
> Who doth the ocean's bounds allot?
> Who all things to perfections brought
> On earth below, in heaven above? –
> Go ask the fool of impious thought
> That dares to say, – 'There is no God!'

Waller's 'On the Fear of God' MacLeod retitled 'Man's Aberration From God':

> As clocks, remaining in the skilful hand
> Of some great master, at the figure stand,
> But, when abroad, neglected they do go,
> At random strike, and the false hour do show;
> So, from our Maker wandering, we stray,
> Like birds that know not to their nests the way.
> In Him we dwelt before our exile here,
> And may, returning, find contentment there:
> True joy may find, perfection of delight,
> Behold his face, and shun eternal night.

And in 1850 MacLeod's *The Geography of Palestine* was introduced to the army school system to help children locate Bible stories as historical events in a contemporary geography. Poetry had its place in this: 'The plan of introducing poetical quotations has been occasionally adapted; if a more frequent use of them, however, seems desirable, a Teacher can have no difficulty in finding quotations to suit his purpose. Any piece of poetry, or any marked and beautiful expression, which conveys the idea you wish to impart concerning any place, is seized by children with avidity, because it gives to the place a more tangible existence.'[16]

The Holy Land was learned according to its place names and main divisions, the chief regions being described under the subheadings of BOUNDARIES, LENGTH, BREADTH, AREA, MOUNTAINS, VALLEYS AND PLAINS, RIVERS, LAKES, WELLS,

POOLS AND HOT SPRINGS, CLIMATE AND SEASONS, FER-
TILITY AND NATURAL PRODUCTIONS, PEOPLE, ORIGINAL
INHABITANTS AND NEIGHBOURING NATIONS, TOWNS. The
first definition to be learned was the names the place as a whole had been
given: THE LAND OF CANAAN, THE LAND OF THE HEBREWS,
THE LAND OF ISRAEL, THE LAND OF JUDAH, THE HOLY
LAND, THE PROMISED LAND, THE LORD'S LAND, or THE
LAND OF GOD, PALESTINE. And there were multiple question-
naires:

1. Where was Caesarea? Give its original name. Who called it Caeserea,
and why? What was remarkable about its buildings? Relate the Scripture
events that happened there.
2. Where is Joppa? What is it now called? What event in Solomon's
life is connected with Joppa? What in the history of Jonah? What circumstances, recorded in the Acts of the Apostles, occurred here? Why
is Joppa now so important a place? What trade is carried on?
3. How far was Lyddia from Joppa? When was this town annexed
to Judea? What miracle was worked here? What is its modern name?
4. What place is supposed to be Arimathea? Who in particular resided
here? What do the Scriptures say concerning Joseph? Describe the position of Ramleh. What trees are abundant in the vicinity of Ramleh?

As for the town of Ballincollig, County Cork, where Thomson
found himself for eighteen months from August 1851, it was a barracks
town of about a thousand inhabitants, chiefly noted for its extensive
gunpowder-mills which stretched for four miles and produced 16,000
barrels of gunpowder a year.[17] To this town of Ballincollig the year
after Thomson's arrival there came the 7th Dragoon Guards, whose
ranks included an orderly clerk who was to play a significant part in
Thomson's life. To see who this clerk was and how he came to arrive
in Ballincollig, it is necessary to have a last look at the life of Edward
Irving.

———————

When Edward Irving was expelled from Regent Square Church in
May 1832, he and 800 of his congregation had first with some reluctance taken refuge in a room rented for seven guineas a week in a
large building in Gray's Inn Road.[18] Their reluctance was due to the
fact that the building was a meeting place for socialists and radicals,
notably followers of the social reformer Robert Owen, who formed
there the first National Equitable Labour Exchange in September 1832,

the month before Irving managed to find premises elsewhere.[19] Thomas Carlyle wrote to his brother John at the time of Irving's first removal to Gray's Inn Road: 'Owen the Atheist, and Irving the Gift-of-Tongues-ist, time about: it is a mad world.'[20]

But it was not really so mad. Owen, like Irving, had announced the institution of a millenium, though Owen's was to be established by human will, not God's. Both centred on a vision of the ideal community: the Irvingites, that of the City of God foretold in *Revelation* to be established by Christ's second coming; the Owenites, the establishment of a network of economically self-contained communities such as tried at New Lanark in Scotland and elsewhere. Owen's community self-help schemes had come to focus on the establishment of 'labour exchanges' where workers could exchange goods to the value of their labour without entry into the money system.[21] Though these exchanges, and the Owenite communities, had no lasting success, they did act as forerunners of the Co-operative Movement in which all customers of a store became shareholders, the profits to be divided as 'dividend' annually. The man who became recognised as a formative influence on the 'Rochdale Pioneers' of the co-operative movement was George Jacob Holyoake, who had become a paid Owenite 'preacher' in 1841.[22]

There were parallels between the organisation of Owen's 'rational religion' and the organisation of the new church that grew around Irving's expelled congregation. The church divided the world into twelve 'tribes' in 1836 to be tended by 'apostles'; Owen in 1838 divided England into twelve dioceses, with a network of 'preachers'. Owen's network was built on an existing structure of support groups organised after 1819 in support of Richard Carlile, who had spent six years in prison from 1819 for blasphemy in selling Thomas Paine's *The Age of Reason*.[23] Carlile had been again imprisoned for blasphemy in 1830, and his common-law (more scandal) wife, Eliza Sharples, had taken over his lectures.[24] After Carlile's death in 1843, funds were raised that enabled Eliza to be settled with her three children as caretaker of a radicals' meeting place at 1 Warner Place, London. Like many such meeting places connected with radical causes in the nineteenth century, it was a temperance hall.

A few doors along from the hall lived a family whose teenage son left home after a row with the family minister over the literal truth of the Thirty Nine Articles,[25] took lodgings with Eliza Sharples and her family, and soon was taking part himself in public discussions. In 1850, when just past his seventeenth birthday he gave a lecture on 'The Past, Present and Future of Theology'. George Jacob Holyoake chaired the meeting, and the name of the young lecturer was Charles Bradlaugh.

That same year Charles Bradlaugh published his first pamphlet, *A Few Words on the Christian's Creed*. It was dedicated to the local minister with whom he had had disagreement:

> Taking the Creed as a whole, it is one of the most ridiculous declarations of faith imaginable, for the believer declares a belief in Father, Son, and Holy Ghost. And how are these pictured in Scripture? The Father is somewhere in heaven, the Son sits at his right hand, and the Holy Ghost flies about in a bodily shape like a dove. What a curious picture to present to any reasonable man – a Father begets a son from nothing, and a dove proceeds from the two of them. I shall say no more on this disgusting part of Christianity – disgusting because so many believe all that is told them by a man who possesses the same powers of comprehension as themselves, and who has a position to maintain in the world – I mean the priest. My blood runs cold to think of the mischief that has been done by those men called priests; they are the bane of society *vi et armis*, and – they rule it wrongfully, they do not give it a chance of obtaining a mouthful of intellectual food without steeping it in the poison of their superstitious dogmas, and till we take the antidote of free discussion we shall never be free.[26]

Bradlaugh was in debt and decided to pay these off by joining the East India Company, paying off his debts with the bounty offered for joining. But he was the victim of a secret trade in men between the Company and the Army, and found himself enlisted against his will. To placate him he was offered the choice of whatever regiment he wanted to join, and settled on the one whose uniform he liked best parading outside the enlistment office window. This was the 7th Dragoon Guards.[27] Bradlaugh was sent to join them in Dublin as an orderly room clerk. In March 1852 the regiment moved south to Ballincollig. There Bradlaugh struck up a friendship with the garrison schoolmaster's assistant, James Thomson, fourteen months his junior. In the words of Bradlaugh's daughter half a century later: 'In the quiet nights, whilst the private was on sentry duty, he and the young schoolmaster would have long serious talks upon subjects a little unusual, perhaps, amongst the rank and file; or in the evening, when Thomson's work was done, and Private Bradlaugh could get leave, they would go for a ramble together. They each became the confidant of the other's troubles and aspirations, and each was sure of a sympathetic listener.' The friendship so established was one 'which lasted for five-and-twenty years'.[28]

The setting of Ballincollig, albeit the gunpowder mills stretched four miles, was rural, and the present-day Irish Army barracks stand not far from the wooded walks by the River Lee of Ballincollig Regional Park. But the area in 1852, for all its beauty of scenery, was still recovering from the ravages of the famine that had gripped the county in the late 1840s. The *Cork Examiner* advertised weekly sailings to Liverpool where twice a week there were sailings on to New York. For £1 deposit at Cork quayside, a berth to America could be secured 'upon the lowest possible terms compatible with a due regard to the comfort of the emigrants'.[29] One person interested in obtaining the lowest possible terms was Sir John Benn-Walsh who owned several estates in County Cork, though he himself spent most of the year across the sea in Berkshire and Cumberland. He acquired in his life 26,300 acres in England, Ireland and Wales, having 'entered Parliament in 1830 as one of the two members for Sudbury, a borough in Suffolk noted for its small electorate (about 750 voters) and notorious for its electoral corruption.'[30]

In 1851 Sir John ended his annual visit to his Cork estates with the noted reflection that he left Ireland 'in far more hope and in far better spirits than on any of the three former occasions since the potato failure'.[31] Firstly, poor rates were diminished 'owing to our having got rid of outdoor relief', and secondly his estates had been 'very much weeded both of paupers and bad tenants'. Though he had 'emigrated several, either with their whole families or in part', this had not generally been necessary. The clearances that year had been managed 'without evictions, bringing in the sheriff, or any harsh measures'. Sums of up to £3 had been enough to have the tenants move on, and having done so the cabins in which they had lived had been then 'immediately levelled'. On his visit the following year, 1852, Sir John was struck by the words of a friend: 'He goes the whole length of saying that the destruction of the potato is a blessing to Ireland. It seems universally admitted that the country has greatly improved; prices are really good for stock, butter, pigs, & sheep, and while in the old days of outdoor relief there were 30,000 souls on the lists out of a population of 70,000, there are now not more than 1,500 and these principally children. Diminished areas and the abolition of outdoor relief have effected these improvements in our condition.'[32] He felt an increased optimism: his visits were no more the 'melancholy visits during the famine years when poor laws were devouring us':

I see the poor law become manageable. I watch the effects of draining & other improvements. If politics will but let us alone, & no tenant right or other device of socialism & Jacobinism marr our prospects, we shall yet regain our property.[33]

There were almost 20,000 soldiers stationed in Ireland in addition to 'Recruiting Parties and Staffs of Militia Regiments, and 13,750 Constabulary and Coast Guards'.[34] The Coast Guards were on the lookout for a rumoured French invasion, whilst inland it was only four years since the suppression of the Young Ireland movement in executions and transportations. The object of military patrols in assisting the civil authorities was defined as 'to arrest illegally armed parties, to prevent houses being broken open by persons searching for arms, and not only to apprehend criminals thus disturbing the country, but to strike a terror in the locality, so as to prevent crime being perpetrated, and to give confidence to the well-disposed, and those possessing arms to defend their house.'[35]

Those allowed arms to defend their houses were of course not the same people whose houses were demolished under army supervision. One such demolition was witnessed by Charles Bradlaugh whilst he and Thomson were stationed at Ballincollig. Bradlaugh described the event and its sequel to an American audience at a public lecture twenty years later:

Those of you who are Irishmen will want no description of that beautiful valley of the Lee which winds between the hills from Cork, and in summer seems like a very Paradise, green grass growing to the waterside, and burnished with gold in the morning, and ruddy to very crimson in the evening sunset. I went there on a November day. I was one of a troop to protect the law officers, who had come with the agent from Dublin to make an eviction a few miles from Innisiara, where the River Bride joins the Lee. It was a miserable day – rain freezing into sleet as it fell – and the men beat down wretched dwelling after wretched dwelling, some thirty or forty, perhaps. They did not take much beating down; there was no flooring to take up; the walls were more mud than aught else, and there was but little trouble in the levelling of them to the ground. We had got our work about three parts done, when out of one of them a woman ran, and flung herself on the ground, wet as it was, before the captain of the troop, and she asked that the house might be spared – not for long, but for a little while. She said her husband had been born in it; he was ill of the fever, but could not live long, and she asked that he might be permitted to die in it in peace. Our captain had no power; the law agent from Dublin wanted to get back to Dublin; his time was of importance, and he would not wait; and that man was carried out while we were there – in front of us, while the sleet was coming down – carried out on a wretched thing (you would not call it a bed), and he died while he was there; and three nights' afterward, while I was on sentry on the front gate at Ballincollig barracks, we heard a cry; and when the guard was turned out, we found this poor woman there a raving maniac, with one dead babe in one arm, and another in the other, clinging to the cold nipple of her lifeless breast. And if you had been brothers to such a woman, sons of such a woman, fathers of such a woman, would not rebellion have

48

seemed the holiest gospel you could hear preached? Two hundred and fifty thousand evictions took place in the twenty years preceding 1866. Two hundred and fifty thousand![36]

But Thomson himself remembered Ballincollig as 'a happy place'.[37] He lived at home with Joseph Barnes and his wife, and their infant son he sometimes carried on his arm while teaching in the school. The Barneses nicknamed him 'Co' as short for 'precocious' because of his wide reading and literary enthusiasms. Shelley had now become a major focus for him,[38] and from this period survive the earliest examples of Thomson's own poetry.

> Still thine eyes haunt me; in the darkness now,
> The dreamtime, the hushed stillness of the night,
> I see them shining, pure and earnest light;
> And here, all lonely, may I not avow
> The thrill with which I ever meet their gaze,
> The while thy soul is floating through some maze
> Of beautiful divinely-peopled trance;
> But now I shrink from them in shame and fear,
> For they are gathering all their beams of light
> Into an arrow – pure, intense, and bright,
> Swerveless and star-like from its deep blue sphere –
> Piercing the cavernous darkness of my soul,
> Burning its foul recesses into view;
> Transfixing with sharp anguish through and through
> Whatever is not brave, and clean, and whole.
> And yet I cannot shrink, although thou piercest
> Into the inmost depths of all my being:
> I will not shrink, although thou now art seeing
> My heart's caged lusts, the wildest and the fiercest;
> The bitterest thoughts which fret my homeless mind,
> My unbelief, my selfishness, my weakness,
> My dismal lack of charity and meekness;
> For, amid all the evil, thou dost find
> Converting, lifting, purifying me,
> A holy love – a reverend awe for thee.[39]

The manuscript of this is dated 1852. In October that year, a month before his eighteenth birthday, he wrote another poem in which the speaker blames himself for having a 'hard, cold, bitter, heart' that nonetheless becomes gentle as a child in the presence of the loved one:

I strive to analyse, in fear and wonder,
The yearnings which thy presence hath inspired,
The restless passion with which I am fired –
Rending my world of common life asunder,

Consuming the foundations of old thought,
Filling heart, soul and brain with only Thee . . .
Oh, dost thou ever dream at all of me:
Yearnest thou ever for a common lot?[40]

Nothing survives to specify for whom these verses were written. Thomson did befriend a girl he taught in the children's class, Matilda Weller, daughter of an armourer-sergeant in Bradlaugh's 7th Dragoons. Matilda though was only a couple of months older than Helen Gray of the family Thomson had visited regularly in London; which is to say that in October 1852 Matilda was just a few months past her thirteenth birthday.[41]

In January 1854 Thomson returned to Chelsea, having been a year and five months in Ireland. He began in his spare time sometimes to use the Reading Room at the British Museum where he tried to keep up with contemporary work, reading the early poetry of Browning and Meredith. But he was not reclusive, and was remembered as 'a high-spirited, pleasure-loving companion, finding matter for merriment under the most unpromising conditions'.[42] He took a leading role in the school debating society, became 'inclined to promulgate sceptical views' and was now considered a Radical.[43] He upset the authorities by telling them, on his first return from Ballincollig, that he felt he had had enough training in teaching and it was time he was properly employed in the job. But he was compelled to remain at Chelsea another eighteen months. During that time his visits to the Grays in the East End became a weekly occurrence.[44]

In 1853 his father died in the island of Arran to where he had retired, by the time of his death having become 'quite imbecile'.[45] In Ireland the 7th Dragoons moved on from Ballincollig to Cahir in Tipperary. From there in July 1853 Thomson received a letter informing him that Matilda Weller was seriously ill. The next day he received another telling him she had died. He was very upset, and hardly touched food for several days. He apparently said little though, and Headmaster Walter MacLeod wrote to Barnes asking what the problem was.[46]

Matilda Weller was buried in Cahir parish church on July 19th:

SACRED
TO THE MEMORY OF
MATILDA WELLER
THE BELOVED DAUGHTER
OF HENRY WELLER
ARMOURER SERGEANT
7TH DRAGOON GUARDS
WHO DEPARTED THIS LIFE
17TH JULY 1853
AGED 14 YEARS

She was too delicate and
Fair a flower
To bloom and flourish in an
Earthly bower
Kindly did God transplant her
To the skies. Her beauty
Will not fade in Paradice.[47]

In Cahir in October 1853 Charles Bradlaugh took advantage of an inheritance to buy himself out of the army. He returned to London, moved in once more with his now widowed mother, and started to earn his living as clerk in a solicitor's office, with a part-time secretaryship in an insurance society. He kept contact with Thomson, and by July 1854 was borrowing some of Thomson's poetry to court Susan Hooper, who was to become Mrs Bradlaugh a year later.[48]

That summer of 1854 Thomson at last received his qualification as Army schoolmaster, and was sent to a garrison in Plymouth where he started work on August 7th.

Flow onward, ye pure sparkling waters
In sunshine with ripple and spray,
For the fairest of earth's young daughters
Will be imaged within you this day,
And tell her, oh! murmuring river,
When past her your bright billows roll,
That thus, too, her fairest form ever
Is imaged with truth in my soul.[49]

51

CHAPTER FIVE

A NEW PAY structure and system of warrant rank for schoolmasters came into being only a month before Thomson took up his first appointment in August 1854. At the top were first class schoolmasters who ranked next to commissioned officers and were paid 7s. a day; second and third class teachers ranked next to sergeant-major and were paid 5s. 6d. and 4s. per day respectively.[1] Newly qualified teachers entered at the third class, and such the majority remained. Promotion, which was by recommendation of an inspectorate, brought no extra duties. This caused some discontent amongst many teachers who saw themselves doing equal work for unequal pay.[2]

A third class schoolmaster was still paid well in comparison with the ordinary soldier. The former received an 8s. 6d. weekly 'lodging and fuel allowance' on top of his pay, and could earn extra money giving private lessons to officers' children. The infantryman who did the actual fighting in wars like the Crimea was paid 1s. a day less 4½d. stoppages for meat and bread.[3] This soldier was now confronted with young schoolmasters who not only had never seen action but had pay, privileges and rank such as they could never hope to attain. And the newcomers hadn't even bought their position – some were from the streets like themselves. Nor could they be ignored. Attendance at school was compulsory for two hours after drill, a privilege for which the soldiers had to pay: sergeants 8d. a month, corporals 6d., drummers and privates 4d. Married soldiers with children at the school also had to find money to have their children educated: 2d. per month for one child, 3d. for two, and a penny for each additional child thereafter.

The Chelsea graduates were as unpopular with the officers as with the men. There was complaint of their 'arrogance of education', and of their over-qualification: 'when a man has gone through a course such as that at Chelsea, he is altogether unfit for the heavy, tedious, monotonous work of a regimental school, it is like employing a razor to cut wood; if he knew a little less, he would be able to teach a great deal more.'[5] Even their uniform added to the trouble, being 'almost indistinguishable from the dress of many officers'.[6] This caused confusion and embarrassment when teachers were saluted by mistake. The uniform was a blue frock-coat braided in black with gold shoulder-knots, with one, two or three stars – according to the class of schoolmaster – on the collar. The frock-coat was worn over grey trousers, the whole topped with a cap which had 'a scarlet band bearing a crown in gold thread'.[7] The general dislike experienced by army teachers in the 1850s was summed up by one of them shortly before he left the service:

> It is a notorious fact that army schoolmasters are the most unpopular body in the whole service. Two-thirds of them are regarded by their commanding officers as a nuisance, by the officers generally as upstarts, who ape to be what they are not, and by the non-commissioned officers as men who are too well paid, have too many privileges, and consequently think too much of themselves.
>
> It has been attempted to create for them a middle-class position, against which the whole constitution of the service is opposed. It refuses to recognise it, and the schoolmaster, neither fish, flesh, nor fowl, disowned by all, having affinity with none, excites the prejudice of every class.[8]

Thomson's teaching began in Plymouth with the South Devon Militia. After a winter in that position he moved north in the spring of 1855 to join the Rifle Brigade at Aldershot, the army's main training camp for the Crimean War. Neither at Plymouth nor at Aldershot did he get on with his regimental commanding officer, the C.O. at Aldershot being recalled by one of Thomson's fellow teachers in later years as 'a rough brute'.[9] But Aldershot was at least handy for London on time off, and Thomson was able to renew his friendship with Charles Bradlaugh. The latter was spending ever greater time on the anti-religious propaganda drive coming to be known as 'secularism'. The word had been adopted by George Jacob Holyoake in 1851 in his weekly paper *The Reasoner*.[10] It was a defiant appropriation of the distinction made in church circles between the secular and the religious, and at the same time it was a gesture to the word's Latin root *'saeculum'* meaning the people of a single generation or era. The 'secularists' therefore were those consciously and publicly disjoining themselves from the practice of religion, and whose focus for what had-to-be-done was on the *'saeculum'* or present here-and-now world.

'Secularism' had been launched at a 'Free Discussion Festival' in London in 1853, the same year that Holyoake had founded the British Secular Institute of Communism and Propagandism.[11] The secularist movement was to remain separate from socialism and communism, becoming in time consistently identified as a kind of anti-Sabbatarian, republican, landownership reform and parliamentary suffrage reform, freedom-of-speech pressure group at the edge of the Liberal Party. Speakers such as Bradlaugh focused much activity on the exposition of contradictions and impossibilities in the Bible. Leaders of the movement regularly made alliances and fell out with one another over such matters as birth control or, more frequently, the distinction between an atheist and what came to be known as an 'agnostic'.[12] In the mid-1850s, within a few years of Holyoake's official 'launch' of the newly named movement, there were thirty-five secularist societies in Britain which Bradlaugh and others began to make their ports of call for weekend lectures or debates.[13] Thomson's own contact with Bradlaugh remained regular, and he told Susan Bradlaugh when passing on a message to her husband who was out of town 'Mr Bradlaugh and myself are such old and close friends that we do not mince words in speaking of or to each other.'[14]

But however close the friendship between them, Bradlaugh had not in 1855 won Thomson over to his point of view, as poems written by Thomson at this time and in the next few years, showed. In July he completed a three-part poem which seemed to say that doubts about religion could usually be attributed to the sins of one's youth:

> My brothers, let us own the truth,
> Bitter and mournful though it be, –
> That we, who spent our dreary youth
> In foul and sensual slavery,
> Are all too slavish, too unmanned,
> For conquerors of the Promised Land.[15]

The poem was in reply to Matthew Arnold's 'Stanzas from the Grande Chartreuse', in which Arnold reflected the doubts he had felt on a visit in France to the head Carthusian monastery there: on the one hand he couldn't accept the reclusive prayer-life of the monks as valid, on the other he couldn't condemn them since he himself had been, from the youthful days when he had been 'purged' of his faith

> Wandering between two worlds, one dead,
> The other powerless to be born,
> With nowhere yet to rest my head,
> Like these, on earth, I wait forlorn.

Thomson was specific about what the monks and everyone else were awaiting. The church might be 'mouldering', a refuge only for some 'ignorant pagan poor', but Christ himself had been divine, and the return of such a divine person was needed to lead modern thought:

> We pine in our dark living tomb,
> Waiting the God-illumined One
> Who, only, can disperse the gloom;
> Completing what the Dead begun.
> Or farther leading us some space
> Toward our eternal resting place.

'Thus religion towers/ Above this sordid, restless life of ours' he wrote another time that year in a poem describing the sight of St Paul's Cathedral as one approached it in London.[16] In that city Thomson on his visits from Aldershot could not only visit Bradlaugh but was able to resume contact with the Gray family, whose daughters were now teenagers, the eldest, Helen, being now aged sixteen. Her sister Agnes recalled Thomson's visits over the years to their East End home: 'Being several years younger than James, I cannot recollect much of him as a boy; but I remember we always thought him wonderfully clever, very nice-looking, and very gentle, grave, and kind. He was always most willing to attend to our whims, but my eldest sister was his especial favourite. Her will seemed always law to him. She was gay as he was grave, but whatever Helen said or did won approbation from him.'[17] There is nothing in Thomson's love poetry that can be unambiguously linked with Helen Gray – or anyone else. However it is worth noting that in 1854, the year that he was posted to his first position as a trained teacher, he wrote a poem 'Parting' which spoke of love surmounting separation.[18] And sometime in 1855 he wrote another that dwelt on the pains of separation, the memory of a loved-one's eyes, and her dread that perhaps 'far away I do or shall forget her guide'. This untitled poem was addressed in its opening line to 'Far-far away my "Sister" dear'.[19] However even if Helen Gray was the 'sister' intended, the annual Spring change-round of troops moved Thomson in 1856 away both from the Gray family in East London and from his 'rough brute' of a commanding officer at Aldershot. Thomson was transferred, apparently with some friends' help, to Dublin.[20] Before leaving he asked Helen's parents' permission to write to her, but permission was not granted. In the words of Agnes, 'he earnestly requested that my sister be allowed to correspond with him, a request which my parents thought it wiser to refuse.'[21]

He spent three years in Dublin, two of them in Richmond Barracks adjacent to the Grand Canal, with a year in the middle garrisoned at Ship Street Barracks beside Dublin Castle. While stationed in the city Thomson wrote more poems than at any other three-year period in his life. The poems varied from occasional cheery bacchanals and drinking choruses, to long self-recriminatory poems about sin and laziness, and more poems that were a kind of 'reply' or retelling of tales told by other poets. In his first winter in Dublin he completed two of these last-mentioned, poems called 'Tasso to Leonore' and 'Bertram to the Most Noble and Beautiful Lady Geraldine'. Amongst the writers who had previously addressed the Tasso story was Byron; his 'Lament for Tasso' of 1818 gave the monologue of the poet hero imprisoned in a madhouse for declaring his love for the Duke of Ferrara's sister. Tasso is unrepentant:

> That thou wert beautiful, and I not blind,
> Hath been the sin which shuts me from mankind

and defiantly ends his monologue by asserting that future generations will visit his cell as a shrine to love and the power of his poetry to link the princess's name with his own in immortality. Thomson's poem had none of this. As with his 'reply' to Matthew Arnold, he introduced a strong measure of sexual guilt, and the hero of 'Tasso to Leonore' is a pathetic figure who thinks humans are puppets in a world defiled by 'Filth of lust and blood of rage'.[22] Only after death can there be a union between Tasso and his lover, and to doubt that there is an afterlife, concludes Thomson's poet in the madhouse, would truly be 'mad – mad – how mad'.

Sexual guilt also featured strongly in 'Bertram to the Most Noble and Beautiful Lady Geraldine',[23] a retelling of Elizabeth Barret Browning's poem 'Lady Geraldine's Courtship'. In Elizabeth Browning's poem a young poet, Bertram, is invited to join the social set at a Lady Geraldine's country estate. He falls in love with her, but overhears her say that she couldn't consider marrying anyone beneath her station. Bertram berates her for thinking herself above any man who is 'only good to God, and nothing more'. But Lady Geraldine tells Bertram she loves him, for since he is rich in virtue, it doesn't matter that he's of low birth. Thomson's version however again deprived the male hero of any inherent worth alongside the woman with whom he is in love. Bertram is a 'torpid and defiled' guilt-ridden character whom no Lady would ever be likely to congratulate for his virtue. The man and the woman don't meet as equals separated by social circumstances: their difference is of fundamental nature and innate worth. Lady Geraldine's job is to save

Bertram – 'Blessed Redeemer of my sinking mind!' he calls her – since he has

> Left faith to die, and nurst the bitter weed
> Which blooms in poisonous gauds of heartless thought

Part of her saving him is the restoration of his 'faith': thanks to her 'numb faith relives', his life once more has a 'goal'. But there's nothing to suggest that the goal is one to be realised in his own lifetime. It's only after death that the man can be worthy of the female, only then can take place what another poem called 'the union that cannot in this life take place'.[24] Such unions though do take place in marriage, and 'Marriage' was the title given another of Thomson's poems written in Dublin in 1855.[25] However the poem was not about marriage as a happy ending to sexual and religious problems, but about their continuance during the narrator's wife's absence. The poem began by addressing a 'noble wife' with the words 'Come to me, oh come to me!' The noble wife must come and help the man whose 'strength, and hope, and faith are waning' and who wants her beside him before his soul be conquered and he 'fail from truth and right'.

There was a lot of failing from truth and right went on around army barracks at the time. Of 102,858 admissions to army hospitals throughout the United Kingdom in one year, 36,048 of them were for 'Diseases Incident to Lust'.[26] In Aldershot for instance the prevalence of brothels and drinking-dens for the forty regiments and 20,000 soldiers at Aldershot meant, according to one Parliamentary Report, that the men were 'cut off from all respectable society'.[27] At Portsmouth – where Thomson was billeted in 1862 – there was a failed attempt to shut down the flourishing brothel trade that serviced the servicemen:

> . . . within a circle having a radius of 1100 feet, there are more than 100 public houses, many of which are known to be brothels in disguise. As an example of the bold and defiant spirits of the prostitutes in Portsmouth I would refer to a display they made only a few months since, when a legal attempt was made to expel them from the houses they occupied or frequented, when on this occasion they mustered in strong force, trooped through the main streets, and made a public exhibition of their famous calling. The magistrates, from prudential motives I suppose, did not persevere in carrying their determination into effect.[28]

To counteract the lure of the brothel and the pub, improvements had been made to garrison libraries and reading rooms, and the new literacy drive of which Thomson himself was a part, could be understood to be part of this. But a contemporary report thought the struggle to change the men's habits was not winning: 'The reading rooms in barracks are not a sufficient check to the strong desire most of the men have for a change of scene; they like to go for a walk to see the shops by day, and the streets lighted up by night, and to escape from an atmosphere of force and restraint, to one of greater freedom; and in seeking for some kind of amusement, they fall naturally into bad company, and involuntarily acquire bad habits.'[29]

The city which Thomson saw when he went on his own walks was another where wealth gained from the industrial revolution – visible here in the society season centred on Dublin Castle itself – contrasted with the slum conditions in areas rapidly overpopulated by those seeking work. In Dublin's case immigration had been accelerated by people driven from the countryside by the famine of the 1840s. An 1857 report analysed the 1851 census to show that almost half of the city's 57,000 families were each then living in a single room. But in 1857 one room to a family was still too much some could hope for:

It is but too common to find more than one family in a room. Some of these rooms are lodging places at night, where there are several beds in the room which had been so densely occupied through the day. One would form the most correct opinion of these abodes by entering one of them at an early hour of the morning, out of the open air. Take one of the courts in these parts as an instance, which is an average specimen, for in such things one must 'nothing extenuate, nor set down aught in malice.' In the court there are eight front doors, or rather door-openings; four rooms in each house; a family in each room. The houses have no rear at all to them. The water is carried by the residents from some distance. The entrance to the court is very filthy, though the court is swept once every morning in the year. The rain in many cases comes in through the roof and into the room on the ground floor. The rent of one of these rooms is one shilling per week. Here the most simple and necessary articles of furniture are wanting . . . A chair, a wash-hand basin, a towel are in many cases things unknown. There are scattered through these parts some whose homes are much more comfortable than these, tradesmen and others in the receipt of good wages; but such cases as I have mentioned are not rare.[30]

In the worst of the slums, cellars had been notoriously overcrowded, though efforts had been made since 1851 to close these up. But they were still to be seen in 1857: 'In going through the city we still find some of these wretched abodes occupied. Many of them can only be entered by a visitor who is a stranger to them, by descending backwards, as a wild animal descends from the top of a tree. In a short time it is to be hoped the remainder will be shut up.'[31]

In what Thomson called his 'purgatorial' Ship Street Barracks,[32] he wrote what was to be the longest of his army poems, a four-part narrative called 'The Doom of a City'.[33] Its 1,714 lines tell of a man with neither 'home nor hope' restlessly driven to leave his city and row out to sea. After storms and an encounter with a sea-monster[34] he arrives at dry land, where he comes on a city whose inhabitants have become petrified statues in the midst of their last everyday actions. He watches as they are given their Last Judgment, a voice from the sky in block capital letters dealing out fire and destruction to successive batches of the damned. The survivors that remain are transformed, and ascend white-robed to Heaven. The narrator then rows back to his own city, and as he approaches it is possessed by divine inspiration to denounce it:

> Thy heritage vast and rich is ample to clothe and feed
> The whole of thy millions of children beyond all real need;
> One of the two main wheels whereon thy Faith doth move
> Is that each as he loves himself so shall he his neighbour
>   love:
> But thy chief social laws seem strictly framed to secure
> That one be corruptingly rich, another bitterly poor,
> And another just starving to death: thy fanes and mansions
>   proud
> Are beleaguered with filthy hovels wherein poor wretches crowd,
> Pining in body and soul; untaught, unfed by those
> Who are good if they merely dribble bland alms upon fatal
>   woes –
> Resigning scarcely aught of their pleasure and pride and
>   content,
> Nor dreaming that all their long life is one huge
>   embezzlement.[35]

Watching the virtuous being saved and taken to Heaven from the city he had visited, he had felt despair then at his own unworthiness:

> As one who in the morning shine
>   Reels homeward, shameful, wan, adust,
> From orgies wild with fiery wine
>   And reckless sin and brutish lust:
> And sees a doorway open wide,
>   And then the grand Cathedral space;

59

And hurries in to crouch and hide
    His trembling frame, his branded face . . .

How can he join the songs of praise:
    His throat is parched, his brain is wild:
How dare he seek the Father's gaze,
    Thus hopeless, loveless and defiled:
How taint the pureness – though he yearn
    To join such fellowship for aye?
He creeps out pale – may he return
    Some time when he shall dare to stay![36]

Thomson afterwards wrote that his idea for the City of the Statues had come from 'the tale of Zobeide in the History of the Three Ladies of Bagdad and the Three Calenders. This episode and the account of the Kingdoms of the Sea in "Prince Beder and . . ." impressed my boyhood more powerfully than anything else in the Arabian Nights.'[37] E.W. Lane's bowdlerised translation of the *Arabian Nights* was the standard edition when Thomson was a boy:

> We set sail with a fair wind, and soon got through the Persian Gulf; and when we got into the ocean, we steered our course for the Indies, and saw land the twentieth day . . .
>   I went ashore in the boat myself, and, making directly to the gates of the town, I saw there great number of men upon guard, some sitting and some standing, with batons in their hands; but perceiving they had no motion, nay, not so much as with their eyes, I took courage, and went nearer, and then found they were all turned into stones. I entered the town, and passed through several streets, where there stood every where men in several postures, but all unmoveable and petrified.[38]

But the *Arabian Nights* were received in Britain and the Western World as just part of that imported view of Middle Eastern culture that included objects and reports on the real ruins lying in real Arabian deserts. These provided museums as well as writers with images in plenty, and travellers' accounts fed Biblical geography such as MacLeod's *Geography of Palestine*, or the sermons of such as John Cumming. The ruins of these past civilisations presented a choice. They could be seen as fulfilment of God's prophecies: proof and warning of the wrath visited on the worshippers of false unchristian gods. Or they could be seen as images of the transience of *all* human office, of *all* monuments to personal achievement: as in Shelley's 'Ozymandias'.

> 'My name is Ozymandias, king of kings:
> Look on my works, ye mighty, and despair!'
> Nothing beside remains. Round the decay
> Of that colossal wreck, boundless and bare
> The lone and level sands stretch far away.

In 'The Doom of a City' the narrator, arriving at the City of Statues, says:

> I plunged into the City of the Dead,
> And pierced its Mausolean loneliness

and in the motionless city comes on a theatre which has an audience of 'tier and tier of serried statues'.[39] The traveller Burckhardt's description of his coming on the deserted city of Petra has resonances both with 'The Doom of a City' and with other poems that Thomson was to write later:

We saw one solitary Arab struggling along without any apparent object, a mere wanderer among ruins; and it is a not uninteresting fact, that this poor Bedouin was the only living being we saw in the desolate city of Petra . . . all along were the open doors of tombs, forming the great Necropolis of the city; and at the extreme end was a large open space, with a powerful body of light thrown down upon it, and exhibiting in one full view the facade of a beautiful temple, hewn out of the rock, with rows of Corinthian columns and ornaments, standing out fresh and clear as if but yesterday from the hands of the sculptor . . . Even now, that I have returned to the pursuits and thought-engrossing incidents of a life in the busiest city in the world, often in situations as widely different as light from darkness, I see before me the facade of that temple; neither the Colisseum at Rome, grand and interesting as it is, nor the ruins of the Acropolis at Athens, nor the Pyramids, nor the mighty temples of the Nile, are so often presented to my memory.

. . . Leaving the temple and the open area on which it fronts, and following the stream, we entered another defile much broader than the first, on each side of which were ranges of tombs, with sculptured doors and columns; and on the left, in the bosom of the mountain, hewn out of the solid rock, is a large theatre, circular in form, the pillars in front fallen, and containing thirty-three rows of seats, capable of containing more than 3,000 persons. Above the corridor was a range of doors opening to chambers in the rocks, the seats of the princes and wealthiest inhabitants of Petra, and not unlike a row of private boxes in a modern theatre.

The whole theatre is at this day in such a state of preservation, that if the tenants of the tombs around could once more rise into life, they might take their old places on its seat, and listen to the declamation of their favourite player.[40]

A vindication of the superior civilisation of imperial England and the Bible on which it claimed to be based, or a reminder that all empires were passing phenomena which left no residual values. Beneath this lay the question: is History an evolutionary linear sequence of progressive moral civilisation, or is it a cyclic structure of repetitive practices under different forms, having no meaning beyond its own existence? These alternatives could be seen as combined in one single eternally unanswerable question facing mankind. The image for this was taken as the Sphinx, in the ambiguous duality of its form – half human, half animal; a face that was the face of a god and was the embodiment of moral value; or a face that was the face of a human, looking on the passing panorama of ultimately meaningless events: its body half-animal – it had no soul.

'Time moves behind her in a grand eclipse' wrote George Meredith of the Sphinx in a poem published in an 1851 collection: 'on her large closed lips/ Hangs dumb the awful riddle of the earth'.[41] The body of the Sphinx who guarded the city of Thebes was female. How different were women from men? Did they know the riddle of the universe? Were they part of the cycle from which men had become separated? Did they have a different consciousness of time? A face over two breasts. Was that a god? Or an animal? Or just another human?[42]

CHAPTER SIX

The Mother – she was very good and sweet

But always sad; and children can discern
The chilly cloud across their morning sun
Of such a mood, and fret that it is stern –

'You sadden us who want whole worlds of fun!'
But [they] see not in this cloud the lingering gloom
Of some retiring tempest which hath done

More fateful ravage than their hearts hath room
To comprehend. She had been wed one year
When suddenly the sailor's solemn doom

Yet less his doom than those who hold him dear,
O'ertook her sire and brother in one ship,
Upon the Goodwins; land & home so near,

Standing they felt their vessel slowly dip
And saw across the waste of savage foam
The boats and men that could not dare the trip.

She got the news; and did not rave nor weep
But walked about the house for many days
As one who walketh in unnatural sleep,

With such a fixed and vacant stony gaze
Doing her household work the while she went.
I think that in this trance of drear amaze

Her spirit was with cruel force distent
To full capacity for all her woe,
And in the process somewhat warped & rent:

For when the stun was past that bitter blow
With almost frantic soreness galled her heart:
She and this brother loved each other so . . .

But as a fire which while its torture burns
Consumes whate'er it doth not purify
So that a void of doleful ruin yearns

Left in her soul drear vacuum – from on high
At length o'erbrimmed with mystic love of God
She learnt strange happiness in misery,

And kissed between its bitter strokes the rod:
In every flower of joy she saw a taint
And bribe [?] to love; with eager steps she trod

Life's thorniest paths until her limbs were faint:
Nor looked for Heaven itself – but welcomed Hell
[If] Hell could [keep her] for ever as a yearning saint

Consumed with love & quenchless fire to dwell
If she might only in pure trance arise
To see her Lord – the Love ineffable

Revealed in glory to her ravished eyes . . .

This is from an unfinished narrative poem written at Ship Street Barracks in January 1858 and abandoned in a barely legible scribble.[1] The poem, evidently using some autobiographical material mixed with fiction, was arranged in two parts: it gave the childhood memories of one who had been orphaned in infancy and adopted by a sailor friend of his late father, to be reared alongside the infant son and daughter of his new foster-parents. The narrator's father had died not long after the mother had died of cholera. This had happened soon after the narrator's birth.

In another piece written by Thomson now, and also left unfinished, the death of a mother again played a significant part. The 10,000-word prose tale *Sarpolus of Mardon* tells the mythical legend of a King and his three sons who, defeated in battle and banished to a magical island, bury their mother in a Temple of the Tombs where the royal dead are enthroned. Having kissed their dead mother, the sons leave King Sarpolus alone to ask questions of the Fate of the royal line:

64

For the moon was high in heaven, and the stars were countless; –
large, beautiful, golden, scintillant, eyes of triumph, strange to sorrow,
all gazing down from their serene heaven into the Valley of the Shadow
of Death. On either side of this rock rose two vast images, King and
Queen; before it was couched a Mammoth-Sphinx upon whose countenance gazed stedfastly a mightier angel, leaning upon his naked sword,
his wings folded in marble patience; and its broad front was overwrought
with wan light and stern shadows of solemn graven words and sculptured
graven imagery yet more mysterious.[2]

Together the sons sing a dirge as they carry their dead mother to
her resting place: the names of the three sons are Roncel, Armon
– and Vanolis. This last name was chosen by Thomson to form the
second part of his pseudonym when, in February 1858, he made his
first appearance in print as a poet. In literary terms the 'Bysshe' was
an obvious reference to Thomson's literary hero Percy Bysshe Shelley:
'Vanolis' is an anagram of the German poet Novalis. Thomson had
begun teaching himself German in his spare time at Aldershot, and
had progressed in German Literature so far as to quote a few lines
of Novalis's poem 'Hymns to the Night' as a footnote to 'Tasso to
Leonore'.[3] The compound 'Bysshe Vanolis' Thomson shortened in
later appearances to 'B.V.', and it is as 'B.V.' Thomson – often
to distinguish him from the James Thomson who wrote 'The Seasons'
and 'The Castle of Indolence' – that he has subsequently been remembered.

The monthly paper in which his first published poem appeared
was called the *Investigator*. Bradlaugh worked on it before taking
over its editorship. He too had a pseudonym under which he wrote,
'Iconoclast'. Why *Investigator*, and why 'Iconoclast', he explained in
his first editorial:

> We are investigators, and our policy is to ascertain facts and present
> them to our readers in clear and distinct language. If we find a mind bound
> round with Creeds and Bibles, we will select a sharp knife to cut the bonds;
> if we find men prostrating themselves, without inquiry, before idols, our
> policy is iconoclastic – we will destroy those idols . . . We believe all the
> religions of the world are founded on error, in the ignorance of natural
> causes and material conditions, and we deem it our duty to endeavour
> to expose their falsity. Our policy is therefore aggressive.[4]

That Thomson only three months after completing 'The Doom of
a City' should make his debut in print in a monthly that announced

itself as 'the only British journal that advocates atheism', might seem strange. But the poem that he published there could be seen as a private rebuke to the hysteria of 'The Doom of a City''s narrator. 'Mr Save-his-Soul-alive-O' derides the Christian who crosses the sea of life shrieking and breastbeating 'Oh! I am drowned!' in a manner liable to upset everyone else in the boat with him:

> The timbers, in fact, are not too sound;
>   The shore's far off, and the chartmark's dim;
> And this coward shrieking his 'Oh! I am drowned!'
>   Will upset us all with him.
>
> To think that a fellow should launch to fight,
>   In the name of Heaven, against Hell and Sin,
> Croaking in such a delirious fright
>   As if the devil must win.[5]

To the readers of the *Investigator* it will have appeared simply as another lampoon on a type of the Christian. They would have been unaware of the existence of 'The Doom of a City', which did not appear in print until twenty-six years later.[6]

In the army classroom religion was considered the chief responsibility of the chaplains who visited to give an hour's lesson twice a week.[7] But the teacher was expected to begin every day's proceedings with a twenty-minute lesson from Scripture, though as mentioned in Chapter Four the lesson was to be general enough as not to upset any specific denomination. No teacher ever complained about having to do this, but the Chaplain General thought many of the teachers' lessons here unsatisfactory. He was also displeased when chaplains complained that many teachers did not join in the visiting chaplains' twice-weekly sessions, but left the classroom or stayed only to keep discipline.[8]

The schools were divided into four grades or classes, all of which were taught in the one room. Those entering at the bottom class, Class Four, were largely illiterate and innumerate. To progress to Class Three in the adult school a soldier had to be able to read reading cards then basic primers and 'to work correctly the four first rules of simple and compound arithmetic and reduction of money'; to reach Class Two he had to be able 'To read correctly; to work correcting sums in proportion, practice and vulgar fractions. To write and spell fairly from dictation. To know the outlines of the geography of the British Empire.' Once in Class Two the aim was to be able to write not just 'fairly' but 'freely and legibly', to spell 'correctly' from dictation, and to do decimals, compound interest, square and cube roots. Class One would add algebra, geometry, 'Light and Heat for Beginners'; and a final Advanced Class would offer trigonometry, hydrostatics and hydraulics.[9] The mathematical side of all this would have been no problem for Thomson. Friends thought he could have made a career as a mathematician, and at Chelsea he had been sometimes coaxed by classmates into sidetracking the teacher with difficult mathematical problems to keep him irrelevantly occupied.[10]

In 1857 attendance of soldiers at the garrison schools was made voluntary and payments for adults in the bottom two classes were abolished. The rudiments of literacy and numeracy thus became free, anything beyond that was what had to be paid for. As a soldier was expected to have progressed beyond the rudiments when applying for promotion to sergeant, Classes One or Two therefore tended, after 1857, to be made up of the small minority of soldiers seeking promotion. But this did not work smoothly, it was soon reported: 'The men in general leave the school so soon as they are called upon to pay, and only return at a subsequent period in order to qualify for promotion; when they find that much of what they formerly learnt has been forgotten.'[11] Irregularity of attendance was also a great handicap:

> . . . of those who attend on any one day, perhaps a third part will not have an opportunity of coming to school again for two or three weeks, whilst others will be able to attend many times within the same period. It is evident that systematic class teaching is out of the question under such circumstances, and that although individuals may derive considerable profit from the schoolmaster's instruction, the general effect must be small. And this irregularity in the attendance militates against the progress even of the few who attend regularly, although of course in a less degree than against that of the others.[12]

Out of a hundred schools picked 'at hazard', only eighteen were found to have any pupils in classes beyond Three or Four – in other words the great majority of army teachers spent their time trying to teach the basics of reading and writing to irregularly attended classes.[13] People like Barnes though continued to show definite success in their results,[14] and Thomson, in a verse-letter to a teacher friend in May 1858, tried to look on the bright side:

> And if now and then a curse (too intense for this light verse)
> Should be gathering in one's spirit when he thinks of how
>   he lives,

With a constant tug and strain – knowing well it's all in vain –
Pumping muddy information into unretentive sieves:

Let him stifle back the curse, which but makes the matter worse,
And by tugging on in silence earn his wages if he can;
For the blessed eve and night are his own yet, and he might
Fix sound bottoms in these sieves too, were he not so weak a man.[15]

The evenings were when Thomson could read, write and continue with his study of German Literature – a study which he shared with the recipient of the verse-letter, James Potterton, who had graduated from Chelsea six months after Thomson.[16] Another friend later recalled that Thomson in his spare time 'worked himself without mercy'.[17]

Sometimes teachers might be asked to perform extra duties, a request that Thomson did not always welcome. Giving lantern-slide lectures was such a duty, there being a wide range of topics available for these, including travellers' accounts of the Holy Land.[18] Barnes in Dublin gave forty lantern lectures to audiences averaging 160 one winter,[19] and Thomson gave Potterton an account of one he had delivered himself:

Lectured last night on English History as showman of certain magic-lantern slides. They were pretty well done, and I knew a little of the subjects; so the speech came rather trippingly from the tongue. With practice of a preliminary hundred or so, I might be able to give a not intolerable lecture. But who would willingly undergo such practice, even if it made perfect?'[20]

Others however were enthusiastic about Thomson's abilities here, and he was asked to repeat one lecture for the exclusive benefit of officers and their families. But when he gave this he cut out all the commentary and remarks which had apparently gone down so well with his first audience, and the performance before the officers was over in minutes, 'a complete fiasco'.[21] This can be taken as an example of the friction between officers and the new Chelsea graduates, friction to which the Commander in Chief at Dublin, the Duke of Cambridge, referred when he spoke of the 'endless trouble' at Dublin caused by these young men who 'considered themselves more like gentlemen than anything else'.[22] It had particularly incensed Cambridge that the schoolmasters after 1854 corresponded directly with the head of their Corps, the Chaplain General, not only bypassing their commanding officers but often reporting them. Further changes in 1857 required teachers to report upwards through the commanding officer, and within two years the whole system was brought under the Army Commander in Chief in a Council of Military Education, whose functions were scrutinised by the Secretary of State at the War Office. In other words by the end of the decade schoolmasters were brought unambiguously into the chain of command and discipline.[23]

In Thomson's verse-letter to Potterton he wrote that he knew as much about 'this world of time and space' as a church mouse knew about the substance and plan of a church or the God for whom it had been built to worship. Joking about some of his companions in Richmond Barracks he added

> And our damned fool Thomson steers through our dusk
> > of hopes and fears
> As some blind bat – blind yet conscious through a dragon-haunted
> wood.[24]

The 'dusk' metaphor is of some interest in that when Thomson appeared for the second time in print just over a month later in July 1858, he temporarily abandoned his first pseudonym for another – the Latin 'Crepusculus'. In fact he used this latter pseudonym for all his signed contributions to *Tait's Edinburgh Magazine*, in which he had twenty of his poems published between July 1858 and July 1860, not long before the magazine went out of business. Founded in 1831 under the Whig William Tait, the monthly was in its last years published from Glasgow under George Troup, journalist founder of Scotland's first daily newspaper the *North British Daily Mail*.[25] Amongst the poems that Troup published was 'Tasso to Leonore' and 'Bertram to the Most Noble and Beautiful Lady Geraldine'.[26] He published nothing controversial or vehement such as 'The Doom of a City'. The poem that appeared in July 1858, 'The Fadeless Bower', was a romantic vignette describing a long-past meeting between the narrator and his now dead lover; the pair had stayed silent and motionless in each other's company, in a 'bower' that would never fade from the narrator's memory. Once again it was to be after death when the man would meet his lover 'in nobler spheres':

> Ah! Alice, if I dream and dream,
> > What else is left me in this life?
> New faces all about me teem;
> > Strange hopes, and woes, and loves are rife;
> I over-lived myself, sweet dear,
> In lingering when you left me here.[27]

In August *Tait's* published another four poems by 'Crepusculus' gathered under the heading 'Four Stages in a Life'. The poems were 'Love's Dawn', 'Marriage', 'Separation', and a fourth poem where the narrator once more looked forward to reunion after death with her whom he called 'My love, whom I have lost this long, sad day.'[28]

Away from *Tait's Edinburgh Magazine* though, Thomson was pursuing a much less romantic strain. He again, as in 'The Doom of a City', described the feelings of one who thinks about entering a church, but declines. However this time it was not guilt about his own supposed unworthiness that kept the outsider outside:

> How sweet to enter in, to kneel and pray
>   With all the others whom we love so well!
> All disbelief and doubt might pass away,
>   All peace float to us with its Sabbath bell.
> Conscience replies, There is but one good rest,
> Whose head is pillowed upon Truth's pure breast.[29]

This would have gone down well at the *Investigator*, but the poem was not published there and did not appear in print until four years later. However Thomson – as 'B.V.' – was published again in the *Investigator* in December, making his debut now as a critical essayist in the same monthly in which he had made his debut as a poet. The American Ralph Waldo Emerson was highly regarded in Bradlaugh's paper; the editor Bradlaugh carried extracts from the essay 'Self-Reliance' in a personal notebook.[30] In 'Notes on Emerson' Thomson focused on Emerson's rejection of that belief in a personal God the Father that engendered widespread personal guilt:

> . . . Emerson, though spiritual and sincere as any; though dissatisfied as any with our present societies, policies and religions, always speaks calmly and hopefully; often with an easy playfulness. 'Our young people are diseased with theological problems of original sin, origin of evil, predestination, and the like . . . These are the soul's mumps, and measles, and hooping-coughs.'
>   The heart yearning to give forth and drink in ever more and more love may create a God for its worship; the passionate soul oscillating fiercely between evil and good may seek a God for its refuge and stay: free from the poverty of longing, securely commanding his passions, he feels no particular need of a personal God, and remains indifferently Pantheistic . . . One submission only can he rejoice in, the being possessed, passive, by the Universal Soul, which is simply essential *Me* of every human

being. 'A man is greater than a crowd.' 'In self-trust all the virtues are comprehended.'[31]

Emerson's 'transcendentalist' thought had been strongly influenced by his interpretation of the German metaphysical philosophers of the turn of the century, and part of his introduction had been in 1830 to read Thomas Carlyle's essay on Novalis;[32] in this Carlyle presented his own interpretation and exposition of the philosophers around Kant: 'Time and Space themselves are not external but internal entities: they have no outward existence, there is no Time and no Space *out* of the mind; they are mere *forms* of man's spiritual being, *laws* under which his thinking nature is constituted to act . . . To a Transcendentalist, matter has an existence, but only as a Phenomenon: were *we* not there, neither would it be there; it is a mere Relation, or rather the result of a Relation between our living Souls and the great First Cause; and depends for its appearance on *our* bodily and mental organs; having itself *no* intrinsic qualities; being in the common sense of that word, Nothing. The tree is green and hard, not of its own natural virtue, but simply because my eye and hand are fashioned so as to discern such and such appearances under such and such conditions . . . There is in fact, says Fichte, no Tree there; but only a manifestation of Power from something which is *not I*.'[33]

It is not to the point whether Carlyle was adequately presenting Kant's views on Space and Time.[34] What mattered was that Carlyle could argue from the religious point of view that if Time and Space were only subjective aspects of the human understanding rather than features of the objective world itself, this cleared the way to resolve certain theological difficulties such as God's supposed knowledge of the end of History set against humans' supposed free will to determine it themselves. To put it another way, it might resolve the problem of the numbered Elect versus the Universality of the Atonement. As Carlyle's essay put it: 'If Time and Space have no absolute existence, no existence out of our minds, it removes a stumbling-block from the very threshold of our Theology. For on this ground, when we say that the Deity is omnipresent and eternal, that with Him it is a universal Here and Now, we say nothing wonderful; nothing but that He also created Time and Space, that Time and Space are not laws of His being, but only of ours.'[35]

This had been, according to Carlyle, source for optimism in Novalis:

For him the material Creation is but an Appearance, a typical shadow in which the Deity manifests itself to man. Not only has the unseen world a reality, but the only reality: the rest being not metaphorically but literally and in scientific strictness, 'a show'; in the words of the poet, '*Schall und Rauch umnebelnd Himmels Gluth*, Sound and Smoke overclouding the splendour of Heaven.' The Invisible World is near us and about us; were the fleshly coil removed from our Soul, the glories of the Unseen were even now around us; as the Ancients fabled of the Spheral Music. Thus, not in word only, but in truth and sober belief, he feels himself encompassed by the Godhead; feels in every thought, that 'in Him he lives, moves and has his being . . .'

'Poetry, Virtue, Religion, which for other men have but, as it were, a traditionary and imagined existence, are for him the everlasting basis of the Universe; and all earthly acquirements, all with which Ambition, Hope, Fear, can tempt us to toil and sin, are in very deed but a picture of the brain, some reflex shadowed on the mirror of the Infinite, but in themselves air and nothingness. Thus, to live in that Light of Reason, to have, even while here and encircled with this Vision of Existence, our abode in that Eternal City, is the highest and sole duty of man.'[36]

Emerson's 'enthusiasm' stood in relation to this vision as the 'gift of tongues' to the Universal Atonement. Emerson described this 'enthusiasm' in his essay 'The Over-Soul':

By the necessity of our constitution, a certain enthusiasm attends the individual's consciousness of the Divine presence. The character and duration of this enthusiasm varies with the state of this individual, from an ecstasy and trance and prophetic inspiration – which is its rarer appearance – to the faintest glow of virtuous emotion, in which form it warms like our household fires all the families and associations of men, and makes society possible. A certain tendency to insanity has always attended the opening of the religious sense in men, as if they had been 'blasted with excess of light.' The trances of Socrates, the 'union' of Plotinus, the vision of Porphyry, the conversion of Paul, the aurora of Behmen, the convulsions of George Fox and his Quakers, the illumination of Swedenborg, are of this kind. What was in the case of these remarkable persons a ravishment has, in innumerable instances in common life, been exhibited in less striking manner. Everywhere the history of religion betrays a tendency to enthusiasm. The rapture of the Moravian and Quietist; the opening of the internal sense of the Word, in the language of the New Jerusalem Church; the *revival* of the Calvinistic churches; the *experiences* of the Methodists, are varying forms of that shudder of awe and delight with which the individual soul always mingles with the universal soul.

. . . The great distinction between teachers sacred or literary – between poets like Herbert, and poets like Pope – between philosophers like Spinoza, Kant, and Coleridge, and philosophers like Locke, Paley,

Mackintosh, and Stewart – between men of the world, who are reckoned accomplished talkers, and here and there a fervent mystic, prophesying, half insane under the infinitude of his thought – is that one class speak *from within*, or from experience, as parties and possessors of the fact; and the other class, *from without*, as spectators merely, or perhaps as acquainted with the fact on the evidence of third persons.[37]

Novalis, Carlyle's essay related out of Tieck's biography, had fallen in love with a thirteen-year-old girl who died when she was fifteen. Novalis's affections moved on elsewhere, but he had idealised the dead girl 'as a saintly presence, mournful and unspeakable and mild, to be worshipped in the inmost shrine of his memory.' The third section of his 'Hymns to the Night', supposedly inspired by his own experience, describes the visionary appearance of the young girl to the poet standing by the heaped earth of her graveside: the heaped earth is what Thomson, in his own translation of the poem, translated as the 'arid mound' of her grave.

Once when I wept bitter tears, when hope was dissolved in anguish, and I stood alone on the arid mound which concealed in its strait darkness the Vision of my Life; lonely as never yet was Being lonely, impotent, an Incarnate Thought of misery: then, as I looked around for help, powerless to advance unable to retire, and to the fleeting extinguished life with infinite longing clung: – there came out of the azure distance, from the heights of my old happiness a twilight-tremor, and at once rent the bonds of birth, the fetters of Light. The earthly splendour fled, and with it fled my grief and sorrow flowed away into a new unfathomable world; thou O Night Inspiration, Slumber of Heaven, possessed me: the ground slowly ascended, and above the ground hovered my released and new-born Spirit. The hillock became a cloud of dust through which I discerned the transfigured lineaments of the Beloved. In her eyes dwelt Eternity: I claspt her hands and the tears came as glittering links of various undisseverable. Milleniums passed by like vanishing storms. On her neck I wept the rapturous tears of the New Life . . . It was my first, my only Vision; and first since then have I everlasting immutable faith in the Heaven of the Night, and its glory the Beloved.[38]

In the pseudonym 'Bysshe Vanolis' that Thomson had first adopted for the *Investigator*, the reference to Shelley would have been approved by readers. Shelley, author of 'The Necessity of Atheism' and 'Queen Mab', was a hero to freethinkers; the poet was amongst those included in the *Half Hours with the Free Thinkers* advertised in the *Investigator* in separate numbers fortnightly before being gathered into anthologies.[39] But a reference to Novalis would have been less welcome, even amongst the small number likely to know his largely untranslated work. Thomson's never-published translation of 'Hymns to the Night' would not have been welcomed by 'the only British journal to champion atheism':[40]

> The stone is rolled away,
>   Humanity arisen:
> And we are thine for aye,
>   Delivered from our prison.
> Before thy bread and wine
>   The sharpest pain and strife;
> The Eucharist divine
>   Dissolves this Earth and Life.
>
> Death to the Feast doth call;
>   The ready virgins bear
> The lamps clear-burning all, –
>   No lack of oil is there.
> Oh, that thy bridal train
>   Now sounded from afar,
> And human voices fain
>   Invoked us from each star!
>
> O Mary, unto thee
>   A thousand hearts aspire;
> In this dark life, thee
>   Thee only they desire.
> They live in hope, forseeing
>   Their rapture unexprest
> When thou, O Blessed Being
>   Shalt take them to thy breast.
>
> So many who woe-waiting
>   With eager spirits burned,
> And from this dark world hasting
>   Themselves to thee have turned;
> And who have helped us long
>   In many a need and pain;
> We come to join their throng
>   Never to part again.
>
> No more the faithful lavish
>   Wan tears on lifeless clay;
> No power can ever ravish
>   What Love doth own alway;

Their yearning grief to heaven,
  The Night their soul inspires;
And o'er them saints in Heaven
  Keep watch that never tires.

Take joy! this life we render
  To life immortal dies;
An inward glowing splendour
  Our spirit glorifies.
To wine of life eternal
  The starry heavens dissolve,
And there in bliss supernal
  As stars we shall revolve.

There Love is freely given,
  There parting is no more;
There swells the Life of Heaven,
  A sea without a shore.
One night of bliss for ever,
  An everlasting trance!
Our sole sun setting never,
  The Father's countenance.

CHAPTER SEVEN

IT WAS TIRESOME to see the Earth as a commodity created by a Supreme Male for a fixed number's eternal profit, the price being the establishment of a much larger eternal underclass who had failed in open competition with their peers. Seen as a myth, as a figurative way of imagining a totality of the world beyond and including the immediate senses, 'Mother Nature' had at least as old, if not an older pedigree than that of Jehovah. For some she might present the image of a supposed pre-industrial Age of Community, for others she could be but one guise of the Supreme Female – God the Mother – who had been evicted with the establishment of a monotheistic but anthropomorphic Cosmic History. Certainly 'Mother Nature' could present a cheerier picture of the planet Earth than that of its being a 5,000-year-old staging-post for billions of human beings on their way to an eternity in the fires of Hell. She hadn't created Time, she was part of it, a manifestation of it, a continuing process from the Past, in the Present, towards the Future. 'Mother Nature' didn't 'create' things like a mad scientist in his garden toolshed. She gave birth to them. She wasn't divorced from that which naturally existed. She was part of it, and it was part of her.[1]

In 'The Doom of a City' the narrator had accused himself of cutting himself off from the rest of the world:

> I shut myself off from the lives around me,
> Eating my own foul heart – envenomed food;
> And while dark shadows more and more enwound me,
> Nourished a dreary pride of solitude;
> The cords of sympathy which should have bound me
> In sweet communion with earth's brotherhood,
> I drew in tight and tighter still around me,
> Strangling my best existence for a mood.[2]

But the narrator in Thomson's 'The Happy Poet' written in April

77

1859 was happy to be on his own. Having realised the 'perfect unity' of space and time, 'I live apart my self-fulfilling life': he wants to write about all the aspects of Nature – birds, beasts, rivers, mountains, flowers, trees, piercing the secrets of 'our great Mother', the mother who 'baring her full breast in solitudes/ Suckles each child as if she had but him.'[3] The poem was completed in Richmond Barracks, the barracks which Thomson had described as his 'castle hight of indolence'.[4] A poem 'The Lord of the Castle of Indolence' again gave the monologue of a detached observer of the universe who felt no guilt in being 'self-sufficing'. This one was happy to watch others toil in vain to change the world while he lay back comprehending 'the heavenly things in earthly symbols writ.'[5]

In Novalis's *The Disciples at Saïs* the student wishing to unlock Nature's secrets would study 'that great Cipher-writing which one meets with everywhere, on wings of birds, shells of eggs, in clouds, in the snow, in crystals, in forms of rocks, in freezing waters, in the interior and exterior of mountains, of plants, animals, men, in the lights of the sky, in plates of glass and pitch when touched and struck on, in the filings round the magnet, and the singular conjunctures of Chance.'[6] They would wish to enter that temple to Isis at Saïs perhaps to decipher the hieroglyphs on the veil of the goddess, which veil it was fatal rashness to attempt to lift. Isis here and in Schiller – whom Thomson was also now reading[7] – can be seen as a kind of iconographic figure representing a different set of fundamental questions from that represented by the figure of the Sphinx. The latter might stand as a sign for the unknowable process of History; whilst Isis might stand as a sign for the unknowable nature of Present reality: whether Berkeley had been right in saying 'all the choir of heaven and furniture of earth, in a word all those bodies which compose the mighty frame of the world, have not any subsistence without a mind, that their *being* is to be perceived or known; that consequently so long as they are not actually perceived by me, or do not exist in my mind or that of any other created spirit, they must either have no existence at all, or else subsist in the mind of some Eternal Spirit'.[8] Whether the 'transcendentalist' philosophy was right as attributed to Fichte by Carlyle in his Novalis essay, namely that 'there is a "Divine Idea" pervading the visible Universe, which visible Universe is indeed but its symbol and sensible manifestation'.[9]

At Richmond Barracks Thomson himself was neither isolated nor deprived of friendship. He had been attached to the 55th Foot the previous Spring, and there were 138 non-commissioned officers and men from the regiment on the school roll. Average daily attendance was nineteen; of children, whose attendance at morning school was more constant and predictable, there were ten boys and eleven girls.[10] For friendly company he had John Grant, at nineteen not long out of the Normal School.[11] He and Thomson began a friendship that was to last for life. They went long walks in the area round the city, and on one occasion discussed the possibility of deserting together by sea.[12] Grant was now included in the circle of Thomson's friends that included James Potterton, Joseph Barnes and his wife, and the Bradlaughs in London. Grant wrote to Bradlaugh in March 1859 requesting that some books unavailable in Dublin be sent over:

> I write, Thomson sitting t'other side of the table, smoking and reading. I fear that we in Dublin shall soon lose him, it being extremely probable that the 55th Regiment will ship to Aldershot within a month. Which leads you to reflect on the universal applicability of 'It's an ill wind that blows nobody good;' and suggests the extreme shortness of the distance between London and Aldershot. He sends his kindest wishes to yourself, Mrs Bradlaugh and the little ones; and desires me to state that he will soon be with you.[13]

Though Thomson had been forbidden to write to Helen Gray from Ireland, he had been given permission to write to her youngest sister Agnes. He told her of his continuing close relationship with Joseph Barnes and his family: 'Poor Mr Barnes's house has been full of sickness ever since Christmas. Did I tell you that I a second time stood god-father to one of his sons: I am getting quite an important and paternal character. Double god-father is almost as respectable as a married man, one would think.'[14]

Another with whom he maintained contact was his monitor friend from Royal Caledonian Asylum days, George Duncan. Since coming to Ireland Thomson had spent his holidays in the home of George Duncan and his wife, Duncan having married in 1855. Mrs Duncan later recalled his visits to them: 'It was like coming to a brother and sister, for he was dearer to us than a friend. Often afterwards did we talk of him and his great talents and how he dreamed the time away, always happy and contented with his Shelley. When a student, he would just glance over a subject, or read it over once, and yet know it perfectly.'[15] Thomson described the location of one of his army holidays – in Belfast – in another letter to Agnes:

> In the hope of adding to your geographical knowledge, let me trouble you with a few words about this great capital of Ulster. People who have seen it call it a fine city: for my part, I can scarcely pretend to have seen it, though I looked about at it for a week. In Christian countries one

expects rain from a canopy of heavy clouds, and hopes for clear skies after; but the Belfast firmament managed to persist in a sulky darkness day after day, while still keeping nearly all its rain to spite and spoil future good weather. East and north-east winds, also, trailed the thick and smutty factory smoke continually about us. The streets of the city are very wide, and so far good, but the houses are not remarkable, and two parallel rows of common buildings – even though half a mile apart – would scarcely make a grand street.[16]

Agnes had begun to write poems herself, and Thomson provided her both with criticism and with books that he thought she should read. In May 1859 he posted her the two volumes of Robert Browning's *Men and Women* which had appeared three years before:

I take the liberty of sending you by this post two volumes of verse which fell into my hands some time back. The author, Robert Browning, is about the strongest and manliest of our living poets. His wife (*née* Elizabeth Barrett, to adopt the style of wedding-cards) is beyond all comparison the greatest of English poetesses – *those whose works are published*, I mean. I happen to have her last book, and will send it to you some day. You will probably not care for these poems at first; but they are worth your study, and you may find, as I did, that they improve much with longer acquaintance. If I might school you a bit, I should order you always to look up a dictionary what words you don't understand, and always to puzzle over difficult passages until they become either perfectly clear or thoroughly hopeless. No lazy reading will ever master a masterly writer. Should you care enough for Browning to wish thoroughly to comprehend him, I shall of course be happy to render you what little assistance may be in my power towards the clearing up of obscurities. The final poem, you will perceive, is addressed to his wife. To the best of my remembrance he used not to write so large a proportion of love-poetry aforetime: his marriage must do its best to excuse the poor fellow for his present extravagance in that article. My notion was that your poets, though always fluttering about Love like moths about a rushlight, generally took good care not to singe seriously their precious selves. This unfortunate Mr Browning, however, seems to have flung himself headlong into the flame, determined to get himself burnt up – wings and all.[17]

He told Agnes to keep the books, as the garrison libraries provided much of his needs and it was awkward for a soldier to carry books around with him from garrison to garrison at the annual changeover.[18]

When that change came in 1859 it was not to Aldershot that Thomson was sent as Grant had expected, but north to the new camp at the Curragh in County Kildare. An army description of the camp made after its construction in 1855 shows how every inch of this city on the plain was calculated proportionately to rank as well as utility.

The huts are distributed in a series of squares, ten in number, for 1,000 men each, placed thirty yards apart . . . These squares have an interior space of 380 by 360 feet, on which the regimental training of recruits, and company drill, etc. etc. take place . . .

The huts, with a few exceptions, are constructed of American white fir timber, deals and battens, of the first quality, excepting the sleeper-sills, door-posts, angle-posts, heel-posts and Meir sill, which are of the best Merriel, Dantzic, or red pine. The joiners' work, including the floors and boarding, was cut of deals or battens when not otherwise directed. The huts are framed, weather-boarded, and lined; the roofs being boarded and covered with asphalt felt, coated with tar, sand and lime; and the walls are paved over with mineral paint externally. Each site is levelled, brick footings are provided, and a space of five feet all round is coated with five inches of broken stones and gravel.

The size common to nearly all the huts may be quoted at 40 feet by 20 feet. The soldiers' hut forms but one apartment, appropriated for twenty-five men, and is finished with the usual in bedsteads, and warmed by a Canadian stove in the centre. The officers' huts are divided into eight small rooms, about nine feet square, with centre passages, and porches at either end for shelter to the end rooms. Porches are also constructed to all doors exposed to the north. The sergeants' huts are divided into six apartments – one half into four rooms similar in size to the officers' quarters, the other half into two rooms. The huts for married soldiers are similar to those for officers; of these there are, at present, but two to each square, giving accommodation to sixteen per 1,000 men, instead of the now apparently authorised rate of six per cent. All huts for officers, non-commissioned officers, and married people, are provided with brick fire-places, open grates, and fenders, to act as fire-screens. The field officers' huts are longer than the others, and are divided as to give each field officer either two rooms about 17 feet 6 inches by 10 feet, or one such room, and two about 10 feet by 9 feet six inches.[19]

But once again the teachers somehow did not quite fit in. Thomson, in his very different description of the site was not only pleased with its spacious setting but surprised by the size of his quarters:

Imagine an undulating sea of grass, here and there rising into hillocks, and spotted with patches of flowerless furze. In the midst, on a slightly elevated ridge, stretches out for about a mile the Camp, consisting of ten squares of dingy red huts – each square holding a regiment – with a somewhat irregular accompaniment of canteens, wash-houses, hospitals, huts for the staff, &c. The squares are lettered A to K, my much ill-used initial, the J, being considered unworthy of a place. In the centre of a line, chosen probably as about the highest spot, stands the Church, the Chapel (Roman Catholic), and the Clock-tower: at the extremities are the white tents of the Artillery and the Dragoons. It is a fine place for freedom and expanse, and in itself much pleasanter than Aldershot, though I could wish to be there for the sake of its nearness to London. Aldershot is set amidst dark heath, the Curragh amidst green grass; and the difference is like that between cloudy and sunshiny weather. It is good to get out here from a town. The sky is seen, not in patches, but broad, complete, and sea-like; the distance where low blue hills float in the horizon is also sea-like, and the uncorrupted air sweeps over us broad and free as an ocean. Last night, for instance, it blew a stiffish gale. Well, the gusts came with a broad rush and sway against a ship's side. The rattling of the windows, the creaking of the window-cords, the sound as of sails flapping, might have made a squeamish stomach sea-sick. I almost fancied that my hut had got under weigh; and hoped that if so it would drift down the Irish Sea, through the Channel, and up the Thames to London. What a pity it held its anchor fast! I have very good quarters for the Camp, better probably than most of the officers. Two rooms, one of them papered, forming the end of the school-hut, are something to boast of for an habitation.[20]

Potterton, fellow-explorer of European as well as English Literature, was now at the Curragh also. German was 'becoming an essential in education', Thomson told Agnes: 'it has the best modern literature in Europe'.[21] Novalis continued to interest him. But where Novalis could confidently present in 'Hymns to the Night' the ecstatic vision of a dead young girl to her mourning lover, Thomson in approaching the same theme still could only present a narrator who looked to the female to provide faith: faith in the afterlife from which, in this case, it was hoped she would materialise. The title of the poem, 'Mater Tenebrarum', was from De Quincey:

> In the endless nights, from my bed, where sleepless in
>   anguish I lie,
> I startle the stillness and gloom with a bitter and strong cry;
> O Love! O Beloved long lost! come down from thy Heaven
>   above,
> Come down for a moment! oh, come! Come serious and mild
> And pale, as thou wert on this earth, thou adorable Child!

Or come as thou art, with thy sanctitude, triumph and bliss,
For a garment of glory about thee; and give me one kiss,
One tender and pitying look of thy tenderest eyes,
One word of solemn assurance and truth that the soul with
   its love never dies!

In the endless nights, on my bed, where sleeplessly brooding
   I lie,
I burden the heavy gloom with a bitter and weary sigh:
No hope in this worn-out world, no hope beyond the tomb;
No living and loving God, but blind and stony Doom.
Anguish and grief and sin, terror, disease and despair:
Why not throw off this life, this garment of torture I wear,
And go down to sleep in the grave in everlasting rest?
What keeps me yet in this life, what spark in my frozen breast?
A fire of dread, a light of hope, kindled, O Love, by thee;
For thy pure and gentle and beautiful soul, it must
   immortal be.[22]

The month that this was completed, November 1859, saw two more poems under the 'Crepusculus' pen-name in *Tait's Edinburgh Magazine*. The poems were 'Bertram to the Most Noble and Beautiful Lady Geraldine', and a poem 'To a Pianiste' in praise of the concert pianist Arabella Godard. Sandwiched between the two poems was a review that shows how distant in opinion *Tait's* under the Christian Troup was from the *Investigator* under the atheist 'Iconoclast'. In a ten-page review of Rev. John Cumming's latest production forecasting the coming end, *The Great Tribulation or the Things to Come*,[23] the anonymous reviewer thought that though Cumming had got his prophetical calculations wrong, nonetheless world affairs were undoubtedly like a stream that, approaching a fall, had got into the rapids, and 'no man doubts that we draw towards grand events'. There were many practical points in *The Great Tribulation* which was overall a book of 'great strength and utility'.[24]

Elsewhere in London away from Cumming's prognostications at Crown Court, the president of the London Secular Society – as Bradlaugh now was[25] – was struggling to keep the secularist message in print. The *Investigator* had collapsed through lack of money in August 1859, but Bradlaugh was now involved in the setting up of a Reformer Newspaper Company Ltd which advertised in February 1860 its purpose in launching a new weekly:

This Company is to be formed for the purpose of issuing a weekly newspaper, price twopence, to be entitled the *Reformer*, of the size of the *Manchester Guardian*, folded so as to form eight pages. It will advocate advanced Liberal opinions, on Social, Political, Theological, and Scientific questions, and will permit free discussion on every statement made, or opinion advanced in its columns, or upon any question of general importance. The present platform of political views will be mainly that advocated by the Northern Reform Union, but every phase of the political question shall have free and unreserved treatment, and the most partial Tory will be allowed to answer the views of the Editor, as well as the most extreme Republican, the promoters being of opinion that no man holds the whole truth, but that it permeates from one extreme to another, and can only be found by a complete ventilation and examination of each man's views. On social science, the promoters intend specially to watch the conduct of the Social Science League, reviewing the course taken by its leading men, and illustrating the general views enunciated at its meetings. The newspaper will contain full reports of co-operative news, meetings and proceedings of trade societies, and co-operative progress throughout the country. It will also contain articles illustrating the connection between physiological and psychological phenomena, and illustrating new scientific discoveries, examining and explaining the various theories in connection with animal magnetism, phrenology, etc., treating fully on the important ground recognised under the title of Political Economy. The present platform, of theological advocacy, will be that of antagonism to every known religious system, and especially to the various phases of Christianity taught and preached in Britain; but every one – Churchman, Dissenter, or anti-theologian – shall have full space to illustrate his own views. The paper will also contain all the important news of the week, summary of Parliamentary debates, reviews of books, etc. etc.; special law and police intelligence; original poetry, etc. The Company will be conducted by a committee of management, appointed annually by the general body of shareholders. The committee will have the financial control of the paper, and will have appointment of the Editor. The Editor for the first six months will be 'Iconoclast', who will be continued in that office if satisfaction be given to the committee of management.[26]

The word 'National' had been added to the title by the time of the paper's first appearance in April: the *National Reformer* was to last for thirty years, becoming in time synonymous with the views of 'Iconoclast', and acting as the vehicle for the greater part of 'B.V.'s published output until the mid-1870s.

Yet to be discovered reading let alone contributing to such freethought publications was risky for army personnel. Soon after the *National Reformer* was launched Thomson was transferred back to

Aldershot. While he was there a soldier in the Royal Artillery who had been passed as suitable for teacher training at Chelsea was refused admission and sent back to Aldershot Camp after freethought material, including Volney's *Ruins of Empires* and work by George Jacob Holyoake, had been found in his possession. The soldier, Thomas Scott, wrote to Holyoake for help to buy himself out of the army, but Holyoake could not raise the money. Scott was court-martialled for insubordination after he claimed that his beliefs were involuntary, was marched under guard to church on Sundays, and having been locked up in the garrison jail, he eventually committed suicide, having been by Holyoake's account 'daily harassed about his opinions'.[27]

Thomson at Aldershot was once again based within travelling distance of the Gray family in East London. George Duncan had been posted abroad in 1860, so that year Thomson decided once more to holiday with the Grays. He was now twenty-five, Helen and her two sisters were aged twenty, nineteen, and eighteen respectively. The holiday was not a success, and it proved to be the last time that he visited the family, as Agnes later recollected:

> At last he wrote saying that he was to have a fortnight's holiday, and would pay us a visit. We were all excited at his coming. I had previously informed him in one of my letters that Helen had become a Ragged-School teacher, and in reply he said he could not imagine a creature so bright, and in his remembrance so beautiful, being arrayed in sombre habiliments and acting such a character. When he arrived, Helen met him in the most demure manner possible, and kept up the deception, or rather tried to do so, for he was not to be deceived. Two days after his arrival, when he was sitting reading, she suddenly sent something flying at his head, at which he started up, saying, 'Ah! I have just been quietly waiting for this! You have been acting a part which does not become you, but you have now resumed your true character, and are the Helen of old.' During this visit we thought him much altered in appearance and manners; indeed we were somewhat disappointed. He was by no means so manly-looking as when he left London, and was painfully silent and depressed.[28]

In September he wrote a poem whose title he changed at the third attempt from 'Love and Sin' to 'Meeting Again'.[29] The poem spoke of meeting someone whose eyes were 'burning with love and woe' and whom the narrator had to leave once more when 'after long bitter years/ We are allowed to meet.' The couple had shared a past 'common sin', which they had both sought to expiate – he 'among the multitude' she in her 'sterner solitary life'.

Ah! can you really love me, whom you know
  So weak and foul of yore:
Dear heart! *I* feel that evil long ago
  But makes me love you more.

Yet still that longing almost swayeth me, –
  That we should sink down deep;
And side by side, from life's sore burthen free,
  Sleep death's eternal sleep.

Biographical connections have been suggested here, though it has
to be noted that the life of a Ragged Schoolteacher need be neither
stern nor solitary, and if Helen Gray's eyes were blazing with love
then it was most likely for someone else, as she was now engaged
to be married elsewhere. However the concluding verse about sinking
down together in death does have a curious prescience with respect to
Helen Gray and Thomson, in that he kept all his life an embroidered
purse that she had given him, and left instructions that it be buried with
him in his coffin.[30]

Despite the evident risks involved that the case of Scott exemplifies,
at Aldershot Thomson began contributing, as 'B.V.', to Bradlaugh's
new *National Reformer*. But far from espousing the paper's atheism,
'B.V.' began his literary career there with a refutation, cast as a letter
to the editor, of 'Iconoclast''s description of Shelley as an atheist.[31]
As Thomson soon added a full essay and a poem on Shelley to follow
this opening *National Reformer* piece, it would be appropriate to reserve
his views on the poet for the chapter that follows.

CHAPTER EIGHT

S HELLEY IN 1860 had not yet been accepted as part of the respectable English literary canon, though he had been taken up by radical freethinkers who looked to works such as 'The Necessity of Atheism' and 'Queen Mab' as key texts in the republican atheist cause. Certainly if one of the many cheap editions of the poem 'Queen Mab' had been found in Gunner Scott's possession it could have been used in evidence against him. 'Queen Mab' criticises 'kings and parasites', the economic system by which 'All things are sold: the very light of Heaven/ Is venal'; and it attacks the 'prolific fiend' Religion – 'Who peoplest earth with demons, Hell with men,/ And Heaven with slaves!' Some of the notes to the poem would have been especially difficult for a soldier to justify to hostile interrogating officers: 'A soldier is a man whose business it is to kill those who never offended him, and who are the innocent martyrs of other men's iniquities. Whatever may become of the abstract question of the justifiableness of war, it seems impossible that the soldier should not be a depraved and unnatural being.'[1]

But 'Queen Mab' was written when Shelley was twenty, and 'B.V.' stated that it should be discounted when considering the poet's mature views on religion. He illustrated this with a résumé of the development of Shelley's theism. Shelley himself, 'B.V.' wrote, had dismissed the materialism of his early works with the words: 'This materialism is a seducing system to young and superficial minds. It allows its disciples to talk, and dispenses them from thinking.'[2] Rejection of the God of Christianity had not made him finally an atheist. 'Alastor', written only two years after 'Queen Mab', was 'pervaded with an indefinite Nature-worship'. 'The Revolt of Islam' was a Manichean struggle of good and evil, the final issue being the triumph of good: 'He declares that he does not speak against the Supreme Being itself, but against the erroneous and degrading idea which men have conceived of a Supreme Being.' The 'Prometheus Unbound' represented the defeat of God the Vengeful Father – 'the tyranny of heaven shall never be reassumed'. But it was not the assertion of a world without God. The most prominent note was pantheistic, though Shelley 'like Plato, among others, before him' believed that a good God had made a good world now ruled by Evil:

> The Good spirit, which at last triumphs, is, indeed, typified in the Titan Prometheus, and not in a man; but no faith in or worship of this deliverer is required from men who would be saved. The Universal Mind is freed and purified; the earth and its moon grow more glorious, and fertile, and beautiful, inspired by the renewed health of the informing spirit. The poem is an apotheosis of the One Infinite Soul, self-subsisting, informing all things, one and the same in all masks of man, and beast, and worm, and plant, and slime.

'Hellas' and the 'Ode to Heaven' contained 'pure Berkeleyan philosophy, with the Kantian extension – that space and time are merely necessary forms of human thought, and have no existence separate from the human mind.' Lastly the elegy for Keats, 'Adonais', should be taken as Shelley's mature position on God and religion: the poem 'simply dwells so continually on the Infinity of God as to overlook, or slightly regard His Personality: it is Spiritualism and Theism, but of the Greeks rather than the Hebrews. The fact is that Shelley, like every other brave Recusant, is credited with much more infidelity than he really had. Finding a vast State Church, based upon politico-theology, everywhere in the ascendant, he was naturally more occupied in negativing dominant assumptions than in affirming his own positive convictions.'

Shelley's idealistic faith was of that type which Wordsworth had had in mind when writing of 'The light that never was on sea or land/ The consecration, and the poet's dream'.[3] The poet's dream, 'B.V.' maintained, was 'the dream, or rather the perception, of the truth of Idealism. It is the vision that our Universe, solid and self-sufficient as it appears, floats fleeting upon a spiritual sea, that a spiritual life, which is Love and Truth, burns and throbs throughout its whole mass, that it is "the apparent picture of the unapparent nature", – the half-veiling, half-revealing robe of the Deity, – the volume of the Scriptures of the Word of God. This is the light which never was on sea or land: even as the passion and thought of the writer are not as the inked paper which is the medium of their communication to his fellow-men. But in thus considering the world only as a great Hieroglyph, it is by no means necessary to consider the cyphers and symbols dead. A loving contemplation of Nature continually suggests the thought that deep in her heart dwells for ever a serene happy consciousness of her life; her life which is the fulfilment of perfect law.'[4]

Shelley was the complete man, an essay of December 1860 and a poem given the poet's name, further suggested. Shelley had faith, and hope, and love. He had faith – in a spiritual Universe described sometimes in cosmic, sometimes in pantheistic terms. He had hope – in the perfectability of human nature and the triumph of good over evil. And he had love – of intellectual beauty, of female beauty, of the world as it wholly existed, though this had only won Shelley misunderstanding:

> I strove to teach them the true God, Whose reign
> Is infinite love for all things that exist;
> And I was branded as an Atheist.[5]

What Shelley had advocated in his life had been that advocated by Christ, and ignored by the churches which claimed to follow him:

'Wherefore I say unto you, all manner of sin and blasphemy shall be forgiven unto men: but the blasphemy against the Holy Ghost shall not be forgiven unto men. And whosoever speaketh a word against the Holy Ghost, it shall not be forgiven him; neither in this world, neither in the world to come.' Which through Scripture we may surely understand to mean, that a man may believe or disbelieve in any book, any historical or legendary personage, any dogmatic formula, and yet be in a state of salvation; that only who rejects and violates the Holy Spirit of love and truth, the Conscience of the World, he cannot (because he will not) be saved. Jesus, though absorbed in his personal mission, could speak this truth of sublime toleration; but eighteen centuries have not taught His disciples the wisdom of believing it and acting upon it. Whom He absolved, they dare condemn.[6]

Shelley, like Emerson and Plato before him, had believed in the necessity of inspiration for the writing of poetry. As Plato's *Ion* had put it in Shelley's own translation, true poets wrote 'in a state of inspiration, and, as it were, *possessed* by a spirit not their own'. The reader reading Shelley's own work could feel that it was 'not self possessed but God possessed'. It addressed the serious issues: 'the existence of God, the moral law of the universe, the immortality of the soul, the independent being of what is called the material world'. Shelley 'attacked not so much Christianity as Priestianity – that blind, unspiritual orthodoxy which freezes the soul and fetters the mind, vilifying the holiest essence of all religion.'

Thomson's admiration for Shelley as a figure of Christ-like uniqueness can be thought of in relation to Shelley's own words in his 'Essay on Love':[7] 'We are born into the world, and there is something within us which, from the instant that we live, more and more thirsts after its likeness. It is probably in correspondence with this law that the infant drains milk from the bosom of its mother; this propensity develops itself with the development of our nature. We dimly see within our intellectual nature a miniature as it were of our entire self, yet deprived of all that we condemn or despise, the ideal prototype of every thing excellent or lovely that we are capable of conceiving as belonging to the nature of man.' Shelley was following Plato, whose *Symposium* he had translated thus:

> He who aspires to love rightly, ought from his earliest youth to seek an intercourse with beautiful forms, and first to make a single form the object of his love, and therein to generate intellectual excellencies . . . For such as discipline themselves upon this system, or are conducted by another beginning to ascend through these transitory objects which are beautiful, towards that which is beauty itself, proceeding as on steps from the love of one form to that of two, and from that of two, to that of all forms which are beautiful; and from beautiful forms to beautiful habits and institutions, and from institutions to beautiful doctrines; until, from the meditation of many doctrines, they arrive at that which is nothing else than the doctrine of the supreme beauty itself, in the knowledge and contemplation of which at length they repose.[8]

Shelley had believed in the capacity of the individual, and the mass of mankind, so to progress. But, 'B.V.' pointed out, he had not expected it to happen in his own lifetime, or even soon: 'Shelley, while singing of the millenial future, and chanting beatitudes of our free and pure and love-united posterity, knew with undeceiving prescience that he could not live to see even the first straight steps taken towards this glorious goal.'[9] However he had made it his life's work: 'He devoted himself heart and mind to the doctrine of the perfectability of human nature, an intrinsic perfectability to eventuate in a heaven on earth realised by the noble endeavours of man himself; not that which is complacently patronised by many so-called Christians, who are agreed to die and accept a perfect nature as a free gift, when they can no longer live imperfect.' But on this belief of Shelley's, Thomson disagreed: 'Though I must consider Shelley mistaken in this belief, I yet honour and not blame him for it. For his nature must have been most pure and noble, since it could persuade his peculiarly introspective mind of its truth. Right or wrong, it is the very mainspring of his philosophic system.'

Unlike Shelley, Thomson wrote, writers when speaking of political progress did not speak out of such a pure and noble nature, and ordinarily did not include Love in the final equation of their plans. Their advocacy of wholesale political change could be seen as a flight from their incapacity to change themselves: 'writers are continually urging political rather than personal reform. But, what possible combination of rotten timbers will build a sea-worthy ship? Republicans, despotic in their own circle, liberals intolerant of adverse opinion. Infidels as fully persuaded of their infallibility as ever was Roman pontiff his; what sort of a polity would these frame, moulding to their will the great inert mass? Yet it is so much easier to reform the world than to reform one's self, it is so pleasant to be comprehensive in our plans, and vast in our aspirations, there is such overwhelming intoxication in crowds and tumults, it is so cheerless to fight vice after vice in the solitary and silent dread of one's own heart, that ninety-nine out of a hundred will for ever persist to understand in a parliamentary sense the "making our calling and election sure".'[10]

But 'Destiny' might have it that the capacity to change was not equally distributed, as the opening of Thomson's unfinished poem of childhood memories had put it:

> The dice to play this dubious game of life
> Are forced into our hands – and we must play –
> But Chance still rules the fortune of the strife.
>
> We throw & throw – we throw our skill away
> If this blind Chance keep stolidly unjust,
> And Destiny finds not a mite to pay
>
> Our winnings, while our bosses pay we must,
> Although with loaded dice becheated still
> Although we stake Heaven's life against earth's dust,
>
> And myriad gains make good no loss's ill –
> Yet some among us play it first and last
> With keen earnestness, as if our skill
>
> Could rule the issue of a single cast
> And count on six instead of empty naught.[11]

For Shelley the Fate-Necessity question had been a theme from the first, albeit that a belief in the forward improvement of human nature, that 'very mainspring of his philosophic system', had been central to

Shelley's answer.[12] The early 'Queen Mab' had contained this deterministic note: 'Every human being is irresistibly impelled to act precisely as he does act: in the eternity which preceded his birth a chain of causes was generated which, operating under the name of motives, makes it impossible that any thought of his mind, or any action of his life, should be otherwise than it is.'[13] There could be no certainty that Man actually had an essential place in the Universe: 'if the principle of the universe be not an organic being, the model and prototype of man, the relation between it and human beings is absolutely none.'[14]

On the one side stood the 'Everlasting No' of Carlyle's *Sartor Resartus*: 'To me the Universe was all void of Life, or Purpose, of Volition, even of Hostility; it was one huge, dead, immeasurable Steam-engine, rolling-on, in its dead indifference, to grind me limb from limb. O the vast, gloomy, solitary Golgotha, and Mill of Death!'[15] On the other stood Novalis, denouncing this very metaphor as the product of an anti-religious hatred in the philosophers of the eighteenth-century Enlightenment: 'this hatred of religion very naturally and consequently extended to all forms of enthusiasm; it anathematised imagination and sentiment – morality and love of art – the past as well as the future; with difficulty it placed man in the rank of natural existence; and it represented the endless creative music of the universe as nothing more than the uniform clapper of an immense mill, which, being moved by the stream of 'chance', and swimming upon it, was supposed to be a self-grinding mill, without architect or miller, a true *perpetuum mobile!*'[16]

The mature Shelley had pointed to the power of Love in decisive, surprising acts of forgiveness – as in 'The Mask of Anarchy',[17] and 'Prometheus Unbound'.[18] As for Platonic love and its search for the perfect form, it could reach its highest expression in poetry itself, as was the matter of Shelley's 'Epipsychidion', which Thomson considered to be Shelley's finest achievement.[19] Concerning poetry, 'The only true or inspired poetry is always from within, not from without,' Thomson, echoing Emerson and the Shelley of 'A Defence of Poetry', wrote in his 'Shelley' essay. But efflux of enthusiasm was by possession, influx, from the spiritual Whole. If the Whole could not be perceived as spiritual, there could be no possession. Which could leave only 'indifferent' Fate, or the 'unfathomable laws' of Necessity.

'You sadden us who want whole worlds of fun', the child in Thomson's unfinished poem of January 1858 had accused the 'Mother'.[20] A paragraph in a centenary article on Burns published in April 1859 had echoes of this language of disappointment in its reflections on Fate:

Fate stands impassive – a sphinx in the desert of life. The rigid lips will not wreath into smiles for all your lamentable dirges; the stony heart will never throb responsive to your yearning, your passion, your enthusiasm. However rich in gifts and graces, you shall not front this fate unvanquishable, unless they be grounded on a stony prudence, armed with iron resolution, fortified with an adamantine self-control. Once it was very different – the men of old had a God; but we, like Burns, are shut out from his presence. They who dwelt at home with their father, happy and loving and beloved, might indulge freely their moods and impulses; we here in prison with a deaf and dumb jailor must guard ourselves as sternly as he guards us. Patience, fortitude; our father may in time recall those terrible *lettres de cachet* which have sealed our doom, and let us see his face again in glad liberty. In the meanwhile, to love our fellow-prisoners, helping and serving them as best we can, is the sanctitude and piety of our miserable existence. And it is also the happiness, such happiness as the dungeon admits . . .[21]

A love born of commiseration was different from a love like Shelley's born of noble optimism and transcendence. A fortnight before Thomson's essay on Shelley appeared in the *National Reformer* in December 1860, Thomson completed a poem 'To the Youngest of Our Ladies of Death',[22] which began thus:

> Weary of erring in this desert Life,
>   Weary of hoping hope for ever vain,
> Weary of struggling in all-sterile strife,
>   Weary of thought that maketh nothing plain,
> I close my eyes and calm my panting breath,
> And pray to Thee, O ever-quiet Death!
>   To come and soothe away my bitter pain.
>
> The strong shall strive – may they be victors crowned;
>   The wise still seek, – may they at length find Truth;
> The young still hope, – may purest love be found
>   To make their age more glorious than their youth.
> For me; my brain is weak, my heart is cold,
> My hope and faith long dead; my life but bold
>   In jest and laugh to parry hateful ruth.

The 'Ladies' could trace their ancestry back to the three sister Fates of Greek legend. But they were more immediately related, like 'Mater Tenebrarum', to the Ladies of Sorrow in De Quincey's *Suspiria de Profundis*.[23] The eldest of the sisters in Thomson's poem, Our Lady of Beatitudes, takes people to Heaven: to call on her the narrator says he is unworthy. Our Lady of Annihilation takes people to Hell: to call on her he is afraid. So he calls on the youngest, Our Lady of Oblivion: she, bearing a poppy, offers opiate sleep to the outcast and the desolate – those oppressed, like her, with 'weary bearing of the heavy Now'. Let her grant him rest from which he might wake renewed, able 'to cope with Life whate'er its mood'. If she cannot manage this, let her take him further, into death itself. Not the death of being delivered to Heaven with its psalms and victorious soldiers, nor to Hell with its burning sinful bodies. A death into the Mother, the forgiving Mother Earth who might at least take him into the useful food-chain of life. One part of him could feed a worm to feed a bird to feed a human, like the sea feeding the sky with clouds dissolved by the sun:

> With cosmic interchange of parts for all,
> > Through all the modes of being numberless
> Of every element, as may befall.
> > And if earth's general soul hath consciousness,
> Their new life must with strange new joy be thrilled,
> Of perfect law all perfectly fulfilled;
> > No sin, no fear, no failure, no excess.

At Aldershot Thomson missed the circle of friends he had enjoyed in Ireland. He wrote to James Potterton, expressing the hope that they could meet at Christmas: 'Why are you not here, O my friend, to partake with me of the German feast, which we prepared so laboriously on the green Curragh? We would plunge headlong into Latin this winter, and emerge Ciceronic next summer. My friends are away, and the heart is taken out of me. What fun in finding some exquisite German sentence, when there is no one whom I can bore with it?'[24] Three months later he complained again to Potterton about the lack of decent company at Aldershot: 'I have been reading fairly in my noble Schiller, but have attempted no translation. How are you prospering with yours and the Reineke? I wish I had a fellow-Christian to read with in the evenings; for the Mess strongly attracts a poor solitary, and plays the deuce with his studies. Having nothing original to write about, I send you some more Heine, to put you in my debt for something.'[25]

In May 1861 the 55th Foot were moved with Thomson to Fort Regent overlooking St Helier in Jersey.[26] From there he again told Potterton that his companionship was missed, and hoped Potterton could come over from London later in the year. The letter, from one graduate of the 'Normal' School to another, made fun of the popular

preacher Charles Spurgeon, and Rev. John Cumming's views on the
Book of Revelation written on Patmos:

> Did Alec Thomson tell you, as I desired him, how I have been looking out
> for your appearance in this beautiful isle? Are you coming this autumn, or
> not? I shall be very glad if you do. There is good sea-bathing very handy.
> Leave the great Babylon, the Queen of Abominations; fly from her, and
> seek Revelations in the remote Patmos. So when you return, you shall be
> able to confound Cumming and outthunder the Boanerges Spurgeon. This
> would be a jolly station for two congenial Normals; for one by himself it is
> not so good. I have none with whom to ramble on Saturdays – a sad want,
> were it not that nearly every Saturday has been wet. Still I have had one
> or two good expeditions . . . Grant has not written for five weeks. Mr
> Barnes I write to now and then . . . We begin at French next month,
> and intend to fasten to it like a bulldog.[27]

From Jersey survives his first albeit fragmentary notebook, which
provides the earliest examples of Thomson's lifelong habit of briefly
noting the day's weather as it developed during a day, recording
passing word-sketches of sea, sky and land. On October 26th 1861
he wrote: 'Noon. Most bright and beautiful. Almost cloudless sky. 5
pm. The sun, large, defined, tremulous, like a beryl or crystal globe
full of amber light, stood on a long low ridge of ashen cloud. Above
it some cloudlets, lustrous as an aureole, floated in the calm element
pervaded with that soft greenish hue so common at sunrise and sunset.
As the sun's broad shield was drawn slowly down, these cloudlets lost
their lustre, and the bank of cloud grew more and more dun except
for the large flecks of fire-snow scattered along its summit. With the
dark brown E. Castle, and the dim St. A shore, and the broad wet
sands, and one boat in the offing, the picture was fine'.[28] These notes
he sometimes worked up into a poem such as 'Havre de Pas' of January
1862:

> Leafless and brown are the trees;
>   And the wild waste rocks are brown,
> Which the warm green sea so stealthily
>   Comes creeping up to drown.
> And the north-west breeze blows chill
>   And the sky is cold and pale,
> And nevermore from this desolate shore
>   Shall I watch my true-love's sail.[29]

He no longer contributed to *Tait's Edinburgh Magazine* which was now in any case going under through lack of money.[30] But in Jersey Thomson found another outlet for his work in the *Jersey Independent*. This was edited by George Julian Harney, a former leading Chartist who only ten years before when in England had published the first English translation of the Communist Manifesto.[31] However Harney was no longer as radical as he had been then, and Thomson's contributions were purely literary and not concerned with radical politics. He contributed some translations of poems by Heine,[32] and an article on Robert Browning's *Men and Women* in which he commended Browning's 'healthy spirit', the evidenced intensity of his love for Elizabeth Barrett, and his 'profound and unsectarian Christianity':

> Many good people, subject from their childhood to religious influences and quite content with their Bible and a few commonplace pious books, have scarcely any conception of the missionary value of such authors as the Brownings in upholding the sway of Christianity over the minds of young and thoughtful persons who turn with contempt from the abounding rash of tracts, and find most clergymen's books vitiated by the special pleading of hired advocates, and scarcely meet with a minister liberal and wise enough to command their intellectual esteem, and know that modern erudition has beaten down and undermined many of what were once considered main bulwarks and buttresses of the Church, and above all ponder frequently on the fact that not a few of those living writers whom they most revere – men like Carlyle and Emerson, Francis Newman and Froude – have found the Christian formula too strait to cover the whole of now-known truth.[33]

In the spring of 1862 he wrote a series of six reminiscing sonnets privately addressed to Joseph and Alice Barnes, telling them what they had meant to him and recalling the experiences they had shared together.[34] He wrote that their friendship had meant more to him than any other, that Joseph had been a guide to him in his youth, and Alice had been a second mother – supreme to him among women 'save only her who died so young'. As for himself, he looked back through 'years of sensual sin and nerveless sloth' to the days when the Barnes's first child had been an infant and Thomson had shared with the family faith, love, and 'hopefulness in mood'. The final sonnet, dated April 10th, gave his declared reason for the subsequent decline in his character – and the special nature of what a previous sonnet had called his 'sanctified' memories:

> Indeed you set me in a happy place,
>> Dear for itself and dearer much for you,

And dearest still for one life-crowning grace –
   Dearest, though infinitely saddest too:
For there my own Good Angel took my hand,
   And filled my soul with glory of her eyes,
And led me through the love-lit Faerie Land
   Which joins our common world to Paradise.
How soon, how soon, God called her from my side,
   Back to her own celestial sphere of day!
And ever since she ceased to be my Guide,
   I reel and stumble on life's solemn way;
Ah, ever since her eyes withdrew her light,
I wander lost in blackest stormy night.

Five days later he wrote a love poem. It began 'Were I a real poet, I would sing/ Such joyous songs to you, and all mere truth'.[35] If intended for anyone, no clue has survived to her identity. Only one reference is extant to an affair of the heart on the island, a single sentence spoken by Bradlaugh after Thomson's death: 'Thomson formed ideal attachments to several women, especially one in Jersey'.[36] Bradlaugh and Thomson had continued to exchange letters while he was in Jersey, and sometimes Thomson's letters ran to nine pages in length.[37]

On the last day of May 1862 the 55th Foot sailed from Jersey to new garrison in Portsmouth. From here Thomson was able on his time off to visit Grant once more, Grant being now stationed at Aldershot. While on a visit there Thomson was with a party of teachers one of whom, an Irishman called Bowen, took a swim for a bet in a local pond where swimming was forbidden. The matter was reported, and Thomson afterwards refused to divulge the names of all those who had been present.[38] He was put on a charge of 'disrespectful conduct' and had to travel from Portsmouth back to Aldershot on September 19th to be court-martialled.[39] Whether because his connections with Bradlaugh and secularist publications had been discovered, or whether he was seen as just another of the upstart young Chelsea set who knew far too much about things a soldier didn't need to know, or whether because he had already been charged more than once for drinking offences:[40] at any rate the court-martial took in Thomson's case a severe view of what was itself not a particularly severe offence. He was reduced to fourth class army schoolmaster, a humiliating position akin to the rank of assistant, no longer in control of the classroom. The little notebook in which he made an occasional entry makes no mention of the offence or the verdict, but an entry made two weeks after the court-martial suggests a difficulty that some of the army officers may have felt in understanding the Chelsea graduate who appeared before them:

> Reading Dante's Purgatory about 10a.m. with the sun shining down slantwise upon my face; the black print grew red and brightened into vivid vermilion as my eyes dilated into that dreamy intentness with which one reads good poetry. Sometimes, not always, I could restore the blackness of the print by letting my eyes fall until nearly closed.[41]

Another entry reads: 'It is melancholy enough to see so many poor mortals, and among them the best and bravest of our kind, wandering every way "about the Earth in search of Heaven" – the Heaven which is infinitely above and beneath the Earth, and can by no possibility be on it.'[42] But the Heaven of Dante's *Divine Comedy* was one Thomson now loved. He copied out large sections of a translation made by C.B. Cayley published in 1854, including the complete Canto 23 and the last four cantos, 30 to 33.

> Afresh her dazzling smile upon me shone,
>   And 'turn,' she said, 'and hark; 't is not within
> Mine eyes that Paradise is found alone.'[43]

The Paradise to be found beyond the eyes of Beatrice, a paradise of light upon light, was not the jeweller's window of precious commodities offered by Cumming in a city built of indestructible material profit for the Tribe of the Father.

> 'Why dost thou so in love my face devour,
>   And the fair garden dost not turn to view,
> Which by the rays of Christ himself doth flower?
> There is the rose, within which human grew
>   The Word of God; there are those lilies, by
> Whose breathing men the blessed way first knew.'[44]

The figure of the Rose contains the ranked Male and Female, with Beatrice enthroned:

> And I beheld her, where herself she crowned,
> Reflecting from her front the eternal rays.
> From regions, wherein thunders highest sound,
>   So far removed is never mortal eye
> That ventures below sea the deepest ground
> As there removed from Beatris was I;

But nought it hindered, since her feature sped
Towards me, thro' where no mingled mediums lie.
  'O Lady, that of all my hopes art head,
  And hast endured, for my spirit's aid,
On Hell to leave the traces of thy tread –
For all the glorious things I have surveyed,
  It is thy power and thy benignity,
That have the grace and strength to me conveyed.'[45]

And beyond Beatrice, there was Our Lady, the Mother of God:

'Thou art that She, who didst our Nature bring
  So high, that its Creator did not spurn
To grow the work of his own fashioning.
Within thy womb began afresh to burn
  That Love, whereof the ardency could raise
This flower, unfolded unto peace eterne.'[46]

And by the grace of Our Lady was granted the power to gaze into the furthest and most intense light, the Supreme of Bliss:

Before this Light we grow of such a bent,
  That thence to turn for any new aspect,
'Tis never possible we should consent,
That good, which is the scope of intellect,
  Being all concenter'd here, and what among
Things else is perfect, being here defect.
Henceforth in utterance shall I be strong
  For even that which I recall no more
Than child, who still at nipple batheth tongue;
Not but that one Appearance only bore
  This living Light, the object of my view,
Which is for ever that it was of yore;
But as upon my sight more vigour grew
  In gazing on a single semblant, hence
My changing made the constant object new.[47]

Within the light seemed three orbs, 'of colours three and one expanse'.[48] And looking into these, beyond human gender, was the mystery of the Person:

O Light Supreme, which dost in Self abide,
  And understanding, understood alone
By self, thy Self dost love and dost arride

That Circle, which appeared in thee grown
  As light from light reflected, having been
A little traversed by mine eyes, anon
Within itself, amidst its very sheen
  Seemed coloured with the semblance of our kind,
Which made me thither all my gaze to lean.[49]

Thomson copied out all this in his fine copperplate hand. But he did not stay much longer in the army. Application was made by the Commanding Officer at Portsmouth, and on October 30th 1862, eight years and 151 days after having been officially enlisted,[50] fourth class schoolmaster James Thomson was 'discharged with disgrace'.[51]

Part Three:
UNARMED MAN

CHAPTER NINE

T HOMSON WAS A few weeks short of his twenty-eighth birthday
when he left the army and moved in with Charles Bradlaugh
and his family at 12 St Helen's Place, Bishopsgate, above the office
of Samuel Leverson, a lawyer to whom Bradlaugh had newly become
articled.[1] Bradlaugh now had three young children: Alice, born in 1856,
Hypatia in 1858, and Charles in 1859.

Bradlaugh was a busy man, on his own account as well as Leverson's.
Republican contacts offered business prospects, and his training as a
lawyer went hand in hand with his development as a venture capitalist. In Garibaldi's new Italy the liberation of Sicily and the South had
opened up commercial prospects to mine undeveloped land. Leverson
became secretary to the Italian Coal and Iron Company, and Bradlaugh
for a while was busy in Italy on this and other deals, including one
entitling himself and Leverson to 'certain rights and benefits under or
a certain interest in a certain Contract or certain Contracts which have
been entered into or are about to be entered into with the Italian
Government or some person or persons on their behalf for the supply
of Rifles Guns and Small Arms.'[2] Bradlaugh's contacts included in
London the exiled Mazzini; and his activities as a Freemason gained
him entrance to the exclusive international lodge the *Loge des
Philadelphes*, whose prominent members included Garibaldi himself.[3]

Bradlaugh's involvement with Leverson had started through their
sharing the legal defence of the French republican Simon Bernard,
accused in 1858 of complicity in the 'Orsini Plot' to assassinate Louis
Napoleon.[4] Bernard and Bradlaugh had become close friends. When
Bernard died and was buried in Kilburn cemetery the occasion provided
an international gathering of republican figures before whom both
Bradlaugh and George Jacob Holyoake gave orations at Bernard's
graveside. The Russians Bakunin and Herzen were numbered amongst
what Bradlaugh called 'the proscribed of all the Nationalities of Europe
mustered round his coffin to do him honour'.[5] This was in November

1862, a few weeks after Thomson had moved in with the Bradlaugh family.

From December 1st Thomson started work downstairs in the office as a clerk and his notebook became busy with abbreviations and memos about 'directly Mr Bradlaugh returns', 'indentures of bond', 'without fail', 'Speak to Mr Rogers', 'Get correspondence copied for Mr Leverson on Monday', 'tomorrow at eleven' and the like.[6] Legal and commercial memos mingled with those about the weekly production of the *National Reformer* which Bradlaugh had now inherited as sole proprietor and editor after the collapse of the Reform Company. There were problems with the paper's distribution, including the refusal to stock it by W.H. Smith, already prominent at many of the new railway stations.[7] And there were editorial disagreements, including a fall-out (one of many) between Bradlaugh and George Jacob Holyoake.[8]

Thomson made a contribution to the paper each week from November 15th 1862 until the end of the year. The poems included an elegy for Elizabeth Barrett Browning, who had died in 1861, and some translations of Heine.[9] And he began the criticism which in a few years time was to become the basis for regular biting satire. In an essay 'The Established Church: its Real as Distinct from its Apparent Strength',[10] 'B.V.' argued that he would only concede the title of true Christian 'to those who thoroughly believe the Bible after having investigated it to the best of their power, who find its doctrines satisfy them, and who sincerely endeavour to act up to those doctrines. How many of such are there? I have known perhaps half a dozen. Has any reader known any more? Will any one dare assert that they are more numerous in England than the equally sincere Secularists or Atheists?'

Bradlaugh remained sole editor until February 21st 1863, when he resigned through overwork and ill-health. Before he resigned he had published 'To the Youngest of Our Ladies of Death'[11] and a review by Thomson of Frederic Harrison's *The Meaning of History*,[12] which book argued, with Comte, that History was the story of progressive advancement in civilisation. Thomson argued otherwise. 'What authority has Mr Harrison or Mr Comte for this charming picture? Do not the traditions of nearly all races lead us back to see our first fathers, not groping their way up from the pit, but descending from the empyrean? What antique records place the iron age first before the golden? What savage tribes have been known to civilise themselves?' A reader wrote complaining about this 'Theist or Christian' reviewer who apparently was blinkered by 'the fable of a "golden age" '.[13] This was not to be the last time that Thomson was to be rebuked for his contributions to the paper.[14]

By the time of Bradlaugh's resignation Thomson had left the Bradlaugh home and taken lodgings in Queen Square, near the British Museum. From Aldershot John Grant wrote to Mrs Bradlaugh joking about Thomson's having 'refused Mr Bradlaugh's boon' and 'having found a conscience after eight years as a third-class army schoolmaster'.

You will I am sure agree with me in thinking that the wretch wants an occasional punch in the ribs or box in the ear just to convince him that he is not entirely spiritual – that there is something the matter with him; and that he ever and anon requires stirring up with a barge pole in order to get him to give forth to us poor mortals what little good he hath in him.

As touching the kind expressions of good will towards the insignificant animal Grant – do you think that he has not for the last four years not known that you have regarded him with a generosity as undeserved as great, and that simply because fortune had been so kind to him as to make him the friend of your friend Thomson.[15]

But though he refused the 'boon' of lodging any longer with Bradlaugh and his family at St Helen's Place, he was glad to accept another job through Bradlaugh's influence. The appointment was a political matter, and Thomson was to work in an office in Southampton Street off the Strand.

Amongst the English republicans with whom Bradlaugh was friendly were W.J. Linton – poet, engraver and publisher – and W.E. Adams who wrote for the *National Reformer* under the pseudonym 'Caractacus'. Adams, unemployed at the end of 1862, was invited by Bradlaugh to come and have free breakfasts at the Bradlaugh family table when he needed them. There Adams found himself eating alongside the former army schoolmaster James Thomson, whom he remembered as being 'of gloomy aspect' though the two conversed 'cordially and pleasantly'.[16] Early in 1863 Adams obtained a job as Secretary to the Polish Defence Committee, founded to organise support for an attempted rising against Russian rule in the then Polish province of Lithuania. But when he was given the chance to earn a more secure living as a journalist with the radical *Newcastle Chronicle*, he accepted the job and headed north.[17] Before he went Bradlaugh suggested that Thomson might be given the secretarial job with the Polish Defence Committee in his place. Adams and the committee – which included John Stuart Mill, as well as W.J. Linton,[18] – agreed, so on April 23rd Thomson began work in Southampton Street where Adams had previously gone daily 'to answer letters, issue appeals, receive subscriptions, give information to visitors, and arrange such other matters of business as required attention.'[19]

Adams in his own words expected Thomson 'would do all that had hitherto been done by me, and indeed, from his superior qualifications, a great deal more.'[20] However after a month had passed the chairman of the Defence Committee, Peter Taylor, wrote to W.J. Linton asking if he knew of Thomson's whereabouts: 'Dear Linton – Do you know Thomson's address or how to get at it? He has not been at S. Street this week, and everything is going to the Devil.'[21] Linton wrote to Bradlaugh next day, May 29th:

> The enclosed from Taylor. I send it to you knowing no other way of getting at Thomson, and wishful not to throw over any one spoken kindly of by you. But for myself I would not stand a second utter neglect of this kind. However, it rests with Taylor.
>
> After some trouble about Thomson, he might at least have written to me in the first instance, or to Taylor now, to account even for 'illness' – which I begin to doubt.
>
> I only asked him for a daily paper, which would have satisfied me of his daily attention. I have had *three* since I left. Row him, please![22]

According to Adams, Thomson had been drinking.[23] But Thomson remained secretary of the Polish Defence Committee until August 25th, though he complained afterwards that he had only been paid once, £11 at the end of July.[24] Adams in his memoirs thought Bradlaugh too tolerant: 'It may readily be imagined how much this collapse must have disturbed and distressed Mr Bradlaugh. But it does not appear that it made any difference whatever in his helpful friendship for the unfortunate poet; for some years afterwards I still found Thomson a member of Mr Bradlaugh's family and the occupant of an important post in the business which Mr Bradlaugh was then conducting.'[25]

Thomson did indeed return later in the year both to the Bradlaugh home and to the Bradlaugh office. Both had moved to different locations in the interim. Bradlaugh and Leverson parted company in September and the former set up office on his own at Windsor Chambers, 23 Gt St Helens – a few minutes' walk from the old office in Bishopsgate. At the same time the Bradlaugh family moved to an eight-roomed house, 'Sunderland Villa', in the semi-rural suburb of Park – now Northumberland Park Road, Tottenham. Thomson's being taken in there as a lodger was of some benefit to the Bradlaughs as well as to himself. He was loved by the children, and loved them himself.[26] Bradlaugh, in addition to his trips abroad, had found like other proselytisers that the burgeoning railway network gave him missionary access to the whole country in a way not possible twenty years before. Many of his weekends were taken up travelling to debates or lectures. Thomson had a function at Sunderland Villa, and Bradlaugh's daughter Hypatia recalled the poet's stay there with affection:

He came when I was about five or six years old, and my earliest recollection of him is sitting on his knee and asking him to make an 'ugly face' for me. First he refused; and when, after renewed and vehement entreaties, he complied, I was so terrified that I incontinently fled upstairs.

My sister was his 'Sunday baby'; on Sunday afternoons she was installed in state on his knee, whilst my brother and I sat more humbly at his feet, to listen with breathless interest whilst he told us wonderful tales of brave knights and fair ladies, boundless seas, high mountains, and wide-stretching prairies. Sometimes the summons to tea would break off our story at a vital point, and then the next Sunday afternoon we would clamour for the end. We of course thought he first read his tales out of books, as we did ours, and it was greatly to our surprise when he laughed and said he had forgotten it, he must tell us a new one. As we grew a little older he told us the stories of the operas, whistling or singing some of the airs to us. I have never seen 'Fidelio', yet he told us the story of it so dramatically that the scenes could hardly be impressed more vividly upon my memory if I had seen them acted instead of merely listening to his description.

On Sunday mornings he mostly took us for long walks. We lived at Park then, and he would take us to Edmonton to see Charles Lamb's grave, or Enfield, or Chingford, or if – as occasionally happened – my father came too, our walk was across the Tottenham Marshes, to give our old favourite, Bruin, a swim.

Nearly all our fairy-tale books we owed to Mr Thomson. Amongst those he gave us were *The Arabian Nights' Tales*, *The Magic Ring*, *Undine*, and *Don Quixote*; there were many others . . .[27]

The visit to Lamb's grave was made in August 1864. Thomson noted 'Plainstone at the top, piece of wood a foot high at the bottom – The grave like an unmade bed; nettles, ragged grass, bare mould for pillow, bare clay for foot'.[28] The fragments of notes that have survived from these years show his continuing habit of noting the weather and making sketches of atmospheric conditions: 'Heavy rain – weather broke. Leaving the office in the afternoon the outer air was warm as if from an oven or as if someone else were breathing on one's cheek. In the country this might have been balmy – sweet with all the perfumes of the renaissance of the year. In London it made me headachey!'[29] On his way to the city from Park in the morning, he described the change from the clean air of the suburbs to a city centre fog:

This morning lovely w' mild brilliance at Park – Last night about full moon in a cloudless sky. After passing the Mile End station this morning noticed the smoke of the chimneys issuing with a peculiar illumination & found that it was because of a lurid background – Looked up at the Sun on my left (nearly ten o'clock) & found that a great cloud was moving to it – in a minute the liquid quivering white brilliance was a red hot cannonball & we were in the midst of a London fog. The latter transition was like a scene at the Theatre.[30]

Sometimes he went on walks alone on Sundays:

Heavy rain all morning; clear afternoon, with fresh breeze. Went after six to Winchmore Hill. On road home, heavy shower, which cleared up as I reached the Edmonton and Enfield Road. There, about the same spot from which I started at the sunset last Sunday, I beheld a magnificent sight. The one rain-sack was drawing off, skirted with wan light of foam; into the immense waste of blue sky above the stars came forth, like ships upon an unknown sea; and behind, from the West, the next storm upheaved a vast livid mountain solidly advancing with mountains and mountain-range shadowed on its enormous breast, and skirted it also, with a foam of warm light. Low dark trees along its base were seen in the sift of yellow stormlight; a massy wall of great trees led right on to it; a large golden planet rode supreme above the flying send in the South. Home in rain & thunder and lightning that seemed to envelope one's face as a veil pressed back by the wind. Dogs & cattle moaned incessantly as if with pain.[31]

In Bradlaugh's home Thomson enjoyed the use of his book collection. Hypatia remembered how her father and Thomson used to sit talking in the midst of it:

. . . the two would sit in my father's little 'den' or study, and smoke. Mr Bradlaugh smoked a great deal at this time, and 'B.V.' was an inveterate smoker; the one had his cigar, and the other his pipe; and while the smoke slowly mounted up and by degrees so filled the room that they could scarce see each other's faces across the table, they would talk philosophy, politics, or literature. I can see them now, in some ways a strangely assorted pair, as they sat in that little room lined with books; at the far side of the table the poet and dreamer, with his head thrown back and with the stem of his pipe never far from his lips, his face almost lost in the blue clouds gently and lazily curling upwards; and here, near the fireplace, my father, essentially a man to whom to think, to plan, was to *do*, sitting in careless comfort in his big uncushioned oaken chair, now taking frequent strong draws at his cigar, transforming the ash into a vigorous point of light, and again laying it aside to die into dull ash once more, whilst he argued a point or drew himself up to write. How often and vividly that once familiar scene rises before my eyes! Of course, whilst with us, Mr Thomson had the use of my father's little library as his own, and many of the books still bear the traces of his reading in the pencilled notes.[32]

The editorship of the *National Reformer*, after Bradlaugh's resignation, had passed to John Watts. He, like Bradlaugh, Holyoake and others familiar on the secularist circuit, was given to issuing challenges to clergymen to meet him in public debate. One clergyman on whom he fixed his sights in 1864 was John Cumming of Crown Court, still drawing the crowds as the predicted final years of the known world began to run out. In May 1864 Watts gave two recitals of the same lecture in the two main halls of secularist activity – Cleveland Hall, Cleveland Street, and the Hall of Science, City Road. The lecture was called 'The Anticipated End of the World. A reply to Dr Cumming', and the *National Reformer* duly praised it as a 'thorough exposure of that superstitious balderdash'.[33] By November Watts was still pursuing Cumming, and issued a personal challenge to him in the *National Reformer*: 'I am willing to discuss with you in these columns, or otherwise, the following proposition: "Have not the teachings of the Bible in reference to the end of the world been entirely falsified?" '[34] But no such discussion appeared.[35]

Under Watts's editorship 'B.V.' became a very infrequent contributor to the paper. For almost a year nothing at all appeared by him, and 1864 added only three small contributions: a satiric jingle about one of Bradlaugh's debating opponents, a translation of a poem by Béranger, and a review of a book of poetry by J.M. Peacock. The latter was a boiler-maker who regularly contributed poems to the *National Reformer*, and Thomson welcomed his poetry with the words 'What we seek in art is the expression of a fellow human nature.'[36] Though not himself now regularly appearing in print, Thomson was nonetheless busy writing in his spare time. By the end of 1864 he had completed two substantial works, a long poem called 'Vane's Story' and a prose work 'A Lady of Sorrow'; the latter had taken him two years to complete.

The person called 'Vane' is the central storyteller in both pieces. 'A Lady of Sorrow' is introduced as an edited selection of Vane's manuscripts communicated 'about three years before his death'.

He was at that time wont to declare that he believed in the soul's immortality as a Materialist believes in the immortality of matter: he believed that the universal soul subsists for ever, just as a Materialist believes that universal matter subsists for ever, without increase or decrease, growth or decay; he no more believed in the immortality of any particular soul than the Materialist believes in the immortality of any particular body. The one substance is eternal, the various forms are ever varying.[37]

'I lived in London, and alone' Vane's manuscripts begin. Vane had become 'possessed' not by a universal soul but by Sorrow described as 'the daughter of Love and Death'. Her image had appeared to him in three progressive phases: as 'Angel', then as 'Siren', then as 'Shadow'. As Angel she had at first shut out totally the city around him, so that 'the whole did not even form a background for the spiritual scenes and personages her spells evoked.' Dressed in a black veil she in transfiguration had revealed herself as 'simply the image of her who died so young. The pure girl was become the angel . . . more intimately known and more passionately loved by me, than when she had walked the earth in the guise of a mortal.' She had led him through the universe from galaxy to galaxy: 'And as we thus wandered, like two children, sister and brother, straying in delight through the palace and domains of Our Father, our beings were ever in most intimate communion'. She had come from her sphere in the afterlife: after Vane's death, their souls would be united in one sphere.

But Vane was unable to keep up the virtuous character required to keep the Angel's company. Sorrow had then revealed herself as the 'Siren', and while he turned to drink and drugs she told him in her song that 'Love, her mother, was dying'. She had shown him the undersurface of things, the hypocrisy of churches, the selfishness under surface piety. After a wild banquet he had wakened to see 'the gleaming sand was a loathsome slime whereon crawled shapes of clammy hideousness . . . and thoughts of horror and feelings of putrefaction crawled within my brain and heart like the swarming of palpable worms'. Eventually he had recovered enough to see himself 'once more a man among men, and vowed – alas, how vainly! – never to harbour *her* more.'

But again he had discovered, as when the image had changed from Angel to Siren, that 'the earth's time passed over me, unperceived, unregarded: but the true time, which is change, wrought within me.' Now far from being able to shut out the city and its inhabitants, as the Angel had enabled him, his surroundings now had become evermore 'ruthlessly real'.

And I wandered about the City, the vast Metropolis which was become as a vast Necropolis, desolate as a Pariah . . . Desolate indeed I was,

although ever and anon, here and there, in wan haggard faces, in wrinkled brows, in thin compressed lips, in drooping frames, in tremulous
gestures, in glassy hopeless eyes, I detected the tokens of brotherhood,
I recognised my brethren in the great Freemasonry of Sorrow. And she,
the sombre patroness of our unassociated fraternity, the veiled goddess
of our lonely midnight mysteries, the dreadful Baphomet in whose
worship we all perished, – she never left me; nay, if so it could be,
she interwrought herself yet more completely with my being. Never more
an Angel, seldom more a Siren; but now a formless Shadow, pervading
my soul as the darkness of night pervades the air. I do well to write
now, for still she is with me, and still this is her dominant metamor-
phosis; and whether it will be the last, lasting until death, or will have
successor or successors, I cannot pretend to judge. But as she is now
thus with me – be it for ever, be it only for a time – I will speak of
the Shadow in the present tense . . .

At first she used to lead me, and still she often leads me, hour after
hour of dusk and night through the interminable streets of this great and
terrible city.

In the Shadow's company the long street becomes a road traversing
a vast desert moorland. Crowds pass, coming up from one horizon
and disappearing below the other. It is impossible to tell whether it
is the same people cyclically returning, or different ones. All pass
before 'a colossal image of black marble, the Image and the con-
centration of the whole blackness of Night, as of a Woman seated,
veiled from head to foot; and the ranks as they pass bow down all
with one impulse, like ranks of corn before a steady blowing wind.'
The Shadow tells him 'year by year the world with its children bows
to the sway of Oblivion. All must move to live, and their moving
moves on and on to death; all life's continual moving moveth only
for death.' The Shadow begins to chant 'the rites of her self-worship
. . . the *suspiria de profundis* of world-weary spirits'. This is made
up of a sequence of thirty-six literary excerpts dating from Biblical
until contemporary times, all on the vanity of life, and on longing
for death. Excerpts from twenty-four works of verse are followed by
twelve excerpts from prose. The prose includes Thomas Browne, De
Quincey, Carlyle, Plato, Bacon, Raleigh, Ecclesiastes, and Jeremiah.
The poetry includes ballads, Shakespeare, Shelley, Robert and
Elizabeth Barrett Browning, Webster, Ebenezer Elliot, Poe – and a
favourite of Thomson's, Spenser:

> He there does now enjoy eternal rest,
>   And happy ease, which thou dost want and crave,

And farther from it daily wanderest.
What if some little pain the passage have,
Which makes frail flesh to fear the bitter wave?
Is not short pain well borne that brings long ease,
And lays the soul to sleep in quiet grave?
Sleep after toil, port after stormy seas,
Ease after war, death after life, does greatly please.[38]

There is no punishment or reward for life: only 'the divine Oblivion'. Vane had thought people were created in the image of God. But the Shadow took him through the city to see 'the mean stupid faces, the mean formless eyebrows, the mean loose or pinched lips, the mean gross or withered bodies, the mean slouching gait, of the mass of them! And what were the chief variations from the prevalent meanness? Despair, ferocity, life-weariness, cunning, starved misery, immense greed or lust.' To see mankind as evolving towards nobler states of civilisation was an illusion: 'Shall man ascend for ever and ever, and the poor toad and sponge never climb a grade?' The coral reefs left by insects are of more use than the libraries and remnants of ancient civilisations. Man has created God, not the reverse: 'Fire the pure, the spiritual, the absolute, fire whose heat is love, and light is truth, *this* indeed subsists for ever in eternity; but all the material atoms and bulks upon which it feeds (and some of which account themselves living beings and immortal spirits during the process of the burning) must sooner or later be consumed.'

The weary are exhorted to come to 'the embrace of me, your Mother! . . . unto me the Divine Oblivion dwelling ever throned in the realm whence you shall not return, even in the land of darkness and the shadow of death; a land of darkness as darkness itself, and of the shadow of death; without any order, and where the light is as darkness; where, O ye weary, sinful desolate, orphan ones, where the wicked cease from troubling, where the weary be at rest!' After this 'revelation of her voice', the work concludes, there is 'utter silence'.

There is Novalis as well as De Quincey – the latter whom the fictitious editor acknowledges – in 'A Lady of Sorrow'. But 'Vane's Story'[39] on the other hand is almost an open tribute to Heine, whose poetry Thomson had now been translating for some years. The difference in German influence is significant, perhaps best introduced by quoting Heine's own words when he compared Novalis with the poet Hoffman: 'frankly confessed, Hoffman was a much greater poet than Novalis, for the latter with his idealistic pictures ever floats in the blue skies; while Hoffman, notwithstanding all his grotesque bogies, still clings fast to earthly realities.'[40] Of Heine's own fine edge between seriousness and deflation Thomson said: 'one can never, however subtle-witted and sympathetic, be quite sure with Heine, and I believe that he could not be quite sure himself, where the seriousness ends and the humouristic irony begins.'[41] The idealisation of the female could not be used as a cover for a sexual taboo. In Heine's sequence 'Germany' for instance the poet meets Hammonia, the titular goddess of Hamburg, who invites him up to her flat and makes tea with some rum in it. She lets him see the future of Germany in a magic kettle, the smell of which is so horrible that he faints. However, he's sworn to secrecy:

> I lifted up the goddess's dress,
>> And placed on her thigh below it
> My hand, vowing secrecy both in my words
> And in my works as a poet.[42]

Thomson described Heine as 'a lusty lover of this world and life, an enthusiastic apostle of the rehabilitation of the flesh.'[43] The romantic afterlife reunion could be a subject of Heine's satire: the sequence 'Atta Troll' presents a dancing bear who reflects on his desire to meet his wife beyond the grave, pinning his faith, he tells his cubs, on the common knowledge that the Great Bear is in the sky above surrounded by all the little bear saints. Heine's last poem '*La Mouche*' or 'The Fly' – a poem to the woman he fell in love with in his last months on his deathbed – describes a visionary dream in which he sees himself lying in a large marble sarcophagus, around which is a frieze representing the gods of ancient Greece together with representatives of religions and philosophy. Over the open coffin hangs a flower in which he sees the face of his beloved.[44] At this moment he begins to hear the swelling uproar caused by the various figures on the frieze arguing amongst themselves, until he is wakened from his dream by the loudest uproar of all, caused by the braying of Balaam's ass.

'Vane's Story' quotes twenty-nine untranslated lines from two Heine poems, and ends with a further twenty-two lines translated by Thomson himself.[45] The poem veers between seriousness and flippancy, and like 'A Lady of Sorrow' it is a supposed posthumous reminiscence, this time an account given by Vane the week before he died, of a recent experience he had had when sleeping on his sofa alone in his room. He had been wakened by the kisses and caresses of a young visitor from her sphere beyond the grave: one whom he had addressed as 'My Own . . . You good Child!' She had asked him about his present state and his thoughts on religion. He had asked her in turn about the region from whence she had come. In fact the focus of the poem's 1,461 lines is the dialogue between Vane and his supernatural guest. It can be summed here as follows:

SHE: Why have you stopped writing love poetry?

VANE: Because you died.

SHE: What about Fame?

VANE: That's no compensation.

SHE: It's better than torpor, and it's better to work according to God's will.

VANE: You work out God's will no matter what you do. And work is overvalued. Mankind is never any the better for it. I just passively endure.

She breaks down at this, her 'true self arrayed in light' struggling to break through the mask of her appearance.

SHE: Do you never kneel and pray?

VANE: God exists or not whether or not we believe in him. He might even prefer people who don't claim to try to know him.

SHE: They say you love sinners, not saints, and stay with friends who are the worst of foes.

VANE: That is something like the truth, though the lambs of Christ are a sleek well-fed flock these days compared with us poor goats fed on their dreary tracts. I've known some saints lived lives of sublimated selfishness, storing up virtue for their own eternity of bliss. Their alms were really loans to God at infinity-per-cent, and God must be hard up to accept them. My heart sides with man, not with God nor with Seraphim. Why should a well-fed lounger like me aim for heaven while the prostitutes thieves and drunks go to Hell for ever? If God thinks he can put a single human being in unquenchable flame –

Then I give God my scorn and hate,
And turning back from Heaven's gate
(Suppose me got there!) bow, *Adieu!*
Almighty Devil, damn me too![46]

His young visitor laughs at 'these old bogey-tales of Hell'. He calls her a 'wicked holy one', though thinks maybe he deserves her laughter. But she still has the feelings for him she had in youth.

SHE: Do you not regret your loss of faith?

VANE: No, I have outgrown penance and dread. Have any of the saints any word for me?

SHE: Shelley and Dante.

VANE   Who's in charge of the universe?

SHE: I've heard many names. The laws seem always the same.

VANE: Take a prayer for me to Demigorgon, with Shelley as your guide. Ask that Our Lady of Oblivious Death be sent to me, to take you and I where we can sleep for ten years and wake refreshed to a life together. I'm tired of this world, the same old hills, trees, ocean, sky:

> The same old way of getting born
> Into it naked and forlorn,
> The same old way of creeping out
> Through death's lean door for lean and stout;
> Same men with the old hungry needs,
> Puffed up with the old windy creeds;
> Old toil, old care, old worthless treasures,
> Old gnawing sorrows, swindling pleasures:
> The cards are shuffled to and fro,
> The hands may vary somewhat so,
> The dirty pack's the same we know
> Played with long thousand years ago;
> Played with and lost with still by Man, –
> Fate marked them ere the game began;
> I think the only thing that's strange
> Is our illusion as to change.[47]

SHE: Maybe I should leave if you find everything so boring.

VANE: By no means. Please kiss my brow. (*She kisses him.*)

> Who wears this burning talisman
> The veil of Isis melts away
> To woven air, the night is day,
> That he alone in all the shrine
> May see the lineaments divine:

And Fate the marble Sphinx, dumb, stern,
Terror of Beauty cold, shall yearn
And melt to flesh, and blood shall thrill
The stony heart, and life shall fill
The statue: it shall follow him
Submissive to his every whim,
Ev'n as the lion of the wild
Followed pure Una, meek and mild.[48]

They go to a dance together – one that's held weekly for clerks and tradesmen. A friend congratulates Vane on how well he looks that night. Vane answers with a parable about a once beautiful garden which contained a fountain overlooked by a marble goddess. Everything went to disuse and decay until an angel visited the garden, and everything came to life again.

Vane and his partner dance ecstatically. Then he wakes up once more on his couch, alone in his room. But he is in evening clothes, with the rose given him by his young visitor. An 'Epilogue' translates Heine to the effect that it's better to be alive making love to a cowgirl or getting drunk with thieves, than to be a dead hero like Achilles – 'though besung by Mighty Homer'.[49]

Neither 'A Lady of Sorrow' nor 'Vane's Story' was published by Watts at the *National Reformer*. Former editor Bradlaugh meanwhile was thriving in business. In 1864 he acquired the St Nazaire Mining Company, for mining in France;[50] and at the beginning of 1865 he launched from 23 Great St Helen's the prospectus for another firm, the Caerhun Slate Co. This was established for 'the quarrying, raising, conveying and selling of slates and other minerals and the purchasing hiring taking on lease or otherwise of the Caerhun Slate Quarry in the parish of Caerhun in the County of Caernarvonshire and of other lands quarries and property for such purposes with power to sell or let or otherwise dispose of all or any property of the Company.'[51] In the Bradlaugh office Thomson, as W.E. Adams found so exasperating, was currently 'installed as chief clerk';[52] and the prospectus for the Caerhun Slate Company was signed on January 4th 1865 by James Thomson, Secretary. By October, when the secretary signed the first report listing the company's subscribers, his own name was listed as James Thomson, Sunderland Villa – 'gentleman'.[53]

CHAPTER TEN

Who am I looking so swellish
  A noble lawyer's clerk:
For a month we have been too busy
  Such loads of overwork!

This coat was Affidavits
  Three copies long;
This hat was a Brief Ferocious
  The Guv'nor come it strong!

These boots were the Correspondence
  Appended to the Brief;
And this pipe was a Bill of Costs
  Clever beyond belief.

Between March and May 1865 Thomson wrote a number of light courtship poems several of them set in the Richmond area:[1] boating at Richmond on the Thames, Richmond Hill, Kew Gardens, and the Star and Garter – the prestigious hotel and restaurant where the children of the Caledonian Asylum Band had played during a festival in 1847.[2] The Star and Garter was certainly a place for the 'swellish', and one poem made it clear the speaker didn't think he or his girlfriend were swellish enough to eat in it:

If you were an opera dancer
  And I were a noble Lord,
We might dine at the Star and Garter
  On the best it can afford:

In the room that looks out on the river
  The room for a Palace we're told

117

With the choicest of wines and dishes
   Served up in silver and gold!

I should love your beautiful body,
   You would love my rank and wealth;
For these you would forfeit your honour
   For that I would ruin my health.

But you are only a shop-girl
   And I am only a clerk
And we've had a shilling dinner
   After our week of work.[3]

Another 'Star and Garter' piece considered what would happen if they did go in and tried to order from the grandiloquent waiter:

How grand must be the people,
   How cool and rich and brave,
Who can order such a creature
   As if he were their slave!

Suppose we plucked up courage,
   And walked right in and bowed,
'If you please Sir two glasses of bitter,
   If we may be allowed.'

Do you think he would deign to serve us?
   Or would he give such a stare
Of dignity dumbfounded,
   That we should cut in a scare:

I'm sure if he did bring them
   In a kind and affable way,
I should pull a halfcrown piece out
   As the poorest coin to pay.

And if he dived into his pocket
   And began to count and range,
I know I should stammer 'Please Sir,
   I really don't want any change.'

It is good to be rich and pious,
   It is good to be strong and tall,
But to have the real grand manner
   Is the best good gift of all.[4]

Thomson gave a courtship sequence the title 'Sunday up the River'.[5] Subtitled 'An Idyll of Cockaigne', it presented a Sunday spent on the Thames at Richmond from the time when the hero waits on the arrival of his girlfriend and sees her hat with its streamers coming across the bridge; through the sail on a rowingboat upstream, he rowing, she steering, with pauses for smokes and Jameson's Irish whiskey; with reflections on her looks, his feelings for her, and on love in general. The sequence like 'Vane's Story' quoted and translated Heine,[6] was whimsical and buoyant in tone on the one hand, and at the furthest other dropped into the female-religiose, particularly a single-verse section which described the love of the woman as 'the Armour of the Lord and the Banner of Heaven unfurled'.[7] Thomson in a joking letter described the reference to religion in the sequence – some of which had been written in Jersey – as indicative of 'a struggle in the hero's mind between the claims of religion and the sentiments of recreation'. The intense athletic exertion of rowing on Sundays, he wrote, might be seen by some as a 'celebration of Muscular Christianity'. The hero's stopping to have a drink though showed that not only had he broken the Sabbath but very quickly 'his Pantheism had already become his Pottheism'.[8]

The remarks were in tune with the drily relaxed attitude to religion of other poems written at this time. The effort, after Heine, to mix urban observation ironically with ancient myth was carried off without apparent strain in a poem in which the courting hero throws his best pipe from Westminster Bridge as a sacrificial offering to those gods who do not allow anyone to be happier than themselves.[9] Another poem 'Virtue and Vice' asked rhetorically whether it would be easier to live with a man who drank and was jolly or a woman who was a dour and sinless saint.[10] And the so much guilt with which Thomson's narrators had been plagued especially in the army poems of the 1850s was answered in eight lines:

> Once in a saintly passion
>   I cried with desperate grief:
> O Lord, my heart is black with guile,
>   Of sinners I am chief!
> Then stooped my guardian-angel
>   And whispered from behind:
> 'Vanity, my little man
> You're nothing of the kind.'[11]

He had written a few courtship poems two years before in the autumn of 1863. These were set not at Richmond but at Hampstead

Heath;[12] and he now fed these 1863 poems into a sequence 'Sunday at Hampstead' with a new central episode describing a party of four couples picnicking there.[13] Places like Hampstead Heath and the Richmond area were not just where courting couples and stylish promenaders 'happened to find themselves' on Sundays. Being there and publicly asserting the right to enjoy oneself on Sundays was part of secularist anti-sabbatarian declaration and campaigning:

> Through all the dreary week, dear,
> We toil in the murk down there,
> Tied to a desk and counter,
> A patient stupid pair!
>
> But on Sunday we slip our tether,
> And away from the smoke and the smirch;
> Too grateful to God for His Sabbath
> To shut its hours in a church.[14]

Sometimes Thomson's longstanding friend James Potterton was in the party with him at Richmond or Hampstead.[15] It was to Potterton that Thomson had sent the letter with the asides about Christian references in the 'Sunday up the River' sequence. Thomson had evidently expected to accompany him that Sunday to Richmond, as he added in the jocular letter that accompanied a copy of the poem. 'Being desperately disappointed that I cannot go with you in the body to Richmond, I herewith send you my spirit for company.' Potterton, fellow-traveller in European literature, was now a fellow Bradlaugh employee. He had left the army in October 1864, and he too had been brought onto Bradlaugh's payroll as a clerk in the Bishopsgate office.[16] When Bradlaugh added yet another company to his stable of interests at Great St Helen's, the Naples Colour Company Limited, Thomson and Potterton were listed amongst the seven nominal shareholders with shares of £10 each.[17] The company produced paint from sand quarried at Castellamare on the coast near Naples, and there were factories both in Italy and in Hatcham, London.[18] Thomson, who had already added French to his knowledge of German, now sought to teach himself Italian – and shorthand.[19] His acquisition of Italian however cannot be taken as a consequence of Bradlaugh's Italian concerns; Thomson learned the language, he told a friend, so that he might be able to read Dante in the original.[20] This he achieved to some effect: in time he came to know much of Dante's original poetry by heart.[21]

Thomson's other army friend, John Grant, was based during the second half of the 1860s at Richmond, London and Windsor[22] – so he also in his time off was sometimes in Thomson's company.[23] This was not so regular an occurrence as in Ireland, and both Grant and Potterton married. But the circle of friends that included Thomson, Grant and Potterton, with the Bradlaughs and the Barneses, were in different ways able to keep in touch. Thomson also wrote regularly to George Duncan – four letters sent between February and October 1865 – and there was occasional contact with relatives. His brother John had visited him in 1864, and Thomson wrote to him three times in the next two years.[24] John had settled as a railway clerk in Manchester, where an uncle was stationmaster.[25] This 'Uncle John' received one letter from Thomson in 1865, as did 'Cousin Helen'.[26]

Besides his Sunday jaunts and city walks in street or park, Thomson for relaxation played billiards, enjoyed evenings at the opera – seeing *Don Giovanni* and *The Barber of Seville* in the space of one summer week[27] – and went regularly to weekend dances organised by secularists at the hall of Science.[28] W.E. Adams saw him at one of these and recalled later that 'Thomson, I remember, entered with what seemed to me quite unusual spirit into the amusement.'[29] But much of Thomson's spare time away from the office was spent neither in social activities nor exercise, but reading and writing at home. This is evidenced not merely by the quantity of work he produced but by the range of literary references it incorporated.[30] Of the poems written in 1865 none were published in the *National Reformer* under John Watts, and the established literary magazines such as the *Fortnightly Review*, *Blackwood's* and the *Cornhill Magazine* only produced rejection slips in answer to submissions.[31] But in the latter part of 1865 Watts was ill with tuberculosis, and Bradlaugh became increasingly concerned again with the running of the *National Reformer*, taking over sole editorship once more in April 1866 on Watts's death.[32] By this time Thomson had become a regular contributor again and had begun solidly to establish 'B.V.' in the *National Reformer* as poet, critic and prose satirist. It was as the last mentioned that he in December 1865 introduced God the Father as the managing director of a squabbling family firm:

Jah was a most haughty and humorous gentleman, extremely difficult to deal with, liable to sudden fits of rage, wherein he maltreated friends and foes alike, implacable when once offended, a desperately sharp shaver in the bargain, a terrible fellow for going to law. The son was a much more kindly personage, very affable and pleasant in conversation, willing and eager to do a favour to any one, liberal in promises even beyond his powers of performance, fond of strangers, and good to the poor; and his mother, with or without reason, is credited with a similar character. Moreover, Jah always kept himself invisible, while the son and mother were possibly seen, during some years, by a large number of persons; and among those who have never seen them their portraits are almost as popular as photographs of the Prince and Princess of Wales. . .

Despite the death or disappearance of the Son, the firm prospered for a considerable time. After severe competition, in which neither side showed itself very scrupulous, the great firm of Jupiter and Co., the old Greek house, which had been strengthened by the amalgamation of the wealthiest Roman firms, was utterly beaten from the field, sold up and extinguished. In the sale of the effects many of the properties in most demand were bought in by the new firm, which also took many of the clerks and agents into its employment, and it is even said adopted in several important respects the mode of carrying on business and the system of book-keeping. But while the firm was thus conquering its most formidable competitor, innumerable dissensions were arising between its own branch establishments; every one accusing every other of dealing on principles quite hostile to the regulations instituted by the head of the house, of falsifying the accounts, and of selling an article which was anything but the genuine unadulterated bread.[33]

If there was buried in this some sly fun at Bradlaugh's numerous financial dealings, there was overt enough criticism not only of Bradlaugh's but of many secularists' assiduous preoccupation with detailed refutations of the Bible. Significantly Thomson here allowed still for the operations of a spiritual agent in the world: not a Spirit of Intellectual Beauty or of Love and Truth, but 'the Comforter':

The humble compiler of this rapid and imperfect summary ought, perhaps, to give his own opinion of the firm and the partners, although he suffers under the disadvantage of caring very little for the business, and thinks that far too much time is wasted both by the friends and enemies of the house in investigation of every line and figure in its books. He believes that Jah, the grand Jewish dealer, was a succession of several distinct personages; and will probably continue to believe thus until he learns that there was but one Pharaoh King of Egypt, but one Bourbon King of France, and that the House of Rothschild has always been one and the same man. He believes that the Son was by no means the child of the Father, that he was really and truly murdered, that his prospectus and business plans were very much more wise and honest and good than the prospectus as we have it now, and the system as it actually has worked. He believes that the Comforter has really had a share in this as in every other business not wholly bad in the world, that he has never identified his interests with those of any firm, that specially he never committed himself to a partnership of limited liability with the Hebrew Jah, that he undoubtedly had extensive dealings with the Son, and placed implicit confidence in him while a living man, and that he will continue to deal profitably and bountifully with men long after the firm has become bankrupt and extinct.[34]

But if 'the Comforter' had had a share in Christ's preaching, this had never made Christ divine. An essay 'Jesus: as God; as a Man'[35] Thomson prefaced with a translation from Heine's '*Reisebilder*': 'These hereditary enemies of the Truth . . . have even had the heart to degrade this first preacher of the Mountain, the purest hero of Liberty; for, unable to deny that he was earth's greatest man, they have made of him heaven's smallest god.' In the essay itself 'B.V.' wrote: 'Jesus, as a man, commands my heart's best homage.' But not homage as God: 'Everything for which we love and venerate the man Jesus becomes a bitter and absurd mockery when attributed to the Lord Christ . . . He went about doing good: if God, why did he not do all good at once? He cured many sick: if God, why did he not give the whole world health? He associated with publicans and sinners: if God, why did he make publicans and sinners at all? He preached the kingdom of heaven: if God, why did he not bring it with him and make all mankind fit for it?' The divinity of Christ was centred on the Atonement – and at this Thomson centred this sarcastic reappraisal:

> The whole scheme of the Atonement, as planned by God, is based upon a crime – a crime infinitely atrocious, the crime of murder and deicide, is essential to its success: if Judas had not betrayed, if the Jews had not insisted, if Pilate had not surrendered, if all these turpitudes had not been secured, the Atonement could not have been consummated. Need one say more? Sometimes, when musing upon this doctrine, I have a vision of the God-man getting old upon the earth, horribly anxious and wretched, because no one will murder him.[36]

Christians might be shocked by his writing such, wrote 'B.V.'. But they had no right to be: 'the orthodox shudder and moan, outraged in their pious sensibilities, when one dares to speak with manly plainliness of their doctrines, which commence by polluting our common nature, continue by insulting our reason, and conclude by damning the large majority of us!'[37]

The satirical thrust at the Atonement was essentially the argument of free will versus God's knowledge – or ignorance – of the future, once again: the Doctrine of the Elect, in other words. This doctrine now became the specific target of 'B.V.''s satire. There was 'One

Thing Needful' for the believers of this doctrine – celibacy. 'When a human soul is born into the world, the odds are at least ten to one that the Devil will get it. Can any pious member of the Church who has thought of this take the responsibility of becoming a parent? . . . Dearly beloved brethren and sisters pause and calculate that for every little saint you give to heaven, you beget and bear at least nine sinners who will eventually go to hell.'[38] One paragraph, in its allusion to the 'moth and rust' of Matthew 6. 19, can be contrasted with the devout use of the same allusion in the letter written by Thomson's mother in 1831:

> When I survey with pious joy the present world of Christendom, finding everywhere that the true believers love their neighbours as themselves and are specially enamoured of their enemies; that no one of them take thought for the morrow, what he shall eat or what he shall drink, or wherewithal he or she shall be clothed; that all the pastors and flocks endeavour to outstrip each other in laying not up for themselves treasures upon earth, where moth and rust corrupt, and where thieves break through and steal; and all are so intensely eager to quit this earthly tabernacle and become freeholders of mansions in the skies; when I find faith as universal as the air, and charity as common as cold water; I sometimes wonder how it is that many misbelievers and unbelievers are left, and feel astonished that the New Jerusalem has not yet descended, and hope that the next morning's *Times* (rechristened *The Eternities*) will announce the inauguration of the Millenium.[39]

His criticism of established British Literature was as outspoken as his criticism of established British religion. From his reading of European authors he felt able to attack not only the narrowness of contemporary British writing but what he saw as the common narrowness of mind in which it was able to flourish. The essay 'Bumble, Bumbledom, Bumbleism' castigated the complacency of British middle-class taste and habit:

> Our present literature is so devotedly subservient to Bumble, that I think it may be safely asserted that there are not half-a-dozen thoughtful and powerful writers now in England, writers able to earn a good livelihood with the pen, who have ever attempted since they were mature frankly to publish their thoughts and feelings on subjects interdicted by Bumble; that is to say, on precisely the most important and urgent problems in religion and sociology. For all thought bearing on the future of our race, and not physico-scientific or artistic, we are nearly in a state of sterile impotence. Pick up a popular French or German book, and note how many problems in morality and religion are touched upon, how much free

and healthy scepticism is carelessly implied or explicitly stated; problems with which no English writer whose book is meant to sell would dare to grapple, scepticism which he dare not avow any more than a Gallic writer dare openly attack the Empire. And then ponder what warm interest in these questions, what freedom in their discussion, what wholesome love of originality, what toleration of honest doubt, what devotion to the pursuit of truth, must have existed for long years among the French and Germans, ere light popular literature could make good use of such problems and flourish on such scepticism. How many English writers of repute, earning good incomes by their writings, would have the courage, however pure and lofty the intent, to treat with the same freedom the same subjects we find treated in a work of Balzac or Heine?[40]

Of living British writers he admired Browning, George Meredith, George Borrow.[41] Dickens he thought 'shallow',[42] Tennyson greatly over-rated:

Scarcely any other artist in verse of the same rank has ever lived on such scanty revenues of thought (both pure, and applied or mixed) as Tennyson. While it cannot be pretended that he is a great sculptor, he is certainly an exquisite carver of luxuries in ivory; but we must be content to admire the caskets, for there are no jewels inside. His meditation at the best is that of a good leading article; he is a pensioner on the thought of his age. He is continually petty with that littleness of the second degree which makes a man brag aloud in avoiding some well-known littleness of the first degree. His nerves are so weak that any largish event – a Crimean War or a Volunteer Movement – sets him off in hysterics. Nothing gives one a keener insight into the want of robustness in the educated English intellect of the age than the fact that nine-tenths of our best known literary men look upon him as a profound philosopher.[43]

The state of British letters had once been much healthier, as he wrote in an essay praising one of his favourite literary masters, Spenser:

What an age was theirs! The Bible newly set free from its monastic prison-house, and the veil of the temple rent in twain from the top to the bottom by the earthquakes of the Reformation; the languages and literatures of Greece and Rome just become universal scholarship, physical science just beginning to awake from its long swoon, and a New World of marvels half discovered in the West. The thirst and the capacity of these men were equal to the most profuse outpourings from all these fountains. Moses and Isaiah, Jesus and Paul, Plato and Aristotle, Homer and Virgil, Plutarch and Livy, El Dorado and the Spanish Main; they would and could absorb all; each new acquisition but made them more eager to acquire. They received all and believed all; devoured and digested all; the richer the feast, and the longer it lasted, the further were they from satiety . . .

Drayton put all England in the most minute detail into one vast poem, the *Polyolbion*. The dramatists put all our history and great part of ancient history, battles, genealogies, conspiracies, sects, schisms, factions, into plays. In like spirit Spenser crushes the whole Chronicle of Briton kings from Brute to Uther's reign into a canto; and all the rivers of England, together with the most famous of the rest of the world, into another, enumerating the fifty Nereids (nearly every name with a distinguishing epithet) in four stanzas. He did not first timidly inquire whether a thing was poetical: he knew it and cared for it, and therefore used it in his poem; and everything he used was poeticised. Fires so great and intense could make fuel of any and every material they met.[44]

Spenser's *Faerie Queene*: an unfinished epic Spenser had planned to be in twelve cantos, demonstrating in adventure the virtues of knights who had set forth at the bidding of she who reigned in 'The fairest City was, that might be seene'. Set in a landscape part fairyland, part Britain transformed by magic, part an imaginary space shared between writer and reader; a poem which glorifies, and was dedicated to, Queen Elizabeth I, 'magnificent empresse renouned for piety, vertue, gracious government'; a poem which sought to celebrate and justify that government, significantly the government of Ireland, wherein Spenser himself was landowner of 3,000 acres at Kilcolman in County Cork, and appointed Sheriff of Cork in 1598. At the heart of the poem, in the Canto that deals most with matters Irish, Britomart – one of the heroines figuring Elizabeth – falls asleep in the Temple of Isis, which goddess here represents 'that part of Justice which is Equity'. In a dream Britomart becomes mother to the lion Bravery by the visitation of Osiris, god of Justice, disguised as an animal at Isis's feet; a priest of the Temple later explains to Britomart how the dream is symbolic prescience of her continuing glorious reign. No disjunction here from the Natural Order. What an age was theirs!

Thomson ignored the political dimension to Spenser's allegory. For him it was in the 'fecund vitality' with which Spenser and his peers had mixed Christianity and Heathenism, sometimes allowing contradictions to lie unresolved, that they themselves had come close to Nature in their work: 'Whatever their religious faith, they, in thought and action, refused to be bound by its narrow limitations, and were forever bursting through their own creeds and systems, as Samson through the ropes and the withes with which he had let himself be bound. A creed or system is a strait-waistcoat for Nature; and if you will persist in trying to force it upon Her, you will soon experience that the great Titaness not only flings it off with wrathful disdain, but makes yourself fit for a strait-waistcoat in recompense for your trouble.'

But a modern writer did not need to produce work that was complex, large-scale and busy for it to be worth reading. The attack on Tennyson had appeared in a review essay on William Blake.[45] Despite the ambition of Blake's longer poems, it was of the shorter poems and songs Thomson felt able to write 'The essence of this poetry is mysticism, and the essence of this mysticism is simplicity.' And the 'mystic' was one of five archetypes praised in an essay 'Open Secret Societies' published in February 1866. These were people the inmost mystery of whose being 'only the initiated' could ever truly hear and read: 'They have not consciously signs of fraternity; yet a brother shall recognise a brother immediately by a glance, a gesture, a casual word, and the two shall be straightway as if they had been intimate from childhood.'[46] This 'B.V.' developed in another essay which can be seen both to connect with the long list of writers quoted side by side in 'A Lady of Sorrow', and with the role he had recently ascribed to 'the Comforter': 'though no word of mine will ever convert any one from being himself into being another Me, my word may bring cheer and comfort and self-knowledge to others who are more or less like myself, and who may have thought themselves peculiar and outcast; it may be to them a friendly voice revealing that they have a brother in the world, and may thus hearten them to put trust in themselves and keep true to themselves, nor succumb to the amiable cowardice of seeking to pretend to believe otherwise than they really do believe, for the sake of fellowship and communion. For the real brothers on this earth are seldom gathered around one family hearth, but are in general widely scattered throughout the kingdoms and nations, and yet more widely scattered throughout the centuries.'[47]

Amongst 'mystics', the greatest had been 'a poor carpenter's son who seems to have had no other learning than such knowledge of the sacred books of the synagogue of his people might easily have acquired, who we are told could read (Luke iv. 16, 20) but who perhaps could not write.'[48] And though the greatest poets and artists such as Dante and Michelangelo formed another 'Open Secret Society' across the centuries, Art whether great or minor was the fruit of a want in the artist's life. 'He sings of that which he cannot enjoy, cannot achieve; if at any time he can enjoy it, can achieve it, be sure that he is not then pondering or singing it . . . life remains and ever is as superior to art as a man is to the picture of a man.'[49]

Singing is sweet; but be sure of this,
Lips only sing when they cannot kiss.

Did he ever suspire a tender lay
While her presence took his breath away?

Had his fingers been able to toy with her hair
Would they then have written the verses fair?

Had she let his arm steal round her waist
Would the lovely portrait yet be traced?

Since he could not embrace it flushed and warm
He has carved in stone the perfect form.

Who gives the fine report of the feast?
He who got none and enjoyed it least.[50]

Meanwhile with Bradlaugh's resumption as editor of the *National Reformer*, 'Vane's Story' had appeared there over four weekly instalments.[51] The paper now allied itself more closely with the National Reform League's campaign for Parliamentary reform, and on the Secularist side it became the official organ of the National Secular Society, which Bradlaugh helped establish on a nationwide scale and of which he became president.[52] The four stated aims of the National Secular Society were both secularist and utilitarian:

1. That the promotion of human improvement and happiness is the highest duty.
2. That the theological teachings of the world have been, and are, most powerfully obstructive of human improvement and happiness; human activity being guided and increased by a consciousness of the facts of existence; while it is misjudged and impeded in the most mischievous manner when the intellect is warped or prostrated by childish and absurd superstitions.
3. That in order to promote effectually the improvement and happiness of mankind, every individual of the human family ought to be well placed and well instructed, and all who are of a suitable age ought to be usefully employed for their own and the general good.
4. That human improvement and happiness cannot be effectively promoted without civil and religious liberty; and that therefore it is the duty of every individual – a duty to be practically recognised by every

member of this Association – to actively attack the barriers to equal freedom and thought and utterance for all, upon political and theological subjects.[53]

Thomson joined neither the National Secular Society nor the National Reform League. But after a demonstration on behalf of the latter on Monday July 22nd 1866 an eyewitness report by 'B.V.' was given the whole front page of the following Sunday's *National Reformer*. The demonstration had been forbidden to meet in Hyde Park, so it had met in Trafalgar Square, where Bradlaugh as vice-president of the League had been amongst those who addressed the crowd from the foot of Nelson's Column. Thomson had gone home after Bradlaugh's speech, but fighting had subsequently broken out at Hyde Park railings where the police, according to the *Morning Star*, 'hit out with their truncheons like savages who, having been under temporary control, were now at full liberty to break heads and cut open faces to their hearts' content.'[54] Thomson, though he missed the fighting, had seen enough to be critical of those who had opposed allowing such a public demonstration to take place:

> If large demonstrations are not held, the upper class journals boast that people do not care for Reform; if such demonstrations are promised, the same journals affect fear, and cry that they are perilous to the public peace. As for the talk about roughs and thieves, every one knows that it is nonsense: a review, a race, a regatta, brings together all the neighbouring roughs; a concert at the Crystal Palace, an Oratorio at Exeter Hall, brings together swell-mobsmen . . . I consider that the authorities and not the populace are responsible for the breaches of the peace, since these certainly would not have occurred had the Park been open and the meeting left to itself . . .
>
> The marching of processions through Western London to various meeting-places would prove a valuable means of education to the unenfranchised pilgrims. As the procession dragged its slow length along between the serene and splendid mansions, gazed down upon by serene and haughty flunkeys, met and passed by serene and lovely ladies (looking with languid curiosity upon the herd of strange animals from some world unknown), the members thereof might gradually master the idea of their ugly insignificance in the eyes of the sublime *beau monde*, and gradually intensify their resolve to emerge from this ugly insignificance by their own energies. Whigs and Tories, rich and noble, will never help the populace; the populace must help itself.[55]

Bradlaugh himself was now seriously interested in becoming a candidate for election to that Parliament he wished to reform.[56] On the financial front, his numerous business dealings had suffered a setback with the 'Black Friday' share collapse of May 11th 1866, when a fraud charge against the firm of Overend & Gurney saw 'investors lose confidence',[57] in other words the market went into Slump ending the period of Boom in which Bradlaugh had been one of the busy speculators. He had returned in haste from Portugal where he had been involved in some business 'to negotiate the supply of horses',[58] though the ambiguity of the phrase 'horse-trading' must be avoided. His offices and personnel remained, though not all the businesses with which he and these had connection. 'I have great facilities for making money, and great facilities for losing it,' was his own estimation of himself as a capitalist.[59] But now he had to cut back on his outlay at his home Sunderland Villa, and the service of its two maids was cut back to one. Thomson too was now soon to be looking elsewhere for a home. This may have been of his own choosing, or for other reasons.

One was that his tendency to episodic heavy drinking had not lessened. Hypatia in later years recalled how 'These fits of intemperance, comparatively rare at first, unhappily became more and more frequent. While Mr Thomson lived with us when he came back after one of these attacks – or was brought back, for indeed it usually happened that some friend searched for him and brought him home despite himself – he was nursed and cared for until he was quite himself again, for it often happened that he was bruised and wounded, and unfit to go out for some days.' Sometimes it was the maid Kate who went looking for him with Mrs Bradlaugh, who 'searched the purlieus of London for him, found him in some poor den, and brought him home to be nursed and cared for.'[60]

There were clergy and journalists ready to accuse Bradlaugh of whatever 'loose living' atheists were supposed to spend their lives pursuing,[61] so outward domestic respectability was very important. Thomson's drinking would in any case have been a bad example to the children, especially when Bradlaugh himself had been nicknamed 'Leaves' in the army as a campaigning teetotaller.[62] Finally there was the fact that Susan Bradlaugh herself was beginning to drink heavily while 'Iconoclast' toured the lecture halls of Britain and did his numerous business deals abroad.[63] The Bradlaugh house at Park was beginning to break up, and Thomson was one of the first to go.

On Thursday October 9th 1866 James Potterton went with Thomson while he searched for lodgings in the city, finding the lodgings north of Oxford Street 'Dusty, fusty, musty, rusty, and *dear*.'[64] Two days later he tried around Pimlico, and wrote afterwards 'Took Bed and sitting room 11 Denbigh Street Belgrave Road SW. 14/– a week with

Breakfast and Tea. Rooms on first floor. Seem decent people. Shall probably settle down.'[65] That weekend Bradlaugh was away as usual, giving three lectures on the Sunday morning, afternoon and evening in Liverpool.[66] Thomson meanwhile, just over a month before his thirty-second birthday, began the life of the single lodger in the single city room.

CHAPTER ELEVEN

I N PIMLICO HE stayed six months at 11 Denbigh Street, a couple
of streets from Victoria Station on one side and Vauxhall Bridge
on the other. Shortly after moving into lodgings on his own he wrote
up a Sunday visit to the park:

The last most beautiful day of the year, one might think; the sun so
warm, and the sky that exquisite blue of late autumn and a few days in
Winter; the blue of warm sunshine in frosty clear air.

After dinner, to Hyde Park & Kensington Gardens; the latter never
charmed me more powerfully. The late winds and the heavy showers
of Saturday had swept off all infirm leaves, so that sometimes, walking
under half-clothed trees, but half-clothed in bright green, one almost
fancied it was spring again. Only the ground was strewn thick with
yellow and russet dead leaves.

Opposite the Palace (about 3 o'clock) was inexpressibly beautiful,
with a subtle & somewhat sorrowful beauty. Three Sundays ago, I had
seen the Palace like a thin dark etching in front of abyssmal sunlight,
the trees on either hand like itself; but as their ring swept round by the
main avenue where I stood (the avenue leading to the Serpentine, and
separated from the Palace by the basin) they gradually showed brown
& green and solid from the shadowy darkness of the west. But today
the sky was quiet over the Palace, soft sad grey, where the sun only
appeared by a rift of white light. Spreading and glowing as from this
grey, were those mottled fleecy clouds which always remind me of
down and plumes, and which indeed, as today, so often are shaped into
vast sweeping wings, suspended in the sky of soft clear azure. (The old
painters and poets may have clothed their archangels and cherubim from
such clouds; they loved just such azure.) The trees had that spring-beauty
that all the main lines of their branching, and much of the most delicate
tracery of their sprays & branchlets, could be distinguished through the
thinned leafage. But this was brown and deep green and bronze, yet
tenderly beautiful as the first green of spring, perhaps more beautiful;
as the tenderness of memory and regret is sweeter than the tenderness
of anticipation and hope. The avenues leading away over the thick dead

132

leaves, under the clear pencilled stems and branches, into the quiet sky of tender azure and soft grey, were wonderfully beautiful and strange, so that discerning the obelisk to Speke down one of them, you found yourself dreaming for a moment that you were in another clime. At four the sky all covered with uniform dusky grey; at five soft rain began to fall.[1]

At the end of January 1867 Thomson's brother John married and came to London on a few days' visit with his wife Julia. Thomson met them at the home of an aunt living in London: 'saw John and Julia at Aunt Susan's' he wrote on February 6th. This was Mrs Susan Birkmyre – twin sister of his father's sister Helen, who had become Mrs Helen McLarty. On Monday April 15th Thomson moved lodgings a short distance to 69 Warwick Street, now Warwick Way. The following Sunday was Easter: on the Friday he was at Hampstead Heath observing what he called 'your future governing classes'; on the Monday John Grant and James Potterton accompanied him to Kew and Richmond.[2]

He was managing reasonably well from his wages in Bradlaugh's office and his still-regular contributions to the *National Reformer*,[3] in which he continued to attack the prudery of English literary taste. He scoffed at the *Saturday Review* when it said Swinburne's *Poems and Ballads* were the kind of literature one would hesitate to read aloud to young ladies in drawing rooms: 'As if there were any great book in existence proper to read aloud to young ladies in drawing rooms! and as if young ladies in drawing rooms were the fit and proper judges of any great book. I should like to watch the smuggest and most conceited of Saturday Reviewers attempting to read aloud to young ladies in a drawing-room certain chapters in the Bible, certain scenes of Shakespeare, certain of the very best passages in Chaucer, Spenser, Dryden, Pope, Swift, Fielding, Sterne, Smollett, Burns, Byron, Shelley.'

I am writing in the interest of strength and health and purity and freedom, at a time when the mass of our literature is infected with servile weakness and disease and that 'obscenity, which is ever blasphemy against the divine beauty in life'. For all obscene things batten on darkness, and light is fatal to them. But for the Bumble who rules us, the naked beauty is obscene and the naked truth is blasphemous; he thinks that the Venus de Medici came out of Holywell Street, and is inclined to believe that all the fossil records of geology were forged by the Devil to throw discredit upon the book of Genesis. One cannot without a keen pang of shame and rage think of what we are when one remembers what we were, when one recalls our old and glorious literature, in the wide world unsurpassed; our literature noble and renowned, ever most glorious when most manly and daring.[4]

Thackeray was but one example of British salon morality. In an essay called 'Sympathy', 'B.V.' argued that true sympathy, in the sense of imaginative identification with someone in a position wholly unlike one's own, was rare and difficult. Thackeray made pretence at such understanding, but this was a sham: 'We all know how Thackeray delighted to dally with this theme: but he never attempted seriously and exhaustively to grapple with it – nor, indeed, with any other problems in whose intricacies our actual system is heavily involved. None more sharply than he could rally the host and the guests after dinner, over the wine; yet the thought seems never to have entered his head (at least in the latter and more famous portion of his career) that he was not at all compelled to be present, a humbug in a gathering of humbugs, that he was quite free to abstain from the dinner and the wine, and that he could have taken up a more honourable and commanding position of attack *outside* the mansion.'[5]

As an office worker living in lodgings writing for the country's foremost atheistic weekly, Thomson was definitely 'outside the mansion' himself. But he knew that that publication gave him a freedom which no other would: 'For me its supreme merit consists in the fact that I can say in it what I like how I like; and I know not another periodical in Britain which would grant me the same liberty or license.'[6] This liberty allowed him to criticise not only the Christians who 'in giving to the poor lend to the Lord, and carefully reckon for compound interest in good repute here and celestial happiness hereafter';[7] it allowed him, however jocularly, to criticise the secularists whose official organ the *National Reformer* purported to be. In 'Sayings of Sigvat' he wrote that if the 'believers' really believed what they claimed to – in the sense of imaginatively understanding it – their belief in the existence of Hell would drive them insane. But secularists could be as naïve in their own ways: 'infidels superabound with belief; they believe that empiricism can discover all the veiled mysteries, that logic can resolve all the world's problems; they believe that human nature can be improved out of man, and that every one can lift himself some fine day higher than heaven, sitting in his own basket; they believe that many an existence depends absolutely upon man's belief in its existence; and they all, above all, believe in themselves – which is the very anti-climax of credulity.'[8]

In two essays in praise of 'Indolence' written in the heat of a sweltering summer 'B.V.' watched cynically those working out their missions 'who are sure that every step is a step in advance, though the quiet looker-on can see that nine-tenths of their movement is that of a squirrel in a cage.'

> March on, march on, O beloved comrades and brothers, charge the ranks of the foe, storm his fortresses, shrink not from heat and fatigue, reck not for hunger and thirst; while I repose here admiring and applauding you, in the cool blue shadow, upon the bladed grass, under the rustling branch-borne foliage; my heart is with you, O my brothers, my soul is plumed with swift love to pursue you when vision falls short; I will rest here that I may the better meditate and realise and acclaim your daring and devotion.[9]

But if Thomson felt isolated he did not feel superior. His own sense of isolation he described in his notebook as a disjunction from Nature, using again the image that has the veiled Isis for background: 'I am conscious of a veil between myself and Nature, which sense and spirit vainly strive to pierce, and behind which they divine manifold beauties and mysteries. Could they pierce this veil they would doubtless find another, still as much hidden, still no more self-revealable, for the increment of knowledge is as zero to the infinitude of the unknown.'[10] Disjunction from Nature he in a poem 'The Naked Goddess' presented as an urban phenomenon, the problem of people who had been educated so that the intellectual and the spiritual was trained to disown the physical. 'The Naked Goddess' proposed a myth in which a goddess appears on a hill above a town, and the townspeople flock up to see her. She is naked and surrounded by wild animals apparently tamed and at peace. The town philosopher and town clergyman are not pleased. The priest thinks she should be better considering her soul and the afterlife, and is upset that she shows no guilt about her body:

> Full of unction pled the preacher;
> Let her come and they would teach her
> Spirit strangled in the mesh
> Of the vile and sinful flesh . . .[11]

So he offers her the gown of a vestal virgin. The philosopher offers a philosopher's gown, promising to educate her, since

What could worse afflict, deject
Any well-trained intellect
Than in savage forest seeing
Such a full-grown human being
With the beasts and birds at play,
Ignorant and wild as they?

But the priest's gown is too small and cramped and her body bursts through it: she throws the gown away, saying

'This cerement was meant
For some creature, stunted, thin,
Breastless, blighted, bones and skin.'

and the philosopher's gown is too baggy:

'This big bag was meant to hold
Some poor sluggard fat and old,
Limping, shuffling wearily,
With a form not fit to see.'
So she flung it off again
With a gesture of disdain.

A young girl and boy are saved in that they subsequently grow up and sail off together to the island over which the Goddess has dominion. This island where they lived happily ever after, a coda to 'The Naked Goddess' concludes, was the lost island of Atlantis.

On his city walks, Thomson noted, he was often lost in thought – thought which he again saw as a self-isolating factor: 'I had walked two or three hours of dusk and night about London, musing so deeply that I scarcely noticed anything – when near home a girl's laugh aroused me, and I saw her walking happy with her lover. But I was startled as I grew conscious of the immense abysses across which my mind perceived her. Her dress had brushed mine a moment back, yet the star glittering above the house in front of me was not more remote than she. In the midst of the ocean or a void of the firmament of space one would not be more isolated than when sunk in deep thought.'[12] His walks were important to him, and bad weather was resented: 'It being a very wet Sunday I had to keep in and paced prisoner-like to and fro in my room. This reminded me of the wild beasts at Regents Park, and especially of the great wild birds, the vultures and eagles. How they must suffer! How long will it be ere the thought of such agonies becomes intolerable to the public conscience, and wild creatures be left at liberty when they need not be killed? Three or four centuries perhaps!'[13]

The despair to which the studious, solitary 'single gent' single-room city lodger might be prone, Thomson now addressed in a poem called 'In the Room'. The poem describes the room of such a lodger, at dusk. Nothing has moved or been touched in the room all day. Then the items of furniture begin to speak amongst themselves. They list complaints – the mirror that it is never cleaned, the curtain that it remains unpulled, the cupboard that it never gets anything but scraps and crusts from the gloomy lodger. The table says the lodger wrote much the previous night; the firegrate that he burned most of it. A letter on the table survives, but it whispers it's too closed up to know what it says within. The mirror says it's fed up with the lodger:

> Write and write!
> And read those stupid, worn-out books!
> That's all he does, read, write, and read,
> And smoke that nasty pipe which stinks:
> He never takes the slightest heed
> How any of us feels or thinks.[14]

The previous lodger, Lucy, hadn't sat for hours 'stark and dumb' by the lamp reading at night, then lain in bed when day came. She'd often adjusted her appearance, smiling, in the mirror; she had paid attention to all the furniture, mended it, dusted it, been cheery and talked to herself. She hadn't bothered writing for hours on end – a note or a letter to a boyfriend had been enough for her. She had had friends too, happy young women like herself who had come and brightened the place up with their laughing and conversation – not like this 'dullard, glum and dour' whom not a single friend comes to visit.

Then the bed speaks. He has seen many changes, he knows how to distinguish the sleeping and the dead, knows when a great change must come to furniture gathered in the same room:

> They get to know each other well,
>   To feel at home and settle down;
> Death bursts amongst them like a shell,
>   And strews them over all the town.
> The bed went on, This man who lies
>   Upon me now is stark and cold;

137

> He will not any more arise,
>   And do the things he did of old.

The lodger will be nailed up in 'a queer long chest' and carried out 'like luggage'. Then a phial on a chair says that he heard, when he was filled, that half his contents would kill a man. The man lying on the bed had drunk the whole contents the previous night.

The only object which has nothing to say is the body itself:

> It lay, the lowest thing there, lulled
>   Sweet-sleep-like in corruption's truce;
> The form whose purpose was annulled,
>   While all the other shapes meant use.
> It lay, the *he* become an *it*,
>   Unconscious of the deep disgrace.
> Unanxious how its parts might flit
>   Through what new forms in time and space.
>
> It lay and preached, as dumb things do,
>   More powerfully than tongues can prate;
> Though life be torture through and through,
>   Man is but weak to plain of fate:
> The drear path crawls on drearier still
>   To wounded feet and hopeless breast?
> Well, he can lie down when he will,
>   And straight all ends in endless rest.

But if it might seem that the changing male narrator in Thomson's poetry had logically arrived at a position of suicide and now had nowhere else to go, 'B.V.' now published an explicit rejection of suicide, albeit the rejection came through a surprising source: the work of the pessimistic Italian poet and essayist Giacomo Leopardi. In a pioneering series of translations from Leopardi's *Opereti Morali*, Thomson introduced readers of the *National Reformer* to Leopardi's essays and dialogues which cumulatively argued that though the myth of an afterlife is indeed an illusion, so is the aim of achieving happiness or improving the human race here on earth. It was not unnatural to wish one were dead; it was modern civilisation that was unnatural. However suicide would be too selfish an act:

> To reckon as nothing the grief for the separation and loss of relatives, intimate friends, companions, or to be incapable of feeling such grief, is not wisdom, but barbarity. To make no account of grieving friends and the home circle by suicide, is to be careless of others, and over-careful of self.[15]

In this Leopardi dialogue though, Plato is accused of making things worse for potential suicides by persuading them they might be punished for it in an afterlife. This appeared in the *National Reformer* in June 1868. A previous nine translations had appeared since December 1867. The themes of these nine pieces from the *Opereti Morali* were not obviously the kind of fare wanted by those who saw 'human improvement and happiness' as the highest duty; or who might see public contentment as a kind of badge to be worn by those who had thrown off the shackles of belief in a vengeful God and the fires of Hell. The themes of the pieces translated were as follows:

1. The sun, tired of going round the earth, tells Copernicus: 'I am weary of this continual going round to give light to a lot of animulcula, that live upon a handful of mud so minute that I, who have good eyesight, cannot discern it.'[16]

2. A philosopher, having discovered how to prolong life, is advised by a metaphysician that he should rather discover how to reduce it to the lifespan of an insect, or else increase its capacity for sensation and action, so that it might fill 'those interminable spaces of time in which our existence rather endures than lives'.[17]

3. A pessimistic satirist, accused of writing books that make people despair of useful action, replies that he cannot stand the deceptions people agree to practise, the false masks they wear to one another: when the human race has perfected itself, he says sarcastically, he will publicly pronounce 'a panegyric upon it every year'.[18]

4. Nature, about to despatch a new soul to an 'excellent person' due to be born, tells the soul this person will be even unhappier than all others, because excellent people always are unhappy, though accorded glory in life: at which the soul asks to be put in the most stupid person Nature can create.[19]

5. Columbus, approaching America, argues the need for reasoned speculative opinion, even though people say the land, if there is one, might be full of marvels and miracles.[20]

6. The corpses in a professor's anatomy laboratory begin to sing, and tell him there is nothing to fear in dying, no pain, because

where there is no consciousness, there can be no consciousness of suffering.[21]

7. A writer, accused of spreading despair, sarcastically pretends to see the error of his ways and to realise the superior nature of the nineteenth century to all previous centuries, what with the nineteenth century's 'profound philosophy of the newspapers'.[22]

8. A seller of almanacs agrees that he doesn't want the new year to be like any of the previous years, he only wants it to be new.[23]

9. An essay on birds argues that they must be the happiest of creatures since they seem designed for motion rather than rest and 'it does not appear that they are subject to tedium'.[24]

10. An essay approves the reported last words of Marcus Brutus that 'virtue was not a reality but a word'; and of Theophrastus that 'The vanity of life outlives its utility'.[25]

When the last of these translations appeared there was a gap of over a year before 'B.V.' appeared in print again. Meanwhile Charles Bradlaugh made his first steps on the road to Parliament when he put himself forward in 1868 as an Independent candidate at Northampton.[26] Though he did not succeed, he won enough support – including a donation of £10 from John Stuart Mill – for him to determine to try again.[27] His ten-point manifesto included compulsory national education and some of the National Secular Society's declared objects: repeal of the blasphemy laws, separation of church and state, revision of the land laws, and the replacement of the House of Lords by a Senate of life peers.[28] Though living on his own, Thomson remained good friends of the Bradlaugh family, spending Christmas at Sunderland Villa with them as he had every year since 1862;[29] ten-year-old Hypatia received a book with some light verse for Christmas written in the fly leaf, wishing her well in the future.[30]

But Thomson's circle of friends had undergone change since the beginning of the year. Joseph Barnes, whom Thomson had called 'dear friend and guide of my youth', had died in October.[31] And James Potterton's company had become less frequent when he decided to resume schoolteaching, and moved with his wife Elizabeth to a small school for girls in Lambeth.[32] Bradlaugh's office moved also in January

1869 – Naples Colour Company, Caerhun Slate Company and all – the short distance from Great St Helen's on one side of Bishopsgate to 23 Palmerston Buildings, 9 Old Broad Street, on the other.[33]

In the early months of the new year Thomson worked on a long narrative poem in the fashionable genre of Oriental tale of dramatic tragic Fate. It was his second venture in the genre, and he a second time went to Stendhal's '*De L'Amour*' to provide a story which he reworked in his new poem. 'Weddah and Om-el-Bonain', which he completed in April 1869, told how an engaged young woman, Om-el-Bonain, is given in marriage to a rival tribe's leader as part of a war pact. Her original lover, Weddah, follows her and hides in a large casket in her room. The new husband, Walid, is made suspicious by the words of a slave, and as if acting on a whim, has the casket sealed, taken away, and buried. Honour forbids that the woman betray her lover by screaming, honour forbids that her lover betray her by shouting out, and honour forbids the new husband should betray himself by opening the casket to display her infidelity:

> But Walid had restrained himself, and thought:
> Shall I unlock the secret of my soul,
> The mystery of my Fate, that has been brought
> So perfectly within my own control?
> That were indeed a work by folly wrought:
> For Time, in this my vassal, must unroll
>   To me, and none but me, what I would learn;
>   I hold the vantage, undiscerned discern.
>
> He summoned certain slaves, and bade them bear
> The coffer he had sealed with his own seal
> Into a room below with strictest care;
> And followed thoughtful at the last one's heel.
> At noontide Amine found her mistress there,
> Benumbed with horror, deaf to her appeal;
>   The sightless eyes fixed glaring on the door
>   By which her soul had vanished evermore.[34]

The poem was in Thomson's lifetime to be considered by a number of people – including the poet Swinburne – as a considerable achievement.[35] But when Thomson first tried to have it published, it was rejected in turn by the *Fortnightly Review*, *St Paul's Magazine*, *MacMillans*, the *Cornhill Magazine*, and *Fraser's*.[36]

In April 1869 he moved lodgings in Pimlico once again, his new address being 240 Vauxhall Bridge Road.[37] His friend James Potterton in Lambeth was now gravely ill with pulmonary tuberculosis. On Wednesday June 23rd Thomson received word that Potterton had died two days before.[38] The funeral took place at Brompton Cemetery the following Tuesday.[39] Thomson did at least have regular contact with family in London at this time, in the person of his Aunt Helen, the widow Mrs McLarty. She lived for some time in Cambridge Street near Hyde Park,[40] and Thomson began to visit her. Mrs McLarty's daughter Helen later recalled the relationship: 'In 1869 my mother met him in London. They were mutually charmed with each other, he visited her frequently in Cambridge Street where she was staying. It was arranged that he would visit her in Scotland the following year and spend some time with her at Clune Park, her residence near Port Glasgow.' But the visit was never to take place, as after Mrs McLarty returned to Scotland she too died, the following summer, of a heart condition.[41]

He noted the address of a 'Cousin Mary' in St John's Wood; and another relative whose address in London he recorded twice around this time – once dated February 27th 1869 – was Helen Birkmyre, daughter of Thomson's Aunt Susan. Helen was in Newcross, c/o 'Miss Sherley's', listed in the London Directory as a 'collegiate school for girls'. In later years Thomson's sister-in-law Julia was to tell Henry Salt that letters passed between the two, and Thomson's answer to Helen's questions was something he would not have wished should be published. Since the letters did not survive it is impossible to say what they contained – or indeed whether it was actually at this particular time the correspondence took place.[42]

In October 1869 'B.V.' resumed his advocacy of Leopardi in the *National Reformer*, launching the first instalment of a biographical introduction to the poet, using as foundation the yet untranslated letters, excerpts from some of which in the ensuing weeks thus began to appear in English for the first time. They were no more optimistic than the *Opereti Morali*:

For this is the miserable condition of man, and the barbarous teaching of reason, that, our pleasures and pains being mere illusions, the affliction which derives from the certitude of the nullity of things is evermore and solely just and real. . . I wish these considerations could make blush those poor stupid philosophers (*poveri philosopheri*) who find comfort in the boundless growth of reason, and think that human happiness consists in the cognition of truth, when there is no other truth than nothingness. . .[43]

A letter from Leopardi to his brother from Rome in 1822 analysed the sense of alienation that living in a large city could bring about:

In a small city we may be dull, but in fine the relation of man to man and to things exist, because the sphere of these relations is small and proportioned to human nature. In a large city man lives without relation at all to what surrounds him, because the sphere is so large that the individual cannot fill it, cannot feel it about him, and thus there is no point of contact for it and him. Hence you may conjecture how much greater and more terrible is the life-weariness (*la noia*) experienced in a large city than that experienced in small cities: since indifference, that horrible passion, or rather apathy, of man, has really and necessarily its chief seat in large cities, that is in the very great societies. The sensitive faculty of man in these places is limited to sight only. This is the unique sensation of the individuals, and is not in any manner reflected interiorly. The one way of managing to live in a great city, and which soon or late all are obliged to adopt, is that of making for one's self as it were a small city within the great; all the rest of the said great city remaining useless and indifferent to the individual.[44]

Meanwhile *Fraser's Magazine* published Thomson's 1865 boating-at-Richmond sequence 'Sunday up the River'. This was heartier stuff than Leopardi:

Let my voice ring out over the earth,
   Through all the grief and strife,
With a golden joy in a silver mirth:
   Thank God for Life![45]

'On to the City of God' read the last line of Arnold's poem 'Rugby Chapel', quoted in an article on Arnold that appeared in the same issue; 'The City of God' read the title of a poem quoted in full in another article, on the poet Palgrave. Susan Bradlaugh passed on a message via John Grant, who was now teaching her son Charles in school alongside his own son Kenneth,[46] that she would like a copy of the issue with Thomson's poem in it. Thomson sent her this, together with a newly taken portrait photograph of himself.[47] The editor of *Fraser's*, J.A. Froude, invited Thomson for breakfast, and loaned him Spinoza in French and four volumes in German of Tieck's *Phantasms*.[48] But Thomson's work never appeared in the magazine again; and his publication in *Fraser's* he later referred to as his 'only production in respectable society'.[49] And though it had brought him a breakfast with the editor, it did not bring him any money, as Froude never sent any payment. The money would have been welcome, as not only was Thomson not well off, his financial outlook was becoming grim. He had started drinking again that year after a year's abstinence;[50] though never mentioned in notebook or diary, any lapses into what Hypatia had called his 'fits of intemperance' could not now expect to end in his being 'nursed and cared for' as when in Bradlaugh's home. And his job in Bradlaugh's office in Lombard Street was in the process of disappearing. Bradlaugh was sliding into bankruptcy, and the Caerhun Slate Company was amongst those shortly to be wound up.[51]

In his room at Mrs Reeve's lodgings, as he approached the halfway mark of his Biblical three-score-and-ten, the lodger James Thomson systematically one night set out to destroy all documentary evidence of his life that had accumulated over the years. On Sunday, November 4th 1869 he made the following entry in his notebook:

> Burned all my old papers, manuscripts, and letters, save the book MSS, which have been already in great part printed. It took me five hours to burn them, guarding against chimney on fire, and keeping them thoroughly burning. I was sad and stupid – scarcely looked into any; had I begun reading them, I might never have finished their destruction. All the letters; those which I had kept for twenty years, those which I had kept for more than sixteen. I felt myself like one who, having climbed half-way up a long rope (35 on the 23rd inst.), cuts off all beneath his feet; he must climb on, and can never touch the old earth again without a fatal fall. The memories treasured in the letters can never, at least in great part, be revived in my life again, nor in the lives of the friends yet living who wrote them. But after this terrible year, I could do no less than consume the past. I can now better face the future, come in what guise it may.[52]

Two months later he finished two verses of a poem that was eventually to run to 1,123 lines, be in twenty-two sections, and take him four years to write. It would tell of a city in one aspect like a reverse picture of the New Jerusalem of *Revelation*: where that Biblical city had eternal light, a River of Life, an ever-present God who would 'wipe away all tears'; this city would always be in darkness, would be crossed by a River of the Suicides, and its citizens would have for inner knowledge, that God does not exist. It would be a city, again, unlike Dante's *Paradise*: here there would be no meeting with the beloved longed for on earth, no 'assurance of salvation' reflected Godward from the eyes of the Mother of God. There would be no help from Faith, Hope and Charity, as in Spenser's *Faerie Queene*, to restore the failing wanderer and prepare him to see the New Jerusalem on its distant mount; no House of Holiness, no Garden of Adonis, no throned Nature on Arlo Hill,[53] before whom Spenser's poem had broken off with what Thomson had called 'the impassioned Theistic prayer':

> Then gin I thinke on that which Nature sayd,
>   Of that same time, when no more Change shall be,
>   But stedfast rest of all things firmely stayd
>   Upon the pillours of Eternity,
>   That is contrayr to Mutabilitie:
>   For, all that moveth, doth in Change delight:
>   But thence-forth all shall rest eternally
>   With him that is the God of Sabbaoth hight:
>   O that great Sabbaoth God, graunt me that Sabbaoth sight!

Instead, in Thomson's poem, there would be a sad and brooding female figure overlooking the city, a colossal statue shaped like the figure 'Melencolia' in the famous etching by the German artist Albrecht Dürer.

The poem would be carefully structured, the underlying theme being, again, a reverse: the reverse of I Corinthians XIII. 13 – 'And now abideth faith, hope, charity, these three: but the greatest of these is charity.' A man would travel round and round in the city, tracing out the points where his faith, hope, and love had each died; his life was like a watch that had ran on though the figures had been removed. Another would be on his hands and knees, crawling up lanes where, he said, he hoped to reunite his present with his past – and go back to the womb. Some would be heard saying they had no hope even left to abandon, that the world was only an engine, grinding out life and death. One would be watched holding forth, to no-one, about how he had strode on regardless whilst a whole landscape had disintegrated around him – and had seen his beloved approach him, dead, holding out her own heart in her hand before her. Another would be watched in a mansion kneeling before the dead body of his beloved, the mansion full of images of her. There would be a cathedral, where a man not unlike Bradlaugh would perorate about how there was nothing to fear, there was no afterlife, no angry God waiting to put everyone in Hell; and a member of the congregation would say so what, he had wanted only an ordinary decent life with marriage and a family – and he had never got that. All this, would be described as on a past visit to this city. And it would end with the Sphinx: the narrator would describe how he had fallen asleep in the cathedral square, where the statue of an angel brandishing a sword stood before a Sphinx; and the narrator had woken three times to the sound of the stone angel disintegrating. First the wings, then the sword, then the trunk. Angel, warrior, unarmed man. Fallen forward, stone on stone, its head between the sphinx's paws.

That already described in this last paragraph, the Past, would take up one half of the poem. But the city would also be described in the Present, as an ever-present reality: a place of relentless thought and consciousness, where the only certainty is the certainty of death. A place where people do not know how they arrived, but know that even if they manage to leave, they will always be forced to return; where the mind cannot fully trust the evidence of eyes and ears, where people can seem like phantoms, where the skeletons can be seen beneath their bodies; a place where the citizens do not yearn for immortality, but see that people who think there is life elsewhere in the universe, delude themselves. A place like a real city, with real ruins, real hills around, a real bay into which a real river runs; a place of night, and of insomnia. All this in the Present, a present ending before the Isis-figure of 'Melencolia': an Isis who has seen beyond the veil, and that there is no veil to see. This balancing of Past and Present in the poem, of Sphinx and Isis, would take twenty-one sections, interweaving, one section in the Past, then one in the Present, then one in the Past, and so on for the poem's entire duration.

But a twenty-second section would precede the poem, separate, as an introductory 'Proem'. It would be an address to the reader from the writer, which would begin by saying that 'prostrate' in the dust was written 'his soul's sad journey' (i.e. the Past) and 'his heart's sad tears' (i.e. the Present); that the poem to follow was neither for the young, nor for those who looked for utopias before death or after it; that a cold anger could prompt such shapings of 'our woe' without the usual comfortable deceits; that most people would never understand what was to follow, that it would be understood only by those made desolate by Fate, 'whose faith and hope are dead, and who would die'. But here in the preface outside the poem, there was to be no mention of 'dead love', or charity's antithesis. For the act of the poem itself was to be like a last act of charity: addressed, like the tacit lore of the 'Open Secret Societies', to the initiate across the centuries, those who would recognise the meaning of the words and see that across Time a brother was greeting them. A sign delivered into the eternal Present of Literature, like the signs given by the brothers and sisters whose words had been sung to herself by the Shade in 'A Lady of Sorrow'.

Thomson was to call his completed poem 'The City of Dreadful Night'. The poem's sections did not come to him in the order in which he finally arranged them. The first two verses he finished early in 1870, and dated 'January 16th'.

Part Four:
THE CITY
OF
DREADFUL NIGHT

CHAPTER TWELVE

JANUARY 16th[1]

Because he seemed to walk with an intent
 I followed him; who, shadowlike and frail,
Unswervingly though slowly onward went,
 Regardless, wrapt in thought as in a veil:
Thus step for step with lonely sounding feet
We travelled many a long dim silent street.

At length he paused: a black mass in the gloom,
 A tower that merged into the heavy sky;
Around, the huddled stones of grave and tomb;
 Some old God's-acre now corruption's sty:
He murmured to himself with dull despair,
Here Faith died, poisoned by this charnel air.

JANUARY 20th

He followed him again through weary roads without suspense, until they came to a low wall where the lights of a villa could be seen beyond the foliage. 'Here Love died, stabbed by its own worshipped pair.' Then through many streets and lanes until the man being followed passed under a narrow arch before a squalid house. 'Here Hope died, starved out in its utmost lair.' He asked the man, When Faith and Love and Hope are dead, how can life go on? The man coldly replied: Take a watch, erase the signs and figures of its face, detach the hands, remove the dial face. The works proceed until run down; though bereft of purpose, void of use, still go.

 Then they moved on again, through squares and streets until once again they stood in the graveyard: 'Here Faith died, poisoned by this charnel air.'

I ceased to follow, for the knot of doubt
   Was severed sharply with a cruel knife:
He circled thus for ever tracing out
   The series of the fraction left of Life;
Perpetual recurrence in the scope
Of but three terms, dead Faith, dead Love, dead Hope.

MAY 22nd

He wandered in a suburb of the north, and came to the junction of three lanes beneath thick trees and hedgerows. The air was misty. He took the left-hand lane and had walked about a hundred steps along the earthen path when he saw something crawling before him, its hindlimbs stretched to push, its forelimbs dragging. He saw it had been a man. It turned and gasped at him, Do you want to rob me of my prize, having traced my sacred secret?

MAY 23th

I could poison you or shrivel you up, the thing said.

MAY 24th

Take pity on me, this is my own lifetrack I'm tracing. Find your own. No-one can trace anyone else's. I've already traced the full length of those other two tracks on my hands and knees.

    But I am in the very way at last
      To find the long-lost broken golden thread
    Which reunites my present with my past,
      If you but go your own way. And I said,
    I will retire as soon as you have told
    Whereunto leadeth this lost thread of gold.

So you know it not, the thing hissed. And to think it had feared him. Back to Eden's innocence, that's where the path went.

MAY 26th

It would become again a baby on its mother's knee, a baby that if it could see the crawling thing it had become, the baby would plunge its face into its mother's breast and scream.

   He left the crawling figure. Why go back, when death was to

come? What had been, never would be again.

JUNE 12th

He sat down, weary, at the foot of a column facing a cathedral. Before him, two figures faced each other – a sphinx, and an angel holding a sword as if to smite.

JULY 7th

He fell asleep, and woke to a crashing noise. The angel's stone wings had fallen to the ground, leaving the figure as of a warrior, facing the unchanged sphinx.

JULY 8th

Again I sank in that repose unsweet,
   Again a clashing noise my slumber rent;
The warrior's sword lay broken at his feet:
   An unarmed man with raised hands impotent
Now stood before the sphinx, which ever kept
Such mien as if with open eyes it slept.

My eyelids sank in spite of wonder grown;
   A louder crash upstartled me in dread:
The man had fallen forward, stone on stone,
   And lay there shattered, with his trunkless head
Between the monster's large quiescent paws,
Beneath its grand front changeless as life's laws.

The moon had circled westward. He long contemplated the sphinx's face. Its vision 'seemed of infinite void space'.

JULY 10th

The City is of Night; perchance of Death,
   But certainly of Night; for never there
Can come the lucid morning's fragrant breath
   After the dewy dawning's cold grey air;
The moon and stars may shine with scorn or pity;
The sun has never visited that city,
   For it dissolveth in the daylight fair.

151

It dissolves like a dream but stays in gloomy thought and weariness of heart, day after day, year after year. And when such a dream recurs, can it be distinguished from real life? For life is only a dream the recurrence of certain shapes we call order and reality, thanks to memory.

JULY 11th

The city has a river to its west and south, a lagoon, sea marshes to the north. Bridges and piers, suburbs.

JULY 15th

To the east the sea, a trackless wilderness north and west, woods and mountains. The city is not in ruins, though within it are ruins of an unremembered past. The street lamps are always on, though there is hardly a light in a house window. The people are sleeping, or dead, or fled from some plague. But sometimes you come on someone, wrapt in their own doom, wandering the streets wearily or sitting sleepless through the night.

JULY 16th

The people you do see are mostly mature men, though occasionally a youth, a woman or a child. If you feel sick with sorrow at meeting a disabled child, think of what it is to meet a child in this place. People hardly ever speak to one another, though sometimes they start raving to themselves. This is ignored, unless by someone standing waiting to rave in turn.

> The City is of Night, but not of Sleep;
>   There sweet sleep is not for the weary brain;
> The pitiless hours like years and ages creep,
>   A night seems termless hell. This dreadful strain
> Of thought and consciousness which never ceases,
> Or which some moments' stupor but increases,
>   This, worse than woe, makes wretches there insane.

JULY 19th

They leave all hope behind who enter the city. They have one certitude, the certitude of death.

AUGUST 26th

How a person arrives there none can clearly know. It is like dying of fever; and leaving the City is like being born. Memory is erased in both acts. But being there, one feels a citizen. Escape seems hopeless, but it does come. One awakens as if new born.

AUGUST 27th

Having escaped, a person can scarcely believe it, and weeps with joy. Poor wretch. Who once has been there, must ever return, with increasing horror:

> Though he possess sweet babes and loving wife,
>   A home of peace by loyal friendships cheered,
> And love them more than death or happy life,
>   They shall avail not; he must dree his weird;
> Renounce all blessings for that imprecation,
> Steal forth and haunt that builded desolation,
>   Of woe and terrors and thick darkness reared.

What men are they who haunt this place? Who have their mouths full of the dust of death, make habitations in the tombs, sigh and pierce life's pleasant veil to see darkness and terror where hope and faith die? They have wisdom but they are not wise, goodness but they do not do good.

AUGUST 28th

They are most rational and yet insane. They have an outward uncontrollable madness, but perfect reason within, which sits wan, cold, and powerless. It sees the madness, sees the ruined future, and tries to pretend that it doesn't.

> And some are great in rank and wealth and power,
>   And some are renowned for genius and for worth;
> And some are poor and mean, who brood and cower
>   And shrink from notice, and accept all dearth
> Of body, heart and soul, and leave to others
> All boons of life: yet these and those are brothers,
>   The saddest and the weariest men on earth.

Some say phantoms haunt the shadowy streets. Others say that these are the illusions of the mentally confused, since no person in the city is wholly sane:

> And yet a man who raves, however mad,
>   Who bares his heart and tells of his own fall,
> Reserves some inmost secret good or bad:
>   The phantoms have no reticence at all:
> The nudity of flesh will blush through tameless,
> The extreme nudity of bone grins shameless,
>   The unsexed skeleton mocks shroud and pall.

He has seen phantoms that were as men and vice-versa. The city seems so awful, maybe phantoms have their proper home there.

———————

A man stood in a square declaiming from a grassy mound, declaiming as if there were crowds listening:

> As I came through the desert thus it was
> As I came through the desert: All was black,
> In heaven no single star, on earth no track;
> A brooding hush without a stir or note,
> The air so thick it clotted in my throat;
> And thus for hours; then some enormous things
> Swooped past with savage cries and clanking wings:
>   But I strode on austere;
>   No hope could have no fear.

OCTOBER 5th

As he had come through the desert, eyes of fire had glared at him, hoarse breath from death was on him, claws and fleshless fingers had grabbed at him, but he had strode on austere: no hope could have no fear. Meteors had crossed the sky, hurled into the earth ablaze with fire; he had reached air again, close by a wild sea-shore, sheer cliffs beside: the sky – moon, star, clouds, blue. The sun rose, burned out black, and the moon fell suddenly to stand over the cliffs. Still he strode on austere: no hope could have no fear. Then along the strand he saw a shape with a ruddy light approaching. A woman was carrying a red lamp, bareheaded and barefoot, anguish and beauty in her face. He fell as if dead, 'hope travailed with such fear'.

> As I came through the desert thus it was,
> As I came through the desert: I was twain,
> Two selves distinct that cannot join again;
> And watched the other stark in swoon and her;
> And she came on, and never turned aside,
> Between such sun and moon and roaring tide:
>> And as she came more near
>> My soul grew mad with fear.

Hell is mild compared with it. A black sign was on her breast, a black band across the shroud in which she was dressed. The lamp she held was her own heart, whose blood drops dripped on the brow of that separated self that lay in swoon before her. She bent, wiping the blood drops away with soothing words of love, pity, woe. Mad with rage and fear the self that remained stood stonebound, watching.

> As I came through the desert thus it was,
> As I came through the desert: When the tide
> Swept up to her there kneeling by my side,
> She clasped that corpse-like me, and they were borne
> Away, and this vile me was left forlorn;
> I know the whole sea cannot quench that heart,
> Or cleanse that brow, or wash those two apart:
>> They love; their doom is drear,
>> Yet they nor love nor fear;
>> But I, what do I here?

OCTOBER 6th

The mansion stood apart in its own ground with lawn and trees, surrounded by high walls. It was wholly lit up inside, though deadly still. Broad steps rose to the open door, inside which there was a large hall with ample stairways on either side.

OCTOBER 13th

He paced from room to room and hall to hall. There was no-one to be found, but everywhere there were shrines with candles before them – portraits, busts and statues of the same young woman, very young and fair. At last he heard a murmur, and through a door he found lying on a bed the Lady of the Images, dead, with folded hands. A young man knelt in the room before her, seemingly praying. A cross surmounted an altar in the room.

OCTOBER 14th

He sat forlornly by the riverside, watching the bridge-lamps make gold bars on the black tidal waters of the river at the foot of the wall. There were elms along the river walk, and he heard what seemed like disembodied voices coming from beneath one not far from where he sat.

OCTOBER 20th

The voices were in dialogue. First voice: So you have come back? I was about to follow you. Second Voice: That I have come back is because there is no hope.

> That I have failed is proved by my return:
> The spark is quenched, nor ever more will burn,
> But listen; and the story you shall learn.
>
> I reached the portal common spirits fear,
> And read the words above it, dark yet clear,
> 'Leave hope behind, all ye who enter here.'
>
> And would have passed in, gratified to gain
> That positive eternity of pain,
> Instead of this insufferable inane.
>
> A demon warder clutched me, Not so fast;
> First leave your hopes behind! – But years have passed
> Since I left all behind me, to the last:
>
> You cannot count for hope, with all your wit,
> This bleak despair that drives me to the Pit:
> How could I seek to enter void of it.

Second Voice: Admission to Hell was denied me, since I had no hope to abandon at the gate. I watched the other spirits giving up their hope, but none would give me first a little bit of theirs to hand over. So I had come back to this Limbo.

The other sighed back, Yea; but if we grope
With care through all this Limbo's dreary scope,
We yet may pick up some minute lost hope.

And, sharing it between us, entrance win,
In spite of fiends so jealous for gross sin:
Let us without delay our search begin.

OCTOBER 23rd

Although lamps burn along the empty streets and the moon may shine, the City is still dark, with pitch black retreats and lanes. Yet the eye begins to see shade within shade, black stirring within blackness. In the silence too the ear seems to hear throbbings, hidden breathings, murmurs, all dubious. But the wonder of it wears away, the weirdest things seem least strange, and the soul is too outworn for wondering.

With the failure of Bradlaugh's businesses – the Caerhun Slate Company was wound up in March 1870 – Thomson was forced to look for other work.[2] He worked as a proofreader then as secretary to two short-lived companies before becoming secretary to the Champion Gold and Silver Mining Company, a company founded to purchase and run mining concerns in the Rocky Mountains of Colorado. Their London office was in Lombard Street, Bishopsgate, not far from Bradlaugh's last premises.[3]

Another effect of Bradlaugh's bankruptcy was that the family home Sunderland Villa was sold off and he and Susan split up – he to lodgings at Turner Street in the East End, she with her daughters to her parents' house at Midhurst in Essex. Thomson still kept in touch with Susan Bradlaugh by letter, and would sometimes take Hypatia and Alice out for the evening when they were in town visiting their father. Hypatia remembered her musical education at Thomson's hands:

He took us to the Monday Popular Concerts when they were much less 'popular' than they are today, and taught us to understand somewhat of the beautiful music interpreted by that unrivalled quartett, Joachim, Strauss, Ries, and Piatti. He gave us the scores of 'Don Giovanni' and 'Le Nozze di Figaro', and took me to see 'Il Barbiere di Seviglia' – my first opera. The memory of that evening remains with me as one of perfect happiness and delight, although, of course, maturer opera goers would be inclined to look on it with scorn. We started in good time from Turner Street (Commercial Road), and walked to Covent Garden; there we waited a long time on the stone steps, and then went up and up until at length I found myself very high up in the world indeed, with all the theatre at my feet, as it seemed to me. Marimon took the part of *Rosina*, and so great was the pleasure she gave me that evening that I have had great difficulty since divesting myself of the notion that she must be in the first rank of singers. Between the acts Mr. Thomson explained the scenes to come, and all the while kept his finger on the line then being sung on the English side of his Italian and English 'book of words', so that I was never at a loss to understand what was going on on the stage. Mr. Thomson seemed to share my enjoyment fully, but his pleasure must have been derived in great part from seeing mine. He also first took us to see the pictures in the National Gallery, the wonders of the old Polytechnic, and to many other places.[4]

When he first found fresh employment after the collapse of Brad-laugh's businesses, Thomson managed over the space of a year slowly to pay off the debts he had built up with his landlady Mrs Reeves at 240 Vauxhall Bridge Road. The weekly amount due for his board and lodgings was 7s. 6d.,[5] but from July 1870 he paid her weekly sums between 9s. and 12s. until on June 19th 1871 he noted: 'Out of debt *chez moi* at last. Hope I shan't get into it again.'[6]

He befriended a fellow lodger Fred Hollett: John Grant was later to describe 'little Fred' as one who 'remained Thomson's friend to the last.' Hollett was for a time 'employed by Lipscombe's the filterers in Regent Street, and occasionally did rockery, grotto and fountain work in gardens, besides turning his hand to ordinary bricklaying.'[7] Grant himself was absent for a year from Thomson's fellowship when he was sent to garrison in Ireland in the spring of 1871. When Thomson became an employee of the Champion Gold and Silver Mining Company he became friendly with two fellow workers there, W.E. Jacques and William Chaplin. He now began to have his Sunday lunch with Jacques and his wife on the other side of Vauxhall Bridge.

Thomson rarely had contact with his brother John, though he did entertain his sister-in-law Julia on a visit she made to London, as he told Mrs Bradlaugh:

October 28th 1871

I had my sister-in-law in town for three or four days the week before last. She is a quaint little creature, whom I feel inclined to like. Unfortunately

I couldn't have any quiet chat with her, as she had come to meet her mother and friends, who had been having a month in the Isle of Wight, and the said friends consisted of one widow, two old maids, and one young maid. Fancy me going to Drury Lane with five of them under my charge! I did it with the utmost coolness and self-possession, I can assure you. Sister-in-law is not very strong, and I think brother is not very strong either.

I spent an evening at Turner Street last week with Hypatia. Mr B. came in before I left, looking better, I think, than I had ever seen him since I came to London. He appeared as though he could have supped off a creature the size of me, and not have been troubled with indigestion if he had eaten it all.

I saw Austin last evening. His wife has a regular engagement now at Sadler's Wells, and has been very well spoken of in the London daily newspapers under the name of Miss Alice Austin . . .

Yesterday I got a letter from Grant. He says that he has written twice to you without answer. A pretty creature you are to grumble about people not writing to you, when you never reply if they do. And you have no writing at all to do except in the way of letters, while some people I know have to write morning, noon, and night, till pen and ink make them feel sea-sick.[8]

'Austin' was Austin Holyoake, who was not only sub-editor of the *National Reformer* but director of the printing and publishing company which issued it at Johnson's Court off Fleet Street, where he lived with his wife Jane Alice and their two young children. Austin was the younger brother by nine years of the now fifty-year-old George Jacob Holyoake, from whom he had maintained an independent line since forming his own company in 1862. He had stayed loyal to Bradlaugh through several arguments between 'Iconoclast' and Austin's older brother, and had acted as helper in Bradlaugh's 1868 Northampton campaign. He was a familiar figure at the heart of *National Reformer* politics, and Thomson had come to know both Austin and his wife well.

Austin Holyoake published some pamphlets written by himself over the years, with titles such as *Does There Exist a Moral Governor of the Universe?*, *Thoughts on Atheism* and *Daniel the Dreamer*.[9] The last was a critique of the *Book of Daniel* as a morass of the incredible and the contradictory. Atheists, by Austin Holyoake's definition, did not actually say there was no God – they had no useful definition of the word which could allow the word enough comprehensibility for it – or 'He' – to be denied. However, Austin wrote, 'The idea of a loving Father, beyond and above all nature, all-powerful, all-knowing, and all-good, who made all things, and who watches over his creatures with ceaseless care, is fascinating; but calm reflection shows that such a being cannot exist, and that it is no use deluding ourselves with the idea.'[10]

Austin Holyoake also compiled non-religious services and formal addresses for secularist funerals and marriages;[11] and he wrote a short guide to elocution for the lower-class secularist, taking as his cue the words of his older brother George Jacob that 'There can be no greater imputation on the intelligence of any man, than that he should talk from the cradle to the grave, and never talk well.'[12] There ought to be elocution classes in every secular society throughout Britain, wrote Austin Holyoake, in which secularists could not only be trained how to speak in public, but how to become 'refined and cultivated talkers'. They 'should carefully avoid the dialect of their district, and aim at speaking pure English. This can only be accomplished by a careful perusal of a good dictionary, and by listening to the most eminent and best educated London actors . . . Where these persons cannot be listened to, London barristers on circuit will be very fair models'. But here as everywhere else clergymen had to be avoided: 'Clergymen, though mostly college trained, have such a vicious style in the pulpit, that all who wish to read cheerfully as well as correctly, had better avoid them.'[13] Secularists should practise the proper pronounciation of words like 'honour', 'honest', 'herb', 'hotel', 'hour', 'heir', 'hospital', 'hostler': for an 'h' wrongly aspirated was even worse than one wrongly silent. The editor of the *National Reformer* was unlikely to disagree with all this: getting rid of his East London accent had been one of the first jobs Bradlaugh had set himself at the beginning of his career.[14]

After a break of some months when Thomson's Leopardi biography had broken off with instalment eleven, the name 'B.V.' had begun to appear regularly again from the summer of 1870. There was a biography in instalments of the French political satirist Paul Louis Courier,[15] translations of Heine[16] and Goethe,[17] and when Thomson wrote his letter to Mrs Bradlaugh describing his Drury Lane visit, the seventh of nine instalments had just been published in the *National Reformer* of a satirical essay, 'Proposals for the Speedy Extinction of Evil and Misery'. This essay, which acknowledged the influence of Swift – though it was more directly influenced by Leopardi, whom Thomson had continued to translate, though no more was published[18] – was probably Thomson's most sarcastic comment ever on the National Secular Society itself. 'B.V.' suggested that the problems of the universe could be solved quite simply by the adoption of two overall aims: the perfection of human nature and the perfection of Nature itself. For this a committee should be appointed to launch the Universal Perfection Company Unlimited, membership of which should be open, like that of the International Congress of Peace held in Geneva in 1867, to those paying a subscription fee of twopence ha'penny. 'No promotion money whatever will be paid in any form; and (for positively the first time in the history of joint-stock enterprise) *the whole of the profits will accrue to each of the shareholders.*' (To Bradlaugh this last passage may have seemed a little jaunty.) Human beings should perfect themselves by abandoning the seven cardinal vices for the seven cardinal virtues, and Nature could be persuaded into abandoning earthquakes and the like if mankind only threatened the ultimate 'strike' against her, universal mass suicide. Since man was so obviously 'the crown and head' of Nature, she could not possibly allow this to happen. Should on the other hand mankind prove incapable of perfecting itself, it would in any case become extinct, 'for every species and genus of imperfect creatures has its limited period no less than every imperfect individual, the perfect only being eternal'.[19]

At Christmas 1871 Thomson had dinner with his new friend Jacques. He apologised to Mrs Bradlaugh at Midhurst for breaking a ten-year tradition:

January 3rd 1872

I hope you have all spent a pleasant Christmas, and will have a happy New Year, and many of them. I was very sorry that I could not come to you, this being the first Christmas I have not passed with you since I came to London. But we were late at business on the Saturday, and had a Board meeting on the Wednesday. I spent the day very quietly at Jacques'; and as for Tuesday, it was so wet and filthy that I didn't know what to do with myself.

I haven't had a word of news about anybody or anything. Grant has not written for several weeks; it is true that I only answered his last letter the other day.

I hope you have more seasonable weather down there than we have in London. Abominable, mild, muggy, drizzling, slushy days and nights make it miserable to go about. I have in consequence been enjoying a thick cold in my head, and an extremely promising sore throat.[20]

His sister-in-law Julia had now begun to exchange letters with him – a correspondence which was to last for the next decade.[21] Julia sent him a Christmas present of a pair of gold-rimmed spectacles, and he described to her in his reply his struggles to keep himself in employment since the collapse of Bradlaugh's businesses.

You think I have left Mr. B., and wonder what I am about, and I often wonder myself. Mr. B. gave up city business altogether more than eighteen months ago in order to devote himself solely to the great business of illuminating the benighted intellectuals of this nation on social, political, and religious matters. For some time after he left I did nothing, an occupation for which I have fine natural talents that I have taken care to cultivate to the best of my abilities. That is, would suit me extremely well on a fortune, or in a semi-tropical climate, but here, without money, it is a luxury too etherial for my taste. Afterwards I did some work in a printing office, reading proofs, revising &c.; and as to this I will only say that if ever you have the misfortune to be condemned to penal servitude, and they offer to commute the sentence for such work in a printing office, you had better far stick to the penal servitude. I then became Secretary *pro tem*, to one of the thousand companies which came into being last year, and in some very hard commercial campaigning have already had two companies killed under me. I am at present astride a third, which may carry me out safely or may not: it has received three or four shots and sabre wounds already, but seems tough and tenacious of life. By the bye, our slain companies brought no one down but the riders; our friendly foes the shareholding public having received all their money back. As I was nearly thirty when I came to London, I could not go through the regular course in any business, and have had to seize whatever honest chance offered. Perhaps some fine day I shall turn up trump and win a good stake; it is much more probable that I shan't. In the meantime, having no one to look to but myself, I quietly take things as they come, and quietly let things go as they go, fortifying myself with that saying of the philosopher that it matters not in this vale of tears, whether we wipe our eyes with a silk handkerchief, or blink through tortoiseshell or gold-rimmed glasses. Perhaps the said philosopher had himself the silk handkerchief and gold-rimmed glasses, or perhaps he did not use a handkerchief nor wear eyeglasses, and was thus enabled to be so philosophical on the subject. Not that I need to wipe my eyes in this vale of tears, for I always find the prospect either much too sad or much too comical for weeping.[22]

However when Julia presumed to congratulate him on having removed himself from a bad influence in leaving Bradlaugh's employ, Thomson was quick to correct her:

So you are rather glad that I am no longer with B., exposed to the contagion of his dreadful heresies. To tell you the truth, I don't think that there's a pin to choose between his opinions as to things in general and my own; only while he considers his opinions of the utmost importance, and is unwearied in the profitable task of trying to convert the world to

162

them, I care very little for mine, and don't believe the world capable of being benefited much by having any opinion whatever preached to it. But you must not blame him or anybody for my wicked opinions, which I have arrived at by the mere force of my own evil nature, influenced very little by the opinions of others. The Sunday-school views of this life and dissolving views of a life hereafter proved quite unsatisfactory to this philosopher many years ago.[23]

The *National Reformer*, having completed its serialisation of 'Proposals for the Speedy Extinction of Evil and Misery', published through five issues the oriental narrative poem 'Weddah and Om-el-Bonain'.[24] Thomson decided to send the copies containing the poem to William Michael Rossetti, brother of Dante Gabriel and Christina Rossetti and former editor of the journal of the Pre-Raphaelite Brotherhood *The Germ*. W.M. Rossetti's edition of Whitman's poems had introduced Thomson to the American poet,[25] and his edition of Shelley in the *Moxon's Cheap Editions* series had been reviewed by 'B.V.' in March the previous year.[26] Rossetti wrote to Bradlaugh that he did not know the work or the identity of 'B.V.' but both he and his brother Dante Gabriel had a 'high opinion' of the poem he had been sent. When the letter was passed on, Thomson replied revealing his true identity.

Mr Bradlaugh had forwarded me your letter of the 4th inst., and I know not how to thank you for your very generous expression of approval of the 'Weddah and Om-el-Bonain'. In sending you this piece I had intended some slight hope of obtaining the verdict of so distinguished and competent a judge, but I chiefly intended it as a sort of apology for my very inadequate notice in the *National Reformer* last March of your popular edition of Shelley, written at the request of my friend Mr Bradlaugh when I had no leisure for anything like a fair attempt to examine and discuss that work properly. Feeling not at all contented with such treatment of Shelley and yourself, I was anxious to show that your too off-hand critic was nevertheless a genuine lover of the poet to whom you have devoted so much worthy labour, and a serious student of poetry.

To clear up your doubt, permit me to state that no living writer can have much less reputation than myself, who am simply known to some readers of the *National Reformer* as B.V., the author of many pieces and scraps in prose and verse which have appeared in that periodical during the last seven years or so. And I am bound in honesty to confess that some of these pieces were amongst the most wicked and blasphemous which even Mr. Bradlaugh ever published. The only production in reputable society which I can cite in my favour is 'Sunday up the River: an Idyll of Cockaigne,' which Mr. Froude inserted in *Fraser's Magazine* for October

1869, and which he and Mr. Kingsley thought very good. The 'Weddah and Om-el-Bonain' Mr. Froude rejected, finding the story beautiful, and the treatment excellent in arrangement and conception, but deficient in melody of versification, in smoothness and sweetness, much less finished in style than the 'Idyll'. Both pieces have been refused by four or five of our chief magazines to which they were sent.

I hope that you will pardon me for saying so much about myself, as I have only done so because your letter seemed to indicate a desire to know something on the subject.

The praise of two such men as yourself and your brother, however much kindliness may have tempered your judgment, is very valuable to me, and I am truly grateful for the generous promptitude and cordiality with which you have rendered it to an obscurer stranger.

While to the public I wish to remain anonymous as a writer, I have no wish to shroud myself from persons I esteem, and am happy to sign myself your obliged and faithful servant,

James Thomson[27]

He returned to his lodgings one day to find that William Rossetti had left him a present of the original two-volume edition from which the *Moxon* Shelley had been condensed. Thomson sent him a note:

I will do my poor best towards reading these noble volumes worthily; and welcome so fair an occasion for studying once more, and with such excellent assistance, the poet who fascinated me in my youth, and of whom my reverence remains undiminished and my estimate scarcely altered after twenty long years.[28]

He now began a correspondence discussing Rossetti's editing and the choice of certain words in the Shelley text.[29] But this new correspondence was interrupted. The Champion Gold and Silver Mines Company was having difficulties in the pursuit of its interests in Colorado, specifically in the final acquisition of a mine it was intended to exploit. It was required that the Secretary go out to attend to this and other matters: accordingly on the evening of April 27th 1872 Thomson left London by first-class train from Euston and travelled to Liverpool, from where he sailed to America.[30]

CHAPTER THIRTEEN

T HOMSON REACHED New York on May 8th and arrived in Central
City Colorado a week later. He described the place in a letter to
Rossetti:

> Every village out here is termed a city: this Central with Blackhawk and
> Nevada, the three virtually forming one straggling town, numbers between
> four and five thousand people. Of these the great majority are miners,
> perhaps a thousand being Cornishmen, who earn from $3 to $4 a day's
> wages, and much more when they take leases or work by contract. The
> stores are well stocked, but nearly everything is very dear. The working
> miner can get most of the mere necessities of life almost as cheap as at
> home; but the comforts and little luxuries are so priced that I find living
> here twice or three times as expensive. A small glass of English beer costs
> twenty-five cents, or say a shilling currency. To get your boots blacked (I
> always clean my own) you pay twenty-five cents, but then they get a 'Dolly
> Varden Shine,' and are wrought upon by a 'Boot Artist'. A 'tonsorialist'
> very naturally charges seventy-five cents or three shillings for cutting your
> hair; &c., &c., &c. We have churches, chapels, schools, and a new large
> hotel, in which a very polite dancing party assembled the other evening.
> This week we are to have a concert, and also a lecture on the Darwinian
> Theory, admission one dollar. We have a theatre, in which we now and
> then have actors. The old rough days, with their perils and excitement,
> are quite over; the 'City' is civilised enough to be dull and commonplace,
> while not yet civilised enough to be sociable and pleasant. There are no
> beggars, and petty larceny is almost unknown; storekeepers extort your
> money blandly and quietly, and the large larceny of selling mines at
> preposterous prices makes the people despise all larceny that is petty.
> You might as well carry a revolver between Euston Square and Somerset
> House as here. I brought one under persuasion, and have never taken it
> out of the bag.
> This Central City is the headquarters of gold-mining in Colorado
> Territory, but it has been very dull for some time past, the working of
> most of the large mines having been suspended, in some cases through

want of capital, in others through litigation (mines are wonderful breeders of lawsuits), and in others because the ores are not rich enough to pay the enormous charges for haulage and reduction and smelting out here, though they would be of immense value in an old country. However, a railroad connecting with the whole east is now within ten miles of us, and is being pushed on rapidly, so things are likely to improve ere long.

The houses, chiefly of wood, and some of them pretty enough in themselves, though spoiled by their surroundings, are huddled and scattered along the bottom and slopes of a winding ravine, intermingled with prospect-holes, primitive log-huts, mill-sheds, of which many are idle, fragments of machinery that proved useless form the first, heaps of stones and poor ores, and all sorts of rubbish. No one has ever cleared up anything here: the streets and roads are usually many inches deep in dust, which the rare heavy rains and the more frequent turning on of some foul sluice make mud which is verily abominable unto one who cleaneth his own boots. Men dig a shaft, shallow or deep, and leave it gaping for any one to tumble into. Trees are cut down, and the stumps all left to make night-wandering safe and agreeable. The hills surrounding us have been flayed of their grass and scalped of their timber; and they are scarred and gashed and ulcerated all over from past mining operations; so ferociously does little man scratch at the breasts of his great calm mother when he thinks that jewels are hidden. The streams running down the ravines, or, as they say here, the creeks running down the gulches, are thick with pollution from the washing of dirt and ores. We are 8,300 feet above the level of the sea, and 3,000 feet above Denver, which lies about forty miles eastward. The highest peaks of the Rocky Mountains hereabout are 14,000 feet; we are among the foothills. To get out of the city in any direction one must climb for a considerable distance.[1]

In describing mines as 'wonderful breeders of lawsuits' he was writing from first-hand experience. The owners of the mines which Champion were buying over had filed a 'vendor's lien' suit asserting property rights until Champion settled the full amount of purchase. And these owners were themselves under litigation from another company claiming precedence on the original stake for one of the mines in negotiation.[2] Thomson had to negotiate with one eye on the outcome of this. He also discovered that the resident agent for Champion Mines in Colorado, T.H. Lowe, seemed to have been fiddling the books. 'I pressed him with the simple question, "Where is the money invested?" I could get no other answer than "You shall know all about it tomorrow" '.[3] But Lowe failed to turn up on that morrow, or on any other morrow for another two months; by which time Thomson had himself taken out a writ, having discovered that Lowe had sold some company machinery. However in the straggling communities along Clear Creek

Thomson came to feel that the people he had to deal with knew more about Lowe's dealings than they were prepared to tell the visitor from London.[4]

He agreed a proposed contract between himself as secretary of Champion Mines and a local banker called Thatcher representing a Mr Stalker for the company previously owning the mines under negotiation. Thomson wired the details of the proposed contract to London, and made a copy for his notebook:

22 May 1872

On £5,000, making £15,000 part purchase money, being paid out of £34,000 debentures deposited, the additional capital raised by issue of debentures to be applied as follows:

First £5,000, retained by Compy, as making capital.

Next £5,000 paid to Thatcher's credit as part purchase money for release of £10,000 debentures Alliance Bank.

Afterwards of every £2,000 realised by Compy, by sale of debentures £1,000 to be paid Thatcher's credit and £1,000 applied at Compy's discretion until balance purchase money paid.

All the above stipulations being subject to provision for payment of interest and debentures issued by the Compy.

Mr Thomson agrees on behalf of the Champion Compy. to execute an agreement with Mr. Thatcher embodying the above conditions if the arrangement pending for release of Vendor's Lien be carried out.

(signed) James Thomson
Secr. Champion Co.[5]

But the directors in London were slow to respond, then there was haggling over an outright cash payment instead, Thatcher threatening to foreclose and sue Champion Mines.[6] On June 22nd he told Thomson that Stalker 'had been to the bank same morning drunk, swearing that he would not give way an inch and saying that he only wanted a shotgun and the other parties in reach and he would soon find the best way of settling the matter.'[7] An outright cash payment of $8,000 was finally agreed, Thatcher looking 'very bitter, making one long wry face over his pill.'[8] But there was the matter of getting the $8,000 out from London, and Thomson had enough bother getting them to send his own wages and expenses. 'My position becoming serious,' he wrote on June 27th before a draft for £100 was sent.[9] By the end of September he was out of money again, and another £100 had to be sent, this time to be split between Thomson and a new agent who had been sent to replace Lowe.[10] But despite Lowe's duplicity and Stalker's threat, a slow-paced decorum seems never to have been breached; even when the writ had been served on Lowe, and Thomson and he found themselves sitting in the same restaurant, they politely ignored each other after first agreeing formally to meet later – though Lowe as usual then failed to turn up.[11] For the next few months Thomson occupied himself checking out other mines in the area, and assessing the company's chances of mining coal as well as silver. Some of the mines to be investigated could only be reached by some stiff hill-climbing: 'very steep, 1100 feet, winded me badly', he wrote of a visit to one such mine on Mount Seaton.[12] A number of them had serious water damage, which was one of the hazards of leaving them unworked during the widespread litigation.[13]

During his six months in America he wrote several times each to Mrs Bradlaugh, Grant, Jacques, Hollett, and Julia.[14] He went long walks, and learned to ride, and regularly visited the settlement at Idaho Springs, to reach which one had to climb a road up out of the valley in which Central City lay, then descend to Idaho Springs on the other side of the Divide. In a letter to Mrs Bradlaugh he described the view he had enjoyed from the summit of the Divide on a recent visit:

In front, down the Canon, beyond Idaho, the ridges of hills & mountains swelling obliquely from left to right, the right being S.W. They were dark with brown patches, and the highest bore some thin sprinkling of snow. Immense cloud shadows, black & irregular, lay upon them. They swell obliquely through one rounded mountain into two high sharp scalped peaks, with many foldings and dells. Behind were white clouds massed and in round islets and the blue sky. The foreground a rough patch with a very few firs and dwarf cottonwood, many stones and tree stumps, thin grass, a single cow grazing. The thick dark green of the firs on the mountains looks fine and short as well mown grass. Two white stems and the multitudinous dazzling twinkle of the leaves of the cottonwood aspens. The sun hot and the 'shoo-flies' countless & busy. The dull tinkle of a cowbell on the righthand slope.

Turning back toward Central, green slope and gulch with shanties and mills. Right and left firs and cottonwood. These are the small bright green firs which turn yellow and russet in needle and apple, and then seen with sun behind them look like withered ferns similarly seen, burning golden & red. Beyond a long massy hillwall dark and brown green with pines. Beyond still a high sharp mountain on the night, brown & dark green. Leftwards a keen steep range, accentuated and abrupt in outline, with white gleaming precipices on the highest left.[15]

He complained of feeling lonely, though on July 31st he enjoyed his first dance at Central City's best hotel:

> Club dance in evening at Teller House. I invited by Potter of the Rocky Mountain Bank. Went with Dowlen. Began 9.30 ended 1.30. Quadrilles very different figures from ours. Hold hands only setting to partners & promenading. Sicilian Circle, with its grotesque of one sex forming ring & the other accompanying it 'basket fashion'. Danced two or three quadrilles & one round dance. Lancers something like ours, Caledonians much the same as ours. Waltz old fashioned, Schottische only first part; no galop, Varsoviana, Mazurka, Cotillon, or Country Dance. Ended with Home Sweet Home Quadrille; grand chain at funeral pace to this air, most of the dancers joining in the song, followed by rapid promenade, three or four times during Quadrille.
>
> Pleasant party, got enough introductions, danced most of the dances, enjoyed myself very well, could have gone on all night tho' I thought that I no longer cared much for such amusement.[16]

He moved a week after his recovery from a bout of fever, to accommodation where he could rely on some company.[17] He described a social jaunt in another letter to Mrs Bradlaugh of August 7th:

> Three charming young ladies in an open carriage, which you may call a buggy if you like, with a gentleman to drive them. Three more of us men on horseback – I am a famous horseman by this time. Lunch of tongue, eggs, sardines, bottled beer, &c., &c. Climb up last mile or two with the most charming of the charming girls on my arm. Ride home by moonlight through pine woods and among mountains. James Peak is more than 13,000 feet high, or 5,000 feet above us here in Central.
>
> We have now a young matron in our house, where four of us held a bachelor's mess. But one of these bachelors (not the present writer) persuaded his betrothed in England to get married to him out here, and out she came the other day, and married they were in this happy mansion, in the evening, by the Episcopal clergyman. We had elegant bridesmaids and a gorgeous supper, worthy to be mentioned with that never-to-be-forgotten breakfast for the wedding of the Grants . . .
>
> The worst of my life here is, that I have not enough to do, and yet am confined a good deal to this place. You will be happy to learn that I am quite clever at cleaning boots, practising regularly on my own, and that I have even made some way in the noble arts of sawing and chopping wood. Our fire fuel is delivered in four-feet logs as thick as my leg.
>
> I still manage to have my bath, having cleverly devised a six-inch ledge to an eighteen-inch tin pan. Kind love to you all, including Mr.

B., to whom, by the bye, I have not written yet. Shameful! but one can't write in this country.[18]

At the end of the month he had a week's holiday and rode on a camping trip north across the mountain range to the region known as Middle Park. His companions included a local judge, Judge Hahn, and the minister Rev. Turner of the Methodist Episcopal church. The group rode fifty miles in the first two days and spent the week exploring, fishing, playing cards in their tents, shooting grouse, and bathing in Sulphur Springs. Sometimes the route lay along narrow precipice roads, as on their first day's ride: 'rough stony road along side of mountain, 1000 to 1500 feet below on left; precipice 60° to 70°.'[19] On their journey back on Saturday August 31st, they found themselves surrounded by cloud: 'Long climb up through timber, ground considerably sodden with late rains. As we approached the top usual mist. Along Mammoth Gulch could only see a few yards above & below. Bitter breeze driving the mist, which became a compound of chill vapour, thin rain, keen sleet, sharp snow. Wentworth, Turner & I halted at lake for a cold bite of grouse, bread, mouthful of brandy & water; Judge & Best went on. Before this weather cleared – Boulder Gulch visible; fine shifting rainbows on tops of pines on farther side. Plenty of snowpatches above & beneath us, as when going.'[20] But the weather closed in again, and they returned to Central through a storm – 'lightnings right in one's face as if a veil blown back against it' – to find Central City temporarily awash: 'Main Street a respectable stream, Pollock's Street a torrent.'[21]

In November, when the weather turned cold enough to freeze the water and when, one albeit 'beautiful bright' day, it was 40° degrees below freezing at 6.30 a.m., he moved lodgings to Teller House itself.[22] There among other hotel entertainments were the barman's stories, such as sights seen at the prostitutes' ball in Massachusetts: 'Four fellows in four bedded attic: three with girls at one time. The prize for best dancer. Girl who had got it four times, refused it fifth. Went & undressed save stockings & garters. Danced wonderfully for five minutes, music playing, ball crowded. Then "Here's the leg that can dance, & there's the arse that can back it up!" Redressed & danced with the others till daylight.'[23] Thomson also observed that one man working a lucrative mine in Central 'would lavish as much as a thousand dollars in a one or two night trip to Denver, between gambling saloons & brothels.'[24]

Having holidayed with the minister Turner Thomson went to his farewell service in town, then returned to church twice to hear Turner's replacement, whom he found 'old & commonplace'.[25] But he was not drifting towards Christian orthodoxy. He sent Charles Bradlaugh at the

National Reformer an essay in three parts called 'Religion in the Rocky Mountains', the third part of which Bradlaugh decided it would be too risky to publish.[26] In the Rockies, Thomson wrote, the daily language and legends of the miners were illustrative of their deep religious faith. One miner argued the case for the Blessed Trinity by comparing it with the barrel of a six-shooter; and as for the ordinary language 'it is common to say of a man who has too much self-esteem, He thinks himself a little tin Jesus on wheels.' The wheels, Thomson suggested, might be a reference to the opening chapter of *Ezekiel*.

Religious legends kept alive included the story of Joseph, refused entry to Heaven for being drunk, who threatened Peter: '. . . by God I'll take my son out of the outfit and bust up the whole consarn!' And there was a famous game of poker – poker being a game Thomson learned to play in Central City – which legend had it was played one day in heaven:

Again it is told that a certain miner, a tough cuss, who could whip his weight in wild cats and give points to a grizzlie, seemed uncommonly moody and low-spirited one morning, and on being questioned by his chum, at length confessed that he was bothered by a very queer dream. 'I dreamt that I was dead,' he explained; 'and a smart spry pretty little angel took me up to heaven.' 'Dreams go by contraries,' suggested the chum, by way of comfort. 'Let that slide,' answered the dreamer; 'the point isn't there. Wall, St Peter wasn't at my gate, and the angel critter led me on to pay my respects to the boss, and after travelling considerable we found him as thus, God the Father, God the Son, God the Holy Ghost and Peter, all as large as life, were playing a high-toned game of poker, and there was four heavy piles on the table – gold, not shinplasters, you bet. I was kinder glad to see that they played poker up in heaven, so as to make life there not onbearable; for it would be but poor fun singing psalms all day; I was never much of a hand at singing, more particularly when the songs is psalms. Wall, we waited, not liking to disturb their game, and I watched the play. I soon found that Jesus Christ was going through the rest, cheating worse than the heathen Chinee at euchre; but of course I didn't say nothing, not being in the game. After a while Peter showed that he began to guess it too, if he wasn't quite sure; or p'r'aps he was skeared at up and telling Christ to his face. At last, however, what does Christ do, after a bully bluff which ran Pete almost to his bottom dollar, but up and show five aces to Pete's call: and "What's that for high:" says he, quite cool. "Now look you, Christ," shouts Pete, jumping up as mad as thunder, and not caring a cent or a continental what he said to anybody; "look you Christ, that's too thin; we don't want any of your darned miracles here!" and with that he grabbed up his pile and all his stakes, and went off in a mighty huff. Christ looked pretty mean, I tell you, and the game was up.'[27]

On December 6th Thomson received instructions to return to London, but a fortnight passed before the company wired his fare, and it was Boxing Day before he received the draft from the Wells Fargo office. He left Central on the morning of Saturday December 28th, and arrived in Denver in mid-afternoon. Next morning he left Denver at 7.40 a.m., passing through Greeley and Antelope on his way to lunch in Cheyenne at 12.30.[28] Here he embarked on the Pacific Railroad and at 3.30 was watching 'antelopes scudding away on the great plains'. He worked at a translation of a Heine poem, 'Where?' The translation he inscribed as 'Englished Sunday afternoon 29/12/72 as I reclined on the sofa in the rushing drawing room of a Pullman's Car, crossing the level yellow green-grass sea between Cheyenne and Pine Bluffs, on the road to Omaha, window open to the mild air, under lovely pale blue sky full of sunlight & flecked with soft clouds:

> Where shall once the wanderer weary
>   Meet his resting-place and shrine?
> Under palm-trees by the Ganges?
>   Under lindens of the Rhine?
>
> Shall I somewhere in the desert
>   Owe my grave to stranger hands?
> Or upon some lonely sea-shore
>   Rest at last beneath the sands?
>
> Ever onward! God's wide heaven
>   Must surround me there as here;
> And like death-lamps o'er me swinging
>   Night by night the stars burn clear.[29]

At a quarter to five he noted the 'long level sunset of intense pale yellow fire burning over long low hills on both sides bounding horizon'. He had tea at Sidney at 5.30, breakfast next morning at 6.20 in Grand Island, then 'afterwards for hours through the great N. Platte valley'. He was at Omaha by lunchtime, Dunlap by 6.30. Early morning breakfast on December 31st was at Cedar Rapids, then he was at Clinton Illinois, and by 4 p.m. had arrived in Chicago, where he booked into the Sherman House hotel, and went for a walk to see the sights 'Walked up and down Madison Street. Wonderful building on each side in the streets at right angle.' He noted the 'vehemence' of people betting at the hotel: 'In the Restaurant Saloon 40 or 50 people intensely excited throwing dice for tickets in lottery & then for its subject a $2000 pair of horses, for which one in the room would give $1500.' On New Year's

Day 1873 he walked about Chicago: 'Madison, Wabash Av., State St., Adams, S. Halstead etc. Down Wabash as far as 16th St., up to where the vessels were lying. – Nearly circumnavigate the burnt district besides going here and there through it. – The difference striking between Wabash Av, unburnt & burnt.' Next day he went to the Suspension Bridge, and to the Falls: 'Four of us sleigh to the Falls – really but a little way under, immense icicles (perhaps more than 50 feet long) & a stream from the fall stopping us . . . The American town seems a large and fine one, many spires & large buildings. The Canadian Vermin who have settled on the Falls seem the most bloodthirsty and rapacious I have ever come across.' On Friday 3rd he had breakfast at Sasquannah 'an hour or so along the Delaware river', dinner at Dixon, and at 5.40 p.m. arrived in Jersey City. On Saturday 4th he 'Walked all up Broadway thro' Central Park and back'. At 4 p.m. he watched the 'extraordinary scene' of a huge traffic crush at the top of Courtland Street on Broadway, with an 'Immense number of people walking both ways, trying to cross'. On the 6th he was still exploring New York: 'Walked morning to lower end of Broadway, to Ferry. Then along East St past & through Fulton Market – Wall Street. After dinner as far as A.J. Stewart's store, – down Broome Street & along Bowery to Canal Street.' On Tuesday: 'Walked up Broadway – Got Whitman's Works ($3.75)'. On Thursday 9th he bought his passage ticket back on the *Baltic Star* to Liverpool, which cost him $89, more than £21 sterling. Then he took a panoramic view of the city and its bay:

Went into Trinity Church & ascended the steeple as high as one can get. Clear pale blue sky, not luminous or transparent, very pale to the south, rather dusky to the north; bright watery sun; water a white frosted silver sheet beyond Battery, dark solid green east & west; numerous steamers with bright white smoke trails; schooners under full sail from North River; fresh N.W. breeze; Broadway to Grace Church; City with serried rooftops & few steeples of brown stone principally; Brooklyn chiefly lost behind ridge; Trinity steeple itself with upward lines of brown stone of stucco, about as shapely as rough-kneaded lumps of dough, one larger Herring lump at every yard.[30]

He had enjoyed his visit to America, he told friends on his return: 'When travelling about I always find myself immensely better than when confined to one place. With money, I believe I should never have a home, but be always going to and fro on the earth, and walking up and down in it, like him of whom I am one of the children.'[31]

Back in Pimlico he moved lodgings a few doors along Vauxhall Bridge Road from Mrs Reeves's lodgings at 240 to a Miss Heywood's at 230.[32] He wrote to Hypatia Bradlaugh at Midhurst.

> If I were only about twenty years old, or if, old as I am, I had a good trade, I would certainly emigrate and become a citizen of the free and enlightened Republic. But for mere clerks and accountants and *sich*, they have more out there than they want.
>
> I don't know when I shall be able to give you a call at Midhurst. I should very much like to do so. Perhaps I shall have little or nothing to do for my Company after next month, and then I may be able to manage a short visit.[33]

He resumed his correspondence with Rossetti about Shelley's texts and sent notes on 'The Witch of Atlas' and 'Epipsychidion'.[34] Of the latter he wrote: 'It has always seemed to me that Shelley never soared higher than this poem, which I find full of supreme inspiration. It is his *Vita Nuova*, tender and fervid and noble as Dante's; and his premature death has deprived us of the befitting *Divina Commedia* which should have followed.'[35] When on April 18th 1873 he sent further extensive notes on the structure of Shelley's lyric drama 'Prometheus Unbound' – 'I have not been afraid of going into minutiae, because nothing, however minute, which affects the perfection of a master-piece, can be insignificant'[36] – Rossetti invited Thomson to visit, and to inspect his 'relic' of Shelley: 'I have for instance a piece of his blackened skull, given me by Trelawney, who picked it out of the furnace, and the regard in which I hold this relic makes me understand the feelings of a Roman Catholic in parallel cases. Possibly you would be at the opposite pole of feeling in this matter.'[37]

Thomson accepted the invitation. But he disclaimed merit as a critic as pointedly as he elsewhere disclaimed merit as either poet or translator:

> 1. I never until reading your edition saw any notes on the text, save those of Mr. Garnett in the 'Relics', and am still quite ignorant of whatever critical comments and discussions have been published, except such as are indicated in your notes. Nor have I ever known personally any reader of Shelley with whom to compare notions on the subject; in fact, I have only come across two people in my life who gave signs of real intelligent interest in the poetry of Shelley, or indeed in any really great poetry, as poetry. I am thus only too likely to vex you with discussion of points long since settled, and with such wrong-headed notions as are the *fungi* of seclusion.

2. Having been used for many years to read his works in editions obviously corrupt, I have naturally taken many more and much greater liberties in guessing at true readings than I should have dreamed of doing had the editions been decently correct. The certainty of numerous errors made the text thoroughly uncertain.[38]

After the twenty-nine-year-old Thomson had visited Rossetti's home at Euston Square, Rossetti wrote up what he thought of his visitor. Rossetti's diary entry for Monday April 28th, 1873 reads: 'J. Thomson called on me. I find him to be a man of about 33 or 34, of appearance and manners rather of the commercial traveller type than the long-headed working man type; in essentials agreeable and well-mannered, and with a good deal of sound knowledge, and readiness in producing it. He learned Italian for the purpose of reading Dante, and seems to have a very competent knowledge of the language and literature. Thinks Leopardi shows some Shelleyan influence, and might possibly have met Shelley: this may be worth looking into. Though he doesn't profess to have devoted himself to the special study of Shelley, I find him very familiar both with Shelley's poems, and with what has been written about him by Hogg, in my memoirs etc. I offered to communicate (and had before made this offer in writing) the more important of his Shelley notes to *Notes and Queries*, and to express therein my high opinion of Thomson's own doings as a poet: in this he acquiesced. His opinions in religion and politics are of course of a very extreme kind, writing as he does in the *National Reformer*: but he does not seem to be mixed up with the practical movements of the Republican etc. party. He knows and likes Bradlaugh: considers him a man of considerable oratorical gift, ambitious, and likely to achieve somewhat. Odger he has rather a distaste for, and other popular leaders he does not seem to know very much about. Thomson passed some of his early youth in Ireland; but, to judge from his speech, he is quite an Englishman, and perhaps a Londoner. He got to know something of Whitman's poems through my selection, and has become a very ardent admirer of them.'[39]

This portrait of Thomson he later complemented in a letter to Thomson's biographer Henry Salt:

He came one evening, when the only person at home with me was my elder sister (authoress of 'A Shadow of Dante'). I saw him partly alone, and partly in my sister's company. Thomson was rather a small man, – say hardly five feet six in height, – with sufficiently regular features, bright eyes, and at that time a cheerful, pleasant manner. There was (but only, I think, in later years) a rather peculiar expression in his mouth; something of a permanently pained expression, along with a settled half-smile, caustic but not cynical, not 'put on', but adopted as part of his attitude towards the world. I had expected to find him rather of the type of the intellectual working-man, but did not find this to be the fact; he seemed to me more of the 'city-clerk' or minor man of business with literary tastes. His manners were good, free from nervousness, pretension, or self-assertion. He talked extremely well, and without, I think, any symptom of defective education, except that his *h*'s were sometimes less aspirated than they should be. Not that he *dropped* his *h*'s, and he certainly never inserted them where they ought not to come. There was no trace of the Scotchman in his pronunciation. We passed a pleasant evening, and I can recollect that my sister, who was an intense religious devotee, received an agreeable impression from his conversation – which shows that he knew when to keep his strong opinions to himself.[40]

Just over a fortnight after his visit to Rossetti, Thomson wrote in his notebook: 'There may or may not be beings superior to us. But I cannot think so ill of any possible supreme being as to accuse him of the guilt and folly of the voluntary creation of such a world and of such lives as ours. I cannot accuse a possible Devil of this, much less a possible God.'[41] That month also he took up once more the poem-sequence he had left off in October 1870. In the margin of the manuscript of a newly completed verse he dated it simply 'May 1873'.

CHAPTER FOURTEEN

M<small>AY</small> 1873[1]: By the riverside he watched another couple sitting under an elm. They were joined in talk, their eyes on the river. First Voice: I never knew another man on earth but had at least some joy or solace in life. I have had none. I didn't ask for fame, rank or riches. All I wanted was homely love, common food and health, and nightly sleep.

JUNE 2nd

'Who is most wretched in this wretched place?
  I think myself; yet I would rather be
  My miserable self than He, than He
Who formed such creatures to His own disgrace.

The vilest thing must be less vile than Thou
  From whom it had its being, God and Lord!
  Creator of all woe and sin abhorred,
Malignant and implacable! I vow

That not for all Thy power furled and unfurled,
  For all the temples to Thy glory built,
  Would I assume the ignominious guilt
Of having made such men in such a world.

As if a Being, God or Fiend, could reign,
At once so wicked, foolish, and insane,
As to produce men when He might refrain!

The world rolls round for ever like a mill;
It grinds out death and life and good and ill;
It has no purpose, heart or mind or will.'

The mill must blindly whirl on. It may be wearing out, but who can know? If man were less dim-sighted he might see one thing – that the mill is indifferent. It does not treat Man harshly. It grinds him some slow years of bitter breath, then grinds him back into eternal death.

JUNE 6th

The river is called the River of the Suicides. Night by night someone seeks oblivion in it:

> One plunges from a bridge's parapet,
>   As by some blind and sudden frenzy hurled;
> Another wades in slow with purpose set
>   Until the waters are above him furled;
> Another in a boat with dreamlike motion
> Glides drifting down into the desert ocean,
>   To starve or sink from out the desert world.

No one tries to save them. People watching think how soon they themselves might seek the same refuge. Why remain in this tragic farce as actors and spectators? To see what next is in the dull play for our illusion. To refrain from grieving dear foolish friends. But those asleep at home, how blest are they.

JUNE 7th

It is strange, wandering the deserted streets, to hear the sound of wheels and ironshod feet. Who could be riding in this Venice of the Black Sea?

> The rolling thunder seems to fill the sky
>   As it comes on; the horses snort and strain,
> The harness jingles, as it passes by;
>   The hugeness of an overburthened wain:
> A man sits nodding on the shaft or trudges
> Three parts asleep beside his fellow drudges:
>   And so it rolls into the night again.

What merchandise? Whence, whither, and for whom? Maybe it's a hearse, bearing away the joy, peace, and all the aborted hopes of the good things which should have been our lot, but which have been strangled by the City's curse.

JUNE 11th

Lo, thus, as prostrate, 'In the dust I write
  My heart's deep languor and my soul's sad tears.'
Yet why evoke the spectres of black night
  To blot the sunshine of exultant years:
Why disinter dead faith from mouldering hidden?
Why break the seals of mute despair unbidden,
  And wail life's discords into careless ears?

Because a cold rage seizes one at whiles
  To show the bitter old and wrinkled truth
Stripped naked of all vesture that beguiles,
  False dreams, false hopes, false masks and modes of youth;
Because it gives some sense of power and passion
In helpless impotence to try to fashion
  Our woe in living words howe'er uncouth.

Surely I write not for the hopeful young,
  Or those who deem their happiness of worth,
Or such as pasture and grow fat among
  The shows of life and feel nor doubt nor dearth,
Or pious spirits with a God above them
To sanctify and glorify and love them,
  Or sages who foresee a heaven on earth.

For none of these I write, and none of these
  Could read the writing if they deigned to try:
So may they flourish, in their due degrees,
  On our sweet earth and in their unplaced sky.
If any cares for the weak words here written,
It must be some one desolate, Fate-smitten,
  Whose faith and hope are dead, and who would die.

Yes, here and there some weary wanderer
  In that same city of tremendous night,
Will understand the speech, and feel a stir
  Of fellowship in all-disastrous fight;
'I suffer mute and lonely, yet another
Uplifts his voice to let me know a brother
  Travels the same wild paths though out of sight.'

O sad Fraternity, do I unfold
  Your dolorous mysteries shrouded from of yore?
Nay, be assured; no secret can be told

To any who divined it not before:
None uninitiate by many a presage
Will comprehend the language of the message,
Although proclaimed aloud for evermore.

JUNE 13th

Near the centre of the northern crest of the City is a bleak level upland. On it sits throned the tremendous image of a winged woman, a bronze colossus on a graded granite base.

JULY 3rd – 5th

He watched a long loose line of people wend their way across the cathedral square, entering the cathedral at its porch. As they entered a hooded figure asked each person from whence they had come to this our City of Tremendous Night. Each answered in turn:

From pleading in a senate of rich lords
For some scant justice to our countless hordes
Who toil half-starved with scarce a human right;
I wake from daydreams to this real night.

From wandering through many a solemn scene
Of opium visions, with a heart serene
And intellect marvellously bright:
I wake from daydreams to this real night.

Then answered in turn, as they passed into the cathedral, a religious recluse, a king, a preacher, a drinker in brothels, a religious painter, a religious poet, a political insurgent:

Thus, challenged by that warder sad and stern,
    Each one responded with his countersign,
Then entered the cathedral; and in turn
    I entered also, having given mine;
But lingered near until I heard no more,
And marked the closing of the massive door.

The interior was gloomy, moonbeams slanting through the windows. There was no music, and no clergy. Men and shadows leaned against the walls, or sat bent in secluded stalls. All waited without a stir, until addressed from the pulpit by a speaker with an enormous head in which two steadfast intolerable eyes burned beneath a broad rugged brow.

The Preacher: O melancholy Brothers, dark, dark, dark! My soul has bled for you these sunless years. Your woe has been my anguish. I have searched the heights and depths, the scope of all our universe, for solace from your wild unrest.

> And now at last authentic voice I bring,
> Witnessed by every dead and living thing;
>   Good tidings of great joy for you, for all:
> There is no God; no Fiend with names divine
> Made us and tortures us; if we must pine,
>   It is to satiate no Being's gall.
>
> It was the dark delusion of a dream,
> That living Person conscious and supreme,
>   Whom we must curse for cursing us with life;
> Whom we must curse because the life He gave
> Could not be buried in the quiet grave,
>   Could not be killed by poison or by knife.
>
> This little life is all we must endure,
> The grave's most holy peace is ever sure,
>   We fall asleep and never wake again;
> Nothing is of us but the mouldering flesh,
> Whose elements dissolve and merge afresh
>   In earth, air, water, plants, and other men.

The Preacher: We finish thus, and all our wretched race shall finish its cycle and be replaced by other beings with their own timespans. We bow down to the universal laws which never had a special place for man; all substance lives and struggles through countless shapes continually at war, interknit by countless interactions. If a person is born on a certain day on earth, all times and forces tended to that birth. I find throughout the Universe no blessing or curse, good or ill: only Necessity Supreme, with infinite Mystery. O brothers of sad lives: they are so brief. If you cannot endure life you are free to end it when you will, with no fear of waking afterwards.

The echo of the preacher's voice died away in the cathedral. The congregation remained motionless as if brooding on his 'End it when you will.'

At 230 Vauxhall Bridge Road Thomson was having trouble paying the rent.[2] He had expected to receive more from the Champion Gold and Silver Mines Company for his trip to America than they had payed him, but as he hadn't a written contract he had had to accept what they decided was his due. However in July 1873 another job came his way through Bradlaugh's contacts, and again it meant travelling overseas. The *New York World* had an office in Fleet Street under its London agent Pierre Girard; and Girard required a reporter, at £5 a week, to travel with the rebel forces of the self-proclaimed Don Carlos VII, pretender to the Spanish throne, currently raising forces to overthrow the new Spanish republic.[3] The Carlist cause was most strongly supported in the north-east Basque and Navarre regions, and thither Thomson was directed to join up with the pretender's troops. Accordingly having arranged for the *New York World* to make payments to his landlady Miss Heywood while he was away, Thomson ticked off in his notebook:– a Spanish conversation book and French-Spanish dictionary; his passport, a pistol borrowed from Bradlaugh, a waterproof coat, hats, two white shirts, flannel shirts and drawers, blanket, rug, towel, soap, horse boots, collars, socks, neckties, eyeglasses, field glasses, gloves, hairbrush, toothbrush, letters of introduction, flask, writing case, bathing drawers, watch, chain, needles, thread, and buttons; and set off from Victoria Station on July 22nd 1873 heading for the French-Spanish border at Bayonne via Dover, Calais, Paris and Bordeaux.[4]

By the 24th he had arrived at the Spanish border about twenty miles from Bayonne, but he had difficulty getting transport to proceed, and returned to Bayonne after spending a night in a hotel at the border. He wired the *New York Herald* for £25 to buy a horse, sending at the same time a description of Bayonne in the summer heat – 'a pleasant place to loaf in'[5] – as his first report: 'Perhaps the streets one likes best are the old narrow ones, with tall houses, all the shutters Venetian-blind fashion, and the shadowy arcades, with many short pillars in front of the stores. As these arcades not only keep out much of the heat, but also much of the light of the sun, the interior of the stores is rather dark, and thus many stalls are placed under the open arches, and much of the work is done outside. Even where there are no arcades it is the custom to carry on the work in the front shop with the door open. Thus you see young girls with nimble fingers, all natty and clean, working away with a will and chatting gaily, with now and then a glance for the passers-by.' He described Carlist recruits at the border, each wearing his brooch 'with the monogram of Carlos Rey' fixed to his beretta. Thomson watched the Basque game of Peluet, noticing its similarity to the Irish game of fives. In his notebook he recorded passing impressions of people seen: 'More than one old woman walking lightly with handkerchief tied obliquely round the head, recalled forcibly the portraits of Dante; network of minute wrinkles, sharp nose, sharp, strong chin, contracted features, intense regard under sharp brows. All give gracious salutations as we go by, for every one here is intensely and obsequiously polite to every one else.'[6]

His money draft came through from London on Saturday July 27th, with the injunction 'Get to the front immediately'. But there was still a delay of a few days getting the money cashed, buying a horse, then getting a pass to allow him to take the horse across into Spain. On the Monday he went bathing in the sea at Biarritz. It was Friday August 1st before he crossed into Spain, his *New York World* contacts having enabled him to join up with a party of seventeen soldiers and some other correspondents, all heading south-west through the mountain passes of Navarre to meet up with Don Carlos and his troops. Thomson had a hard time with his horse's saddle, which kept slipping; but on the evening of Saturday August 4th he reached Aranaz with his companions and began to enjoy the hospitality that the Basques were offering all connected with the Carlist entourage. His Sunday at Aranaz he later described to a secularist readership:

The next morning being Sunday we all went to mass, and I accepted holy water (I hope my Freethinking friends will pardon me). The church was fine and large, as are all the churches in the country, a very smart Madonna was carried down it for our adoration, and we had a stirring sonorous sermon in Basque, of which I could understand only a few adopted Spanish words. In the afternoon we went again to the house of the gracious Senora, where we had not only more chocolate, but some fandango (I hope my Calvinistic friends will forgive me), two priests approving by their presence. In the evening, yet again fandango, with polka, scottische, Biscay reel, and a sort of waltz (I despair of the forgiveness of my Calvinistic friends), and we did not yet get back to bed till midnight, our kind hostess decisively refusing to let us pay anything.[7]

Next day they travelled further into the mountains: 'Monday 4.8.73. Late starting; at 6 for Escurra. Route mounting for two hours. Horse awfully fatigued. Arrived at crest three grand eagles floating under the intense pale blue sky. What augury? Afterwards had to walk on foot all the way – more than three hours, with hot sun & route ascending somewhat & descending much, bad & stony. Almost knocked up, carrying heavy bag & field glass, & walking in cavalry boots. Arrive at noon. Drank wine & breakfasted & soon felt refreshed.' On Wednesday 6th they set off again at 5 a.m. before the intense heat built up: 'Very bad route across mountains, much mounting at first. After one hour both straps of my saddle broke & I had to march on foot for four hours to Lacunza – Grand mountain to left above this town; with magnificent rampart of grey-white rock crowning it'. They entered Lacunza to cheering and 'bewildering vivas', it being assumed that they were the vanguard of the Carlist army, expected in the town shortly thereafter. Don Carlos himself did arrive soon after: 'He shewed himself on the balcony; frenetic exultation of the people, all gathered. After he parted, a band of loud music; women & girls & some men dancing the fandango.'

From Lacunza Thomson travelled with Don Carlos's army marching south to Puente de la Reina. Days of marching passed, as Thomson put it, 'like a military promenade'.[8] They would be called at dawn or before, and after washing and dressing would be given a cup of very thick chocolate with two or three fingers of bread and a glass of water. There would be a march till noon, with a short break around 10. Eggs, milk, fruit and vegetables would be bought in a hurry and food prepared, often with much competition for the use of a wood fire on a stone floor. Lunch – which Thomson and others from England called 'breakfast' – would be followed by a smoke and perhaps a glass of *anisau* or a local white brandy. Then siesta, indoors on a bed or floor, or outdoors in the shade. At four or five the march would resume till nightfall when billets had to be sought, while attendants looked after the horses and saw to dinner. After dinner there was time for some relaxation before bed: 'If the resting place was largish, we had decent beds in curtained alcoves; if not, we had mattresses on the floor; and in either case we slept the sleep of the just.'[9]

The Basques had given the Carlists strong support in the previous war of succession, and they did so likewise a second time. The new pretender promised the preservation of their *fueros* – certain independent rights held by their own assemblies – and he was identified with Catholic Church traditions that the Basques largely wished to maintain. The new republic on the other hand had a proposed constitution which included the separation of church and state. Thomson's opinion was that though the Carlist cause with its 'God, Country and King' motto might be thought reactionary by his freethinking friends, the Basques deserved respect rather than sneers: 'They are still faithful to their

King and their Church, precisely because they have always preserved their freedom under these. The priests spring from the people, just as the Irish priests used to be with their flocks before newspapers and emigration spread among the latter swarms of novel ideas.' He equated the Basques with the Jacobites, and of Don Carlos he concluded: 'If he was not King of Spain, he was certainly King of Navarre, not only by the grace of God (who is generally held responsible for the monarchy of monarchs), but also by the manifest will of the people.'[10]

They reached Puenta de la Reina, south of Pamplona, on August 14th. Here as elsewhere in the region they were received with local enthusiasm. After a day's rest in which Thomson went to a 'bull-teasing' the march set off again at 3 a.m. on Monday 16th for the ancient town of Estella, which they reached at 4.30. At 5.45 Thomson at last was able to note 'heard first firing'. There was skirmishing and rifle fire in Estella for the rest of the day, shots being fired at one point from the attic of the house in which Thomson with some soldiers had been lodged. Thomson recorded one soldier shot dead, and that 'the swallows kept dashing about in the line of fire evidently excited yet not scared away'. More Carlist battalions arrived, and the republican forces began to gather eleven miles to the east of Allo. Thomson with his immediate party was moved to Dicastillo four miles short of Allo, and here he remained some days, taking the chance to write a letter to Julia. With some staff officers he moved nearer the fighting now taking place, but in driving rain 'couldn't see at all' what was happening to the south. He gathered statistics on the numbers wounded and killed, and in better weather on the 25th saw 'flashing of arms among trees' and a bayonet charge by the Carlists. That evening there was a victory march into Estella:

> About 5 marched to Estella, which we reached about 7. Immense cheering at Di Castillo, *en route*, and grand reception at Estella . . . Place full of soldiers and people – Illumination – Bands playing late at night. Before we left Di Castillo saw the dead & wounded – One poor fellow very bad – Corpse naked in coffin – others sewn-up like mummies in shrouds – Dead carried off in large box – turned out into grave – service at house – box back for future services.
>
> As we approached Estella saw smoke of fort set on fire this morning. Still burning with shells occasionally exploding.
>
> *Times* had special messenger last night (Sunday Monday) at 2 in the morning that Estella was taken – Sent off telegram – We didn't know till after getting up in the morning – Our lodging out of the way; didn't hear shouting & music after midnight.

There were a few days' rest and drilling before the troops marched southwest to Viana, where more skirmishing took place. Again Thomson was distanced from the fighting itself, though later in the day he entered Viana where the republicans had surrendered and 150 prisoners been taken. On September 2nd he received a letter from London dated from eleven days before, recalling him. An earlier letter had not reached him. The *New York World* was not pleased with his performance, having only received three reports.

Heading back in the direction of the French border therefore Thomson set off north-east with some troops to Alsasua, where he was detained three days with sunstroke. His daily notebook, now abandoned apart from occasional fragments of names, records that on September 6th he was with troops marching for Santesteban. But there he was laid up ill for fully ten days before travelling on to Bayonne via Aranaz and Vera at the border. He arrived back in London on September 23rd, having sent another two reports since his letter of recall. Hypatia Bradlaugh in her memoir of her father recalled the whole *New York World* episode with some scepticism: 'During the Carlist War, in 1873, Mr Bradlaugh obtained for his friend an appointment to go to Spain as special correspondent to a New York paper; but alas! he was taken "ill" whilst about his duties, wrote irregularly and infrequently, and as a climax wrote three lines describing an important event when three columns were expected. He was consequently recalled, and when he got back my father found, to his additional vexation, that he (Mr Thomson) had lost the Colt's revolver which he had lent him.'[11] Thomson himself maintained that the infrequency of his reporting had been due to the poor lines of communication established by the Carlists, and that people had expected dramatic reports from a situation in which nothing particularly dramatic had occurred.[12]

The day after his return he wrote to his sister-in-law telling her that he was back from Spain with a cold in his left eye and a staved right thumb, war-wounds 'worse than fell to the lot of most warriors in Spain'.[13] Pierre Girard at the *New York World* told him he could not be expected to be paid for his full duration in Spain since he had been recalled weeks before he managed to arrive back, and because in any case they thought his performance unsatisfactory. So once more Thomson was disappointed in payment. Out of work, he wrote in November to Alice Bradlaugh: 'My eye is quite well again, thank you. I only want some good employment for it and its fellow. The time was very tedious during the weeks it remained bad, as I could hardly read, write, smoke, or do anything but lounge indoors unoccupied. Mr Girard has now no work for an assistant, and I have not managed to get hold of anything in the City yet, though, of course, I have been making every effort.'[14]

While in Spain Thomson had not completely laid aside his unfinished poem sequence. He had worked on it during the two spells he was detained on his way home in September across north-east Spain at Alsasua then at Santesteban. And despite what he told Alice Bradlaugh in November, he had not remained wholly unoccupied at 230 Vauxhall Bridge Road since his return. His manuscripts show that during the weeks of October 1873 he dated as largely complete the remaining parts of the poem he had last dated before his departure for Spain.[15]

OCTOBER 1st – 2nd

How the moon triumphs through the endless nights, stars throbbing and glittering. Men look at the stars and think the heavens respond to what they feel. In the moonlight boats glide past the reflected bridge trembling on the black stream. Cold windows in the city become shining crystals, and the glistening dew on lawns looks like fairy lakes. With such living light shines the dead eyes of sightless heaven, in which we read pity or scorn.

Fond man! They are neither haughty nor tender, there is no heart or mind: 'They thread mere puppets all their marvellous maze':

> If we could near them with the flight unflown,
>> We should but find them worlds as sad as this,
> Or suns all self-consuming like our own
>> Enringed by planet worlds as much amiss:
> They wax and wane through fusion and confusion;
> The spheres eternal are a grand illusion,
>> The empyréan is a void abyss.

OCTOBER 4th

Wherever men are gathered in the City, all the air is charged with feeling and thought. All the shouts, cries, laughs, curses, prayers are wrought into the air's vibrations, and unspoken passions and meditations are carried into it with our breathing. No man there breathes earth's simple breath as he would do if alone on a mountain or at sea;

he is constantly nourished on what will warm his life or will hasten his death, he in turn affecting his neighbours as they affect him:

> That City's atmosphere is dark and dense,
>   Although not many exiles wander there,
> With many a potent evil influence,
>   Each adding poison to the poisoned air;
> Infections of unutterable madness,
> Infections of incalculable madness,
>   Infections of incurable despair.

───────────

Of all things human which are strange and wild, perchance the wildest and most strange to wanderers in the sunless city is that man moans repeatedly how Time is deadly swift, how life is fleeting, and how naught is constant on the earth but change.

OCTOBER 6th

The congregation still muses on the preacher's 'End it when you will'. Suddenly a voice cries out, shrill and lamentable.

OCTOBER 11th

The Voice from the Congregation: The preacher has spoken sooth. We have no personal life beyond the grave, there is no God, and Fate is indifferent. But can I find the comfort which I crave? In all eternity I had one chance for the few years' term of life: for intellectual advancement, a home with a wife and children, social pleasure; for the enjoyment of Art, Nature, works of imagination; for the pleasure of mere being – a careless childhood, a passionate youth, for the gaining some wealth in maturity, for the calmness of old age: all the prerogatives of Man, working out his place in the universe through History, calculating the likely future progress of the world. All this chance was never offered me before, and never will be again: the past is silent, Blank Blank the infinite To-come.

> And this sole chance was frustrate from my birth,
>   A mockery, a delusion; and my breath
> Of noble human life upon this earth
>   So racks me that I sigh for senseless death.

My wine of life is poison mixed with gall,
   My noonday passes in a nightmare dream,
I worse than lose the years which are my all;
   What can console me for the loss supreme?

Speak not of comfort where no comfort is,
   Speak not at all: can words make foul things fair?
Our life's a cheat, our death a black abyss:
   Hush and be mute envisaging despair.

His voice ceased, and there was silence for a while. Then the preacher spoke again: My poor Brothers, it is thus. Life itself holds nothing good for us, but it will end soon and never be again. We know nothing before our birth and will know nothing after we have been consigned to earth. I ponder these thoughts, and they comfort me.

OCTOBER 24th

The colossal winged woman to the north of the city sits massively leaning forward with her cheek on her left hand, her forearm upright, her elbow on her knee. Across a book in her lap she holds a pair of compasses. Her eyes gaze full set, wandering in mazes of thought, seeing no outward sight.

OCTOBER 26th

Words cannot picture her, but all men know the image made by the sad artist 360 years ago: the instruments of carpentry and science scattered about her feet, the wolf-hound sleeping there.

OCTOBER 28th

Scales, hour-glass, bell and magic square above her, the grave, solid infant looking heavy-eyed at the stone tablets it is bearing. The woman's folded wings, like a mighty eagle too impotent to lift her earth-born strength and pride.

OCTOBER 29th

Man's delusions: The hours are heavy on him, and the days. The burden of the months he scarce can bear. Often he secretly would rather sleep between his periods of pleasure. Yet in his marvellous fancy he must make quick wings for Time, this Time which crawls blindwormlike like a monstrous snake spreading poison forever round the world.

> And since he cannot spend and use aright
>   The little time here given him in trust,
> But wasteth it in weary undelight
>   Of foolish toil and trouble, strife and lust,
> He naturally claimeth to inherit
> The everlasting Future, that his merit
>   May have full scope; as surely is most just.
>
> O length of the intolerable hours,
>   O nights that are as aeons of slow pain,
> O Time, too ample for our vital powers,
>   O Life, whose woeful vanities remain
> Immutable for all of all our legions
> Through all the centuries and all the regions,
>   Not of your speed and variance *we* complain.
>
> *We* do not ask a longer term of strife,
>   Weakness and weariness and nameless woes;
> We do not claim renewed and endless life
>   When this which is our torment here shall close,
> An everlasting conscious inanition!
> We yearn for speedy death in full fruition,
>   Dateless oblivion and divine repose.

With the wings given the huge seated woman there is the light wreath which mocks her forehead: the forehead that is knotted with thoughts and dreams. There is the bunch of household keys, the housewife's gown voluminous and indented, rigid like burnished metal; her feet thick-shod to tread all weakness down. The comet hangs over the sea; there is the rainbow, and the imp with the dog's head holding out in its pinions the woman's name: 'Melencolia'.

> Thus has the artist copied her, and thus
>   Surrounded to expound her form sublime,
> Her fate heroic and calamitous;
>   Fronting the dreadful mysteries of Time,
> Unvanquished in defeat and desolation,
> Undaunted in the hopeless conflagration
>   Of the day setting on her baffled prime.

Baffled and beaten back she works on still,
   Weary and sick of soul she works the more,
Sustained by her indomitable will:
   The hands shall fasten and the brain shall pore,
And all her sorrow shall be turned to labour,
Till Death the friend-foe piercing with his sabre,
   That mighty heart of hearts ends bitter war.

But as if blacker night could dawn on night, there is a sense more tragic, desperate and fatal in her regard.

The sense that every struggle brings defeat
   Because Fate holds no prize to crown success;
That all the oracles are dumb or cheat
   Because they have no secret to express;
That none can pierce the vast black veil uncertain
Because there is no light beyond the curtain;
   That all is vanity and nothingness.

From this her throne in the north the City's patroness and queen looks over her capital of grief and lamentations; over the river with its isles and bridges. The moon and stars circle from east to west in the sea of air before her, shadows and gleams glide round her.

Her subjects often gaze up to her there:
The strong to drink new strength of iron endurance,
The weak new terrors; all, renewed assurance,
   And confirmation of the old despair.

And so it was finished. Thomson checked with William Rossetti that the animal at the feet of the sitting woman in Dürer's *Melencolia* – the model for his 'bronze colossus' – was in fact a wolfhound.[16] He considered beginning the poem sequence with this 'Melencolia' section, but decided to leave it as the conclusion.[17] He put the six verses dated June 11th 1873 (previously numbered as Section 15) at the beginning, and called them the 'Proem'. The remaining twenty-one sections he arranged to alternate between even-numbered sections written in the Past Tense, culminating in the disintegrating figure that faced the Sphinx in Section 20; and odd-numbered sections written in the Present Tense, concluding with the Isis-like figure of Melencolia in Section 21. The provisional title 'The City of Night' he changed to 'The City of Dreadful Night'.

On March 22nd 1874 the Proem and the first five sections of 'The City of Dreadful Night' appeared in the *National Reformer*. Quotes from Dante and Leopardi were placed beneath the poem's title.[18] Sections 5 to 10 appeared on April 12th, Sections 11 to 16 on April 26th, and the last five sections were published on May 17th. There was a heavier than usual demand for the issues in which the poem appeared. Soon they were out of print. 'The City of Dreadful Night' was to remain out of print for another six years.

CHAPTER FIFTEEN

O N APRIL 10TH 1874 Austin Holyoake died of consumption and he
was buried in Highgate Cemetery a week later. The service used
was the secular service composed by Austin Holyoake himself for his
Secularists' Manual:

> We this day consign to the earth the body of our departed friend;
> for him life's fitful dream is over, with its toils, and sufferings, and
> disappointment. He derived his being from the bountiful mother of all;
> he returns to her capacious bosom, to again mingle with the elements.
> He basked in life's sunshine for his allotted time, and has passed into
> the shadow of death, where sorrow and pain are unknown. Noble he
> performed life's duties on the stage of earth; the impenetrable curtain of
> futurity has fallen, and we see him no more. But he leaves to his sorrowing
> relatives and friends a legacy in the remembrance of his virtues, his ser-
> vices, his honour, and truth. He fought the good fight of free enquiry,
> and triumphed over prejudice and the results of misdirected education.
> His voyage through life was not always on tranquil seas, but his strong
> judgement steered him clear of the rocks and quicksands of ignorance,
> and for years he rested placidly in the haven of self-knowledge. He had
> long been free from the fears and misgivings of superstitious belief. He
> worked out for himself the problem of life, and no man was the keeper
> of his conscience. His religion was of the world – the service of humanity
> his highest aspiration. He recognised no authority but that of Nature;
> adopted no methods but those of science and philosophy; and respected
> in practice no rule but that of conscience, illustrated by the common sense
> of mankind. He valued the lessons of the past, but disowned tradition as
> a ground of belief, whether miracles and supernaturalism be claimed or
> not claimed on its side. No sacred Scripture or ancient Church formed
> the basis of his faith. By his example he vindicated the right to think,
> and to act upon conscientious conviction.[1]

Bradlaugh added a graveside farewell to the 'staunch friend, and
your most loyal brother and true servant to the cause of progress'.[2]

193

Thomson had been an almost daily visitor at Austin's for the previous two months.[3] He wrote an account of the funeral – 'as quiet and simple as I could well make it'[4] – for the *National Reformer*.[5]

A few days before Austin's death Thomson received a letter from Bertram Dobell, a secondhand bookseller and collector who owned a shop in Haverstock Hill. Dobell wrote to 'B.V.' at the *National Reformer* when the first instalment of 'The City of Dreadful Night' had been followed by two issues of the weekly paper without the poem's continuation. He had followed 'B.V.''s contributions to the *National Reformer* since the appearance of 'To Our Ladies of Death' nine years before. Thomson replied to Dobell's letter:

> I have just received from Mr Bradlaugh your note about myself, and hasten to thank you heartily for your generous expression of approval for my writing. While I have neither tried nor cared to win any popular applause, the occasional approbation of an intelligent and sympathetic reader cheers me on a somewhat lonely path.
>
> You must not blame Mr Bradlaugh for the delay in continuing my current contribution to his paper. He is my very dear friend, and always anxious to strain a point in my favour; but as an editor he must try to suit his public, and the great majority of these care nothing for most of what I write. As for this 'The City of Dreadful Night', it is so alien from common thought and feeling that I knew well (as stated in the Proem) that scarcely any readers would care for it, and Mr B. tells me that he has received three or four letters energetically protesting against its publication in the *N.R.*, yours, I think, being the only one praising it. Moreover, we must not forget that there is probably no other periodical in the kingdom which would accept such writings, even were their literary merits far greater than they are.
>
> I address from the office of the *N.R.*, because I am just now rather unsettled, and not sure what will be my private address for some time to come. Whilst preferring to remain anonymous for the public, I have no reason to hide my name from such correspondents as yourself. – I am, dear Sir, yours truly,
>
> James Thomson (B.V.)[6]

He owed the landlady of his lodgings at 230 Vauxhall Bridge Road more than £32,[7] and on April 13th he moved lodgings to 60 Tachbrooke Street, leaving a box of books as surety on his debt.[8] To his sister-in-law Julia he wrote: 'Please note that I have changed my address, moving, however, but a short distance, as this neighbourhood suits me. I do not yet know whether I shall stay here long; but the house is nice and clean, and the landlady seems a decent body. As inscrutable destiny decides that I am to lodge with married women and old maids alternately, I am with a family woman this time, though I have really not yet learnt whether the husband is dead or living.'9

When 'The City of Dreadful Night' had completed its irregular course in the *National Reformer* Thomson sent copies to Thomas Carlyle, George Eliot and William Rossetti.10 There is no record of a reply from Carlyle, but George Eliot wrote as follows:

> The Priory
> 21 North Bank
> Regent's Park
> May 30 1874

Dear Poet, – I cannot rest satisfied without telling you that my mind responds with admiration to the distinct vision and grand utterance in the poem which you have been so good as to send me.

Also, I trust that an intellect informed by so much passionate energy as yours will give us more heroic strains with a wider embrace of human fellowship in them – such as will be to the labourers of the world what the odes of Tyrtaeus were to the Spartans, thrilling them with the sublimity of the social order and the courage of resistance to all that would dissolve it. To accept life and write much fine poetry is to take a very large share in the quantum of human good, and seems to draw with it necessarily some recognition, affectionate and even joyful, of the manifold willing labours which have made such a lot possible.

> Yours sincerely,
> M.E. Lewes.11

Thomson replied from 60 Tachbrooke Street:

Dear Madam, – Having been absent for several days, I am only now able to thank you for your very kind letter, for your generous expression of praise, and for your yet more generous trust, though this, I fear, will prove to be misplaced.

I have no Byronic quarrel with my fellows, whom I find all alike crushed under the iron yoke of Fate, and few of whom I can deem worse than myself, while so many are far better, and I certainly have an affectionate and even joyful recognition of the willing labours of those who have striven to alleviate our lot, though I cannot see that all their efforts have availed much against the primal curse of our existence. Has the world been the better or the worse for the life of even such a man as Jesus? I cannot judge; but I fear on the whole considerably worse. None the less I can love and revere his memory. A physician saves a life, and he does well; yet perchance it were better for the patient himself and for others that he now died. But it is not for me to introduce such thoughts to you.

I ventured to send you a copy of the verses (as I ventured to send another to Mr Carlyle) because I have already read, whether rightly or wrongly, through all the manifold beauty and delightfulness of your works, a character and an intellectual destiny akin to that grand and awful Melancholy of Albrecht Dürer which dominates the City of my poem.

I cannot conclude without expressing to you my gratitude for many hours of exquisite enjoyment. – I am, Madam, with profound respect, yours sincerely,

James Thomson (B.V.)[12]

Two days later on June 20th he sent a postscript:

In my note of Thursday I omitted to qualify, as I intended, the general statements by the distinct admission of what, however, is in all likelihood quite obvious – that the poem in question was the outcome of much sleepless hypochondria. I am aware that the truth of midnight does not exclude the truth of noonday, though one's nature may lead him to dwell in the former rather than the latter. Pardon me for troubling you on so small a matter.[13]

Rossetti had recently married and was away on honeymoon when the poem was delivered to his home at Euston Square. Thomson apologised later for having sent 'such a raven's croak' to greet the newly married couple on their return.[14] But Rossetti was impressed by 'The City of Dreadful Night', and in a footnote to an edition of Blake's poems that he brought out later in the year he referred to it as an 'extremely remarkable poem, of philosophic meaning and symbolic or visionary form'.[15] The *Academy* – to which Rossetti contributed art criticism – carried a review stating that in his poem 'B.V.' had demonstrated a more thoroughly worked out system of pessimistic thought than Leopardi himself.[16] Thomson dismissed this comparison, though he wrote to the *Academy* thanking it for calling attention to 'an atheistical writing (less remote than, say, Lucretius) treating it simply and fairly on its literary merits, without obloquy or protesting cant'.[17] Rossetti invited Thomson again to Euston Square, this time for dinner. But Thomson declined on the grounds that he was 'a barbarian who has not evening dress'.[18] Having been assured that formal dress was unnecessary, he then accepted the invitation; but he did not turn up, and only apologised to Rossetti some months later.[19]

At Johnson's Court Thomson helped proof-read the weekly galleys and did sub-editorial work. Sub-editor Charles Watts's young son was apprenticed there, and the youth sometimes worked under Thomson's supervision.[20] Like Agnes Gray and the Bradlaugh sisters, he remembered Thomson as an instinctive teacher who tried to broaden his literary horizons: 'I can well remember the great pains he took in developing my then slight interest in literature'.[21] In 1874 though Thomson's connection with the *National Reformer* and the printing office was episodic: in the first six months of 1874 'The City of Dreadful Night' was the only contribution 'B.V.' made, and his attendance at Johnson's Court was often only required on Tuesday and Wednesday evenings. He had hope of more secretarial work: 'I am promised regular employment beginning next week, but am not sure how long it will last,' he told Dobell on May 10th.[22] He worked some irregular hours in the city trying to help launch another mining company, but soon the unnamed company was shortly 'doubtless foundering' and his diary entry for June 1st reads 'W.D.B. settled up with me. Compy. a failure.'[23]

In July his precarious financial position improved when he was given a weekly double column in the *National Reformer* under the title 'Jottings'. This he chose to sign not 'B.V.' but simply 'X'. It was what could be called a resident diarist's column, sarcastically commenting on religious or political events that had been seriously and unsarcastically already reported somewhere else. Among the stories that 'X' re-reported were the tale of a lay preacher who had advertised himself as 'Happy William the Converted Basket-Maker';[24] the difficulties allegedly experienced by the son of Alexander Dumas in accepting the Virgin Birth;[25] a Chicago priest's being discharged for giving a 'racy' commentary on *Genesis*; the report of a Mexican couple burned at the stake for sorcery; the *Christian* magazine's 'Department for Requests for Praise and Prayer'; the interruption of a Florida preacher's sermon by frogs; an eccentric minister's discourse on *John* XXI. 16, which he had titled 'Popping the Question'; the report of a Tyrolese play in which God the Father had been depicted on stage smoking a pipe 'in a grotesque costume, wearing big leather gloves, and walking up and down on a rainbow, at one end of which was the sun, and at the other end the moon'; and an advertised new history of merchant and ancient shipping, whose prospectus announced that it would begin with Noah's Ark.[26]

Pope Pius IX was thanked for having issued, along with an irrelevant encyclical letter, a handy syllabus of 'the principal errors of our time'.[27] The hymns of the globe-trotting American evangelists Moody and Sankey were a favourite target: 'A large number indeed turn on that unnatural metaphor of blood washing white, which would be as disgusting as it is absurd to anyone hearing it for the first time. Mr Moody, after the manner of his kind, is very fond of graphic illustrations. Let him bring before his audience a begrimed handkerchief and a bowl of bullock's blood, and wash the former clean and white in the latter, and he will give the most striking illustration of his doctrine of the Atonement that can be given.'[28] Another favourite of 'X' was the conflict between the separate Christian churches. A vicar was quoted as having stated 'Popery is the religion of false human nature, and is thoroughly congenial to it; no wonder at its growth, when it finds such a congenial soil in which to flourish. It is the masterpiece of Satan.' On which 'X' commented:

> Once more, How these Christians love one another! Better the Atheist than Roman Catholic or Protestant in the eyes of the other of these. One wonders where the false human nature comes from. Perhaps it is forged and uttered by Satan; but then, God can't have created us all. I thought the Protestant doctrine of original sin made human nature so vile that the worse it is the more true it is; so that false human nature would be better. Never mind; let us leave these Christians to their mutual love.[29]

Amongst topical political comment was criticism of farmers for locking out members of the National Agricultural Union 'in the hope of destroying unionism – that is to say, unionism of labourers, that of farmers being of course another and sacred thing'.[30] The new Disraeli government was attacked for aiming to restore grammar schools to the control of the established Church – 'the first decidedly reactionary measure on which the Tories have ventured'.[31] Royal commissions of enquiry were described – in an essay later to be reissued as the title-piece of a pamphlet – as no more than government confidence tricks to remove the object of enquiry from its rightful place under public scrutiny: 'the appointment of one being merely a dodge by which people who don't want to act on what they and everybody else see quite well with their naked eyes, set a number of elderly gentlemen to pore upon it with spectacles and magnifying glasses until dazed and stupid with poring, in the hope that this process will last so long that ere it is finished the public will have forgotten the matter altogether.'[32] And in another attack on the rulers of the day 'X' quoted Shelley:

> Having had occasion recently to read carefully certain poems, I am tempted to quote one thoroughly, simply to show how very different is the state of our country now to that of fifty-five years ago. The poet was an aristocrat; his name was Shelley. The title of the verses is 'England in 1819' Some of our readers may remember that year as the year of Peterloo:

An old, mad, blind, despised, and dying king, –
Princes, the dregs of their dull race, who flow
Through public scorn, mud from a muddy spring –
Rulers who neither see nor feel nor know . . .

The contrast between '19 and '74 in most points is really astounding.

For the old, mad, blind, despised, and dying king, we have a queen quite young (about thirty by the effigy on this year's coin); thoroughly sane; not blind, but with a most sharp eye on the main chance; revered; and very much living.

Instead of the princes, dregs of their dull race, flowing through public scorn, and from a muddy spring, we have the present Duke of Wales, the Duke of Edinburgh, the Duke of Connaght: Could contrast be more complete?

Instead of the rulers who neither see nor feel nor know, we have rulers who certainly see what the Licensed Victuallers want, who feel that they themselves very much want to keep their places, and who are truly knowing – except as to the meaning of their own Bills.[33]

And so on for another ten lines of Shelley's poem. But not all the 'Jottings' were satirical or querulous. Occasionally the diarist's own positive tastes were revealed, as when an obituary tribute was paid to the French painter Corot,[34] and when 'X' enthused over the Monday concerts given each winter at St James's Hall: 'looking back through several years, I reckon that these concerts have yielded me more and more pure delight than all the other public entertainments of London put together . . . Can anyone tell me of such another investment for time and money in London or elsewhere on earth? Two and a half hours of Paradise for a shilling!'[35] Thomson in fact told Dobell that should he want to meet Thomson any week, St James's Hall on a Monday night would be a good place to do so: 'If you like chamber music, and can spare the time, I shall be happy to meet you any Monday at St. James's Hall. I usually go there with a friend, another melomaniac. You get Orchestra ticket, Piccadilly entrance, and get to Orchestra from Piccadilly Place, a narrow passage a few steps farther on. Be careful not to fall into the abomination of the Christy Minstrels, who are in the Minor Hall! Concert commences at eight. I usually get there about seven, as the doors are open, and one can sit and read or chat while waiting. In the Orchestra you can easily see whether a friend is present, and get beside him.'[36] The other 'melomaniac' mentioned was John Grant, now back in London from Ireland. Together he and Thomson heard Joachim play the violin in Beethoven's *Kreutzer Sonata*; and one weekend they had a kind of music festival when they heard a concert including Wagner at the Albert Hall on Friday, Beethoven's Septet at St James's Hall on the Saturday, and another chamber recital on Monday evening. The weekend of the Oxford-Cambridge boat race they walked to Putney and back to see it;[37] and on the Monday they took the Bradlaugh girls to hear another of the Monday concerts which, Thomson told the girls' mother Susan, were his 'only dissipation'.[38]

Sometimes Grant and Fred Hollett were together in Thomson's company as when the two friends helped him move lodgings from Vauxhall Bridge Road to Tachbrooke Street.[39] He saw W.E. Jacques again now too, once again making regular visits to the home of Jacques and his wife for Sunday dinner. The three played cribbage or went out to the familiar leisure haunts of Regents Park, Kew Gardens, Hampstead Heath.[40] Occasionally William Chaplin – also of Champion Gold and Silver Mining – was present.[41] One weekday Thomson and Jacques had a 'run round' the Archway area: 'Archway Tavern, Junction Road &c. Walk up Seven Sisters Road'.[42] But on weekdays it was Hollett was Thomson's most frequent companion at this time. He became a familiar with Hollett's family, was invited to tea with his brother in Battersea, and daily visited his sister Loisa with fruit and ice when she was ill and Fred had to be out of town for a few days. Hollett and Thomson went to a police fête at Crystal Palace at the beginning of July 1874: 'Supper at Shakespeare – Home at 12 midnight. Lovely day & evening – Large number at fête.'[43]

After 'Jottings' by 'X' had begun that month in the *National Reformer*, new contributions by 'B.V.' began also to appear soon after. There was a biographical introduction, in six instalments, to Walt Whitman, of whose voice B.V. said: 'It is not, as none knows better than himself, a voice for drawing-rooms': instead it was 'indisputably the greatest native voice yet heard from America'. The essay praised Whitman – the man's ability to get on easily with his neighbours in the street, his work helping injured soldiers during the Civil War, and his physical health. Good health was not characteristic of most great poets:

> . . . for the last century we can perhaps cite only Robert Burns; and he perished in misery at thirty-seven. The greater part of our noblest modern poetic genius have been shrined in disease or deformity; Shelley never had good health, Keats died of consumption at twenty-four, Byron and Scott were lame, Schiller with difficulty kept alive till forty-six, Heine

200

lay helpless in paralysis seven years before his death, Lenau died young in a mad-house, Alfred de Musset was an old man at forty, Leopardi was irretrievably shattered at twenty.[44]

The Whitman essay was followed by another, this time over eight instalments, which looked at some posthumously published work by John Stuart Mill. In 'Mill on Religion' 'B.V.' wrote that he had never been amongst those who 'worshipped' Mill. However, he went on: 'I have always regarded him with great respect as a sincere and very brave man of most generous sympathies, and also with considerable admiration as a patient, acute, and unprejudiced thinker.' For this same reason 'B.V.' had been horrified when reading Mill's posthumous *Autobiography* to see Mill describe himself as 'one of the very few examples, in this country, of one who has not thrown off religion, but never had it'. 'B.V.' was horrified that this was a *posthumously* published remark in that though Mill had published during his lifetime passages that were 'depreciative of Christianity', he had never openly stated that religion never had had any significance for him from the first. Yet the *Autobiography* contained a statement that 'B.V.' found even more disturbing. In this Mill wrote of his father: 'I think that few men of my father's intellect and public spirit, holding with such intensity of moral conviction as he did, unpopular opinions on religion, or on any other great subjects of thought, would either practise or inculcate the withholding of them from the world, unless in the cases, becoming fewer every day, in which frankness on these subjects would either risk the loss of means of subsistence, or would amount to exclusion from some sphere of usefulness peculiarly suitable to the capacities of the individual.' This 'B.V.' attacked at length:

> I can understand a heretic keeping quiet, who does not set himself up as a teacher or leader, or who has a scornful indifference for all creeds and systems; or because he is hopeless of any improvement in mankind, and believes that if dragged out of one pitfall, they immediately stumble into another as deep and dangerous. But I do not understand how one who believes in the improvability of mankind, and the manifold harmfulness of religion, a Liberal leader and teacher, a man of intellect, public spirit, and intense moral convictions, can conceal his heresy rather than 'risk the loss of his means of subsistence.' These unfortunate words imply about the meanest doctrine of the apostolic life of a champion of Truth I have ever heard or read; and they are the more lamentable and astounding as coming from a really brave, high-minded, and disinterested reformer . . .
>
> As things are, in Britain, the tremendous task of openly attacking, hew-

ing down, and extirpating the mental and moral tyranny of a supernatural religion, whose roots cling deep in the past, whose branches and scions extend over all regions of the earth, whose evil shadow chills and darkens our richest fields of culture and civilisation, is left almost wholly to us of the *National Reformer* and the Secular Societies, to us who for the most part are poor, uneducated, and uninfluential; while thousands and thousands of men with wealth, leisure, scholarship and influence, who in their hearts and minds are just as antagonistic to Christianity as we ourselves, submit to be negative if not positive dissemblers and hypocrites, rejecting on us the heavy burden of odium and disabilities, which they by a manly avowal would at once remove from us without bringing it on themselves.

Had the early Reformers and Freethinkers availed themselves of the excuse now sanctioned by John Stuart Mill, we should now be under the absolute despotism of the Holy Roman Catholic Church, with all its incredible dogmas and degrading superstitions; for they would have kept their free thoughts to themselves. What would Wycliffe, Luther, Huss, Savonarola, Sarpi, Knox; what would Berquin, Dolet, Des Periers; what would Bruno, Campanella, Vanini; what would Socrates and the two Zenos, Epictetus and Marcus Antoninus; what would Puritans, Huguenots, and Covenanters; have thought of a theory of apostleship based on 'intense moral conviction', allowing silence and inertia, which mean dissimulation, in cases where there is 'risk of the loss of the means of subsistence'; they, most of whom risked their lives, and lost them abundantly?[45]

The series 'Mill on Religion' ran from November 1874. That month Thomson was forty, an event he noted glumly: 'Cold. Forty years old today – Third day of fog. Congenial natal weather. No marvel one is obscure, dismal, bewildered and melancholy.'[46] Things were changing at the *National Reformer*, and Thomson's future there was beginning to look uncertain. Bradlaugh – now earning £1,000 a year from lectures and publications,[47] and becoming more intent on a parliamentary career – had introduced a new member of staff to whom he showed an apparent favouritism which made others feel crowded out. This newcomer was the twenty-four-year-old Annie Besant, who had left her minister husband and two children to come to London, where she had seen Bradlaugh lecture at the Hall of Science. She had subsequently described him in words reminiscent of Thomson's description of the atheist preacher in 'The City of Dreadful Night': 'The grave, quiet, stern, strong face, the massive head, the keen eyes, the magnificent breadth and height of forehead – was this the man I had heard described as a blatant agitator, an ignorant demagogue?'[48]

Besant a month after seeing Bradlaugh had given her first public lecture herself, 'The Political Status of Women', which 'Iconoclast' had then described in the *National Reformer* of August 30th as the 'best speech by a woman to which we have ever listened'. In that same issue had appeared the first of what was to be Annie Besant's weekly commentaries under the pseudonym 'Ajax', and her first review, of a book called *Practical Politics for Plain People*. Besant was put on a salary of a guinea a week, the same as that received by Charles Watts, deputy editor and manager of the printing and publishing company bequeathed by Austin Holyoake.[49] Watts was not pleased, nor was another secularist associated with the paper, at twenty-four the same age as Besant, George William Foote. Foote, a republican interested in Literature, admired Thomson's work and now befriended him. Foote thus in the last months of 1874 joined Thomson more than once on his city walks: 'Met G.W.F. about 11 at Angel. Train to Finsbury Park, dinner Alexandra Hotel near Alexandra Palace. Walked Wood Green, Lordship Lane, Tottenham, Back Seven Sisters Road – Wood Green Station to Holloway (G.N.R.) Train to High Street. Tea & chat at Foote's till 11. 'Bus to Regent Circus.'[50]

The new year saw the dominance of Bradlaugh and Besant only increase at the *National Reformer* as Thomson told Dobell on January 18th:

> I'm still on the staff of the noble *N.R.*, but have been crowded out of late. C.B. and Ajax take up much room, and we wanted to bring in other things. I'm always willing to give way, especially when doing so saves me from writing nonsense. I resume in next week's number.[51]

As the months progressed his contributions to the *National Reformer* began to dwindle. In May he told Dobell: 'I don't do any more "Jottings", simply two or three columns on one or two topics of the day, a sermon or religious meeting, or any nonsense of the sort.'[52] Reporting on a Bishop Ellicott who had predicted the imminent end of the world, he took the opportunity to have another swipe at John Cumming, who just before the end of the world that he had been predicting for two decades, took out a mortgage on his house for twenty-one years: 'The end of the world has been looked for often enough at a fixed date, from the times of the early Christians to the other day in Chicago; but scarcely before this age did ecclesiastics of good repute venture to predict the end in words, and utterly ignore it in act. We in our blessed age have had Dr Cumming frightening many people half out of their slender wits with his Great Tribulation, and at the same time taking a lease which ran years into his own millenium; and justifying himself with coolest effrontery on the ground that "the expectation of prophecy should not override common sense". "While a Cumming lives there will be guile" is a right old proverb, which I have heard him quote myself.'[53]

He contributed an essay on Stendhal – 'As a nation we import corn and cotton, not literature and ideas'[54] – and two reports, on June 13th and 20th, of a public debate on the topic, 'Is Christianity Superior to Secularism?' These were Thomson's last contributions to the *National Reformer*, for he now broke irrevocably with Charles Bradlaugh, the end of the relationship taking place in heated argument. Hypatia Bradlaugh thought the fault lay in Thomson's unpredictable behaviour after his return from Spain. Thomson, she recalled, was then 'unhappily one not to be relied on; and on a special occasion when he was left with the responsibility of the paper he disappeared and left it, as far as he was concerned, to come out as best it could. At length, in 1875, in spite of all my father's forbearance and affection, Mr Thomson for some reason felt injured; but whatever might have been his grievances, they were in fact utterly baseless. Mr Thomson resented his supposed injury by an open insult, and from that moment the friendship between the two was dead.'[55] Bradlaugh said that drink was the trouble, Thomson being now 'utterly accursed' by it.[56] He gave Thomson a dismissal slip stating drunkenness as the cause of dismissal,[57] an act for which Thomson never forgave him. It would have been difficult enough for him to obtain new employment citing years of work on the country's leading atheistic newspaper, without having to add that he had been sacked from it for drunkenness.

But now another new friend came to Thomson's rescue. After the publication of the essay on Whitman, a poem 'Genius and Health' had appeared in the *National Reformer* addressed to 'B.V.'. The poem had agreed with the sentiments of 'B.V.''s Whitman essay regretting lack of good health in poets. But it had taken issue with the pessimism of 'The City of Dreadful Night'.

> We weep for Leopardi's fate,
>   Have pity, wrath for Dante's doom;
> Yet still believe that to be great
>   We must abhor the Creed of Gloom:
> Genius has martyrs, but its kings
> Have stalwart arms and mighty wings.[58]

The writer was William Maccall, a freethought journalist of many years, and a regular contributor to the *National Reformer*. Maccall was another native of the Firth of Clyde, born in Largs in 1812.

Moreover, as Unitarian minister at Greenock in 1833, he had come to know the Margaret Hatrick who in later years had become the Mrs Gray in whose East London home Thomson had spent much of his childhood and youth.[59] Maccall still had contact with Mr and Mrs Gray, now living in Snaresbrook.[60] He and Thomson began a lasting correspondence, and the Grays were frequently referred to, as Maccall later remembered: 'It was at their house, and as the playmate of their children, that James Thomson spent his happiest days. These days he seemed in his letters to me never tired of recalling. I often pressed him to renew his relations with the hospitable friends of his childhood, who were as willing as in the past to welcome him. But his constitutional shyness, or some other cause, hindered him from gratifying a desire which evidently stirred him deeply.'[61]

Among the journals to which Maccall had contributed in addition to the *National Reformer* was a monthly called *Cope's Tobacco Plant*, a literary-cum-advertising journal sponsored by the Cope Tobacco Company of Liverpool. Thomson described the monthly in one of his last 'Jottings' as 'one of the most daring and original publications of the day . . . It attacks cant of all kinds with rare boldness.'[62] The editor was John Fraser, another of Maccall's Scottish friends. An introduction was arranged, and in September 1875 Thomson made his first contribution to what was to be his monthly source of income for the next five years.

CHAPTER SIXTEEN

'IN LANE'S ADMIRABLE and delightful *Account of the Manners and Customs of the Modern Egyptians*, which forms so worthy a pendant to Sir Gardner Wilkinson's book on the ancient, we read (chap. xv.): – "The most prevalent means, in most Muslim countries, of exciting what the Arabs call 'keyf', which I cannot more nearly translate than by the terms 'placid enjoyment', is Tobacco".' So began Thomson's first contribution to *Cope's Tobacco Plant* in September 1875, an essay entitled 'Stray Whiffs from an Old Smoker'. The essay roamed from methods of smoking in Egyptian culture, to Baudelaire's discussion of 'keyf' in *Les Paradis Artificiels*'; from languid smokers in the East who concentrated on the smoke, to hurrying smokers in the West always busy doing something else; from the difficulty of smoking little Spanish cigarettes without burning oneself, to the story of a 'young student friend, perhaps a little beyond his depth in Berkeley' who only smoked 'when the speculative mood was strong upon him, in front of a blank wall'; thus trying 'to gaze the wall, as it were, into his retina, and perchance to draw it along the optic nerves into his central brain: to perceive it as an immediate sensation, not outward, but internal'. As for the smoking habits of the writer himself:

> There are some who can smoke with enjoyment and profit when writing: this I cannot do, either with a cigar or a pipe, when the writing requires reflection; for either the thought is distracted by the smoke, or the fire goes out in the interest of the thought. But how delightful and inspiring are a few whiffs in the pausing-spaces, when the brain teems with new ideas gradually assuming form, and the palate yearns for the Tobacco savour with a thirst as keen as the water-thirst of the desert – the desert whose cruel mirage, while it cannot be drunk, cannot even be smoked.

Cope's Tobacco Plant had ten pages of two columns text with two concluding pages of advertising. Thomson was given room to write

206

at length. He developed the reference to Baudelaire in his opening article into a 3,000-word essay in the next month's issue, condensing from *Les Paradis Artificiels* an account of three phases of hashish smoking.[1] Next he translated Theophile Gautier's account of smoking hashish at the Hotel Pimoda in Paris, where Baudelaire and he had been amongst the regular hashish smokers: 'It being understood that I am ruthlessly compressing, I retain the first person in the narrative, in order to avoid circumlocution,' Thomson prefaced his translation. This contribution again ran to around 3,000 words.

I rose with effort, and went towards the door of my room, which it took me a considerable time to reach: by my reckoning, ten years. Daucus-Corota followed me sneering, 'If he walks at this rate, he will be old when he arrives.' However, I got into the next room, which was indefinitely prolonged, the light at its extremity seeming remote as a fixed star. Disheartened, I was about to stop, when the small voice said, 'Courage! she awaits you at eleven o'clock.' By an enormous projection of volition, I managed to raise my feet, rooted like trees on the ground, while the monster with legs of mandrake-root parodied my efforts, and drawled, like a psalm, 'The marble gains! the marble gains!' In effect, I felt my extremities petrify; I was statue to the middle, like the prince in the *Thousand and One Nights*; my heels resounded formidably upon the flooring; I was fit to play the commander in *Don Giovanni*. I reached the landing of the staircase, and tried to descend. Dimly lit, it assumed in my dream gigantic proportions; the top and bottom, in shadow, appeared to reach heaven above and hell beneath. 'This staircase must pierce the earth through and through,' I said to myself, in continuing to walk mechanically; 'I shall reach the foot on the morrow of the day of judgment.' The figures in the pictures regarded me with compassion; some contorted themselves painfully, like mutes striving to give warning in a supreme crisis; the stairs were soft, and sank under me; new landings, new degrees, presented themselves continuously to my resigned steps; those which I had passed came and placed themselves before me again. By my reckoning, this lasted a thousand years. At length I reached the vestibule, where another persecution not less terrible awaited me. The Egyptian monster, holding a taper in its claws, barred the passage with intentions manifestly hostile. Its greenish eyes flashed, its lion's croup quivered savagely; and Daucus-Corota urged it on: 'Bite him! bite him! flesh of marble for a mouth of brass is a splendid feast.' Unaffrighted by this horrible brute, I passed on. A breath of cold air struck my face; I saw the cloudless, star-lit sky: I was in the courtyard, which had assumed the dimensions of the Champ-de-Mars, and was surrounded by enormous buildings, which would have covered twenty times the real area of the Isle St Louis. I thought with terror of the magicians who, in one evening, could construct such edifices. Daucus-Corota joined me: 'You cannot arrive at eleven o'clock; it is already fifteen hundred years since you set out. Half your hair is now grey. Better come up again.' As I did not obey, he entangled me in his legs, and, using his hands like cramp-irons, hauled me up the staircase, and set me again in the room where I had escaped with such agonising efforts. Then I became wild and delirious. He cut capers to the ceiling, crying: 'Imbecile! I gave you back your head, but, first, I took out the brains with a spoon.' I felt a horrible melancholy; for putting my hand to the skull, I found it open; and I lost consciousness.

Coming to myself, I saw the room full of men in black, who said sadly to one another, 'Time is dead: henceforth there will be neither years, nor months, nor hours; Time is dead, and we attend his funeral.'[2]

Thomson – or 'Sigvat', as he called himself in this monthly – now contributed a fantasy smoking experience of his own. The smoke was of ordinary tobacco, the essay beginning with a description of a typical evening in 'Sigvat''s room at home:

It was the last evening of the year, and I was alone in my room. The curtains were drawn, the fire was burning brightly, I had just taken my tea, and was having the delicious after-smoke; for no smoke is more delicious than that immediately following tea, when one's mind is lucid and active again after the afternoon sluggishness, with a long evening before it for intellectual enjoyment, whether of reading or writing or simple meditation. On this occasion I had purposed to do some writing; but I felt so warm and cosy and nobly indolent, leaning back in the easy-chair, with my feet towards the fire on another chair, and gazing with half-shut eyes into the ruddy glow and dancing flames, that, when the one pipe was finished, and by previous covenant with myself I was bound to set to work, I calmly refilled the beloved pipe and set myself to deliberate enjoyment thereof, while my mind was borne slowly hither and thither through the serene twilight of remembrance and reverie.[3]

Or

The smoke preceded a vision; not a hallucinogenic nightmare like Gautier's, but of the return of she whom 'Sigvat' described as 'the beautiful, the ever-young, who is so gracious and loving when it pleases her to visit me'. It was December 31st, the Feast of St Sylvester, and his young visitor was dressed in the robes of that saint. She took him on a magic sleigh through the skies to an Arctic region where a Fair of St Sylvester, with stalls and entertainments, was in progress. In the middle of the fair stood two back-to-back giant images, of the Old Year and the New Year: one consumed all the events of the past year in his pipe, the other, a baby, blew soap bubbles representing the events to come. 'Sigvat's' young guide told him to buy a gift for her at one of

James Thomson 1860: Frontispiece to *Poems, Essays and Fragments*

James Thomson *c.* 1881

the stalls before she should take him back to his room. He bought her 'a golden bracelet, a Serpent of Eternity, with carbuncle eyes, and a certain Name enammeled within'.

When 'The Fair of St Sylvester' appeared in *Cope's Tobacco Plant* in January 1876, Thomson was a few weeks settled in new lodgings once more, having moved north in December from Pimlico to Bloomsbury.[4] He had been found his new place by George Foote, himself now a lodger in the home of Austin Holyoake's widow Jane Alice. She had remarried in 1875, and was living with her two children and new husband at 12 Gower Street near the British Museum. Foote had had enough of Bradlaugh and Besant at the *National Reformer*, and had decided to launch a new freethought paper in competition to it, to be called the *Secularist*. He planned that Thomson should be a regular contributor, and the lodgings he had found him were at 12 Alfred Terrace just round the corner from his own. 'I want to be near Foote for the *Secularist* business, and also near the British Museum for the Reading Room,' Thomson told William Rossetti.[5]

Jane Alice's new husband Theodore Rich Wright was another *National Reformer* exile, and author of the *Practical Politics for Plain People* which had been the subject of Annie Besant's first book review. A partner in a legal recorders' firm in the Strand, he was described in Besant's review as 'a disciple, though a discriminating one, of J.S. Mill.'[6] He was an advocate of land nationalisation – though 'of the land *only*' – and a republican; he was against compulsory education, and though a believer in parliamentary reform and women's suffrage, he thought a system should be found for government other than by party.[7] His article 'Secular Politics' which appeared in the first issue of the *Secularist* on New Year's Day 1876, said that though most papers were owned by Whig or Tory interests, the *Secularist* would be different: 'no question of whatever kind will be treated from a class point of view'. Party allegiance, wrote 'T.R.W.', was not the answer to the problems facing Britain and the world: 'for the material, moral and intellectual – in short, for the *secular* improvement of mankind, we trust mainly to individual influences.'

These influences were to be helped though through the medium of secularist organisation. This organisation, as G.W. Foote maintained in his opening 'Secular Principles and Policy', had been focused too narrowly of late: 'Secularism is something more than a mere hostile attitude towards Christianity, and its teachers must set themselves to provide some positive sustenance for the multitudes who have thrown off effete superstitions, and can find no edification in the weekly explosion of discarded errors.' It was neither sufficient nor even necessary for a secularist to deny that there was a God; what was important was that Nature was governed by discernible laws, and if there was a Supreme Being, that being was also subject to them. It was belief in supernatural revelation, miracle and the power of prayer that was the obstacle to progress, for which progress 'the experimental method of science' provided the way forward. Secularism as described by Foote was 'catholic enough to embrace all who are disposed to set their faces towards the new day long since heralded by voices of prophetic song. In Secularism there is a common platform for Theists, and Pantheists, and Atheists, for all, in fact, who have fully recognised the universality of causation, the supremacy of reason, and the independence of ethics from theological dogmas.'[8]

Wright, Foote and Thomson were to be the most regular contributors to the *Secularist* in the next twelve months: Thomson contributed to all but four of the weekly issues of 1876. The opening number carried an article by 'B.V.' called 'Secularism and the Bible'; this complemented Foote's attack, and had as unstated but implicit reference the lectures and writings of Charles Bradlaugh:

> . . . it seems to me that Secularists, or those who think themselves Secularists, have given a great deal too much time to this volume. An opponent really overmasters us when we are always or nearly always thinking of him, when we occupy ourselves with little or nothing else. It may be well to be thus possessed by the object of our love, it must be hurtful to be possessed by the object of our dislike. For many years past, if I am not mistaken, the professors of Secularism who decry the Bible as human and fallible have squandered far more study upon it than have any save a few of the professors of Christianity, who extol it as infallible and divine.
>
> One error in the Bible clearly proved is as fatal to the claim of infallibility as a thousand; half a dozen gross errors and contradictions constitute a multiplication and over-abundance of proof which must convince anybody open to conviction. The indefinite accumulation of errors and contradictions is worse than waste of time in people who have no further end in view, scholarly or philosophical.

In the next issue 'B.V.' began a review of a critical biography of Heine by William Stigand; it served as the opening for his own appreciation of the poet, phased over six weeks. In this he himself quoted and translated from several of Heine's prose works, Stigand's translations being so 'criminally unfaithful' that he wondered why the publishers Longmans had allowed their name to be used on such a production. With Stigand himself 'B.V.' had had no prior dispute: 'Of

Mr Stigand I knew nothing before reading this work, except that I had seen his name subscribed to what seemed respectable verse in some magazine many years ago. This I never attempted to read, having such respect for respectable verse that I always keep at a most respectable distance from it: and I was equally ready to respect the respectable man by whom it was perpetrated.'[9] With regard to Thomson's own translations of Heine's poetry, the issue of February 5th contained the first of thirteen that appeared over the months:

> All sadly through the stern ravine
>   There rides a horseman brave:
> 'Ah! draw I near to my darling's arms,
>   Or near to the gloomy grave?'
>   The echo answer gave:
>   'To the gloomy grave!'
>
> And as the horseman onward rode
>   A deep sigh heaved his breast:
> 'If I thus early go to the grave,
>   Well, in the grave is rest!'
>   The answering voice confessed:
>   'In the grave is rest!'
>
> Slowly adown the rider's cheek
>   A tear of sad thought fell:
> 'If but in the grave there is rest for me,
> For me in the grave 'tis well!'
>   Whereto the echoing knell:
>   'In the grave 'tis well!'[10]

George Jacob Holyoake had been persuaded at first to join the paper, but the criticism of Bradlaugh became too pointed for him, and he left.[11] Though Foote wrote in an editorial that Holyoake's departure had not caused an appreciable drop in circulation, nonetheless Foote as sole proprietor was having difficulty meeting the paper's expenses. It would be necessary, he wrote, for friendly readers 'to lend me whatever pecuniary assistance they can'.[12]

Thomson was affected by this in that his was one of the running expenses that Foote apparently was unable to meet. In March Thomson had to apply for more money from his editor at *Cope's Tobacco Plant*, John Fraser, as he was having difficulty keeping up with his weekly payments at 12 Alfred Terrace.[13] There, along with four other lodgers, he paid rent to the landlord Mr Gibson, and board for his meals to the housekeeper, Miss Sarah Scott. However Foote did find sufficient funds to have the *Secularist*'s publisher Charles Keen publish two twopenny pamphlets in quick succession of essays by 'B.V.' that had previously appeared in the *National Reformer*: 'The Story of a Famous Old Jewish Firm' then followed by 'A Commission of Enquiry upon Royalty'. By April 6th, 400 of the first had been sold; a week later the *Secularist* announced that the second pamphlet was 'now ready'.[14] That month Thomson began to do some tutoring at 12 Gower Street, where Jane Alice's children by her first marriage, Percy and Adeline, were now aged fifteen and thirteen respectively. He began to tutor Adeline in Italian for two afternoons a week. This became an episodic arrangement – both Italian and French being taught – recurring irregularly for short periods during the next few years.[15]

The Wrights' home at 12 Gower Street became in fact another in the line of Thomson's secondary domestic bases. It was here that he now evidently had a more or less standing invitation to Sunday dinner, and his Pimlico friend Jacques – along with Fred Hollett and John Grant – effectively disappeared from his social life. He became familiar with the secularist social set attached to the dissidents at 12 Gower Street, visitors who would come for musical-social gatherings and to whose homes Thomson would occasionally be invited with the Wrights and G.W. Foote. There were the Mitchells of nearby Oakley Square, whose nineteen-year-old daughter Clara usually sang when music was to be part of an evening's proceedings; sometimes she stayed late at Gower Street on Sundays, and Thomson would walk her home.[16] There was occasionally George Flaws, who wrote regularly for the *Secularist* under the name of 'Gegëef'.[17] And there was Josef Trouselle, who was something of the circle's resident composer and musician. He organised Sunday musical evenings for piano, voice and small ensembles at his home in Blandford Place – off Baker Street between Thomson's lodgings and Hyde Park. Thomson went to a number of these in April and May. On Sunday April 9th he noted the evening's entertainment at Trousselle's as 'Bach, Handel, Clementi, Wagner, Cards.' Trousselle was a Wagnerite: there were excerpts from *Tannhäuser*, *Götterdämmerung*, and 'Acts 1 and 3 of *Lohengrin*.'[18] Piano transcriptions were used: on one occasion Thomson heard a forty-five minute transcription for piano duet of Beethoven's 'Eroica' Symphony.[19] He was always late home from these gatherings, usually well past midnight. Sometimes he went accompanied by another of this secularist set, Ernest Hember, who lived in Islington and would call up for Thomson on his way to Blandford Place.[20]

He no longer went weekly to the Monday concerts in St James's

Hall, though he and the Wrights did go once in February to hear Joachim again in a concert of music by Beethoven and Mendelssohn. And it was a musical publication that was at the centre of a row which Thomson now stirred up between the *National Reformer* and the *Secularist* factions, when he reviewed Annie Besant's *Secular Song and Hymn Book*, which she had edited on behalf of the National Secular Society. The contents 'B.V.' described as 'so exceedingly, so incredibly bad, that I am compelled to infer that Mrs Besant knows nothing of music; and that she has no ear for melody, no sense of rhythm.' He quoted a chorus of one of her songs

> To arms! Republicans!
> Strike now for liberty!
> March on: march on: Republicans!
> We march to victory!

and commented: 'It may be excusable in a young convert, carried away by her first zeal to rave in this manner, but it seems to me quite inexcusable in the National Secular Society and its President to authorise and warmly approve the raving. Mr Bradlaugh used to declare, with clear common sense, that anybody advising Republicans to appeal to physical force must be either mad or a traitor to the cause; and here he himself, and Mrs Besant and his Society, are not only advising but urging and exasperating the Party to do this very thing. Are they traitors to the cause or only mad?'[21] Bradlaugh attacked Thomson's review the following Sunday, and 'B.V.' replied to the attack in the next *Secularist*:

I am told that Mr Bradlaugh, as Mrs Besant's chairman at the Hall of Science last Sunday evening, insulted the audience with some very foolish words about my notice of the *Secular Song and Hymn Book* in your paper of the 8th inst. If Mr Bradlaugh has anything to urge in defence of that book and offence of my rather lenient criticism, let him urge it in the *National Reformer*, so that I may see and if need be answer it. I supported my general charges with specific citations; if he can vindicate these, he had better do so at once, and I will then furnish him with others for the exercise of his ingenuity, those given being but samples of the many I noted. Reviling an absent man to a crowd of people, the majority of whom may know little or nothing of the matter in question, especially when the reviler has a paper at his command, seems to me a very cowardly trick.[22]

It was George Jacob Holyoake who now replied from the columns of the *National Reformer* on Bradlaugh's behalf. He criticised the review by 'B.V.' and stressed the importance of Secularist unity. This only stung Thomson to attack Bradlaugh more sharply:

> ... when he is challenged to meet directly and openly direct and open criticisms, he has nothing to reply; he seduces or alarms a veteran and disabled rival into saying something for him and for the wretched book he has imposed on the party, in his own paper. Such cowardice and meanness are so unworthy of the Mr Bradlaugh I once knew, that I have still some difficulty in realising how eminently worthy they are of the Mr Bradlaugh I want to know no more. All his old courage seems to have evaporated in immeasurable boasting and bullying and buncombe; while as to the 'clash of intellect' for which he was wont to profess such eagerness, he appears to have at length grown marvellously aware that he has himself no intellect available for the clash.[23]

Foote, Theodore Wright and others were still nominally members of the National Secular Society on whose behalf the *Secular Song and Hymn Book* had officially been issued. Their complaint was that the society was administered by an executive in London which society the president Bradlaugh dominated. Their complaints in a way prefigured internal British political party debate in the second half of the twentieth century, in that they wanted annual party conference to be the shaper of party policy, not an executive under a party leader making policy decisions behind closed doors. This was one of the demands made by Foote when he listed proposed amendments to the society's stated principles, objectives and constitution: this he did prior to putting himself forward for the position of vice-president at the annual conference to be held in Leeds in June. The society's four principles he proposed enlarging to include the statement that the pursuit of the public good should be through 'the progress of Science' and 'the preservation and promotion of international peace and amity'; that against 'the mistaken selfishness of individuals' there should be 'practical recognition of the brotherhood of man'. The 'specific present objects' Foote listed remained essentially the same as before, these including repeal of the Blasphemy laws, disestablishment and disendowment of the Church, and 'the promotion of a purely secular system of national education'.[24]

Foote failed in his attempt to become vice-president, and the conference was rowdy, Bradlaugh on a technicality refusing to accept the votes of the Glasgow branch who backed Foote's candidature. It would not have affected the outcome – Foote lost by 292 votes to 51[25] – but Bradlaugh's behaviour at the conference was the focus of an attack

'B.V.' made when he wrote up the proceedings for the *Secularist* on his return from Leeds with Foote: 'He was accuser, witness, inquisitor, judge, all in one. He was a king of France of that *ancien régime* he denounced with pen and tongue, holding a bed of justice; he was Judge Jefferies trying a rebel. He continually interrupted Mr Foote with an insolence equally disgraceful and ludicrous. When Mr Foote wanted to reply to statements made after his first speech, the dictator decreed, "I don't allow you to speak again." He coerced his society with the lofty threat echoed by Mrs Besant, "If you choose Mr Foote, I resign" . . . Whatever the next Conference may bring forth, the National Secular Society in the meantime under its old constitution must be regarded as in no sense National, as but a petty small fraction of the great Freethought party, a fraction too appropriately stigmatized in its own hymn book as "Bradlaugh's Band".'[26]

Thomson after he had first left the *National Reformer* had refused to shake Bradlaugh's hand when it was offered.[27] Now while Thomson attacked Bradlaugh's behaviour towards Foote, Foote in an open letter attacked Bradlaugh's behaviour towards Thomson – though not mentioning him by name:

> Your malicious slander cast against my dearest friend, I was blamed for not repudiating; but in truth I dared not trust myself to speak of it. It was characterised by some of your own supporters as 'brutal', seeing that the mouth of the slandered man was stopped. My friend may be left to make his own defence, and to inflict on you, as he assuredly will, condign retribution. When last he and you met, you respected him sufficiently to proffer your hand, but he disrespected you sufficiently to decline it. His name will live when yours is forgotten; his memory be treasured when yours has fled. I would rather touch his hand dead than yours living; and I, and those who love and honour him, shall love and honour him the more since your reviling has supremely attested his worth.[28]

George Holyoake had not remained silent since Thomson's sharp reply to Holyoake's criticism of the songbook review. Before the Leeds Conference, Holyoake had again ventured forth in the *National Reformer* calling Thomson's review of Stigand's *Life of Heine* 'gross, coarse, and libellous', and the review of *The Secular Song and Hymn Book* 'mostly untrue and entirely unfair'.[29] This time Thomson had rounded on Holyoake himself before dealing again with Bradlaugh: 'I am very reluctant to occupy my time and your space with answering the unscrupulous twaddle of a very vain and spiteful old man, who in his best days was remarkable for what I will call inaccuracy, and whose memory is now like a magic-lantern with new sets of slides at his pleasure.'[30]

Stigand's *Life of Heine* had been reviewed not only in the *Secularist* but in *Cope's Tobacco Plant*. In the latter 'B.V.' had written:

> This pretentious work of nine hundred pages is one of the most disgracefully bad ones we ever came across; and the disgrace is shared by current criticism, which for the most part has lauded the book, instead of severely castigating it . . .
>
> Let no English reader think he has the true Heine here; for passed through Stigand, he has lost nearly all his wit and humour, quite all his poetry and music, and a large part of his mere common-sense and grammar. If Bismarck should demand the extradition of Mr Stigand for a criminal attempt on the life of the most brilliant of Germans, and for coarse and gratuitous insults to the German nation, we should be apt to respond: Take him, and welcome, if you will but engage never to let him get pen in hand again to write himself down what Dogberry has written down long before him.[31]

But his contributions to *Cope's Tobacco Plant* in 1876 were largely a continuation of his previous advocacy of French authors. A three-part autobiographical essay on Saint-Amant was followed by a four-part essay on Rabelais. Both acknowledged the information contained to be a distillation from published sources in French and English. In the latter essay 'Sigvat' wrote 'I am inclined to look up to Rabelais as the greatest genius in French literature. Perhaps the very finest work in the literature has been done by Pascal, but Pascal's finest work is a series of fragments; and while as profound, he is narrow as an artesian well, in comparison with the oceanic amplitude and energy, as well as depth, of Rabelais.' *Cope's Tobacco Plant* was not an anti-clerical sheet like the *Secularist*. But 'Sigvat' could still make comments there that would not have been passed in the 'respectable' monthlies such as *Fraser's Magazine*. He quoted the stories of Rabelais's last hours: 'When he had received Extreme Unction he declared that they had greased his boots for the long journey. When the attending priest asked him whether he believed in the real presence of Jesus Christ in the wafer given him for the Communion, he answered, with a respectful air: 'I believe in it, and it rejoices me; for I seem to see my God as when he entered Jerusalem, triumphant and borne by an ass.'[32]

But this was satire in passing. Elsewhere in *Cope's* that year he gave a warm welcome to George Meredith's *Beauchamp's Career*, and began a fourteen-part critical biography of Ben Jonson.[33] At the *Secularist* on the other hand anti-clerical satire was a regular feature of 'B.V.''s contributions. He had fun satirising an Anglican minister who had been taken to court for refusing to administer communion to a parishioner whom he thought did not believe in the Devil or Hell.

> . . . for my own part, I do not see how the Church could get on at all without a Devil and hell, especially in competition with the other Christian sects, which make unlimited use of both. The Devil is in fact as essential to the Christian schemes as a leader of the opposition to that great political blessing, government by party. If he were to die, or be deposed, it would be necessary to elect another to the vacant dignity. You cannot put the leadership in commission as the unfortunate Liberals were taunted with doing, in their demoralisation after their disasters of the General Election and Mr Gladstone's sudden retirement. Just as Mr Disraeli lamented the withdrawal of Mr Gladstone, complaining of the embarrassment caused to the Government by having no responsible leader opposed to it, so we can imagine dear God lamenting the absence of a Devil, and declaring that the Christian scheme could not work well without one. His utter loss would make the government of the world retrograde from an admirably balanced constitutional monarchy to a mere Oriental absolute despotism. You must choose someone to lead, if only in name and time, as the Whigs chose Lord Hartington. But though Lord Hartington is still tolerated by us English, a Lord Hartington of a Devil, be it said with all respect to both his lordship and his Devilship, would scarcely be tolerated by either the celestial or the infernal benches.[34]

And in 'Some Muslim Laws and Beliefs' 'B.V.' regretted that he had not been reared to believe in a Muslim heaven which, he thought, sounded like an eternal feast for the unjaded male appetite, and a lot more desirable than the Christian Heaven foretold in *Revelation*.[35] The *Christian World* – which Thomson at the *National Reformer* had found a regular source for satire in his 'Jottings' columns – attacked the *Secularist* for publishing this. 'B.V.' it said 'seems to have surpassed the general run of sceptics of his class in hysterical buffoonery and blasphemous irreverence.'[36] 'I have yet to learn that there is anything hysterical in a jolly burst of Rabelaisian laughter,' Thomson commented. Far from apologising for having shown disrespect towards the *Book of Revelation*, he elaborated further.

> Luther, indeed, who was not afraid to pass an independent judgment, said 'I look upon the Revelation as neither apostolic nor prophetic'; but it is received as both by our English Protestants, and continually referred to by them as the record of a genuine and authentic vision. But I assert

without fear of contradiction, that if they had never known it, and some missionary brought home an account of its marvels as belonging to the faith of some Polynesian islanders, they would be filled with wonder and compassion at the monstrous superstitions of these poor heathen barbarians. Yes, Exeter Hall and the readers and writers of the *Christian World* itself, would assuredly invoke help to enlighten the degraded idolators who believed in a Heaven whose God was to look upon like a jasper and a sardine; in the midst of whose throne, and round about whose throne, were four beasts, a lion, a calf, a man-faced monster, an eagle, each with six wings, and full of eyes before and behind and within; which beasts never rested day nor night from saying Holy, holy, holy, Lord God Almighty; and which, moreover, worshipped a lamb with seven horns and seven eyes, a figment more extravagant than the many-headed and many-armed idols of India. Our civilised gentlemen of the *Christian World* can only believe that they believe these things, because hallowed associations and unreflecting faith blind their judgment to the obvious absurdity of the imagery, and the conspicuous non-fulfilment of the prophecy, which again and again claims to announce events then at hand, to come quickly.[37]

The charge against him of blasphemy, he argued, was illogical. 'If the writer in the *Christian World* were accused of blasphemy for reviling Jupiter and Venus, Brahma and Vishnu, Baal and Moloch, the Goddess of Reason and Mumbo Jumbo, he would reply, I cannot blaspheme false gods, meaning simply gods in whom he has no faith. Just so, I say that I cannot blaspheme the trinity-in-unity of the Christian, which to me is non-existent, absurd, impossible.' And the State Church 'B.V.' repeatedly continued to attack: 'our fat Church still keeps to the text, "By grace ye are saved;" but its grace now is chiefly of deportment. It boasts that its clergy are gentlemen; and they may be, as a rule, in society, though we unbelievers seldom find them so in controversy; and it seems to be persuaded that we should continue to keep up this supply of gentlemen, when every profession, every trade shows gentlemen quite as good, with the advantages of more intellect, more experience of life, more courage and more sincerity.'[38] The Archbishop of Canterbury's salary was a disgrace: '£15,000 a year and a palace rent-free, and the members of the Cathedral body of Canterbury each with our several hundreds a year and our snug residences!'[39]

Yet if the State Church was corrupt, the Nonconformists had no more integrity: 'The various sects of Nonconformists, who all join with us in attacking the State Church, will all join the Churchmen to maintain against us their common fetish, the Bible.' To the Protestant, 'B.V.' wrote, the Bible was every bit as infallible as the Pope to the Catholic. Thus, 'taking western Christianity in particular, both the Roman embodied in Mary and the Protestant embodied in Jesus, we affirm that it no longer has real life, but only the "ghastly affectation of life". Reason and science have disembowelled it, have removed its heart and brain. It is ready for the historical embalmer.' Moreover there was a third blight on British society in addition to the Established and the Disestablished Church:

But for many, perhaps the majority of us, who are not only Secularists, but Republicans, there is a third great obstacle, the Throne, which is now little else than a costly sham. Yet, sham as it is, it is still as strong to obstruct, being encompassed and fortified by the power of the nobles, the degraded and degrading snobbishness of the middle and lower classes. The artisans and labourers generally, as we know, care nothing for it or are distinctly hostile. We have had some great monarchs, though the greatest we ever had was crownless, and we can yield to monarchy in the past something of such historical respect as we yield to Christianity. But who that is not a very serf by nature can feel any genuine respect for monarchy as we have it in these days? when the main duty of the King or Queen is to countersign the decrees of Parliament; a duty which the Lord Chancellor or the Speaker could perform just as well and with more promptitude. One need not dwell on the character of the reigning house, which, brought ignobly to the throne, has been consistently ignoble from the first until the accession of her present Most Gracious Majesty. A much nobler royal family would be just as superfluous now as the present; we have outgrown the need of a paternal or guardian king. Nor is the question of principle really affected by the fact that this ignoble family, like other species of the lower animals, is excessively prolific, and that every prince or princess born of it, costs us several thousands a year. We should not grudge the money for service rendered; the gravamen of our impeachment is that no monarch now can render service of value.[40]

Thomson's break with Bradlaugh meant that he was now also, to his regret, estranged from Bradlaugh's family. He could no longer write to Susan, or take her daughters out for an evening's music. Even when he did see Alice and Hypatia at a social in the Hall of Science, he was unable to go over and speak.[41] Before the break he had coined pet names for them (Fatima and Lina, a joke about one being fat and the other lean) and had corresponded with them, for the good of their language skills, in French.[42] However he did occasionally accompany others to music. He took Adeline Holyoake to see Cherubini's opera *The Water Carrier* and went with Foote to

Wagner's *The Flying Dutchman* and a 'Wagner Night' promenade concert.[43]

G.W. Foote, like Bradlaugh and Watts, spent many of his weekends lecturing in secularist halls around the country. In September 1876 Thomson accompanied him when he went to Leicester where he gave three Sunday lectures, morning noon and afternoon: 'Did Adam Fall and Did Christ Save Us?'; 'The Gospel of Secularism'; and 'The Turks and the Koran'.[44] Thomson stayed over the weekend at the home of Josiah Gimson, director of an engineering firm and prominent at the Leeds conference in supporting Foote's bid for the vice-presidency and his suggested amendments to society rules. The Leicester branch was very much in the *Secularist* camp. Prosperous leading members with whom Thomson and Foote also spent time that weekend were the elastic manufacturer Michael Wright and his two businessmen sons Phil and James.[45]

Back in London Foote continued to be his most regular companion not only on *Secularist* business but occasionally on Thomson's afternoon city walks. Thomson usually read or wrote at home in the evenings, and wrote – sometimes in the British Museum – in the mornings. He began to note signs of bad health in his diaries during 1876. On February 28th the unexplained word 'Accident' appeared, and Thomson was daily visited by a doctor for two weeks before he ventured out of doors. On Sunday April 2nd he went with the Wrights to Hampstead; on the 5th he noted 'slept at home again'. He also at other times during the year recorded feeling bilious, and passing blood.[46] Then on November 11th 'Accident' once again appeared, unexplained. This time he stayed indoors for a week. Then in the final month of the year the seasonal 'at homes' drew him into the social life of that section of literary Bloomsbury with which the Wrights and Foote had some marginal points of contact.

He needed no introduction to William Rossetti who lived nearby in Euston Square. His single previous visit had been in April 1873; now he was invited again to dinner on January 1st 1877. Other guests included the German-born poet Mathilde Blind in whose company Thomson thus found himself for the third time in four days.[47] He had accompanied Foote and the Wrights to a social evening at her home in Torrington Square on December 29th, and the following evening she had been amongst the guests at 12 Gower Street. Blind greatly admired the paintings of Rossetti's father-in-law, Ford Madox Brown, with whom she became a lodger. Madox Brown was at the New Year dinner, and he was impressed by Thomson's conversation: more impressed, he told his son-in-law, than he had been with the poet Swinburne's.[48] He invited Thomson to join the guests the following week at the Madox Browns' in Fitzroy Square.

Meanwhile a sequence of events had begun to take place that was to bring the schism in the secularist community to a public and dramatic climax. For Thomson the practical outcome was to be his source of earnings restricted once again to a single monthly publication.

CHAPTER SEVENTEEN

O N JANUARY 7TH 1877 the day before Thomson's visit to Madox
Brown's home in Fitzroy Square, the sub-editor of the *National
Reformer* Charles Watts was charged with having published and sold
obscene literature. The charge related to an 1832 pamphlet *The Fruits
of Philosophy: or the Private Companion of Young Married People* by
the American Dr Charles Knowlton. The printing plates for this had
been part of the stock of the freethought publisher James Truelove
which Watts had purchased on behalf of the *National Reformer* on
Truelove's death in 1874. Having bought the late Austin Holyoake's
printing works the same year, Watts had kept *The Fruits of Philosophy*
in print as one of several freethought publications offering advice on
contraception. The booklet sold about 1,000 copies a year.[1]

The Fruits of Philosophy made clear that it was aimed only at
married couples and was not about sex outside of marriage. It described
the female reproductive organs, menstruation, semen and pregnancy;
advised married males having sexual intercourse to practise 'entire
withdrawal' or use a baudruche, a covering 'of very delicate skin'. The
wife who wanted to practise contraception should prior to intercourse
insert in her vagina 'a very delicate piece of sponge, moistened with
water, to be immediately afterwards withdrawn by means of a very
narrow ribbon attached to it', the sponge preferably 'moistened with
some liquid which acted chemically upon the semen'; or better, she
should practise 'syringing the vagina immediately after use with a
solution of sulphate of zinc, or alum, pearl-ash, or any salt that
acts chemically on the semen'. The booklet concluded by saying
that sexual satisfaction was healthy when achieved in a way that was
'controlled by reason and chastened by good feeling'; masturbation
was unhealthy, the popular belief being reiterated that the 'unnatural
habit of onanism or solitary gratification . . . not unfrequently leads to
insanity'.[2]

In 1876 a part-time bookseller Albert Cook who had previously been jailed for selling books deemed to be obscene, had bought up copies of *The Fruits of Philosophy*, put in new title pages, added illustrations, and raised the price from fourpence to one shilling and eightpence. He was arrested on obscenity charges, tried on December 8th, and sentenced to two years' hard labour.[3] Watts, although he had stopped selling the book after Cook's arrest, was then also charged, in January. He decided to plead guilty, and was fined £500 with costs. At this point Bradlaugh sacked him and Watts came over to join the ranks of the disaffected secularists centred on Foote, T. R. Wright and the Leicester group. Bradlaugh and Besant founded the new Freethought Publishing Company, republished Knowlton's book themselves as a matter of principle, and were then prosecuted, it being charged that they

> . . . unlawfully and wickedly devising, contriving, and intending, as much as in them lay, to vitiate and corrupt the morals as well as youth of divers other liege subjects of our said lady the Queen, and to incite and encourage the said liege subjects to indecent, obscene, unnatural, and immoral practices, and bring them to a state of wickedness, lewdness, and debauchery, therefore, to wit, on the 24th day of March A.D. 1877, in the City of London and within the jurisdiction of the Central Criminal Court, unlawfully, wickedly, knowingly, wilfully, and designedly did print, publish, sell and utter a certain indecent, lewd, filthy, bawdy, and obscene book, called *Fruits of Philosophy*, thereby contaminating, vitiating, and corrupting the public morals.[4]

By the time the trial began in June sales had reached 133,000.[5] Bradlaugh and Besant were found guilty, fined £200 each and sentenced to six months' imprisonment. But right to appeal was accepted prior to execution of sentence, and the appeal was won on a technicality 'that the words relied upon by the prosecution as proving their case ought expressly to have been set out'.[6] During all this time the rival *Secularist* group did not support them. Foote wrote that the fine had been heavy but Bradlaugh and Besant had 'brought it upon themselves'.[7] The movement was seriously split over the court case, some resigning from the National Secular Society on the grounds that birth control was being wholly identified with Secularism in a way they could not accept. For others it was a free speech issue, but that in this specific matter Bradlaugh the Malthusian was prepared to defend free speech so long as it was freely expressing what he believed in himself: people like Watts who disagreed were free only to move on.[8] Thomson saw nothing to admire in Bradlaugh's behaviour. He accused him, in a letter to Dobell, of seeking martyrdom and self-publicity by defending a booklet 'tainted with the worst species of quack doctor'.[5]

Charles Watts after being expelled from the *National Reformer* had taken over a weekly recently founded by George Jacob Holyoake, the *Secular Review*. Watts and Foote decided to amalgamate their two papers into the *Secular Review and Secularist*, and this first appeared under their joint editorship in July. The following month the anti-Bradlaugh faction at last formed their own distinct alternative to the National Secular Society, the British Secular Union.[10] This held Sunday evening lectures and debates in the Cleveland Hall, Cleveland Street, near Fitzroy Square. Theodore Wright was one of the lecturers who took part, but more frequently he presided as chairman. The *Secular Review and Secularist* became the new group's official weekly organ.

The paper's opening number in July 1877 carried the first of a two-part review essay by 'B.V.' of Flaubert's newly published and as yet untranslated *Trois Contes* (*Three Tales*). The review included a 1,500-word plot exposition of the first tale, concluding: 'Such are the outlines of the story, which thus outlined may seem nought; but as told by Gustave Flaubert it is a most impressive little masterpiece.'[11] But the review was to be Thomson's only work for the *Secular Review and Secularist*. Watts had hired Thomson to help him sort out his residual accounts at Johnson's Court; this had involved Thomson's negotiating with a lawyer appointed by Bradlaugh.[12] But Thomson found Watts – who did not like the result of Thomson's investigations – slow to pay both for the accounts work and for the Flaubert review.[13] He did pay up for both, but Thomson never wrote for the *Secular Review and Secularist* again. So in August 1877 *Cope's Tobacco Plant* became his only regular source of income.

Publication of his first collection might have helped. But since Bertram Dobell had failed through lack of sufficient money to publish it in 1874, other publishers to whom the manuscript was subsequently offered had rejected it for publication.[14] Thomson found the behaviour of the publishers Henry King especially exasperating; they went so far as to advertise publication in the *Academy*, then changed their minds.[15] 'This is bad treatment' Thomson wrote,[16] but he was determined to keep trying, as he told someone who wrote asking if he could supply a copy of 'The City of Dreadful Night'. Thomson's letter was headed 7 Huntley Street: he had not moved lodgings, but Alfred Street had been renamed and renumbered:

I regret that I cannot oblige yourself & friend in the matter of the City of Dreadful Night. Much to my surprise it went out of print immediately on publication. I am left with a single proof copy & I have been unable to get others for friends. An advt. in the N.R. might bring a few copies of the numbers in which it appeared, which were scattered, if I remember rightly, through March, April & May 1874. As to its republication, I have been disappointed four or five times, but shall make an attempt to carry it through this winter. Verse by an unknown man is always a drug in the market, & when it is Atheistic it is a virulently poisonous drug with which respectable publishers would rather have nothing to do.[17]

His visits to the Rossettis and the Madox Browns at the beginning of 1877 had not been the prelude to frequent social intercourse with that artistic enclave, though he was at Euston Square again for 'at homes' twice in the summer.[18] Mathilde Blind and the Madox Browns, were there, and two more poets he met on these occasions were Arthur O'Shaughnessy, and Philip Bourke Marston who stayed round the corner in Euston Road. Marston thought highly of 'The City of Dreadful Night', and had called at the offices of the *National Reformer* for a copy after its publication.[19]

Thomson saw less of Foote for a while after Foote had become engaged at the beginning of 1877, married soon after and moved from Gower Street. But Foote's wife fell seriously ill and died only a few months later.[20] Thomson – who had had to bill Foote for his first six months' work at the *Secularist* the previous year – was irritated by a tendency in Foote to deflect questions about money still owed onto a discussion of Foote's personal tragedy.[21] However he and Foote began to pick up their close relationship again, Foote accompanying him regularly on his afternoon strolls. Of his other acquaintances, Thomson still saw Trousselle occasionally, their mutual interests not being solely confined to music: 'Evening: About to write when Trousselle came in (top heavy) & dragged me out to billiards. Saw him to tram-car. Then walked – bed about 2.'[22] The Wrights' place at 12 Gower Street had a billiard table, and billiards became part of the Sunday routine there after dinner. Thomson played Theodore, Percy, Adeline and visitors such as the children's uncles Walter and William Holyoake. A couple of times Thomson met Fred Hollett, and he continued irregularly to exchange letters with Grant, his sister-in-law Julia, and William Maccall.

'I have not forsaken the briary path of Secularism, or whatever path I trod in public,' he wrote.[23] But in *Cope's Tobacco Plant* it was the path of briary pipes he was increasingly expected to tread. The fourteen-part biographical essay on Ben Jonson that had run from November 1876, had in its final seven instalments made a kind of tobacco-trawl through the plays, citing tobacco and smoking references.[24] Then for the next seven months from April 1878 Thomson's work was to present 'Tobacco Smuggling in the Last Generation', a résumé of a Parliamentary Report or 'Blue Book' on the of course outrageous nature and effects of the tobacco duties. This was not something that could be thrown off, but involved a lot of preparation work in the British Museum. Thomson was in this as in other tobacco-focused articles, directed by Fraser as to which areas should be covered. In the final instalment 'Sigvat' summed up:

> I have thus summarised as well as I could in the space what appear to me the most significant points in the Blue Book. The facts speak for themselves without any elaborate commentary. On the one side a government, whose leading financial policy was the protection of the landed interest at the expense of all the other interests of the country, callously avowing that its sole object was to extort as much out of Tobacco as possible, regardless of the well-fare or ill-fare of importers, manufacturers, distributors, and consumers, the great bulk of the last being of the poorer classes to whom it was (as it is) a real necessity of life; a costly coastguard and Customs and Excise whose vaunted vigilance and detective service were proved altogether untrustworthy, and which mainly relied upon the infamy of delation; restrictions very harassing and injurious to the honest trader, quite inoperative against the contrabandist: on the other side a vast trade, giving millions to the revenue, in which legal dealing meant ruin, and good men were driven into smuggling and adulteration against their will; the poor forced to forego their best and most harmless solace, or have it vilely debased when not illegally introduced; the revenue suffering incalculable loss through the abominable and preposterous rapacity of the duties.[25]

Twice that year he privately described feeling a sense of alienation, using each time the image of a veil that conceals reality. In May he wrote: 'I often now write, as I wonder whether others ever write, conscious of a sort of dim veil separating the inner from the dictating mind. Reading over such exterior writing, I may judge: It is correct; it will do; but my inner self disclaims all responsibility for it, and simply refuses to be concerned in or about it.'[26] And in September he wrote again: 'Of old I was conscious of an impenetrable veil between my inner and my outer self; I have to live, think and work with the latter, and cannot get at the former, cold and vague and dim aloof. This is a painful puzzle, to be shut out and cut off from one's own very self, and conscious of the disabling separation.'[27]

His sister-in-law Julia surprised him that autumn by suddenly turning up at his lodgings in London. She stayed the night – 'told me all', he recorded. 'All' was that her marriage with John was falling apart. Thomson decided to stay out of the argument, 'would have nothing to do with it', he wrote, returning a diary of his brother John's that Julia had left with him.[28] But he continued to correspond with his sister-in-law. And in September 1878 he began writing poetry again, after a lapse of years.

> I had a Love; it was so long ago,
>   So many long sad years;
> She died; and then a waste of arid woe,
>   Never refreshed by tears:
> She died so young, so tender, pure and fair;
> I wandered in the Desert of Despair.[29]

Once again, the dead young lover. But this time there was to be no fancied visit. Such a myth was explicitly rejected. There had been a time once when he had constantly complained of his love's absence, and would have loved to have had her back with him. But then he had half believed she was in Heaven. Now, even if there *was* a God to offer him the chance to be young again with the girl as his bride, he would reject God's offer:

> For she has perfect and eternal rest,
>   She is not evermore,
> Save as an image graven in my breast;
>   And I am near the shore
> Of that Dead Sea where we find end of woes
> Unconsciousness, oblivion, and full repose.

He would not tear her from her present resting place, nor take the responsibility of bringing children into this world.

> What profit from all life that lives on Earth,
>   What good, what use, what aim?
> What compensation for the throes of birth
>   And death in all its frame:
> What conscious life has ever paid its cost?
> From Nothingness to Nothingness – all lost!

He added in the manuscript: 'Above merely rough copy pencil draft; too hard and harsh in both conception and execution for attempt at polishing

– Far more truth than poetry in it. Writing the foregoing lines I have felt like a man making his Will at the gates of Death, summing up Life's scores and settling accounts when about to leave its inn. Yet I do not truly feel very near to Death, for with a seeming partial revival of the creative energies, in thought and imagination, it is impossible to realise death, even when absorbed by its sombre fascination. It may be merely the throes of some new birth that give the lethal illusion; for birth is so like death.' A verse followed:

> I do not hate a single man alive,
> > Some few I must disdain;
> I have loved heartily some four or five,
> > And of these there remain
> Just two, I think, for whom I would outface
> > Death gladly; for the one, death and disgrace.

He was two months short of his forty-fourth birthday. He certainly disdained Bradlaugh, whilst Potterton, Barnes – and Bradlaugh before the quarrel – can probably be counted amongst the men once loved. Of the 'just two' remaining, Grant and Hollett seem the likeliest references, though neither were at this time a regular part of his daily life.[30]

The following month Theodore Wright put up money to hire the South Place Institute in Finsbury for the new winter season of Secular Union evening 'services'.[31] These were duly written up each week in the group's newspaper, the name of which had reverted under Charles Watts to the *Secular Review* after Foote had resigned the co-editorship of the *Secular Review and Secularist* in February.[32] The reported 'services' usually consisted of lectures together with songs and recitations, with Theodore's wife Jane Alice often reciting poetry. Hood, Charles Mackay, and Shelley were amongst the poets she chose to recite, and the *Secular Review* reported on one occasion that she 'read a short poem by Longfellow descriptive of the honours of war, in that cultivated style for which she is well known.'[33] Trousselle conducted a small choir, with Mendelssohn and Balfe being featured along with what was described as 'the usual part-songs'.[34] There was classical music on piano sometimes with violin accompaniment: Chopin, Sarasate, 'Variations on William Tell'.[35] Admission was 3d., 6d., or 1s. Charles Watts reported after one meeting: 'It was exceedingly gratifying to find a large and most respectable assembly testifying by their presence to the progress which Secular principles are making among the middle classes.'[36]

After a year's absence Thomson had been to Rossetti's home at Euston Square once more in June,[37] and between November and

December 1878 he was at three more 'at homes' there in the space of four weeks.[38] The guests included the painter William Bell Scott – whose name Thomson underlined in his diary – and the translator C.B. Cayley, whose translation of Dante's *Paradiso* Thomson had once copied out at such length. Rossetti had some sympathy with the views of the British Secular Union set, and he accepted an invitation to speak on Shelley at South Place. His lecture was called 'Shelley as Man, Poet, and Thinker'. Theodore Wright was once more in the chair, and Jane Alice, according to the report in the *Secular Review* gave a 'beautiful and impressive' rendering of Shelley's 'To a Skylark'.[39] George Foote accompanied Thomson to Rossetti's on his last visit there that December. Foote's own lectures at South Place and elsewhere now included 'Why I am not a Christian'; 'Thomas Paine: Republican and Freethinker'; 'Walt Whitman, Poet and Person, the Bond of Universal Democracy'; 'Woman's Rights and Woman's Wrongs'; 'John Milton: Man, Poet and Politician'; 'Religion without a God'; and 'Byron and Shelley: The Poets of Revolution and Progress'.[40] Foote included George Meredith amongst those contemporaries he admired, and went so far as to write to Meredith at his home in Box Hill, Dorking, expressing disappointment that Meredith's poetry was not more widely available. Meredith, who had evidently been apprised both of 'B.V.''s poetry as well as his praise of *Beauchamp's Career* replied to Foote: 'To feel that men like you and "B.V." read and have taste for what I produce, is full of encouragement to me to write on with good heart . . . As to my poems, I have lost the ardour for publishing them; perhaps in a year or two they may appear; I am well content to remain unpublished while the poems of "B.V." are withheld.'[41]

Foote had been lacking an editorial position since leaving the *Secular Review and Secularist*. He decided it was time to launch another secularist paper under his own direction, this one a monthly to be called the *Liberal*, the editorial address once again being 12 Gower Street. He wanted Thomson to be a regular contributor again, but Thomson was wary about Foote's ability to pay.[42] However any potential source of income could not be ignored: money was by now so scarce with Thomson that he frequently missed his meals at home, settling for a local coffee house rather than run up a meals bill with his housekeeper Miss Scott.[43] 'Dinner & tea out' became a common entry underlined in his diary. John Fraser at *Cope's Tobacco Plant* remained his only provider. 'I have not earned a penny save from him for the whole year,' Thomson told Dobell two days before Christmas.[44] But when the *Liberal* made its first appearance in January 1879 it carried, after Foote's editorial, an opening article by 'B.V.'. This attacked Disraeli's foreign policy as indicative of a lack of principle in government, monarchy and church. 'B.V.' however feared rather than hoped for a republican revolution under the prime minister:

> What I fear is the unfitness of large and influential masses of the people, if not indeed the main part of the people, for a Democratic Republic when the inevitable recoil from the Charlatan's Imperialism arrives: our lords spiritual and temporal have managed to keep so many of us, and particularly their noble selves, in such dense undisciplined ignorance or, worse, gross misunderstanding, of the mutual relations of the various classes in a well-ordered State, of their mutual and common duties, of their common inalienable rights, of the science and art of good citizenship . . . Wherefore I, though a Republican in principle, am by no means in a hurry for a Democratic Republic in Great Britain, preferring to wait until we are taught and trained into something like fitness for it; and therefore I do not regard the present costly and bloody burlesque of Imperialism with any the less disfavour because it is likely to precipitate the advent of such a Republic.[45]

On January 4th he was at the Madox Browns' in a company of about thirty for a gathering which included a formal talk on Tolstoy's *War and Peace*. There was a 'pleasant smoke upstairs to end with', when Thomson chatted with Edmund Gosse about Swinburne, and with Madox Brown himself about Meredith, Byron, Browning, and the 'political slog' in the *Liberal*.[46] The next issue of that paper advertised a forthcoming review by 'B.V.' of a biography of David Hume written by T.E. Huxley. Thomson was annoyed with Foote over this, as he hadn't in fact agreed to do the review.[47] However next month it duly appeared, and in his review 'B.V.' proceeded to describe Hume as one whose 'calm and subtle Scepticism, so irritatingly obnoxious to the dominant dogmatism of British thought, has gathered such thick clouds of prejudice about him, steamed up and steaming up evermore from those humid flats and sluggish swamps which form so large a part of the intellectual realm of our happy nation, that it requires the keenest and strongest and steadiest insight to see the philosopher and his philosophy in plainness and truth.' Huxley's achievement was remarkable in seeing through the prejudices here that normally blinded not merely the British churchgoing public but 'the bulk of the self-termed Freethinkers, who are always so eager to get hold of any great name as a catch-word and a battle-cry, having been just about as ignorant and foolish and bigoted in reckless laudation as the bulk of non-thinkers in their timid execration.' T.E. Huxley's courage was of a kind unusual in Britain: 'You may safely call upon a Briton to confront battle or shipwreck, a Polar winter or tropical desert, all dangers and hardships of land and sea; but do not expect him to face like a man any thesis which threatens ruin, or havoc, or even serious disturbance, to his old familiar dogmas about God and the soul.' Hume the supposedly 'wretched Infidel' had shown such a calmness on his deathbed – 'It is difficult to be more detached from life than I am at present' he said then – that his demeanour could be seen as refutation of those who saw his infidelity as 'one of the three unclean spirits like frogs that come out of the mouth of the dragon, and out of the mouth of the beast, and out of the mouth of the false prophet – Rev. xvi. 13; as certified by that profound Christian Apocalyptic interpreter, his countryman *in this world*, the Revd Dr Cumming'.[48]

At *Cope's Tobacco Plant* 'Sigvat' was kept focused on factual tobacco matters through 1878 and into the spring of 1879. The seven-part 'Tobacco Smuggling in the Last Generation' was followed over four months by 'The Tobacco Duties',[49] then in March 1879 began the first instalment of 'Tobacco Legislation in the Three Kingdoms'. This was to run until the end of the following year. However during the time that this last series made its appearance, Thomson was given room to contribute once again on matters literary. He had already in February 1879 managed to squeeze in something reflecting his musical interests, but the terms of reference of that article emphasised the peculiar constraints under which it was written. After twice going to see Bizet's opera *Carmen* he had given readers a full plot-description of the 'success of the year 1878 in London' – an 'opera of tobacco' which centred on 'a fascinating girl, who makes cigars in Seville'.[50]

But in April appeared the concluding second part of an essay on John Wilson ('Christopher North') that had been held over for more than a year;[51] and in that same issue 'Sigvat' gave a long welcome to a republication of George Meredith's novel *The Ordeal of Richard Feverel*.[52] Foote sent the review to Meredith at his home in Dorking, and he replied: 'I have read Mr Thomson's article on my book, with the singular pleasure we feel when it is evident we have been loved of old date, and by the very worthiest, and that nothing but love can have that way of speaking. The mental stature of the critic is the point; after which the sincerity. He who does me the honour to praise me in this instance, is to be valued in both respects. I wish that work of his were forthcoming.'[53] The work referred to was Thomson's still unpublished first collection of poetry. Foote showed Thomson the letter, and he decided to write straight to Meredith himself.[54] On July 5th he received Meredith's reply: 'I am glad to be in personal communication with you. The pleasant things you have written of me could not be other than agreeable to a writer . . . when a friend unmasked your initials, I was flattered. For I had read the "The City of Dreadful Night", and to be praised by the author of that poem, would strike all men able to form a judgment upon eminent work, as a distinction.'[55]

By this time Thomson had contributed more reviews for Fraser. Huxley's *Hume* which he had reviewed for the *Liberal* was one in a biography series called *English Men of Letters*. Fraser agreed that Thomson should review it again for *Cope's*, together with others in the series as they appeared. Despite the title of the series, Scottish writers Burns and Scott were included along with David Hume.[56] Taken with the essay on John Wilson and a three-part essay on a new edition of James Hogg,[57] 'Sigvat' in 1879 devoted a significant amount of his literary column space to Scottish writers. The Burns biography was by John Shairp, Principal of St Andrews University and Professor of Poetry at Oxford. Thomson was as acerbic in his review as he had been of Stigand's *Heine* three years before. Professor Shairp he wrote had 'crowned all his splendid achievements by one of the worst essays on Burns that we have ever come across':

A Scot, he has no national fervour; an old student of poetry and at least a would-be poet, he has no poetic sympathy; a successor of Matthew Arnold, he has no sweetness and very little light. Of course we speak of him as he shows himself in this, the one book of his that we have read; and having read, are little likely to read another. This Oxford graduate and professor has none of the liberal grace and urbanity of culture, but writes with the stark dogmatic narrowness of some provincial Calvinist. He might be one of those Auld Light ministers whom Burns scarified; he seems to resent the Address to the Unco Guid or Rigidly Righteous as aimed by anticipation at himself; he is continually sermonising on the great-hearted poet as a Sunday-school teacher might lecture his class on a life which was an awful warning. He is Cauld Kail in Aberdeen (or should we say St Andrews?) preaching against hot haggis; the coldest of cold water prelecting on the ardours of whisky. His voice is pitched to the pious twang of the Pharisee who thanked God that he was not as this Publican. He is a raven croaking immensely self-satisfied over a dead thrush. His blood is of the fishy temperature, and he swims serene in a sea of moral platitudes. His body may be in a great University, but his mind is in a little conventicle. He is frigid as the book of Euclid, writing on the most passionate of poets; he is bitter as the dogma of eternal damnation, discoursing on the sweet-souled singer; he is dull as ditch-water for quenching this fiery genius. Burns could cordially sympathise with a wee field-mouse and a mountain daisy: this man has no sympathy even with a Burns.[58]

Throughout 1879 Thomson's health continued to worry him. The word 'bilious' appeared at intervals in his diary, with notes on pains in his chest and back, and references as in 1876 to his having passed blood.[59] Occasionally alcohol was mentioned, though never as to connect it with stomach or other disorders. 'Slight bilious indigestion. Listless & sleepy. Beer early for early bed'.[60] 'The dull rheumatic pains shoulders & right arm continue; slight, but I rather fear after father. Tried moderate Irish whisky instead of beer last two nights'.[61] He complained of insomnia, and itching of the skin: 'Have got into bad way of waking two or three hours before I want to get up (before 5 or 6), & being unable to sleep afterwards. Hence I arise weary at last; & am very drowsy after tea, when I want to read or write. This morng. awoke at 5.40; this evg. had to lie down, & slept from 6.30 to 8.30, losing two good hours. Have been much annoyed lately by itching here, there, & everywhere, in bed, though uninfested by bugs or fleas, & tho' my skin is quite clean. Sponge every morning, & would at night, but the bath leaks a little'.[62] Another time when bothered with pains in his stomach he wrote: 'Got a decent sleep last night by drinking some hot rum & water instead of beer. Don't remember ever feeling quite so before. Castor oil to-morrow morng. if not better; more rum & water to-night, tho' I wd. rather not have it as a matter of taste'.[63]

Sometimes he sat up late with fellow-lodgers at Huntley Street – a Mr Hawkes, and a teacher called Hopkirk.[64] He still had regular Sunday lunch at Gower Street, gave some tuition to Adeline, played billiards with her or Percy, worked in the British Museum on weekday mornings, walked often with Foote in the afternoons, read or wrote at home in the evenings. But his relationship with Foote was beginning to cool; as Thomson had feared, Foote was proving slow in paying for contributions to the *Liberal*. Yet in September Foote offered to publish Thomson's book manuscript, and got as far as having publication costed. But again there was delay, and Thomson demanded his manuscript back, accusing Foote of 'bad faith'.[65] He recorded that he 'shook hands coolly' with Foote when he met him at Gower Street,[66] but soon he was writing to him in angry tone: 'It seems you are past all shame for breaking promises.'[67] The two men began to ignore each other when together at Gower Street or when they happened to be in the same coffee-shop nearby.[68] Yet the name 'B.V.' continued to appear in the *Liberal* until the end of the year, Thomson having given Foote a review of a collection of poetry which appeared over four months from September. The collection was by James John Garth Wilkinson, and was unusual in that it claimed to be the product of automatic writing – hence the title of the book *Improvisations from the Spirit* and the title of Thomson's review essay, 'A Strange Book'. Wilkinson was a leading translator of Swedenborg, medical practitioner and early advocate of homoeopathy.[69] He was also the first to publish – anonymously – a printed text of Blake's *Songs of Innocence and Experience* in 1829, and these poems had had a discernible influence on the products now claimed to have been written under spiritual dictation. The review provided Thomson with an opportunity not only to draw attention to a writer whom he considered to have been unjustly neglected by all but Emerson, but enabled him further to define his mature position with respect to the role of inspiration and 'possession'. Again he could cite a tradition that extended from Plato to Shelley, but now he was quite unambiguous in denying the ubiquity of a 'Comforter' or of any supernatural agent:

> To myself, ecstasy, trance, inspiration, vision, revelation, are no less simply human and natural, though so much less common, than sleep and waking; are just as susceptible of scientific explanation, though our science is not yet subtile and comprehensive enough to pervade them, as spring-tides or summer flowering and fruitage or the *aurora borealis*.[70]

And 'inspirational discourses' claiming to come from the Holy Spirit should be treated with total scepticism: 'I have heard but one, from a woman who seemed a cleverish actress,' 'B.V.' wrote. Taking this at its face value it would confirm that the outpourings of the 'gift of tongues' were no longer the practice of his mother's circle by the time of her son's earliest recollection.

More jobbing work centred on the tobacco world came Thomson's way at *Cope's* when a journalist died who had contributed a monthly satirical miscellaneous column, and Thomson was asked to take it over.[71] 'Cope's Mixture' was a miscellany of jokes about anti-smokers and like matters, in tone not unlike the anti-clerical 'Jottings' Thomson had provided for the *National Reformer*. He took it over for five months. Meanwhile his patience was finally running out with G.W. Foote over financial matters, and he billed him for £16 10s. owed. Foote wrote back deferring payment, telling Thomson that the language of his demand had been 'gratuitously insulting'.[72] Thomson wrote to Maccall that he had now 'definitely broken' with Foote.[73] The December 1879 issue of the *Liberal* proved in any event to be the last. *Cope's Tobacco Plant* was once more Thomson's only publishing output and source of money.

It was Percy Holyoake – nineteen in November 1879 – who now frequently accompanied Thomson on his afternoon city stroll. The route taken by Thomson he only at intervals recorded in his summary of the day's events, but entries show a regular walk to have been along Oxford Street as far as Hollis Street, or Orchard Street, or on to Marble Arch. Sometimes he went further, into Hyde Park along the north side as far as Kensington Gardens, or down to the Serpentine and Rotten Row. Places also mentioned are the Strand, St James's Park, 'Regent St etc', Fleet Street, Hampstead Road, Hollas Street, King's Cross, Oxford Circus, Regent's Park, Great Portland Street, Bond Street, 'Soho, Wardour Street etc', 'Charing X etc.', Holywell Street, and Newgate Street.[74]

The pocket diaries he used were published by T. & E. Smith, a week to an opening, with a blotter bound in between each double page. Besides the information about holidays and postal times at the front, there was a page of 'Simple Rules of Etiquette' for the use of those engaged in formal 'at home' visits and the like.[75]

If the sexes are the same, always present the inferior in social rank to the superior.

A gentleman should be introduced to the lady, not the lady to the gentleman.

An introduction given to a lady at a ball does not entitle a gentleman to bow to her on a future occasion; if he commits that error, the lady is not bound to acknowledge his salutation.

Persons meeting as mutual friends, not introduced, should not claim acquaintance: if they meet elsewhere a bow implies acquaintance.

Morning calls are usually made between the hours of two and four.

If walking with a friend, you meet or are joined by a third, it is unnecessary to introduce the one to the other.

At evening parties do not remain till the close. Put your gloves on prior to entering the room.

In conversation avoid political, commercial, or religious subjects. Scandal is inexcusable.

Daily in these diaries Thomson began his entry by writing up the weather, sometimes the direction of the wind, often amending the entry through the day according to his divisions of morning, afternoon evening.

DECEMBER 1879

Cold; snow-powder morng. & evg.

Snow-powder on ground – Fine & very cold. W. working round to S. & W. from N. & N.E.

Cold, rather thick but dry. No water for bath.

Very cold. N.E. Dry.

Cold. Slight snow; fine morng., livid day. Snowing pretty heavily at night. (9 p.m.)

Not much snow; not so cold; bright; some thaw; little wind, but northerly.

Keen frost, fine day.

Fine, some thaw.

Dull, some thaw, cold night.

Dull, thaw, fair aftn; dirty – Water again free.

Foggy morng; electric lamps twice in Readg. Room, B.M. Fine aftn. Coldish – water free.

Foggy morng & evg.; fine aftn. thaw; water free.

Black fog morning nine; thaw still; lamps in Readg. Room all morng.

Mild, dull, dry overhead.

Mild, moist, muggy; fog with dusk.

Fog settling into thick yellow after noon. Just managed to read without lamps in morng. Moist.

Cold, frost, dull.

Thaw but coldish. Pleasant aftn.

Frost morng., slight thaw aftwds, no fog, inclined to rain.

Cold, but still thick-paste thaw.

Cold, dull; thaw eveng.

Mild, muddy, fine aftn., some rain early morng. Very dark fog at night.

Muddy, humid, mild; fog evg.

Frost, then some thaw; viscid mud; but sun & moonshine.

Black fog midday; & until night.

Dull & coldish, not foggy.

Cold, some sunlight & moon.

Slight rain early; thaw, slush. High wind – both nights.

Dirty; very mild; sunshine – Evg (10) colder, with splendid gibbous moon.

Colder, windy; fine morng. with clouds, midday sharp short rain with some thunder & lightning.

Very mild; some rain; dirty & windy.

JANUARY 1880

Still very mild; clouds & some winds –

Fine day; breezy, mild; fairly dry underfoot.

Very fine day, little cooler; large red sun sinking Hyde Park.

Very fine; not cold.

Dull; but dry; cooler.

Dull & cool; dry.

Fog settled down dense morng. & mid-day; less so about three.

Fog again all day; slight drizzle. Very chary again of their electric light at Museum.

Fog again all day. B.M. still very stingy with its light.

Dull, coldish. Some drizzle.

Dull, cold. E.

Cold, dull, dry.

Dull, fog; mid-day fog & snow; dusk sleety drizzle; 9 o'cl wet snow.

Dull, cold, dry.

Splendid aftn. (for us), sun & sky. Dusk fog & sleet; evg. snow; night, snow, sloppy & slushy.

Rain or drizzle all day; slush of despond; milder since snow.

Dull, muddy; but not rain.

Dull, frosty; sun mid-day.

Very cold southerly wind; frost; sunshine – moonlight –

Very cold, not so much wind, bright. At 4 p.m. large luminous red sun sinking behind Hyde Park, & dim moon high in the south.

Fog all day; but not too dark for Readg. Room; cold but no wind.

Fine, cool; snow shower at noon. Thick halo round moon.

Dull; some rain; greasy –

With that last entry for Saturday January 23rd, Thomson stopped writing in the diary for over a month. When he commenced again on March 4th he recorded that Dobell had found two partners, Reeves & Turner in the Strand, who were prepared to share the cost of publication of Thomson's first book of poetry. After six years *The City of Dreadful Night and other Poems*, ascribed openly to 'James Thomson ("B.V.")', was underway. 'I take no share of risk & have one-third profits (if any)' wrote Thomson. 'Fair for a first book, as I have certain gain of an independent name.'

CHAPTER EIGHTEEN

T HE BOOK WAS dedicated 'To the memory of the younger brother of Dante GIACOMO LEOPARDI a spirit as lofty a genius as intense with a yet more tragic doom'. Thomson received his first copies on April 6th. He sent one to William Rossetti thanking him for having 'done more both in public and private than anyone else to prepare the way for it,'[1] and sent a copy also to his sister-in-law Julia: 'Send reluctantly because likely to shock and depress you; advise you to skip first three pieces (first 77pp.), written under evil inspiration of insomnia.'[2] The first three pieces were 'The City of Dreadful Night', 'To Our Ladies of Death', and 'In the Room'.

George Meredith wrote on April 27th:

Dear Sir, – I will not delay any longer to write to you on the subject of your book, though I am not yet in a condition to do justice either to the critic or the poet, for, owing to the attack I suffered under last year, I have been pensioned off all work of any worth of late; and in writing to you about this admirable and priceless book of verse I have wished to be competent to express my feeling for your merit, and as much as possible the praise of such rarely equalled good work. My friends could tell you that I am a critic hard to please. They say that irony lurks in my eulogy. I am not in truth frequently satisfied by verse. Well, I have gone through your volume, and I have not found the line I would propose to recast. I have found many pages that no other English poet could have written. Nowhere is the verse feeble, nowhere is the expression insufficient; the majesty of the line has always its full colouring, and marches under a banner. And you accomplish this effect with the utmost sobriety, with absolute self-mastery. I have not time to speak of the City of Melencolia. There is a massive impressiveness in it that goes beyond Dürer, and takes it into upper regions where poetry is the sublimation of the mind of man, the voice of our highest. What might have been said contra poet, I am glad that you should have forestalled and answered in 'Philosophy' – very wise writing. I am in love with the dear London lass who helped you to the 'Idyll of Cockaigne'. You give a zest and new attraction to Hampstead Heath . . . Yours very faithfully,

George Meredith[3]

Thomson had reviewed Meredith's new novel *The Egoist* at the beginning of the year in *Cope's Tobacco Plant*, another 3,000-word article in which he wrote 'I have long deemed Mr Meredith's dialogue not only the best of our age, but unsurpassed, if equalled, in our whole literature.'[4] In that same issue there had been in addition to the Meredith review the sixth instalment of 'Tobacco Legislation in the Three Kingdoms', the second 'Cope's Mixture' miscellany, and a review in the *English Men of Letters* series of a Spenser biography by R.W. Church, Dean of St Paul's. The Dean's literary style was judged to have suffered from the verboseness of pulpit oratory:

We think it was Voltaire who termed the adjective the natural enemy of the noun; we have seldom seen, though we have pretty often heard, the hostility so desperate as in the Dean's style. Two or three robust adjectives make a dead set upon a single noun, when any one of them would have been quite sufficient to do for it. The three are generally synonymous, or so nearly synonymous that one includes the other two. One clause or short sentence with quite superfluous kindness repeats in other words what a predecessor has said; or now and then, by failure of memory, in trying to repeat repeats with a difference. The booklet is substantially not a bad one; but it needs thorough revision in order to concision.[5]

As he noted in his diary, his combined contribution to this issue of *Cope's Tobacco Plant* amounted to three-quarters of the paper's nineteen and a half pages of text.[6] Throughout 1880 his 'Tobacco Legislation in the Three Kingdoms' continued to appear, and there was a six-part biographical essay on Whitman that can be seen as a companion piece to his 1874 Whitman essay in the *National Reformer*.[7] There were more reviews of *Shelley*, *Burke*, *Thackeray* and *Milton* in the *English Men of Letters* series.[8] 'Sigvat' was not so severe as he had been in his reviews of *Burns* and *Spenser*, but he criticised the overall editor of the series John Morley for too often allowing his biographers a looseness of style and incorrect grammar.[9] He listed over fifty examples of the latter in a review of Mark Pattison's *Milton*.

Foote had in January gone over once more to Bradlaugh at the *National Reformer*, and complained to Dobell of Thomson's 'bitterness' towards him.[10] Dobell told Thomson of this, and the diary then recorded: 'G.W.F. more impudent & insolent still; thinks to brazen it out. My regard has declined with his fortunes! as if I had not gradually found him out appropriator of the money entrusted to him by a very poor "friend", a shameless parasite for years, a dishonest debtor, a lazy beggar; a fellow who won't try to earn an independent livelihood by regular work because he "must have excitement", who takes articles (not necessaries) for w^h he has no prospect of paying, who chuckles the chuckle with a base ring in it that his crs can get nothing out of him, who turns round & insults his best benefactor in cowardly reliance upon that benefactor's continued forbearance, &c., &c.!'[11]

He told Dobell not to send any review copies of *The City of Dreadful Night* to Foote or to Watts, as both were 'not trustworthy'.[12] But the publication of his book did link him once more with some friends of whom he had seen little for some while. Grant, now left the army and a teacher in St Stephen's National School in Pimlico, visited Huntley Street and collected a copy.[13] Fred Hollett, now married and settled in Lambeth[14] – Thomson had kept him supplied by post with *Cope's Tobacco Plant*[15] – visited also.[16] Trousselle and Hember distributed adverts amongst the South Place set, and the latter took a dozen orders.[17] Mathilde Blind, whom Thomson bumped into at Regent's Park gate out walking one day,[18] invited him to visit, as did her friend Philip Bourke Marston, who thought the poem 'The City of Dreadful Night' was 'wonderful'.[19] At the British Museum the Superintendent of the Reading Room, Richard Garnett – who had sometimes been in Thomson's company at the Rossettis – told him that Karl Marx's daughter Eleanor thought so highly of the Heine translations at the end of his collection that she had copied them out for her father.[20] Karl Marx and Thomson subsequently exchanged letters.[21] Richard Garnett shared Thomson's interest in Leopardi, and he borrowed the manuscripts of Thomson's Leopardi translations.

Around this time Thomson also renewed contact, briefly, with his old friend Jacques. The reunion was nothing to do with Thomson's new literary success. What happened was that Jacques' name appeared in the papers when he sued the London Tramways Company for wrongful dismissal and damage to character in dismissing him from his job as office manager, alleging fraud. Thomson visited Jacques again, had Sunday lunch with him in Fentiman Road near Vauxhall Bridge, and attended the court proceedings. The judge found 'not a scintilla of evidence' to substantiate the fraud charges, the employers being deemed to have behaved in a way that was 'reckless, unscrupulous, mischievous, erroneous and unjust'. The jury awarded Jacques £1,000, and Thomson had a celebratory meal and glass of wine with Jacques and his solicitor.[22] But Jacques then disappeared once more from Thomson's daily record of events.

Bradlaugh and Thomson were irrevocably gone their opposing ways, but at the *National Reformer* Bradlaugh accepted adverts for *The City of Dreadful Night* and gave it a welcoming review: 'We have during the last few years had many applications from correspondents at home and abroad for copies of this journal containing the poem "The City of Dreadful Night", but in consequence of the issues being out of print every applicant has been disappointed. Now we are glad to say that the author has collected a few of his poems together in one volume, and has published them with "The City of Dreadful Night" to head the list. Our old readers will be glad to have anything from "B.V." in handy form, and those of our later circle, who know not the charm of his pen will do well to read this book, if only that they may then learn how much of harmony and power, how much of beauty and softness, how much of sad despair and biting mockery, how much of grandeur and of bitterness, how much of the conception of life's misery and of wasted hope may be welded by poetic genius into a chain of linked words, powerful enough to hold the most unwilling reader . . . We trust that this volume may have a sufficiently wide circulation to encourage the publication of a number of other poems which we know to exist from the same pen, a pen which long ago made music in our ears, and which though to-day unfriend with us is now happily freshest to us by the older yet clearer memory of the author's kindness thirty years ago. If our readers who have any love for poetry and who do not know "B.V.", will but buy his book for our sake, we feel sure that having read him they will then try to make some others, too, sharers of the feast which in this little volume his pen has provided.'[23]

The volume itself sold briskly enough for Dobell and Reeves to decide within two months of publication that a second collection could safely be launched later in the year before reaction to the first had died down.[24] In preparing this second volume Thomson was able to give Reeves – with whose family he was several times asked to have Sunday dinner – a selection of generally favourable reviews of *The City of Dreadful Night*. These were for inclusion at the back of the new collection. The *Fortnightly Review* praised 'the writer's absolute and courageous content with circumstances which have a sordid side to them' but thought the title poem an unsuccessful attempt to weld two wholly different schemes: 'The fragments of each scheme are exquisitely finished; there is no redundancy or weakness in any single poem; but the attempt to fuse two incomplete schemes is not a complete success.' Other sometimes-qualified praise included quotes from the *Westminster Review*, the *Pall Mall Gazette*, and the *Academy*: 'Not since the days when Mr Swinburne and Mr Morris startled the reading world has any volume called forth more decided and sterling praise than this one before us . . . The longest piece in the book, "The City of Dreadful Night", is nothing but an allegorical representation of the misery and hopelessness of human life'.[26]

One review not included was Bradlaugh's, though Thomson had noticed its appearance, without comment, in his diary. Bradlaugh meanwhile was at the centre of another public controversy by this time. He had finally been elected Liberal member for Northampton in 1880 but had been denied his seat in Parliament. The problem was the Oath of Allegiance required of each new member on presenting himself to the House of Commons for the first time. Bradlaugh had requested 'to be allowed to affirm as a person for the time being by law permitted to make a solemn Affirmation or Declaration instead of taking an Oath'.[27] A Commons select committee decided against Bradlaugh's request. He then said that he would take the oath, though he would consider himself 'bound not by the letter of its words, but by the spirit which the affirmation would have conveyed'. This was not agreeable to many MPs, who complained that a declared atheist should not be allowed to take an oath the basis of which he did not believe. A second select committee decided Bradlaugh should after all be allowed to affirm, but this was rejected by a Commons vote of 275 to 230. Bradlaugh next day made his maiden speech at the Bar of the House, after which the Speaker asked him to withdraw. He refused, the Sergeant-at-Arms was called, and eventually it took a dozen policemen to have him removed and imprisoned in the Tower of the House of Commons. He remained there overnight before being released next day. Thomson was unsympathetic: 'C.B.'s arrest & imprisonment in morng. papers. The imbecile bigots have been playing his game as if he dictated all their moves; given him twentyfold notoriety, his very breath of life, multiplied the sale of his paper & pamphlets &c., &c.'[28]

Meredith invited Thomson to come and visit him at Box Hill,[29] and on June 29th, five days after Bradlaugh's imprisonment, Thomson took the train from Victoria to Dorking. The two writers had a stroll before lunch and after dinner, and discussed Swinburne, Shelley, Keats, Milton, and Meredith's own work. 'A day to be marked with a white stone' Thomson wrote in his diary. But despite his progress in literary contacts, and despite his book's having sold well enough for Reeves 'unasked' to give him £10 share of the profits in August,[30] Thomson was still having difficulty keeping up his weekly payments at Huntley Street. 'Mr T has still the pleasure of being in debt through Mr F's lack of common honesty,' he wrote to Foote.[31]

And his health seemed to be getting worse. He wrote a long letter of apology citing '5 weeks illness' to Marston for failing to turn up for an appointment at his home in Euston Road.[32] Throughout these five weeks the diary remained blank. It was blank again through September[33] before in October he wrote to Fraser 'Will be very much obliged by an advance, my long illnesses having thrown me back.'[34] He complained of his health to Dobell when sending him one of the reviews of *The City of Dreadful Night* that were to be bound in the new book:

7 Huntley Street, Gower St WC
Saturday October 9th 1880

Dear Sir,

Yours with *Westminster Review* notice to hand. I have been going through the notices, marking what shall be printed on the fly-leaf. I am engaged to dine with Mr Reeves tomorrow, but have written not to wait or alter his hours for me, because if it is as wet as today I shall scarcely venture. The bitter nor'easter of Saturday night gave me a chill that kept me in all Sunday (this is why I didn't give you a call). Since then we have had but one decent day, and I have had hints of rheumatism. As an agreeable addition, I now have a slight cold in the left eye, the eye which kept me from reading, writing, and smoking, five long weeks some years ago. So I must be careful.

I hope to be at Museum all the mornings next week (you can always see me there by enquiring), but at home all the evenings from tea-time, say 4.30 or 5 – unless I cannot go to Mr Reeves's tomorrow, and so call one evening in the Strand.

Yours truly,
James Thomson[35]

Fraser sent him £22 for recent contributions and offered more on account, though Thomson told him the £22 was 'too liberal for what it covers'.[36] He spent his afternoon stroll that day 'paying slight debts and shopping'. Then the diary entries stopped again, this time for two months.[37] The sole exception was a shakily written entry for October 15th recording a visit to Philip Bourke Marston's. He stayed overnight, was introduced to Marston's playwright father, noted the blind poet's special printing press which saved him from having to dictate his poems. In a letter to Dobell ten days later he apologised for his handwriting, saying it was caused by rheumatism in his right hand.[38]

When the new collection *Vane's Story* appeared, it bore the dedication 'Inscribed to the memory of the poet of poets and purest of men
PERCY BYSSHE SHELLEY with the gratitude of love and reverence of
the author'. Rossetti had regretted that Thomson's first volume had
omitted the poem 'Weddah and Om-el-Bonain',[39] and he was pleased
to see it follow the title poem in the new book. Amongst those who
expressed admiration for this poem was the poet Swinburne, whose
praise of its having 'forthright triumphant power' Rossetti passed on
to Thomson.[40] He replied with thanks on December 15th, telling
Rossetti also that Dobell and Reeves had now decided to press on
with a third substantial collection of Thomson's work, this time of his
prose:

I am much obliged to you for sending me Mr. Swinburne's remarks
on the 'Weddah'. When you next write to him will you please say that
I count the value of such generous praise from such a poet simply ines-
timable. It immensely surpasses the most sanguine expectations I could
have cherished had I known that he was going to give out any opinion
at all on the poem.

I am also very much gratified by Mrs. Rossetti's sympathy with 'Vane's
Story', a piece too wild and capricious for most minds to follow. It is in
fact a piece of pure phantasy, wherein I threw the reins on the neck of
Pegasus and let him go whither he would. Hence I purposely made the
title equivocal to the ear. Writing simply for my own pleasure, I enjoyed
the writing.

My own intention, as you will readily believe, was to start the
volume with 'Weddah'. But the publishers represented that there would
be all sorts of blundering and confusion in the orders, and that people in
general are shy of asking for a book whose title they don't exactly know
how to pronounce. As these appeared valid business arguments, I reluctantly yielded the first place to the fantastic 'Vane', keeping, however,
'Weddah' on the first page.

I have been unwell for a very considerable time, and have only
just now been able to resume and finish what was nearly completed
before my illness, the preparation of a volume of prose requested by
the publishers. It contains merely reprints, mostly from the *National
Reformer*; but careful revision was required, and there was, and still
is, some difficulty in the selection. However, I hope the first half of
the matter will be in the hands of the printers by about Monday, and
the other within a week after. But you need not mention the subject
until we are further advanced.

I hope you have all been keeping well.

Pray tender my respects to Mrs. Rossetti, and kiss for me the miraculous little lady who at four and a half could listen to several pages of 'The City of Dreadful Night'.[41]

Amongst the reviews of *Vane's Story* 'Weddah and Om-el-Bonain' was singled out for praise by the *Westminster Review* and the *Athenaeum*. The former called it 'one of the finest narrative poems that has been written in modern times', the latter commented 'As a piece of solid, vigorous, and masculine narrative, it would be difficult to find its superior among the writings of contemporary poets.' The *Pall Mall Gazette* was not alone in expressing disappointment that most of the poems in *Vane's Story* dated from the 1850s and the 1860s. It welcomed works 'rescued from unjust neglect', but concluded: 'We are loth to think of Mr Thomson's contributions to English song as remaining in the place of splendid promises never quite fulfilled.'[42]

Though he had sent a copy of the poem 'The City of Dreadful Night' to George Eliot after it appeared in the *National Reformer* in 1874, Thomson had been unable to locate her address in 1880 to send her a copy of the book now containing the poem.[43] When he did hear of George Eliot again soon after the publication of *Vane's Story*, it was to learn of her death. On December 29th he attended her funeral at Highgate Cemetery with Percy Holyoake and Theodore Wright:

> With T.R.W. & Percy to George Eliot's funeral. Most dismal day, drizzle settling into heavy rain – ¾ hour waiting at the grave: we secured footing on a plank; other outsiders on swampy clay & drenched clay-sward. No arrangements for comfort save broken red brick up path to grave, & sawdusted planks for mourning-coach intimates & reporters. For distinguished people present see newspapers. Dr Sadler conducted service in Chapel & mumbled something over grave – scarcely a word to be caught at two yards' distance. Coffin polished oak, covered with camellias & a few violets & lilies of the valley. Brick sarcophagus, to be lidded. It struck me no pauper's funeral could be more dismal. Nothing to see but expanded umbrellas.[44]

They walked back to Gower Street in the rain, to dinner, and billiards. Thomson had eaten at Gower Street on Christmas Day, and he now noticed the 'third turkey' being served.[45] He himself at Huntley Street was still entering 'Dinner & tea out' nearly every day in his diary, keeping down the bill owed Miss Scott for meals. Meanwhile *Vane's Story* helped him renew old contacts as *The City of Dreadful Night* had done. Grant called up late on New Year's Day for *Vane's Story*,[46] and Mathilde Blind also borrowed a copy.[47] He spent an evening with

Marston and others at Blind's home where she gave a recital of a 900-line poem on Celtic legend, 'Oram and Mona'. Thomson described the poem as 'a good & strange story to be preserved among Xns. in connexion with St Columba'.[48] As the early weeks of 1881 got under way he worked on the first proofs of his forthcoming prose anthology, finished instalment fourteen of 'Tobacco Legislation in the Three Kingdoms', and posted it to Fraser with an enquiry about three biography reviews that he had on hand. Then came news from Fraser that *Cope's Tobacco Plant* had ceased publication.[49] Thomson's one source of assured income was now gone.

Dobell suggested he do a couple of small critical biographies, of George Eliot and Heine, the latter based on Thomson's already published material on the poet.[50] He and Reeves would publish these in addition to the forthcoming volume of Thomson's prose. The two publishers supplied Thomson with George Eliot's works, and he began reading his way through them. 'But how exist meantime?'[51] he underlined in his diary. Then came a request from his secularist friends in Leicester. They were due to open a new hall in March, and Michael Wright wrote asking him if he would compose a poem for the occasion. Thomson set to work, and in two weeks the poem he sent was 'joyfully accepted'.[52] It was printed as a leaflet to be sold at the opening of the hall, and on March 5th Thomson travelled by train to Leicester with Theodore and Jane Alice Wright.

> We gaze into the living world and mark
> Infinite mysteries for ever dark:
> And if there is a god beyond our thought
> (How could he be within its compass brought?);
> He will not blame the eyes he made so dim
> That they cannot discern a trace of him;
> He must approve the pure sincerity
> Which, seeing not, declares it cannot see;
> He cannot love the blasphemous pretence
> Of puny mannikins with purblind sense
> To see him thoroughly, to know him well,
> His secret purposes, His Heaven and hell,
> His inmost nature, formulating this
> With calmest chemical analysis,
> Or vivisecting it, as if it were
> Some compound gas, or dog with brain laid bare.
> And if we *have* a life beyond our death,
> A life of nobler aims and ampler breath,

What better preparation for such bliss
Than honest work to make the best of this?
Our creed is simple, All men are one man! –
Our sole commandment, Do what good you can.[53]

They stayed at Michael Wright's home in Regent Street Leicester for four nights. On the Sunday the hall was opened with four 'services' morning afternoon and evening, including an overflow in the society clubrooms because of the crush. Thomson's 'Address on the Opening of Leicester Secular Society Hall' was read each time by Jane Alice, with 'endless speeches' and a dinner that Thomson described as 'Three courses & enough dishes to last me for many years to come.'[54] On the Monday they were taken round the Wrights' family factories, with dancing in the evening, toasts in champagne, bed not reached until after midnight. On Tuesday morning they were shown round Josiah Gimson's engineering factory, then Jack Barrs, a twenty-nine-year-old tea merchant – he described himself on the census form that year as 'Tea dealer and local atheistic lecturer (occasionally)' – took them out to his villa 'Forest Edge', set in grounds in the village of Kirby Muxloe, four miles away. Jack introduced his twenty-year-old sister Harriet, known as 'Dick'. After tea the whole party returned to Leicester where they went to see the Carl Rosa company in Benedict's opera *The Lily of Killarney*. Next day Thomson returned to London. 'Very pleasant visit. All of us *plus* Adeline & Percy *must* go in summer,' he wrote.[55]

The George Eliot booklet was taking more of his time than he had anticipated. He decided to abandon it and go on with the Heine, meantime daily continuing with corrections of proofs now received of his prose collection. He toyed with several titles for this: *Collected Essays*, *Studies of Life and Thought*, *Essays Serious and Fantastic* (or *Fanciful*) and *A Lady of Sorrow with other Essays and Phantasies*. Finally he agreed on the title favoured by Dobell and Reeves – *Essays and Phantasies*.[56] He was invited round for tea once again with Mathilde Blind,[57] and was likewise twice invited to the home of Francis J. Furnivall, editor of what became the Oxford English Dictionary and founder of numerous literary societies. Furnivall sent him a couple of tickets for a performance of *Hamlet*.[58] Still Thomson pursued Foote for money: 'Mr T is in need of the money which Mr F. owes him, & of which part payment was promised a year ago.'[59] Foote in April launched another secularist monthly, the *Freethinker*, and the same month *Essays and Phantasies* appeared. Its 320 pages of text contained nineteen pieces beginning with 'A Lady of Sorrow', which Thomson had completed in 1864. In fact the bulk of the book was material from the *National Reformer* of the 1860s, only the last fifty pages having some samples of work done for the *Secularist* and *Cope's Tobacco Plant* four years previously. That month of publication Thomson again stopped making entries in his diary.[60] Bertram Dobell (who also kept a diary) visited 7 Huntley Street on April 21st and 'found he had again relapsed'; nine days later he noted that Thomson was 'still very queer but I hope recovering'; on May 7th – 'Saw Thomson and was very sorry to find him in a very bad condition'. The following week he 'found him better'.[61]

On June 4th Thomson's hope to return to Leicestershire in the summer was realised. He was away for seven weeks, noting in a retrospective diary entry that he had spent three days with Michael Wright in Leicester, a week with his sons Phil and James in Quorndon, a day in the company of Josiah Gimson, and 'all the other 5½ weeks with the Barrs at Forest Edge, Kirby Muxloe, 4 miles out of Leicester. Unbounded hospitality; splendid holiday.'[62] The Barrs had a lawn for lawn tennis, and much time was spent playing this. 'Home at length from Forest Edge,' Thomson wrote on July 23rd. 'Seven weeks holiday, most of it thoroughly enjoyable. Made fair progress in lawn-tennis. Man could not have kinder hosts.'[63]

On his return he found that F.J. Furnivall, in launching a new Browning Society to meet monthly at University College in Gower Street, had put Thomson down to speak for an hour and a quarter, with half an hour for questions, the following January. Furnivall had taken the absence of a reply from Huntley Street as indicative of Thomson's assent. Though annoyed, Thomson agreed to give a paper for thirty minutes, with no questions to follow.[64] Meanwhile he had to earn some money, and this speedier than a Heine booklet was likely to bring about. He began work daily in the British Museum on Browning's *The Ring and the Book*, and managed to place the resulting essay with the *Gentleman's Magazine*.[65] He decided also to try to utilise the analysis of Shelley texts made in his correspondence with William Rossetti in 1873, specifically Thomson's copious notes on Shelley's lyric drama 'Prometheus Unbound'.[66] The *Athenaeum* accepted these for publication in five instalments, and the first of these duly appeared on September 17th 1881. Thomson was by this time newly back from another visit to George Meredith, a visit he described to his new friend Harriet 'Dick' Barrs in a letter to her at Forest Edge:

Tuesday I spent with George Meredith at Box Hill; a quiet, pleasant day, cloudy but rainless, with some sunshine and blue sky in the afternoon. We had a fine stroll over Mickleham Downs, really parklike, with noble yew-trees and many a mountain-ash (*rowan*, we Scots call it) glowing with thick clusters of red berries, – but you have some at Forest Edge . . . M. read me an unpublished poem of considerable length, which, so far as I can judge by a single hearing (not like reading at one's leisure), is very fine, and ought to be understood even by that laziest and haziest of animals, the general reader. He says that having suspended work on a novel, poems began to spring up in his mind, and I am glad that he thinks of bringing out a new collection.

Jack tells me that he has all of 'Omar Kháyyám', four hundred lines, by heart. Tell him from me that he is a prodigy, and profoundly impresses me with a sense of my own ineptitude. For, as long as I have read 'Omar', I don't think that I could repeat half a dozen verses without book . . .

Friendly regards to all friends there from all friends here. With best wishes, yours truly,

James Thomson[67]

Jack and Harriet Barrs had kept in touch with Thomson since his return to London in July. Jack on a visit to the city went with Thomson and Percy to Parliament to see Bradlaugh once again expelled when attempting to take his seat: and that same evening the trio went to the Hall of Science with Jack's younger brother Harry Hood Barrs, a London solicitor.[68] The latter kept in touch with Thomson after Jack had returned to Kirby Muxloe. Harry called at Thomson's 'latish' on September 1st, and was loaned some Heine on September 10th.[69] A week later Percy and Thomson visited him and they walked about the city 'to & fro until 1.40 am'.[70] Jack Barrs wrote inviting Thomson back to Forest Edge, but Thomson said he needed to stay in London to try somehow to earn some money. His three books had only brought him £25 in more than a year since August 1880, and this had included £5 'on account'.[71] Thomson explained his position in a letter to Julia, telling her at the same time how much he had benefited from his summer break:

I enjoyed myself immensely at Forest Edge, near Leicester, and came back several years younger than I went down. They kept me there and in the neighbourhood seven weeks, and then I could only get away with extreme difficulty, and on a pledge to go again at Christmas; and they began urging me to come down before I was back three weeks, saying that I could get all the books I wanted down there, which was nearly true, and could work there as well as here, which was very far from true, the society and recreations being much too tempting. I have very rarely met with such liberal kindness from old friends, and I have had three or four as good as a man could wish; and the Leicester people knew very little of me personally, welcoming me for the sake of my beautiful and pious books and articles.

These books have brought me a little money directly, which I had scarcely hoped for, as two of them are in verse and all three of them are full of the most unpopular heresies. What I did hope for they now seem about bringing me; that is, enough reputation to secure work which was denied to the mere anonymous heterodox journalist. We shall soon see.[72]

On September 18th Michael Wright, commissioner of Thomson's Leicester Secular Hall poem, died at his home after a lingering illness. Thomson did not attend the funeral, and explained why to Jack Barrs: 'The simple fact was that I could not afford to come . . . I am in deep tribulation owing much more at home than I ever owed before, and with my poor landlord depending on me for about £15 to meet his rent by next Monday – I am not entitled to any further advance on a/c from the Publishers . . . Foote is making some money, and owes me £20; but of course I get nothing but promises from that skunk.' Four days later he wrote acknowledging receipt of a cheque for £15, telling Jack that landlord Mr Gibson and housekeeper Miss Scott would be relieved.[73] He wrote to George Meredith reminding him that he had promised to put in a word for Thomson with John Morley, editor of the *Fortnightly Review* and the *Pall Mall Gazette*[74] – and the same John Morley whose editorship of the *English Men of Letters* series Thomson had severely criticised. A letter of introduction was sent, and on October 21st Morley told Thomson he would accept verses, reviews and articles for both magazines so long as Thomson could 'hit their tone'.[75] 'If I get on well with this connexion I shall probably be inspired to set about versifying again,' Thomson wrote to Dobell.[76] He gave Morley the 1859 poem 'The Deliverer' and handed in two reviews, of Ingelow's *Don John* and Mead's *Philosophy of Carlyle*.[77]

He tried unsuccessfully to borrow £6 from Harry Barrs, and his request for a similar amount was refused by Theodore Wright in Gower Street and Josiah Gimson in Leicester.[78] Gimson apologised, saying he would have done so 'with pleasure' had he been able.[79] Reeves came up with another £10 in October, and Thomson ordered a new pair of trousers from a tailors, to be ready at the end of the month. He went to the inaugural meeting of the Browning Society at University College on October 28th[80] then on October 29th he asked Harry Hood Barrs to instigate proceedings against Foote for £20 7s. 10d., this including £5 17s. 9d. claimed as still outstanding for contributions to the *Secularist*.[81]

He began work on a completely new poem for John Morley using notes made ten years before when working on 'The City of Dreadful Night'. The poem, 'A Voice from the Nile' was the song sung by the Nile on its progress to the sea, and the notes – from the *Encyclopaedia Britannica* and elsewhere – detailed the record of civilisations present and past to be found on the Nile's banks: the temple at Säis, the pyramids, the city of Memphis. There was a description of the statue of Ozymandias, and of the Sphinx:

> Ozymandias – seven foot cubits: 'I am Ozymandias, King of Kings; if any one desire to know what a prince I am, & where I lie, let him read my exploits.'
> Sphinx: head & neck 27 feet high, breast 33 feet broad, entire length about 130 feet, paws 50 feet in front. Red paint tablet & altar. Fragments of an enormous head resting underneath chin. Human female, leonine male.[82]

But the poem was not completed in London, for Thomson finally agreed to Jack Barrs's persistent requests that he return to join Jack and his sister at Forest Edge. So in November 1881 Thomson found himself once again resident guest in a domestic setting in the country.

CHAPTER NINETEEN

STONE ON STONE

a
sequence with introduction and key
from the diaries 1877 – 1881 of James Thomson

based on
a computer-generated random number sequence
and providing 100 written entries from the period

———

TO THE READER: This chapter appears at this point as a necessary part of the underlying structural argument of the book.

It does not need to be fully digested on first encounter, and the reader may prefer after a short read, to progress to Chapter Twenty, p. 281, seeing STONE ON STONE as a place to return to at leisure and as interest commands.

INCLUDING THE DAY he was born and the day that he died, James Thomson lived for 17,360 days. He kept two notebook diaries (one for business, one personal) while in America in 1872, and a notebook diary while in Spain in 1873. After this he maintained each year a commercial pocket diary, and these have survived for the years 1874 to 1881, with the exception of 1875 which is missing. The commercial diaries, which end with the entry for October 29th 1881, have frequent blanks, sometimes for days, sometimes for months at a time. Between January 1st 1877 and October 29th 1881 the ratio of written entries to blanks is as follows:

Year	Entries	Blanks
1877	213	152
1878	236	129
1879	200	165
1880	152	214
1881	161	141

The reader can have a general understanding of what follows if it is simply borne in mind that most entries make references to an essay, article or review in hand, or the books being read for such. The work is in most cases for Cope's Tobacco Plant, which Thomson abbreviated as T.P.

Again, throughout the period Thomson's landlord was Mr Gibson (Mr G.), his housekeeper was Miss Scott (Miss S.); and his most frequent companions were the Wrights of Gower Street (T.R.W. and Mrs W.) with Percy, Adeline, and Foote (G.W.F.). When not working at home in 7 Huntley Street he worked in the British Museum (B.M.).

As for the footnotes, if followed, not every reference is given. Where mention of a work recurs, for example the 13-part 'Tobacco Legislation in the Three Kingdoms', it retains the same number as

255

first given it. Punctuation varies, and sometimes titles of books are not underlined.

The first diary entry describes the occasion of Thomson's handing the publisher Reeves the manuscript for the second collection, Vane's Story.

Adeline	Adeline Holyoake	M.W.	Michael Wright (of
Annie	Mr Gibson's daughter		Leicester)
Athnm.	The Athenaeum	N.R.	National Reformer
Brawn	Printer	S.R.& S.	Secular Review &
B.M.	British Museum		Secularist
B.S.	British Secular	T.P.	Cope's Tobacco Plant
	(Almanack)	Parris	Lawyer used by
C.B.	Charles Bradlaugh		Bradlaugh
Clifford	Professor Clifford	Percy	Percy Holyoake
C.M.	Clara Mitchell	Miss S	Sarah Scott,
C.W.	Charles Watts		housekeeper at Huntley
Fraser	Cope's Tobacco Plant		St
	editor	S.R.T.	Smoke Room Table
Mr G.	Mr Gibson, landlord		(Review part of Cope's)
G.W.F.	George William Foote	W.L.Sugden	Secularist, architect of
Wm. H.	William Holyoake		Leicester Hall
	(Austin's brother)	T.R.W.	Theodore Rich Wright
Hatton	Cope's London agent	Whittle	printer
Hawkes	fellow lodger in Huntley	The W.s	The Wrights of 12
	Street		Gower Street
Mr Klein	Violinist	Mrs W.	Jane Alice Wright
lr(e)s.	letters	W.M.R.	William Michael
			Rossetti

TUESDAY AUGUST 17th 1880

Still glorious weather. To Reeves, with Dobell. Dr. Kaines, jolly. Handed him Vane's Story, Weddah, Two Lovers, to begin, & 17 minor poems to end vol. He, <u>unrequested</u>, handed me £10 on a/c.

(*Facing page*) Tuesday 17.8.80: Handed Mr Reeves Vane's Story, Weddah & Two Lovers to begin, with 17 minor poems to end a second vol. When gap can be estimated will send pieces of intermediate length to fill up. Vol to be same size as first; 184 pp. text, with 8 for title pp., dedic^n (Shelley) & contents.

R., <u>unasked</u>, handed me cheque for £10 on a/c of first vol., which he reckons has already paid its expenses, & of whose profitable success both he & D. feel sure. <u>N.B.</u> Other publishers all firm that <u>no</u> vol. of verse, however good, can now pay its expenses, unless bearing one of three or four famous or popular names. Yet this vol. by an unknown writer, burdened with the heavy dead weight of the sombre & atheistical & generally incomprehensible City of Dreadful Night, has paid its expenses.

Pall Mall, Academy, Fortnightly, Westminster. Not even Lit^y World, younger sister X^n World, raves against the Atheism in these days!

MONDAY JUNE 11th 1877

Hot but cloudy. Morning & Evg. Ben Johnson VII.[1] Thunder, or rather lightning shower, in evening. Raining a good deal at night – Usual summer – three hot days & a thunderstorm.

TUESDAY JANUARY 2nd 1877

Evening: Children's & Adult's Party at Cleveland Hall. Xmas tree, tea, &c. Wrights, Trousselles, Bostons, Gilliames, Hember &c. Home about 2.30 a.m.

x G.W.F. told me of his engagement (Sunday night).

WEDNESDAY JANUARY 14th 1880

Dull, cold, dry. Morng. Up late – Stupid. Readng. Steinmatz on tob^o.[2] Aftn. (& bfe dinner) Stroll. Evg. Readg. Dobell's Tob^o pamphlets & the vol of reviews (miscellaneous). Coals (1) – [Curry at home].

TUESDAY MARCH 29th 1881

Glorious day – Cold N.E. out of sun. (Miss S. out before dinner for once). Morng. up late. Opinion proofs not come.[3] Note from Mr Reeves: F.J. Furnivall &c. Answd (See his envelope). Wrote Mr. F. 5.30 tomorrow. Aftn. Stroll. Orchard St &c. Left leaves for Percy. Evng. Notices prose vol. to Atheneum & Acady . . . (nearly same). Coals (part Mr. G rest Annie – Sunday) Dinner & tea out.

---

[1]'Ben Jonson', Nov. '76–Dec. '77. T.P.
[2]Steinmatz: *Tobacco, its History Culture Manufacture and Adulteration*, 1857 or *The Smoker's Guide, Philosopher and Friend*, 1877.
[3]Press opinions of *Vane's Story* to be bound with *Essays and Phantasies*.

SATURDAY OCTOBER 25th 1879

Fine day; rather cooler. Morng. B.M. (till 2.30 from 10) Tob⁰ Legisl^n
VI.[4] After dinner stroll. Evg. Gower St. Mrs W. much better, but not
down stairs. Looking at proof Strange Book III[5] &c.

THURSDAY JANUARY 24th 1878: [Blank]

SATURDAY MAY 3rd 1879: [Blank]

SUNDAY MARCH 24th 1878

Sharp northerly dust. squall aftn. Shedding some keen dry snow.
Walk morng. & aftn. Paid papers to date (Discontinued Daily News).

SUNDAY FEBRUARY 13th 1881

Dull but no rain till night. Morng. With Percy to beyond Marble
Arch. Evg. They all to S. Place concert, I home, finished Leicester
draft Address[6] (50 lines); Bed 1.30.

TUESDAY MAY 13th 1879: [Blank]

MONDAY MARCH 19th 1877: [Blank]

THURSDAY FEBRUARY 11th 1880: [Blank]

TUESDAY MAY 21st 1878

Sharp thundershower aftn. Morng. B.M. Hogg.[7] Reading. Aftn. Chat
& doze. x Evg. Began Leopardi Trans.[8] fair copy. Still rather bilious.

---

[4]'Tobacco Legislation in the Three Kingdoms', T.P. March '79 – Nov. '80.
[5]'A Strange Book' – Garth Wilkinson's *Improvisations from the Spirit Liberal* Sep.
– Dec. '79.
[6]Poem: 'Address on the Opening of the New Hall of Leicester Secular Society'.
[7]'James Hogg, The Ettrick Shepherd', rev. of *Works* ed. Rev. T. Thomson, 2 vols.
1865–66. T.P. Aug. – Oct. '79.
[8]Thomson had been dating translations (unpublished) of Leopardi until Nov. '77.
(See n. 25 chap. 11).

TUESDAY OCTOBER 14th 1879: [Blank]

MONDAY AUGUST 23rd 1880

Morng. B.M. Carducci.[9] Aftn. Stroll, Oxford St &c. Evg. Notes from Heine & Carducci, with After Mentana & note to Ballantyne, Hanson & Co. for early estimate no. of pages required.[10] (Fish, capital, supper).

10.30 p.m. Moon shining in broken steadfast field of white cloud; splendid planet in pale blue lake a dozen feet below it; the south an open pale blue sea; zenith & all northward vast dark cloud with rifts & lakes of deep dark blue.

TUESDAY SEPTEMBER 20th 1881

Miss S. out. President Garfield died last night. Morng. B.M. Finished Ring & Book notes. Aftn. Stroll. Evng. Revised R^g & B^k for <u>Gentleman's Magazine</u>.[11] Revised & posted Part II proof Shelley.[12] <u>Ath^m</u>. <u>Dinner & tea out</u>. (G.W.F.)

FRIDAY APRIL 13th 1877

Dullish & mild. Wet evg. X Wrote G.W.F. paper. C.B. Watts A/cs. <u>Mudie</u>. After tea A/cs with Miss Scott till Monday last. Evng. reading <u>Epictetus</u>[13] & noting. <u>Academy</u> & weekly ed^n <u>Times</u>.

TUESDAY NOVEMBER 11th 1879

Murky – got colder – drizzle evg. Morng. B.M. Finished extracts <u>Egoist</u> II.[14] Aftn. Adeline, French: Took back <u>Egoist</u> II. Took also <u>T.P.</u> for Novr. Evg. Writing Fraser, &c.

SATURDAY JUNE 7th 1879: [Blank]

[9]Thomson read Carducci (1836–1907) without publishing criticism or translation.
[10]For *Vane's Story*.
[11]Browning's 'The Ring and the Book', *Gentleman's Magazine*, Dec. '81.
[12]'Notes on the Structure of Shelley's "Prometheus Unbound" ', *Athenaeum* 17 Sep.–19 Nov. '81
[13]'The Discourses of Epictetus' (trans. G. Long) S., 14 Apr. – 12 May '77. Also reviewed T.P., April '77.
[14]'George Meredith's New Work: *The Egoist*', T.P., Jan. '80. 3 vols.

TUESDAY JUNE 19th 1877

Still fine, with fresh breeze. Renewed ticket B. Museum. From 11.30 to 5.20 Elliot Stock's reprints: Bunyan, Herbert, Milton, Walton. Posted at 5.25, with note, to Fraser. Walked evg. after dinner. No tea.

WEDNESDAY AUGUST 13th 1879

Clouds wool-white morng; iron-grey aftn. Perhaps storm coming. Rain at night; no storm. Morng. B.M. Improvis^{ns5} (Jowett's <u>Plato</u> &c.) Aftn. Stroll Oxford St. Evg. Improvis^{ns} (Referring to <u>Dante</u> & vol. itself).

SUNDAY OCTOBER 10th 1880

Engagement Mr Reeves, Sunday at one. Very wet – Could not venture to Mr Reeves'. Dawdled a good deal; but revised ag^n Opinions of the Press on 1st Vol. for fly-leaf end of 2nd, wrote Printer with them, wrote also announcements 2nd Ath^m & Acady.

SATURDAY MARCH 24th 1877: [Blank]

SATURDAY SEPTEMBER 20th 1879: [Blank]

WEDNESDAY JUNE 25th 1879

Heavy rain morning – one or two slight showers later. Morng. B.M. Tob^o Legisl^{n4} – Index Statutes Realm. Evg. <u>Men of Letters</u> Readg. Defoe [15] again more carefully.

MONDAY JANUARY 28th 1878: [Blank]

FRIDAY DECEMBER 13th 1878

Very fine. Cold. Fog evg. Morng. Walk with G.W.F. Marble Arch, Regent St. Aftn. Adeline (French) then (4.30 – 6.30) W.M.R.'s – Mrs Garnett, Mrs Petruzzi, Moore (?) Carmichael (<u>Secularist</u>, &c.), O'Shaugnessy, Payn, Dr Todhunter, G.W.F.

---

[15]William Minto's *Defoe*, T.P., Aug. '79.

THURSDAY JANUARY 20th 1881

Bright cold day, but little wind. Pleasant out. Morng. Up late again. B.M. for short while. Aftn. Called on Marston for a walk, he engaged for Canonbury. Strolled, then Gower St. Evg. Finished Silas Marner. Then looking at Adam Bede.[16]

WEDNESDAY SEPTEMBER 14th 1881

Fine day. Proof from Ath^m of 1st part Notes on Shelley's Prometheus Unbound.[12] Returned corrected. Asked for ms. with proof in future. Posted part II to Editor – Note as to ms. with proof. Posted to Meredith leaves on Stigand & Heine[17] – aftn. Sent him note evg.

THURSDAY DECEMBER 6th 1877: [Blank]

SUNDAY JANUARY 7th 1877

Dined Gower St. Short stroll in evg.

TUESDAY MAY 1st 1877

Cool – cloudy – shifting wind. Morng. Epictetus IV (long).[13] Aftn. Adeline – Clara – Miss Bolingbroke. Evg. Trousselle called after tea – Home with him – Books – Lessing, Emilia, Musical – Lee & Mad Cooper – Home by eleven. Drank much beer. Note from G.W.F.

THURSDAY MAY 3rd 1877: [Blank]

FRIDAY AUGUST 10th 1877

Stupid note from Watts. Answ^d sharply. Show card[18] & paper from Fraser. Acknowlegd. Will do what I can.

---

[16]Reading for projected George Eliot booklet.
[17]'Heinrich Heine' (response to Stigand's *Heine*) S., 8 Jan. – 12 Feb. '76; also T.P., April '76.
[18]A new 'Seaside' Cope's Card; required description sent to Fraser 3 days later. Cope's annual cards issued to subscribers with prose essay and droll captions to a cartoon, often of literary allusion.

SUNDAY APRIL 15th 1877

Dry, cloudy, cool. Walked before dinner & afternoon. Evg. Eastern Crisis[19] for Watts. (5½ narrow fos.)

THURSDAY JULY 24th 1879: [Blank]

THURSDAY JUNE 7th 1877: [Blank]

TUESDAY JULY 1st 1879

Heavy rain with gale almost incessant till 4 p.m. Brief clear up, then shower, then clear. At 9 (dusk) great haggard rack to N. sweeping from W. across very pale blue skimmed milk sky, & beneath it the brick-dust yellow rift ominous of storm. 1st of July & no summer yet! Morng. finished Defoe;[15] read again end Burns.[20] Evg. Began Legisl[n] IV.[4] Reading Lavengro &c.[21] Aftn. Dawdled – couldn't get out.

TUESDAY SEPTEMBER 16th 1879: [Blank]

WEDNESDAY SEPTEMBER 20th 1879: [Blank]

FRIDAY FEBRUARY 19th 1880: [Blank]

MONDAY AUGUST 29th 1881: [Blank]

SATURDAY FEBRUARY 27th 1880: [Blank]

MONDAY JANUARY 1st 1877

Always very wet & mild. Floods. Heavy storm of wind & rain in morning. Dined W.M. Rossetti's (7). He & wife, Madox Brown & wife, F. Hueffer & wife, Miss Blind, Mrs Petruzzi, Wallis, Theophile Marzials.

Madox Brown's drawing of Mrs. R & baby. Home after one.

MONDAY APRIL 18th 1881: [Blank]

FRIDAY JUNE 6th 1879: [Blank]

[19]'The Eastern Crisis' S.R., 22 Apr. '77.
[20]'Principal Shairp's *Robert Burns*', T.P., Sep. '79.
[21]Thomson read and reread works of George Borrow without writing about him.

TUESDAY MARCH 26th 1878

Cold. Morng. B.M. Vols <u>Athenaeum</u> 1877. Aftn. Walk with G.W.F. Evg. Langham Hall. G.W.F's 2nd Reading. Rossettis & Madox Brown. Chat with W.M.R. on Shelley matters.

FRIDAY JULY 18th 1879: [Blank]

SATURDAY AUGUST 10th 1878: [Blank]

TUESDAY FEBRUARY 23rd 1880: [Blank]

FRIDAY FEBRUARY 7th 1879

Mild, dull, wet. Gleam (watery) of sun & sky in aftn. Some wind – smoke. Morng. & evng. Reading for <u>Tobacco Legisl^n</u>.[4] Aftn. Stroll to Strand. Lre from G.W.F. Advt. <u>Heine</u> article still in <u>Secr. Rev^w</u>.[22] (The fellow advt^d me falsely as contributing to <u>B.S. Almanack</u>.)

TUESDAY AUGUST 21st 1877

Fine, with short showers & very black masses of sailing cloud fold beyond fold. Morng. B.M. Reading <u>Noctes</u>.[23] Aftn. Longish walk. Evg. Copy^g from G. Meredith's poems. Heavy rain at night & early morning.

TUESDAY MAY 27th 1879: [Blank]

THURSDAY JUNE 28th 1877

Fine. Morning – to City – tobacco. Noon to 4. B. Museum – H.H. Furness's <u>Variorum Shakespeare</u> Vols I & II.[24] Posted notice to Fraser with letter. Evg. to Trousselle's by appoint^{mt}. He at Art Social Union. Chat with Mrs T.

TUESDAY NOVEMBER 13th 1877

Fine, cold. Damp underfoot. Morng. B.M. <u>Noctes</u>. Finishg. Wilson's

---

[22]Article not supplied from Thomson.
[23]'John Wilson and the *Noctes Ambrosianae*', T.P., Apr. '78; May '79.
[24]*Romeo and Juliet*; *Macbeth* (Philadelphia 71, 73) T.P., Sep. '77.

Memoir. Aftn. Walk with G.W.F. (Clifford's Friday, if fine). Evg. Leopardi – draft trans.[8] Reading Holcroft's Memoirs.[25]

THURSDAY FEBRUARY 21st 1878: [Blank]

WEDNESDAY APRIL 20th 1881: [Blank]

SATURDAY NOVEMBER 16th 1878

Fine day. Morng. B.M. till 2.15. Extracts Seven Sisters. Wrote Maccall & G.W.F. Posted back revised proof Social Notes[26] recd. this morng. Aftn. Stroll – first since Monday. Evg. Ring & Book (Count Guido Franceschini, again.)[11]

MONDAY MAY 3rd 1880: [Blank]

THURSDAY MAY 23rd 1878

Cloudy & cool. Aftn. sun. Morng. B.M. Reading Hogg.[7] Aftn. Walk G.W.F. (Waldstein. Browng. burlesque, Inigo Long at Lewes') Evg. Lazy readg. x Athenaeum. Barbera of Florence to bring out supplement to Le Mounier's Leopardi, Correspondence & early writings –

MONDAY NOVEMBER 1st 1880: [Blank]

WEDNESDAY MAY 2nd 1877

Cool & cloudy. x Tobacco Plants – Only about half of Ben Jonson VI[1] in. x C.B. v C.W. Lre & particulars claim from Mr. R. Thomas. x called on Watts. Answd Solrs lre in writing in full – 3 to 6 – Wrote G.W.F. (thanks & no promise on Sunday) Posted Epictetus[13] to Brawn.

TUESDAY OCTOBER 9th 1877: [Blank]

WEDNESDAY APRIL 17th 1878

Showers. Thunderstorm with heavy hail & rain aftn. Forked lightning. Cold still on me: brains running away in phlegm. Aftn. Walk. Evg. Ordeal of Richard Feverel.[27]

[25]Thomas Holcroft's *Memoirs* (3 vols) ed. Hazlitt, 1816.
[26]'Social Notes on Tobacco', T.P., Jan. '79.
[27]'An Old New Book': Meredith's *Ordeal of Richard Feverel*, T.P., May '79.

WEDNESDAY JULY 10th 1878

Cloudy – cooler. Morng. & Evg. Blue Book for No. VII. (Conclusion).
Aftn. Gower St. Adeline, <u>Lohengrin</u> – C.M.

SUNDAY MARCH 23rd 1879: [Blank]

FRIDAY AUGUST 12th 1881: [Blank]

THURSDAY FEBRUARY 20th 1879

Fair cool morng. Livid snow storm aftn. Held up evg. & night.
Morng. & Aftn. (till dark with storm, 3.30) B.M. <u>English Men of
Letters</u> for Fraser: reading <u>Gibbon</u>[28] & writing. C.M. Gower St. (Mrs
W. & Adeline in vain last night; ball this evg.) – Met Adeline & Edith
twice in strolling. <u>Carmen</u> at Her Majesty's – Gallery stalls 1/6 – Home
about 12; Bed before one.

THURSDAY APRIL 14th 1881: [Blank]

SATURDAY FEBRUARY 20th 1880: [Blank]

TUESDAY APRIL 1st 1879: [Blank]

SATURDAY OCTOBER 11th 1879: [Blank]

MONDAY JUNE 25th 1877

Morning reading. Aftn. Dozing. Eveng. About to write when Trousselle
came in (top heavy) & dragged me out to billiards – Saw him to tram-car
– Then walked. Bed about 2.

WEDNESDAY MARCH 26th 1879: [Blank]

THURSDAY DECEMBER 25th 1879

Black fog midday; & until night. Morng. (late) Answg. Fraser's, with
receipt. T.R.W. & Percy went to Wm H's! Dined Gower St. Only Mrs
Gilder besides. Billiards &c. evg. Home 12.20 or so. Bed past one. All
up. <u>Dinner & tea out.</u>

[28]'JC Morrison's *Gibbon*', T.P., June '79.

(*Facing page*) Note from Fraser: P.O.O. £7.15/- for Decr. TP (Legisl^{n4} & Mixture[29]; Box of cigars for Xmas smoke; Art essay all right[30] – hope to send cash soon. Answd with formal receipt & thanks: cigars not yet to hand, probably tomorrow; returned yesterday revised proofs Egoist,[14] Mixture,[29] Figaro,[31] – two lines added in first & alter^n as to Peacock. Receipt dated 27th where P.O.O. paid.

FRIDAY JUNE 29th 1879

Reading and sorting lres &c. x Evg. at Gower St. Chat with T.R.W. as to G.W.F., & Watts, &c.

MONDAY SEPTEMBER 27th 1880: [Blank]

SUNDAY JULY 22nd 1877: [Blank]

WEDNESDAY FEBRUARY 13th 1878: [Blank]

SATURDAY JUNE 30th 1879

Reading &c. Proof Flaubert I.[32] 'Watts will write on business next Tuesday.' Posted back proof corrected. Sorting letters & old papers.

SUNDAY MARCH 18th 1877: [Blank]

SATURDAY NOVEMBER 15th 1879

Fine & cold. Castor oil in morng.; kept in. Morng. Evg. Cope's Mixture.[29] Coals (2) Saty night & Sunday – No dinner.

THURSDAY MARCH 3rd 1881

Heard Big Ben last night & morng. – S.E. by E. No rain – but very cold wind & murky day. Morng. Note to Lead with 3 more corrections Address.[6] Note from M.W. as to train &c. Aftn. To Mrs W. She writes

---

[29]'Cope's Mixture', T.P., Dec. '79 – May '80.
[30]Fraser had written the day before asking Thomson to do a quick 'redaction' of a paper 'Educational Uses of Art' to be given somewhere by an unnamed friend. Thomson sent paper retitled 'Art as a General Educator'.
[31]About 400 words in defence of editor of *Figaro* jailed for libel, T.P. Jan. '80.
[32]Flaubert's *Trois Contes*, S.R. & S., 7 July, 21 July '77.

5 o'c. train Saty. & rehearsal tomorrow aftn. Evng. Sorting papers &c. <u>Dinner & tea out.</u>

MONDAY MARCH 24th 1879: [Blank]

WEDNESDAY NOVEMBER 19th 1879

Dull morng. Fine day, but colder; clear young moon. Morng. B.M. Correctg. Proof <u>Spenser</u>[33] as cut down, & cancelling 8 more lines. Writing Fraser &c. Aftn. & Evg. Making up parcels (3) books to return to Fraser. Reading <u>Egoist</u> III[14] again.

WEDNESDAY MAY 1st 1878

Warm wet morning. Sun aftn. Some thunder & lightning evg. Morng. Blue Book II.[4] Aftn. & Evg. Clearing out old papers.

MONDAY JANUARY 3rd 1881

Dull coldish morng.; fair aftn. Morng. B.M. Legislation.[4] T.R.W. came. Aftn. Short stroll. Miss S. not home from brother's till evg. Evg. Reading papers &c. too sleepy for work. <u>Dinner & tea out.</u> <u>Bought fish for supper.</u>

SATURDAY DECEMBER 15th 1877: [Blank]

MONDAY JANUARY 27th 1879

Glum & raw. Very bilious with diarrhoea. (passing blood). Quite unable to work. Reading 'Shirley'[34] again. Lre from G.W.F. (<u>Liberal</u>) Answd. already.

SATURDAY AUGUST 30th 1879

Fine day, eveng. & night. Cloudy sky, splendid ¾ moon with (Jupiter?) breadth Alfred Place behind it. Morng. B.M. Strange Book III. (till 2.30) – Aftn. Stroll. Got Morley's Burke.[35] Evg. Dawdled. Burke, <u>Lavengro</u>[21] (again). <u>Dinner & tea out.</u>

[33]R.W. Church's *Spenser*, T.P., Jan. '80.
[34]Thomson also copied out 2 sections of Charlotte Bronte's *Villette* (Ms. Don. e.45).
[35]John Morley's *Burke*, T.P., June '80.

FRIDAY MARCH 23rd 1877: [Blank]

FRIDAY MAY 28th 1880: [Blank]

SUNDAY FEBRUARY 23rd 1879

Snow morng. & aftn. No walk. Gower St. Billiards after tea. Sunday Social (Mr Klein) Mead at South Place, Mild sloppy night.

WEDNESDAY JANUARY 16th 1878: [Blank]

MONDAY OCTOBER 15th 1877: [Blank]

TUESDAY JUNE 18th 1878

Dull morg. & evg. Lightning at dark without thunder or rain. Morng. & Evg. Blue Book V.[4] Aftn. Paper & doze. Very bilious.

WEDNESDAY JANUARY 27th 1880: [Blank]

MONDAY NOVEMBER 17th 1879

Dull, moist, mild. (Better today – not quite settled) Morng. B.M. Adding to Mixture[29] & note to Fraser, having recd. from two more scraps & lre by first post. Aftn. Stroll. Got 5 Men of Letters. Evg. Resumed writing Egoist[15] (till past ten) Moisture that seems rather exuded from stones than fallen from the clouds. Dinner & tea out.

TUESDAY OCTOBER 1st 1878

Dull. Soft rain. Morng. & Evg. Rich[d] Feverel[27] (Finished – *16* ruled fos). Posted to Fraser, with note as to Meredith, & cutting down, if needful, this & B.B. VII. Aftn. Stroll. B.M. closed 1st – 7th. Evg. Reading Feverel.

SATURDAY JANUARY 10th 1880

Dull, coldish, some drizzle. Posted T.P.'s in morning. One to Julia, & also last May number with article on Richard Feverel.[27] Morng. B.M. (10.30 to 3) Finished Legisl[n] VIII.[4] (15 + fos) & began Legisl[n] IX.[4] (Many in aftn. wanting seats.) Stroll at dusk; greasy or sloppy. Evg. Pottering & reading a bit. Dinner & tea out.

THURSDAY JANUARY 23rd 1879

Bitter east wind. Whirlwinds of dust from East, South & North along Oxford St. Morng. B.M. Began writing Huxley on Hume.[36] C.M. Criterion next week; Adeline, & Mrs W. if well. Aftn. Walk. Evg. Huxley on Hume (Posted first 9 fos. to C.W. 'Rest tomorrow if time. Foote had no right to advertise it!') Address for proof. Dinner & tea out.

TUESDAY NOVEMBER 25th 1879

Dull, damp; glimpse red sun aftn. Some rain or sleet evg. Morng. B.M. Ruskin's Oxford Lectures & Modern Painters.[30] Aftn. Adeline (French). Took back Egoist III.[14] Left Shelley[37] & Burke.[35] Evg. Ruskin's lectures.

SUNDAY JULY 27th 1879: [Blank]

SATURDAY DECEMBER 6th 1879

Not much snow; not so cold; bright; some thaw; little wind, but northerly. Morng. B.M. Readg. for Raleigh. Aftn. Stroll. Evg. Finished S.R.T. Thackeray[38] (9 ruled note fos. 75–83).

Saty. night. Lre from G.W.F. in answer to mine of Thursday. Will make it his first aim to pay off indebtedness to me. My language gratuitously insulting; will not submit his conscience to my castigation; &c. Not worth answering. Coals (2) Dinner & tea out.

FRIDAY APRIL 5th 1878

Some showers – thunder – cool. Morng. B.M. Ingram's Poe. Aftn. Walk. Evg. W.M.R. Shelley memoir[39] – Poetaster (finished) Card from W.M.R. – will forward Shelley notes.[12]

[36]T.H. Huxley's *Hume*, T.P., June '79.
[37]J.A. Symond's *Shelley*, T.P., Feb. '80.
[38]Trollope's *Thackeray*, T.P., July '80.
[39]Shelley, *Poetical Works*, ed. W.M. Rossetti, T.P., April '78.

TUESDAY JANUARY 4th 1881

Dull & cool – no rain – crescent moon. Morng. B.M. Legisl[n].[4] T.R.W. ag[n], Karl Marx 'Capital'.[40] Aftn. Bit of a stroll. Evg. Copying out five sonnets for Miss Blind's friend Mr Hall;[41] reservg. copyright of one not hitherto published. Coals (1).

WEDNESDAY MAY 11th 1881: [Blank]

MONDAY AUGUST 30th 1880: [Blank]

WEDNESDAY MARCH 17th 1879: [Blank]

TUESDAY MARCH 25th 1879: [Blank]

TUESDAY OCTOBER 23rd 1877

et & mild. Up soon after 8 (good sleep at last) Morng. Trans[n] (draft) Leopardi.[8] Addressed T.P.'s for Octr. & Posted. Aftn. Pottering about. Evg. Looking thro' mss. Progress, Leopardi, &c.

SUNDAY DECEMBER 21st 1879

Cold, dull; thaw eveng. Serpentine with Percy. Evg. Billiards with Adeline.

WEDNESDAY MARCH 7th 1877

Cold, Slight snow. Sunshine. Heavier snow midday. Letter from Fraser. Programme &c first rate. Name price.[42] Wrote Fraser. Kept draft with his note. Wrote Dobell. Note from W.L. Sugden. Black suit from Moses (4 & 42) £4. 10/-

SUNDAY APRIL 18th 1880

Splendid day – Park & Gardens lovely. Morng. Kensington Gardens & Hyde Park with Percy. Aftn. To site of Holborn fire &c. Evg. Home at nine. The Ws. billiards.

---

[40]Thomson made no published comment. But see note 21 chap. 18.
[41]'. . . friend also of Madox Brown and Rossetti, Casine Hall'. To Dobell, 10 Mar. '82.
[42]This 'programme' took 13 days' work and was posted on March 5th. No trace in T.P.

SATURDAY SEPTEMBER 14th 1878

Fine. Morng. City for tobacco – walked. Aftn. Late dinner; short doze. Evg. Finished Blue Book VII.[4] (34 ruled note folios!) Wrote Fraser about cutting down Richard Feverel.[27]

MONDAY OCTOBER 20th 1877

Morning B.M. Only writing letters. (Electric lamps) Aftn. Short stroll. Posted T.P.s for Octr. Evg. Writing Julia.

WEDNESDAY AUGUST 25th 1880

Dull all day; no rain after early morng. about six. Dobell called; I at B.M. Morng. B.M. Carducci[9] – Very drowsy (awoke early) Took to Edinburgh Review 1879: The Mirabeaus. Campanella. & True Story of the Cenci. Aftn. Thought rain coming on; dozed. Eveng. Ranieri: Sodalizio –

(*Facing page*) Wedy. Edinburgh Rev April, '79 – True Story of the Cenci, after Signor A. Bertolletti. Beatrice, by baptismal certificate, 22 years 7 mos. old when executed. Case, as summarised in Review does not seem to me absolutely conclusive as to her alleged son; tho' certainly the presumptive evidence appears very strong. The famous picture in the Barberini Palace decidedly not her portrait; but pretty surely by Guido Reni, & of a favourite model of his, as same head & face are in two other specified pictures by him in Rome.

TUESDAY DECEMBER 21st 1880

Fine cold day. Morng. B.M. Began Legisl[n] XIV.[4] Aftn. Doze. Evg. Began Whitman VI.[43] (6 fos.) x Percy called evg. I must spend Xmas & following day with them.

THURSDAY JUNE 6th 1878

Warm – fairly fine. Whitewashing & papering my room. Morng. Strolled. Aftn. Chat G.W.F. & doze. Evg. Dobells (Don't remember G.W.F. sending stamps for Rhoda Fleming.[44] G.W.F. says he sent.) Slept so-so on sofa front parlour.

[43]'Walt Whitman', T.P., May – Dec. '80.
[44]Meredith novel of 1865.

271

WEDNESDAY FEBRUARY 23rd 1881

Light snow all day; murky; cold; milder night, heavier snow. Morng. Dobell called: two hrs' chat. Aftn. Doze. Morng & Evg. Revised proofs pages 113–144 (first 3pp of Indolence)[45] Wrote to Leicester for proofs & copy.[6] Coals (2) Tea out.

SATURDAY MARCH 20th 1880

Cold foggy morng. Boat race put off till Monday. Cold E. bright day. x Mr Harper died quietly at 11.32 a.m. x Morng. B.M. Finished Legisl^n 9 & began 10.[4] Aftern. came rest of proofs from Edinbro'.[46] Aftn. walk with Percy Rotten Row (nearly empty) Evg. Correcting proofs, to post tomorrow.

(*Facing page*) Saty. 20.3.80 At 3 p.m. came last proofs from Edinbro'; but only 184 pp. text, instead of 192 as I directed exclusive of title-pages, Dedicn & Contents, with which they make up 192. Corrected in the evg. to post tomorrow. Lre from Dobell with a few Prosp^s (his name on) x 1000 to be printed; 50 large paper copies. Scribbled him note: All proofs now to hand. May call tomorrow eveng. Can't promise.

MONDAY AUGUST 9th 1880: [Blank]

THURSDAY OCTOBER 11th 1877: [Blank]

SATURDAY JANUARY 1st 1881

Dull & rather cold. Morng. Waited till 11.15 for Dobell – then B.M. merely dawdling over Athnm. &c. Aftn. Shoes & head.[47] Evg. Cutting out notices George Eliot[48] & critiques on my 2nd Vol. Grant called late. Mrs G. ill again. Gave him 2nd vol. Dinner & tea out.

THURSDAY FEBRUARY 25th 1880: [Blank]

SUNDAY NOVEMBER 16th 1879

Cold & mirk. More castor-oil – in all day. Percy morng. Evg. Finished Cope's Mixture[29] (11 ruled note fos.) Post with note tomorrow. Also note to Whittle for proof.

---

[45]'In Praise of Indolence' for *Essays and Phantasies*.
[46]*The City of Dreadful Night, and other poems*.
[47]Diary 9 April '81: 'Evg. Usual headwashing & shoe cleaning.'
[48] Obituaries.

SUNDAY DECEMBER 29th 1878

Fine mild morng – wet eveng. Stroll with T.R.W. & Adeline. Dined Gower St. Billiards after tea; Prutz. Hoyac. G.W.F. Adeline & self. Gave G.W.F. proof Liberal.[49]

FRIDAY JULY 1st 1881: [Blank]

WEDNESDAY APRIL 23rd 1879: [Blank]

TUESDAY AUGUST 12th 1879

Bright; cool S.E. breeze. Morng. (till 2.45) B.M. W's Improv^{ns}.[5] Aftn. Haircut. After tea stroll. Evg. Looking up Defence of Poetry & trans. Ion in Shelley, & my own Blake[50] for Improv^{ns}. Dinner & tea out.

THURSDAY JULY 29th 1880: [Blank]

WEDNESDAY OCTOBER 22nd 1879

Drizzle & damp. Morng. B.M. Finished Tob^o Legisl^n V.[4] (Reading Room open till 7, with electric lamps.) Aftn. City for Tobacco – ¼ lb. Evg. Whitman[43] & Romany Rye.[21]

(*Facing page*) Wedy. 22nd. Posted Fraser Tob^o Legisl^n V.[4] (19 ruled note fos., 56–74) with note: too many extracts from Calendar State Papers (again)? Cancel items you find uninteresting; if you have any cash to spare, would be glad of some, as am getting heavily pressed at lodging – pardon my troubling you.

Wrote Mr Whittle, printer, to let me have proof in good time of Strange Book III,[5] if it is to appear in Liberal for Novr. Two or three ugly errors in Octr. Section, 11.

TUESDAY MAY 14th 1878

Morng. Lazy. Aftn. Dozed. Evg. Shelley.

---

[49]Either article 'In the Valley of Humiliation' or poem 'Two Leaves from a Fadeless Rose' (both *Liberal* Jan. '79).
[50]Gilchrist's *Life of Blake with Selected Poems* ed. D.G. and W.M. Rossetti. Thomson's essay review of this was in N.R. 14 Jan. – 6 Feb. '66.

SATURDAY APRIL 5th 1879: [Blank]

MONDAY SEPTEMBER 8th 1879

Fine fresh breeze – white clouds. Shine. Morng. B.M. Tob^{o}
Legisl^{n} V.[4] Aftn. Chat at Gower St. Party last night. Mrs Trouselle
– the Meads (his vol poems!) – then stroll. Began reading Morley's
Burke[35] for S.R.T. Romany Rye.[21] Tea out.

WEDNESDAY SEPTEMBER 1st 1880: [Blank]

FRIDAY NOVEMBER 19th 1880: [Blank]

TUESDAY MARCH 16th 1880

Morng. Finished Mixture[29] 10 fos. posted with lre. [*Scored out*:
Working at proof pp 81–96 & choosing additional pieces to fill up
gaps.][46]
Aftn. Late chop & stroll – called at Gower St. Evg. To Reeves;
long chat; advts, binding, &c. wrote Dobell all about the business.
Coals (1) Dinner & tea out.
   (*Facing page*) Tuesday 16.3.80. Lre from Fraser with second halves
5 £5 notes: vol 1000 two advs, Liberal &c. Answ^{d} formal receipt for
£25.14.6, for T.P. Jany. Feby. Mar. & Burke[35] S.R.T. not yet out.
Questions & suggestions & requirements as to Card.[51] Enclosed the
remainder of Mixture.

SUNDAY MAY 22nd 1881: [Blank]

FRIDAY JUNE 25th 1880

Showery aftn., heavy eveng. Some thunder. Morng. B.M. Legisl^{n}
XII.[4] Reading & writing. Aftn. Stroll. Soho, Wardour St &c. Note
from Mr. Reeves: Sunday, 12.30. Evg. Finished Whitman IV.[43] (18
fos. 152–169).
   (*Facing Page*) Friday: 25.6.80. Mem. from Mr. Reeves (W.D.)
Glad to see you next Sunday as soon after 12.30 as convenient.

TUESDAY AUGUST 30th 1881: [Blank]

---

[51]April issue announced new card 'Cope's World Fair', a skit on *Vanity Fair*. One
of annual cards and supplements to subscribers, as n. 18.

WEDNESDAY MAY 25th 1881: [Blank]

THURSDAY AUGUST 16th 1877

Fine. Morning B. Museum (T.L. Peacock in Edin. Rev. & Prof Wilson for condensed Noctes)[23] Aftn. Walked, then dozed. Evg. Began letter to C.B. Sec. Rev & Sec[t] Must stop free sending. G.W.F. 9.30 till past 12. Bed at one.

MONDAY APRIL 1st 1878

Sun & snow showers. Morng. B.M. Quarterly vols. Aftn. Walk. Evg. Rhoda Fleming.[44] Trousselle called. Tried piano. New nightshirts (two).

FRIDAY JANUARY 9th 1880

Fog again all day. B.M. still very stingy with its light. Morng. B.M. Reading & correctg. T.P. (came first post); Writing Geo Meredith & Fraser. Aftn. Gower St. Chat with Mrs. W. G.W.F. came in (no notice of each other). Evg. Correcting T.Ps to keep & addressing others. Dinner & tea out.

(*Facing page*) Friday 9.1.80. Tobacco Plant for Jany: Tob[o] Legisl[n] VI 5 cols full.[4] Mixture[29] & 'Figaro'[31] 3 cols full. G. Meredith's 'Egoist'[15] 3 cols full. Dean Church's Spenser;[33] S.R.T. 2 = 3 = 13 cols = 14! Just two-thirds of the whole space (19½ cols!) (F. has in hand S.R.T. Shelley,[37] Burke,[35] Thackeray,[38] Milton;[52] also Tob[o] Legisl[n] VII.[4] I have in hand W. Whitman I.[43] 19 ruled note fos; & have nearly finished Legisl[n] VIII.)[4]

Wrote Geo. Meredith answering his of 27th Novr., & forwarding two copies of T.P. by Bookpost. Wrote Fraser, thankg. him heartily for his noble bountifulness, & forwardng. Geo Meredith's lre of Nov. 27 to read.

SUNDAY SEPTEMBER 26th 1880: [Blank]

THURSDAY APRIL 12th 1877

Cool. Aftn. 2 to 5 at Johnson's Court. Bradlaugh didn't come, tho' his own apptmt. Sent Parris, with no powers to settle.[53] Made out gen[l]

[52]Mark Pattison's *Milton*, T.P., Aug. '80.
[53]Legal wrangle consequent on Watts's expulsion from N.R.

joint a/c the two Bs answrd. objections we knew of & so matter stands open. Gower St. till 9.30 T.R.W. not home.

SUNDAY AUGUST 17th 1879

Much rain all day from 7.30 to 6. Stroll evg. with G.W.F. whom I met. Dawdled over papers all day. Bilious at night.

FRIDAY OCTOBER 11th 1878: [Blank]

SUNDAY DECEMBER 9th 1877: [Blank]

THURSDAY DECEMBER 26th 1878

Sudden thaw. Water down front from roof to kitchen. Up late. Breakfast late. Got from G.W.F. <u>Secularist</u> 77. (No. 74 wanting) & Swinburne's Academy notes – took <u>R. Feverel</u>.[27] (F. has still my Donne & one MS book) Aftn. Short stroll. Evg. Reading. Young party in parlour – singing & playing.

SATURDAY MAY 15th 1880: [Blank]

TUESDAY AUGUST 16th 1881: [Blank]

MONDAY APRIL 30th 1877

Cool & cloudy. Morng. <u>Incidence & Increase Taxat</u>n[54] Posted 2.40 to Watts, with proof <u>Plain Statem</u>t, & note 'I prefer *not* to have my name attached to Confce Circular.'[55] Aftn. Adeline (Italn again) – Clara & Kate. Lre from Julia. Eveng. <u>Epictetus</u> IV.[13]

SATURDAY APRIL 10th 1880

World Fair Cards & Keys from L'Pool.[51] Morng. B.M. Leopardi (Cugnoni & Viani)[56] – Aftn. City for walk & tobacco. Evg. Gower St. Billiards with T.R.W. <u>Coals</u> (1) <u>Dinner & tea out</u>.

[54]'The Incidence and Increase of Taxation'. S.R., 13 May '77.
[55]A conference at Nottingham in May, first since June '76 conference at Leeds.
[56]Leopardi: Prose – *Opere Inedite*, (Cugnoni G.) 1878; *Opera* (ed. Viani, P.) 1845 etc; *Appendice all' Epistolaria e agli altri scritti giovanili di G Leopardi* 1878. (In B.M. catalogue.)

FRIDAY JUNE 21st 1878

Splendid summer at last. Morng. Trübner's: Times worse than ever, we let things drift, no speculation. City for tobacco. Aftn. W.M.R.'s at home: Mrs Fraser, Miss Robinson, (Handful of Honeysuckle), Miss Carmichael & friend who sang, Theo. Watts, Gosses, Tademas, Conways & Col. Higginson. Miss Blind, & O'Shaughnessy. C.B. Cayley. Evg. Gower St. Mrs W. lost her voice. x Saw Thatcher, Central City, Inns of Court Hotel.

TUESDAY JULY 26th 1881: [Blank]

SUNDAY NOVEMBER 18th 1877

Fine day. Hawkes, & walk with Percy before dinner. Dined Gower St. Hember in evg. Home 10.30. Bed 12.30.

FRIDAY JULY 2nd 1880

Showers & sun. Note from Hatton; Answd. morng. B.M. morng. Legisln. XII.[4] readg. & writg. Aftn. City for tobacco. Evg. Writing up this diary; reading.

MONDAY APRIL 21st 1879: [Blank]

TUESDAY SEPTEMBER 27th 1881: [Blank]

SUNDAY JANUARY 24th 1880: [Blank]

SUNDAY FEBRUARY 17th 1878: [Blank]

TUESDAY FEBRUARY 8th 1881

Dull, but milder; slight rain. Fine moon in deep blue sky far beyond grey clouds. Morng. Up late. Aftn. Hair cut; Gower St with M.W's lre. Evg. Wrote to Fraser. (Draft on his of 4th). Daniel Deronda &c.[16] Breakfast & tea out. Late fire.

THURSDAY JUNE 5th 1879: [Blank]

TUESDAY APRIL 29th 1879: [Blank]

SATURDAY MARCH 1st 1879

Dull morng., fine aftn. & night. Morng. B.M. Tob⁰ Legisl ̱ ̱ II.[4] (Man with <u>Rymer</u>, wh. he didn't look into). Revising proof <u>Tob⁰ Duties</u>[57] (2 cols). Aftn. Stroll with Percy. Evg. Gower St. Billiards. Mr Mitchell & Walter Holyoake.

SATURDAY APRIL 14th 1877

Cool. Cloudy. S.E. breeze. Two letters with photo from Maccall. Letter from Foote: 'Get letters Queen Sq.[58] &c. I'll send P.O. Monday.' Morng. & Evg. till 2.20 & 10.40 <u>Epictetus</u> II.[13] (Paid for this week's papers.) <u>Secularist</u> No 68 – Long's Epictetus (2) & Reading. <u>Secr. Rev ̱ ̱</u> No. 37 – Clerical Modesty[59] – & A/cs. Trouselle called at tea-time – Wagner festival.

SATURDAY AUGUST 3rd 1878: [Blank]

SATURDAY NOVEMBER 15th 1879

Fine & cold. Castor oil in morning; kept in. Morng. Evg. <u>Cope's Mixture</u>.[29] Coals (2) Saty night & Sunday. <u>No dinner</u>.

(*Facing page*) <u>Saty. 15th</u> Lre from Fraser, enclosg. proofs of Dean Church's <u>Spenser</u>[33] as first set up, before cutting down. Trial of Strafford wanted back – any time next week.

THURSDAY JANUARY 1st 1880

Still very mild; clouds & some wind. Saw Old year out & New Year in at Mitchells' – Wrights, Novras, Totty Schwagmann, Mrs Watts. Morng. (Late) B.M. Carlyle's Cromwell for <u>Legisl ̱ ̱</u>[4] Aftn. Stroll – shopping again. Evg. Called Gower St. Home 8.40. (G.W.F. advt in N.R. <u>Liberal</u> suspended. <u>Coals</u> (1) <u>– unused. Dinner & tea out</u> (so Tuesday & Wednesday).

(*Facing page*) <u>Thursday</u> 1.1.80 New Year's card from Julia. G.W.F.'s advt. in N.R. <u>Liberal</u> suspended through pressure of engagements (!); hopes to resume it soon – He has article in N.R.

---

[57]'The Tobacco Duties', T.P., Dec. '78 – Mar. '79.
[58]Foote was away on a lecture tour in Scotland. Thomson in London on April 6th had visited 'Mr & Mrs Foote, 15 Queen's Square'.
[59]'Clerical Modesty', S.R., 15 April '77.

MONDAY NOVEMBER 29th 1880: [Blank]

SATURDAY JUNE 19th 1880

Morning: To Miss Blind's with note explaining my position with regard to Geo. Meredith.[60] She kept me to lunch & chat. Aftn. Stroll, Regent's Park & Portland St. Evg. Fred called, wife ill. Mr Cooke. Stroll. Dinner Out (Cold hash &c.)

WEDNESDAY MARCH 20th 1878

Hair cut. Calico 5/2. University 7/6. Morng. & Aftn. Walk. Have done no work, not knowing what to do.

FRIDAY OCTOBER 19th 1877

Posted Fraser Jacobite Ballads.[61] After supper (till 2.a.m.). To Anna Linden San Francisco News Letter (Prose & verse)[62] Up at one. No sleep till seven. For the last fortnight my old friend Insomnia has been with me.

MONDAY FEBRUARY 17th 1879

Fog morng. Some sun midday. Wet evg. Cool, N.W. Morng. Up late. Dawdled. (Poor strange cat in back coal-cellar & under kitchen since Saty. morng.) Aftn. Stroll Oxford St., Also before dinner. Evg. Reading Erasme: Eloge de la Folie (Biblio: Nationale)[63] Slight bilious indigestion. Listless & sleepy. Beer only for early bed.

TUESDAY NOVEMBER 4th 1879

Cloudy & cool. Morng. B.M. Finished extracts from Egoist I:[14] not all I wanted, but promised to return vol. this aftn. Aftn. Adeline – French. V's Louis XIV. Evg. Resumed S.R.T. Burke.[35] Then Egoist II, brought by Percy. Coals (1).

[60]She had invited him to visit on Sunday 20th but he was afraid an expected invitation from Meredith might turn up at the last minute to clash with that. He did go to Blind's on the 20th, and Meredith's on the 29th.

[61]Review of *English Jacobite Ballads, Songs and Satires* etc. Towneley Mss. ed. A.B. Grosart, Lancaster, Private ed. 125 copies: T.P., Mar. '78.

[62]Verses with prose intro., in reply to a poem by Anna Linden addressed to *Cope's* about smoking, published in San Francisco.

[63]Two French versions from the 1870s of Erasmus's *In Praise of Folly* are listed in the B.M. catalogue.

SUNDAY SEPTEMBER 16th 1877

Posted Fraser New Republic.[64] Dined T.R.W.'s. He to lecture. Evg. Mitchell's & Trousselle's. Both Hembers. New Piano & cards. Home 1.30. Bed 3 a.m.

SUNDAY APRIL 24th 1881: [Blank]

THURSDAY OCTOBER 27th 1881

Morng. & evg. Readg. Mead's 'Philosy. of Carlyle'. Evg. Began article on it. Aftn. Strolled Regent St. Called at Photos. Proofs 7 or 10 days, not 2 or 3. Ordered trowsers 16/-. Wenkheim. Monday evg.

[64]Review: *The New Republic, or Culture Faith and Philosophy in an English Country House* (2 vols) T.P., Oct. '77.

CHAPTER TWENTY

Poor men, most admirable, most pitiable,
With all their changes all their great Creeds change:
For Man, this alien in my family,
Is alien most in this, to cherish dreams
And brood on visions of eternity,
And build religions in his brooding brain
And in the dark depths awe-full of his soul.
My other children live their little lives,
Are born and reach their prime and slowly fail,
And all their little lives are self-fulfilled;
They die and are no more, content with age
And weary with infirmity. But Man
Has fear and hope and phantasy and awe,
And wistful yearnings and unsated loves,
That strain beyond the limits of his life,
And therefore Gods and Demons, Heaven and Hell:
This Man, the admirable, the pitiable.

'A Voice from the Nile' ll. 140–156

The setting at Kirby Muxloe Thomson had described to Bertram
Dobell during his first stay in June:

We are here four miles from Leicester, with railway station a few
minutes off, in a pleasant villa, surrounded by shrubbery, lawn, mead-
ow, and kitchen garden. Host and hostess (sister) are kindness itself, as
are all other Leicester friends. We lead the most healthy of lives, save
for strong temptation to over-feeding on excellent fare, and host's evil
and powerfully contagious habit of sitting up till about 2.a.m. smoking
and reading or chatting. I now leave him to his own wicked devices at
midnight, or as soon after as possible. Despite the showery weather we

281

have had good drives and walks (country all green and well-wooded), jolly little picnics, and lawn-tennis *ad infinitum*. (*N.B.* – Lawn-tennis even more than lady's fine pen responsible for the uncouthness of this scrawl.) In brief, we have been so busy with enjoyment that this is the first note I have accomplished (or begun) in the seventeen days. I say *we*, because Adeline is still here. She leaves about end of week, and I shall then spend a week at Quorndon, where three of Mr Wright's sons live managing factories there. Thence I return here for two or three days, and perhaps shall have two or three with old Mr Wright in Leicester before homing. You see I mean to have a good holiday before setting to work again.[1]

He had kept in touch with Harriet during his week in Quorndon, sending a letter to her at Forest Edge with an account of his doings:

Dear Miss Barrs – Raining hard since six in the morning (not that *I* was up to see it begin), despite the fair promise of yesterday and the steady rise of the glass during the last two days. General despair as to hay unmown, or mown and lying unstacked. Special despair of B.V. (Beautiful Virtue, mind!), who has to scrawl instead of rambling, while the Wrights are engaged in the factory till one.

Phil Wright having all his things in the other sleeping chamber, I have the honour of sleeping in the wonderful bedstead which Mr and Mrs Noah used in the ark some short time ago. Under the beneficent protection of the good angel with the scanty wings and the ample nose, and sustained by a flawless conscience, I slept the sleep of the just.

James Wright and wife were in town (Leicester) yesterday, and I stayed dinner in Regent Street, James coming by same train to Quorn. Phil awaited us with boat. In the evening we were again on the river, which is not only of fair breadth, but really very pretty about here, and I renewed my friendly acquaintance with the water-rats, from whose charming society I have for several years been debarred by the force of circumstances I was unable to control. The W's have fishing rights opposite factory, and not only pike, perch, tench, and so on, are to be caught (they tell me), but also trout. Unfortunately I am no more a fisher of fish than of men (including women), but if others bring good trout to table, I am resolved, at whatever sacrifice, to bear my part of the burden of eating them . . .

I must not inflict any more of my pluvial *ennui* upon you just now, as I am about writing for the first time to my good landlady, who is a credit to her sex, and who may be getting anxious about her model lodger.[2]

A highlight of that summer holiday for Thomson had been a weekend visit to Belvoir Castle about twenty-five miles from Leicester with Jack, Dick, and a friend of the Barrs called Mary Patten.[3] That trip Thomson had recounted to Percy Holyoake, who like Adeline had spent some of

the summer at Forest Edge and was party to the banter and summer inti-
macies: 'Saturday we drove *via* Melton to Belvoir: Sunday and morning
of Monday in grounds and castle, Monday afternoon drove back. Cousin
Dick can tell you all about the shady alleys and arbours, and all the
sunny terraces and slopes, from the pit of despair to declaration covert
and fix-the-day secret bower. The subject is too young and tender for
my rusty pen . . . Adeline and yourself will be glad to learn that the
tennis-court is being beaten flat after the rain. With a good rolling it
will be in first-class condition.'[4]

Now four months later Thomson was back. On December 1st
1881 Dobell heard from him again:

> You see I am down here, drawn by urgent invitations, and glad of
> the change, as I was not feeling well in London, although of course the
> country here is very different in November and December from what it
> was in June and July. The home comfort itself.
>
> You asked about the *Pall Mall Gazette*. Morley don't find an opening
> for me there at present, but he has accepted a piece of two hundred
> lines blank verse, 'A Voice from the Nile', which I did down here
> and sent for the *Fortnightly*. He says that he likes it very much; can't
> promise positively for January number, but will try. The 'Deliverer'
> duly appeared in November. I am doing now another which I shall
> offer him, and have planned yet another. As the *Gentleman's* proof of
> the 'Ring and the Book' came and was returned yesterday fortnight, I
> presume it is in this month . . . My host found that it had not arrived
> last evening . . . Please remember me to Mr Reeves, and tell him
> my little literary news, and say that I will write him soon. As the
> *Athenaeum* printed the fifth and last instalment of my Shelley notes on
> the 19th November, I am about writing to offer articles on any books in
> my scope.
>
> My photos reached me (i.e. six of them) on Wednesday, Novem-
> ber 23, which made me forty-seven, a month after the sitting. Percy
> Holyoake has one for you, and one for Mr Reeves. They are very
> poorly done though they took so long, but friends say a good like-
> ness.[5]

He was writing poetry once more. On his forty-seventh birthday
he had dedicated some birthday verses to Harriet Barrs, though
they were not celebratory. People of his age, the poem said, had
only 'long-dead joys'; people of hers still had 'hope and joy and
love'. There was nothing after death, and the only hope was that
work done by people living now might eventually pay off for future
generations – 'our children's children's children's heritage'. This was
no secure prospect:

> But if it prove a mirage after all!
> Our last illusion leaves us wholly bare,
> To bruise against Fate's adamantine wall,
> Consumed or frozen in the pitiless air;
> In all our world, beneath, around, above,
> Only one refuge, solace, triumph, – Love,
> Sole star of light in infinite black despair.[6]

The Heine booklet remained unwritten, though he continued to prepare the lecture for the Browning Society that was to be given on January 27th. 'The time has chiefly been spent in distractions with guests here, so that I have even yet about half a day's work on the fair copy of the Browning notes to do,' he told Dobell on December 31st.[7] His chief distraction, according to Frances Gill, a visiting friend of the Barrs, was Harriet Barrs herself. 'Don't you see that Thomson is in love with your sister?' Frances told Jack after her visit to Forest Edge.[8] Jack refused to believe this, and dismissed her opinion as 'silly', the whim of a 'neuropath' – 'an excitable woman of five & thirty & quite capable of evolving other people's love stories from her own lightly balanced fancy.'[9]

Harriet did have two young suitors trying to court her at Forest Edge, one a veterinary student called John Parr.[10] Harry Barrs did some investigating of the matter, and assured his older brother there was nothing to worry about over Thomson's feelings for 'Dick'. Any fuss was merely 'a mare's nest':

> There is nothing between Dick and B.V. but friendship of which I am glad. Poor Parr is evidently altogether out of it. Well, he's not the first fellow who has been jilted and won't be the last. Don Cupid has evidently been 'playing it' in the Barrs family just lately.[11]

A postscript added 'Am on the warpath after tonight. B.V. versus Foote'.

In a poem 'A Modern Penelope' written in January, Thomson described a young woman sitting crocheting in her chair; this woman was the object of two suitors' attentions – 'You have caught twin loves in the toils of your art'.[12] Another poem 'The Sleeper', which Harry Barrs described as 'B.V.''s poem about Dick',[13] described a woman similarly seated, this time dozing:

> She is not surely all awake,
>   As yet she is not all asleep;
> The eyes with lids half-open take

A startled deprecating peep
Of quivering drowsiness, then slowly
The lids sink back, before she wholly
    Resigns herself to slumber deep.

The side-neck gleams so pure beneath
    The underfringe of gossamer,
The tendrils of whose faery wreath
    The softest sighs suppressed would stir.
The little pink-shell ear-rim flushes
With her young blood's translucent blushes,
    Nestling in tresses warm as fur.[14]

In fact between November and the following March Thomson wrote
1,400 lines of verse at Forest Edge, enough for him to begin supplicating
Dobell to publish a third collection of his poetry. One poem was based
on the visit to Belvoir Castle the previous summer, describing how when
Jack and Mary walked on ahead in the grounds:

We roamed with many a merry jest
    And many a ringing laughter;
The slow calm hours too rich in zest
    To heed before and after:
Yet lingering down the lovely walks
    Soft strains anon came stealing,
A finer music through our talks
    Of sweeter, deeper feeling.

Yes, now and then a quiet word
    Of seriousness dissembling
In smiles would touch some hidden chord
    And set it all a-trembling:
I trembled too, and felt it strange; –
    Could I be in possession
Of music richer in its range
    Than yet had found expression?[15]

'Richard Forest's Midsummer Night' was a long narrative describing
the stealthy evening meeting of two lovers;[16] 'He Heard Her Sing'[17]
was a rapturous idyll – the metre based on Swinburne's 'Hymn to
Proserpine', he told Dobell[18] – in which a lover secretly listened to
the object of his desire singing her heart out in a boat on a lake. There
was nothing secretive about Thomson's composing these poems. He sent
them to the *Cornhill Magazine* and other publications, and 'He Heard

Her Sing' Jack saw 'written down morning after morning until finished & had barely a correction before being sent off to the magazines.'[19]

But with six days to go before the Browning lecture Thomson was causing his Forest Edge friends some dismay about whether he could stay sober. Percy wrote: 'After all our united efforts, we are done in the end . . . Dick is very cut up about it as well she may be, after all the trouble she had taken, and the promises he had given her to be good, however genius is its own reward.'[20] At this time a letter reached Thomson from Julia, now living in Stretford and separated from his brother John, in which she requested him to describe to her what he could remember of his early childhood.

My Dear James,

Aunt Mary has swooped down again & is staying with your brother, she came to see me on Saturday & made several statements which bother me a good deal, perhaps you can clear some of them up for me. Were you old enough to remember anything connected with your Father and Mother, because I want you to help me, or if you forget there may be some person who knew them.

Now for my reasons. Mrs Millar when I saw her said your mother was a bright good woman, & that your father ill used her, & went into bad company & that she had bruises & marks on her when she died, & that she was quite as good as he in every way when he married her. Aunt Mary's story runs thus – that the marriage as far as your father's well fare went was a mistake from the first. There never was a nicer man & she was a very strange woman, & they lived right enough until he had a moon stroke & then *she* was unkind to him.

Now, which is true? does it not look like a page of 'The Ring & the Book' with its conflicting evidence.

In what year did the moon stroke occur? Tell me that if you have any means of knowing.

You see they know I am pretty nearly at their mercy in these details, & I am determined to get at the truth & tell it. Let me know as soon as possible & I will write you again as soon as possible.

Aunt Mary is going about her peace making in a funny fashion, quite the wrong way to gain her point, as you would say if you knew all, papa is quite disgusted. I wish I could have a long talk with you & yet I don't think I could talk much about it. It is a mad world & a wicked one to be sure.

I hope you are getting on well & comfortably. I am sending this to you at Leicester not knowing where you are. With kind love,

I am,

Your affectionate Sister,

Julia.[21]

To this Thomson replied:

I was just past eight years old and at the school when mother died, so I can only give you very early impressions. These are, that father and mother were very happy together when he was at home, until, when I was about six, he returned from his last voyage, paralyzed in the right side, the result, as I understand, of a week of terrible storm, during which time he was never able to change his drenched clothes. Before then I think he was a good husband and a kind father; her I always remember as a loving mother and wife. He may have been a bit gay, in the sense of liking a social song and glass, being, I believe, much better looking and more attractive in company than either of his sons. She was more serious, and pious too, following Irving from the Kirk when he was driven out. I remember well Irving's portrait under yellow gauze, and some books of his on the interpretation of prophecy, which I used to read for the imagery. The paralysis at first unhinged father's mind, and he had some fits of violence; more generally his temper was strange, disagreeable, and not to be depended upon. I remember him taunting her with being his elder. Mother must have had a sad time of it for a year or so. His mental perturbations settled down into a permanent weakness of mind, not amounting to imbecility but very, very different, I should say, from his former brightness and decision. Before I went to the school he used to take me to chapels where the members of the congregation ejaculated groaning responses to the minister's prayer, and to small meetings in a private room where the members detailed their spiritual experiences of the week. Good, bad, or indifferent, these were not the sort of things with which he had anything to do in his days of soundness. The right hand remained useless, but the leg had gradually grown strong enough to walk well, though with an awkward dragging pace.

I think mother, who was mystically inclined with Edward Irving, had also a cloud of melancholy hanging over her; first, perhaps, from the death of her favourite brother, John Parker Kennedy, drowned on the Goodwin Sands; then probably deepened by the death of my little sister, of whom I remember being devotedly fond, when she was about three and myself five, of measles caught from me. Had she or someone else lived, I might have been worth something; but on the whole, I sincerely judge that it was well for both to die when they did, and I would not, for my own selfish comfort, call them back if I could. At first I would doubtless have done so, but not for many years past.

We also had good friends, mother and daughter, named Smith, whom I knew some years on in my holidays, and then lost sight of. Speaking generally, you know far more of my family than I do, who have been Ishmael in the desert from my childhood.[22]

He sent Furnivall the lecture for the Browning Society, but telling him he was not well enough to read it in public. Thus on January 27th Furnivall, who liked the lecture 'tremendously', delivered it himself.[23] The lecture ranged from the sequence 'Men and Women' of 1856 to the poem 'The Two Poets of Croisic' of 1878. Thomson praised Browning's 'passionate, living, triumphant faith in Christ', a belief which maintained not the redemption of a few but 'the immortality and ultimate redemption of every human soul in and through Christ'. The latter tenet was illustrated by quoting Browning's 'Apparent Failure' which suggested that even suicides, contrary to church doctrine, might find forgiveness. Browning's 'The Two Poets of Croisic' Thomson thought demonstrated a sound principle by which one might decide which of two poets was the better:

> . . . End the strife
> By asking 'Which one led a happy life?'
>
> If one did, over his antagonist
>   That yelled or shrieked or sobbed or wept or wailed
> Or simply had the dumps, – dispute who list, –
>   I count him victor.[24]

On the 26th, Harry Barrs had described Thomson as being in a 'shockingly bad' state.[25] Four days later Percy wrote to Forest Edge that Thomson had told him 'grim Fate had his head in Chancery', and that he wanted to go back to Kirby Muxloe, where he hoped, once again, to pick up with the projected Heine booklet. 'He has sworn an oath not to touch spirits again – a thing he has never attempted to say before,' wrote Percy; 'packed up all his "comforts" (corks and all). He is fearfully cut up "that damned infernal fit" came on him whilst with you.'[26] He needed new clothes, and Percy took him to a tailors to be measured,[27] but later Dobell found him drunk again, and Percy 'relieved him of about half a pint of firewater from various pockets, he protesting that "how it was done" was beyond him.'[28] Still he hoped to make it to Forest Edge, though the Wrights' home just round the corner he now considered beyond his reach:

> 7 Huntley Street
> Monday February 6th 1882

Dear Percy, – Will you let me know whether the arrangement for Leicester holds? A really pious Sabbath has restored me to my mind, such as it is. Of course I am still weak and nervous in body, and if I am going to go will be grateful for help in packing, &c. I write because my clothes are so fluffy that I don't think I shall have the courage to enter no. 12.

I will ask all the news when I see you.

Yours truly
B.V.[29]

He made it back to Leicester. William Maccall, still keeping in touch after eight years, thought Thomson now sounded more optimistic. He seemed, Maccall later recalled, 'escaped for a time from the dungeons and despairs of the Inquisition, and to be gladdened for an instant by the sun'.[30] At the time he told Thomson: 'I take a deep and tender interest in you for your own sake and also for the sake of romantic memories that carry me back to the old days by the "Banks of Clyde" '.[31]

In Kirby Muxloe Thomson began writing poetry again. Two poems again brought the imagined Visitor to the solitary narrator. In the first the Female was no longer young, but dead, an old and worn phantom. In the second it was only the phantom of passing Time that was left, and behind that the phantom of Death. 'The Poet and His Muse' brought the poet's muse from her grave, only to accuse him:

> 'My hair dishevelled dank with dews of night
>   From that far region of dim death I come,
> With eyes and soul and spirit void of light,
>   With lips more sad in speech than stark and dumb:
> Lo, you have ravaged me with dolorous thought
> Until my brain was wholly overwrought,
>   Barren of flowers and fruit;
> Until my heart was bloodless for all passion,
> Until my trembling lips could no more fashion
> Sweet words to fit sweet airs of trembling lyre and lute.
>
> We tell no tales more, we whose tale is told;
>   As your brain withered and your heart grew chill
> My heart and brain were turned to churchyard mould;
>   Wherefore my singing voice sank ever still;
> And I, all heart and brain and voice, am dead;
> It is my phantom here beside your bed
>   That speaketh to you now;
> Though you exist still, a mere form inurning

289

The ashes of dead fires of thought and yearning,
Dead faith, dead love, dead hope, in hollow breast and brow.'[32]

Then on February 23rd 1882 he completed at Forest Edge the first forty lines of the poem he was to call 'Insomnia'.[33]

FEBRUARY 23rd. He heard midnight strike, and one by one the others left the room, each assured that sleep's alchemy would transmute leaden weight to gold; just weary enough to nestle into divine unconsciousness, assured of waking in the morning with richer zest from the womb of night.

FEBRUARY 24th. He, weary and haggard with endless nights unblessed by sleep, went into the desert of Night, expecting no oasis of slumber, like one going to his tomb knowing that he alone would not be granted oblivion. Eternity like this could not be worse, as fatigue and pain seem eternal in each passing instant.

He lay down and closed his eyes as if the mockery of sleep might win real sleep. Then he grew aware of a Presence watching, its shadow on him. He heard the chimes of One. He opened his eyes and saw the Image still as stone, its remorseless eyes on him.

Wherefore I asked for what I knew too well:
    O ominous midnight Presence, What art Thou?
Whereto in tones that sounded like a knell:
    'I am the Second Hour, appointed now
To watch beside thy slumberless unrest.'
Then I: Thus both, unlike, alike unblest;
    For I should sleep, you fly:
Are not those wings beneath thy mantly folded?
O Hour! unfold those wings so straitly folded,
And urge thy natural flight beneath the moonlit sky.

FEBRUARY 25th. The Image: I can only open my wings when you lie in genuine slumber, and do not know I am here. Sleep only can stir my wings; sleep, and you will be borne gently across the night on my pinions.
He: I know both you and I want the same end. What could be more gladly brought than sleep, whose absence is longed for equally only by Love and Death?

Then he let his eyelids fall, and saw the night before him as a waste of ridges, hour by hour apart, dividing deep ravines. Sleep's flying hour was a bridge across these ravines, but he, whose hours stood fast, must climb painfully down each side and climb more painfully up the other. Thus he went down into the first ravine, stumbling and bruised, to a rushing torrent-brook at the bottom, from which he escaped feeling faint as death. Then he climbed with bleeding hands and feet the scarp facing him until he lay on the ridge of sand and gravel at the top. He heard the bells chime Two –

FEBRUARY 27th. – and knew there was a change of Watchers in the room, without a stir or sound beside his bed. Only silence and 'the muffled pulsing of the night's deep dread'. The moonlight now slanted on the bedroom wall and on the corniced ceiling. A shrouded form stood by the bed like a black sepulchral column. It was the Third Hour of the Night.

FEBRUARY 28th. Something transcending all his former fear came through him. He did not have the heart to say a word to the phantom, but closed his eyes and set himself to climbing down then up the next tremendous gulf.

Men sigh and complain how life is brief. Yes, eternities of bliss are transient and minute. But suffering can seem eternal. The darkness of the next ravine was beyond description. When such agonies and horrors of darkness drown the soul, to be is not to be: in the memory only ghastliest impressions remain, the chaos of possession by demons. He reached the next ridge and lay shuddering. The bells chimed Three.

MARCH 4th. The Image of the Fourth Hour stood over him. But there was Something beyond it not there previously, something more dreadful but with an inexorable fascination. It was a formless Shade from the regions of the dead. Dismayed by the menacing fascination of it, he shut his eyes and went into the next gulf as into Hell. What depths he descended and what gripped his heart are horrors that will never leave him.

MARCH 6th. If he had any hope it was that he would be smashed on the rocks of the raging torrent at the foot of this ravine, and his mangled body be carried by the torrent to the sea. But some mysterious instinct bore him on until he climbed to the next ridge. He heard four o'clock strike, saw the image of the Fifth Hour. Over and behind it again stood the shadow that was not the shadow of the

Hour – Death – fascinating but repulsive: 'Despair's envenomed anodyne to tempt the soul'.

MARCH 7th – 8th. He closed his eyes, but could no longer lie pretending to sleep beside the two watchers. Trembling he rose and dressed, descended the stairs with furtive footsteps and left the slumbering house. He alone was forced to move through the unmoving hours. He paced streets silent and chilly in the moonlight, thinking of his life as a series of failures.

> Against a bridge's stony parapet
>   I leaned, and gazed into the waters black;
> And marked an angry morning red and wet
>   Beneath a livid and enormous rack
> Glare out confronting the belated moon,
> Huddled and wan and feeble as the swoon
>   Of featureless despair:
> When some stray workmen half-asleep but lusty
> Passed urgent through the rainpour wild and gusty,
> I felt a ghost already, planted watching there.
>
> As phantom to its grave, or to its den
>   Some wild beast of the night when night is sped,
> I turned unto my homeless home again
>   To front a day only less charged with dread
> Than that drear night; and after day, to front
> Another night of – what would be the brunt?
>   I put the thought aside,
> To be resumed when common life unfolded
> In common daylight had my brain remoulded;
> Meanwhile the flaws of rain refreshed and fortified.

Days passed, and nights as ghastly. Let them be buried with their sufferings. He feels rage and self-scorn at how weak, proud, and infinitely inane his words seem. But how to return from those Inferno-like depths to nights of sleep?

> How do men climb back from a swoon whose stress,
> Crushing far deeper than all consciousness,
>   Is deep as deep death seems?
> Who can the steps and stages mete and number
> By which we re-emerge from nightly slumber? –
> Our poor vast petty life is one dark maze of dreams.

292

With the completion of 'Insomnia' Thomson now wrote to Dobell:

> I have been taking poetical stock with result set forth on other leaf. There seems to be enough in hand, half old and half new, for another volume. I understand from Mr Reeves that, with Forman's Keats, and half a dozen other works, his hands are quite full for the season. Being, as usual, since the *Tobacco Plant* was cut down and uprooted, in sad want of cash, I should be very glad to sell the whole copyright out, but suppose it would be impossible to get anything for it. You may have noticed a little skit of mine, 'Law *v* Gospel', in this week's *Dispatch*. Yesterday I sent another on the Prince Leopold grant. If the *Dispatch* will take such things, it will help a little.[34]

'Law *v* Gospel' satirised the prosecution of a Salvation Army youth charged with obstruction for selling the army's *War Cry* newspaper in the streets.[35] The defence – which lost – had quoted the Salvation Army's claim to have sobered up a thousand drinkers; unselfishness would never be understood by most Christians, the poem stated, and the Apostles in their poverty would never have survived a similar prosecution. But at Forest Edge Thomson's drinking was now beginning to upset the domestic scene to an extent that made his further stay unlikely. On March 20th Harry Barrs, having been told the latest news by Jack, wrote to him in reply: 'I am very sorry to hear of B.V.'s stupidity or lunacy or whatever it may be. I suppose there is no help for it, & that he *must* leave Forest Edge. I am sure that whilst the fit is on him the only way to stop his drinking is to lock him up, & this one can scarcely do. Poor fool! he ought to know better than to throw up the best & last chance he will have.'[36] A week later Thomson was still in Kirby Muxloe, and he went in to Leicester where he bought six second-hand books including Dante's *La Vita Nuova* and Stendhal's *De L'Amour*.[37] But within days he was finally ordered to leave Forest Edge and he returned to London. Jack Barrs later described what happened in an 1898 interview with Thomson's biographer Henry Salt. Salt's notebooks record what Jack Barrs ('B') said, as follows:

'On one or two occasions T had been affected by drink while at Leicester. At last he began introducing into the house small flasks of brandy purchased from a neighbouring public house. B having detected from T's appearance & temperature that something was wrong, a search was made & some flasks were found in his bedroom. The contents were taken away, but nothing was said by T. Then same symptoms reappeared, but for a long time no flasks could be found, until Miss Barrs happened to see B.V. take something from an ivy-covered tree-stump in the garden! A search was again made, & a number of small flasks found & confiscated. Still B.V. said nothing. Then one day, when he was to have gone into Leicester with Miss B., he evaded her on some excuse & disappeared. In the evening a message was sent from the inn that he was there, ill, & Percy Holyoake found him lying with his head on the table. He was brought back & put in the coach-house for the night, still imploring for brandy – wine & beer, which were offered him, being rejected as useless. (He was found to have several sixpences tied up in corners of his handkerchief!) As Miss B. objected to having him in the house, he was sent back to London the next morning, though, as B. felt, he was not fit to go.'[38]

CHAPTER TWENTY-ONE

From H. Hood Barrs to J.W. Barrs[1]

April 17th: 'Went to Wright's & Gibson's on Saturday, but there was no news – except that he was still on the warpath and in very full paint.'

April 21st (Section of letter headed 'B.V.'): 'This gent was at Bow Street thrice last week. He had a good lecture from Flowers, who, it seems, had heard who he is. He is better now, and swears of all stimulants. How long will it last? He has *two* black eyes, & would have had more had nature blessed him with more visual organs – a broken nose & cut forehead!!!'

From James Thomson to J.W. Barrs

April 22nd: 'I scarcely know how to write to you after my atrocious and disgusting return for the wonderful hospitality and kindness of yourself and Miss Barrs. I can only say that I was mad. In one fit of frenzy I have not only lost more than I yet know, and half murdered myself (were it not for my debts I sincerely wish it had been wholly), but justly alienated my best and firmest friends, old and new, both in London and Leicester.

As, unfortunately for myself at least, I am left alive, it only remains for me to endeavour my utmost by hard and persistent struggling to repay my money debts, for my debts of kindness can never be repaid. If I fail, as very probably I shall fail, the failure will but irresistibly prove what I have long thoroughly believed, that for myself and others I am much better dead than alive.

As apologies would be worse than useless, I will conclude by simply expressing my deep gratitude for your astonishing undeserved goodness to myself, and my best wishes for the welfare of you and yours.

P.S. Percy called yesterday & said he would call again today. When I have seen him, or at any rate this evg. or tomorrow, I will write on matters of business.'

April 22nd (second letter sent by afternoon post): 'In case Percy should not be able to come I will add a few business lines for aftn. post to what I have already posted to Kirby.

At the beginning of the week I must get a new lodging & when settled will let you know address . . . I do not know what to turn to yet, but must evidently resolve without delay.'

| From Percy Holyoake to J.W. Barrs

April 22nd: 'The ways of the "Great Pitiable" have been curious. Thrice to the Police Station & once to Bow Street (*en passant* I might observe that in the far-distant freethought future, that spot will no doubt be the "Mecca" of the party). Mr Flowers however seemed to know who he was in spite of his false name "John Turner", gave him a sensible talking to, & at length let him off. Truly it must have been a comic scene to see "B.V." marched up in a very undress style, *sans* hat, & leopard-like apparel. Gibson's patience came to a point when the poet successfully stood a six hours' siege in the W.C. – *vide* Miss S. The police could not come in to "chuck him out" & B.V. would not come out to be run in. When I saw him on Thursday he was perfectly well, simply highly coloured. He knew you had been, that is all. He gives up all hope of coming down to Forest Edge again, & says "My only hope lies in total abstinence", which he is going to try. On Monday night he is going to find some new rooms, as Gibson says he won't have him for £2 a week.'

April 24th: 'I am quite with you as regards the total abstaining. This a mere phase, "only that and nothing more". Yesterday while talking over the business with him, I asked if he had begun the period of probation, or if he had entirely given up beer. He said, no, to both questions, "but –" and there was evidently so much meant by that word that I think I ought to treat it with a capital "B". And there in my opinion the matter will end. He can hardly do much more than he is in the way of wearing out the "friends". He was taken to the Salvation Army the other night, but up to the present he is not on the rolls. He stoutly maintains that he arrived in London with the grim determination of cooling down, but the "singing in the head" (doubtless a kind of mental "Lorelei") came on, & that put an end to good intentions . . . Flaws hopes to get £50 for B.V.'s new vol. from Sampson Low & Co.'

From James Thomson to Bertram Dobell

May 4th: (from 7 Huntley Street): 'I am here for a few days until I can get another place.

Will you please let me have back the pieces of verse I sent you, as I want to correct and make fair copies. No word yet from any of the magazines.

I will try to call up some evening.

Hoping you are all well.

From Percy Holyoake to J.W. Barrs

May 5th: 'Thomson is again on the loose. And such a loose – escorted to the station by three of the defenders of the peace. Yesterday evng. Mr Gibson sent for, & told me that B.V. was breaking out, & said that he refused again to leave the house. Eventually was put outside, & lay on the doorstep until the police came. The three men were not enough to take him, & so drove him home. I went to the station & explained the whole matter, & saw him put into the cell amongst some of the most inferior dossit in the way of drunken prostitutes as you would wish to see. The inspector asked me to go down to Bow St this morning to speak to the magistrate, so I went, but the poet (who was let out on bail at 6 this morning) did not put in an appearance, so they are going to issue a summons. Isn't this encouraging? – just as Flaws had got on excellent terms as to an American edition of the "Night". I must say that the police are very good to him; they sent for the doctor in the small hours of the morning, but of course the old humbug cd. not so easily summon *him* as the police. I give up entirely. More as the carnival passes.

P.S. *On no* account write to Huntley St.'

Description by W. Stewart Ross, given to Thomson's biographer Henry Salt, of a meeting he and G.G. Flaws (pen-name 'Gegeef') had with Thomson some time in May 'after his return from Leicester'

'The glance of a moment sufficed to show Gegeef and myself that our companion was in the sodden state which succeeds a prolonged debauch. And shortly we found it only too evident that the debauch had ended only because the oil of Mammon had ceased to feed the fire of Bacchus. Gegeef advanced a small loan, and in spite of his remonstrances, the bar at the Holborn Restaurant was the only mart in the whole world in which Thomson would consent to have the little sum disbursed. . .

297

He stands before me now as distinctly as he did nearly seven years ago among the well dressed people at that glittering bar – he the abject, shabby, the waif among those who had never even knocked at the door of Renown, which he had knocked and entered, *maugre* his rags and hunger. They, with their fashionable garments, shining hats, and gold chains, stood apart from him as they would a tramp or beggar. Gegeef stood close on the one side of him, and I on the other, to prevent his noticing the "respectable" stand apart from him. He observed our strategic movement, and recognised it with a faint smile, in which there was a mixture of kindness and contempt.'

From H. Hood Barrs to J.W. Barrs

May 9th: 'As perhaps you know, this gent is off again. Fought his way into Scott's the other night! He owes about 50/- at Bow St for fines! Very bad.'

From Percy Holyoake to J.W. Barrs

May 10th (telegram): 'Gibson seeks instruction from magistrate today as to charging the Hopeful with arson.'

May 11th: 'Doubtless you are still wondering as to my telegram of yesterday. Decidedly I think it is nothing more or less than arson. About 9 o'clock yesterday morning Gibson sent across for me to have a look at his back-kitchen, where they had confined B.V., who was hopeless drunk, during the night. It was simply paved with charred papers, rags, rubbish, &c. It appears that at about 5 in the morng. G. awoke with a distinct idea of fire hovering about, so he descended & found the rubbish well alight & our hero calmly surveying the scene from his arm-chair, refusing any word of explanation, or anything of the sort. Judging from what I saw, he had secreted a box of matches (*not* vestas) & built the fire on the wooden table, feeding with the old dusters he could get about the house. There can be not the slightest doubt that it was fired maliciously. G. had been shipping into him exceedingly during the evng., & that was his set-off. There is just the chance that he thought he might get choked, but he was not drunk enough for that. G. said he wd. see the magistrate about it, & the end of the matter is that he was strongly advised to eject him & let the police deal with him as circumstances occur. Well, yesterday Flaws fetched him away from Scott's & took him to "Dyott's Chamber", a bed & bugs, fourpenny sort of place where if business *is* bad, you can have a "twopenny rope" & do a little "musth falling" [? illegible] – but I wonder. Arriving there, B.V. was hungry & he was dispatched for forage & returned – Flaws waiting in the meanwhile – triumphant with two sausages, & immediately set down amongst a motley area expecting I suppose that they would be cooked for him. However Flaws set him on the right track, & then left him for the night, giving him 2/-. This morng. Gibson was saying how relieved he felt at being rid of such a nightmare, & crowing that, if ever B.V. did turn up there again tight, he'd get a warm reception. Now listen, the whole time G. was thus yarning, B.V. was upstairs in one of his unlet rooms!! Miss S. had neglected to obtain the key from Thomson, & he had slipped in upstairs while they were at breakfast. About 10 he was bundled out again – he had left *his mark* in the room – saying he should go & see some friends in the Park, & since then no one seems to have seen him. I've been with Flaws at several of the lodging houses hereabout . . . I'm open to bet if he gets one clear pound in his pocket he's down to Leicester within three hours. He wants to talk with *you*. Miss S. says that you and Mrs Thomson are the two he is most anxious to see at present.'

May 12th (telegram): 'For creating a disturbance at Gibson's this morng. Turner was sentenced to fourteen days.'

May 12th (letter): 'Perhaps there never was a more pitiable sight than B.V. in the dock this morng. Y'day evng. it struck one that money was coming into him a little faster than was good for him, so I made a few inquiries at the shops where he was in the habit of dealing. At the newsvendors a curious tale was told. He had been pestering them all day for money, & was refused, he being so drunk. At 6 o'clock he walked in for 26 copies of the 'sixpenny novelette', which was also refused him. Then a battle of words ensued, in which doubtless the poor old lady came off second best. Thomson would have some things – so he suddenly helped himself to 2 copies of the Prayer Book, morocco bound, 2/3d each, one copy *Shelley* at 3/6, 5 copies of the Novelette, one copy *Theatre*, and other sundries to the tune of 11/3, & bolted before the old dame could stop him. He being an old customer, she hesitated to give chase.

Nothing did I see of him till about 9 last eveng., when he was lying on the doorstep at Gibson's in the most filthy condition I *ever* saw him, simply nauseous. Move he could not. Tactics failed, suasion failed, force failed. At about 11 Gibson & friend took him to the before-mentioned "Chambers", but he was refused admission. At 2 o'clock this morning he was thundering at Gibson's door, demanding entrance. Twice the police turned him away, but to no purpose, for back he came again, & was then charged as "drunk & disorderly". Safely at the station, searched

& locked up, then soon he bothered the officials for whisky! Gibson took him over some coffee & toast. When this morning I got down to the Court, it was not open so I wandered down the Strand hoping to find Henry & asking him his advice – Wright being dead against my interfering. Fortunately I met Henry and both of us went into Court. Gibson said nothing more than he possibly could; he didn't want any punishment, simply protection. Then poor old B.V., shaking from head to foot, mud-splashed, "black, greasy & unkempt", faltered in, with "I won't go near you again, Mr Gibson". Then came the ultimatum of 20/- or 14 days, and he was removed. Up jumped Henry from the solicitors' table; "I would ask your worship's advice about paying the fine." "Well, do you think he will keep sober? I understand the case I think; it appears to me that he has *delirium tremens*. If you can give an understanding that he will be all right, I'll let him out on his personal security."

Of course in the face of this nothing could be done; so both magistrate, Henry & myself thought that he wd. be the gainer of this temporary detention. You see, by speaking after he went below, B.V. cd. not hope to be paid for, & it saved him doubtless some suffering. Never again do I want to see such a picture. The case coming on comparatively early, no reporters were present, so it will not be in the papers; had they been, I shd. have asked them not to send it in.

Now what do you think is to be done? One thing is pretty certain – that he will want a complete rig-out before he leaves the House of Correction. H. and I are going to meet him this day fortnight. Writing all this may seem pretty cold-blooded & callous, when the whole business might have been settled for £1, *plus* former arrears perhaps. We both of us debated the question for some time. Had he been out on these terms, where wd. he have gone? The police would not take so much care of him again as they have done hitherto; being officially an "incorrigible" he wd. doubtless have received pretty rough handling.'

From H. Hood Barrs to J.W. Barrs

May 12th: 'B.V. was sentenced to 14 days in the Bow St Police Court this morning 20/- or 14 days for annoying Gibson. I was there & asked Vaughan whether he would advise me to pay the fine or not. He said *not* – so I did not, especially as his opinion concurred with mine. Inspector Galy asked him on order to brace up very determinedly & so we left the poetic blackguard to take "a spell in a cool cell of stately Pentonville".'

From Percy Holyoake to J.W. Barrs

Sunday, May 28th: 'The plot certainly thickens. On Thursday at 12.15 I left B.V. en route for Morley; at 3 o'clock, with some several guineas in his pocket, he convivialised at the "Bedford Head", and then he went straight to Miss Scott, made over – in a manner oft before rehearsed – his goods & chattels, & announced his intention of jumping off the Viaduct. However, as night wore on, his downy home became dearer, so "for the last time" he turned in with the youngster George, & slept quietly till 1 o'clock, when the whole house was roused by the cry of "Brandy". And he lay in bed & chimed out as nearly as possible this one request, and so on till 4, when he got up saying "he would do it", dressed *minus* boots & hat, & left the house, & has since been lost sight of.'

May 31st: 'Gibson this aftn. says he must take exceedingly severe measures, & purposes ejecting B.V. & chattels once more. Tomorrow we shall see if he has succeeded. Yesterday aftn. he was on the high road to recovery, but this morning at 5 o'clock he went out, & returned with more than a full complement. This is the last straw for G., & much as he regrets these semi-brutal measures he has to again throw him out. Clarke called this morng. expecting to find you in town. I was unfortunately out. I have written to Liverpool in reference to a "retreat", & am awaiting reply.'

Account of June 1st given Thomson's biographer Henry Salt by T.E. Clarke.

'On the 1st of June, 1882, I went by appointment to meet James Thomson, at Philip Marston's rooms in Euston Road. When I arrived, between seven and eight o'clock in the evening, I found three persons there – Marston himself, Mr William Sharp, and a third whom I did not know; a man with a careworn, tragic face, a remarkably furrowed forehead, and a leaden complexion; a ghastly figure. He was half-lying, half-sitting on the sofa, and it was clear that something was very wrong; in fact, I had not been long in the room before he sank back on the sofa, with some incoherent muttering, and relapsed into total unconsciousness.

It was explained to me that Thomson, for this was the author of "The City of Dreadful Night", had arrived at Marston's rooms early in the day, and had spent the morning with his host. They had read poetry, they had talked, doubtless there had been whiskey. Towards afternoon Thomson had asked if he might lie on Marston's bed, and

301

there he had spent the rest of the day until shortly before my arrival, when he had made his appearance in the lamentable state I have described. I was taken into the bedroom, and found some marks of blood on the sheets.

What was to be done? Thomson could not be left on Marston's sofa; so much was clear. Marston was blind and helpless; he occupied the second floor of the house; his father had the first floor. But Dr Marston was quite useless in an emergency. His ceremonious, old-world courtesy never forsook him, but his faculties did; he was every whit as helpless as his son. Somebody asked where Thomson lived, and somebody else, Philip Marston I think, was able to produce an address that had once been his. Here was a gleam of hope. We left Mr Sharp to watch the sick man, and Philip and I went off to find his lodgings. The usual things happened; we were misdirected by others; we lost the way for ourselves; we got the right number in the wrong street, and the wrong number in the right one, but we found the place at last.

A shaggy-browed man in his shirt-sleeves answered my ring, holding a candle above his head and scowling at us from the dark doorway.

"Live here? Mr Thomson? No, he don't," he snapped rudely.

"We were told he used to lodge here," I ventured to suggest.

"He tried to burn this here house down one night," retorted the man more rudely than before, "and he don't come here again if I know it."

"He's been taken very ill," I urged. "He can do no harm now. Won't you take him in if we bring him?"

The man emphasised his refusal with an oath, and slammed the door.

"That's cheerful," remarked Marston, after a short pause of astonishment. "Now what are we to do?" A question to which I had no answer ready.

However, we could not go back exactly as we had started; so we called upon a doctor, and took him with us to Marston's rooms, where nothing had happened in our absence.

Thomson could not be roused, and the doctor, after examining the pupils of his eyes and feeling his pulse, recommended his immediate removal to hospital. Mr Sharp and I carried him downstairs, put him in a cab, and took him to University College.

The house-surgeon was sewing up a yawning gash in a man's head, and could not attend to him; so he lay huddled upon a bench until the house-physician could be fetched. We had to wait some time. The wounded man chatted cheerfully; his companion, who had inflicted the gash, endeavoured to persuade him that it was done out of pure friendship; the inevitable woman who was at the bottom of the quarrel agreed with both; the surgeon went on with his work, paying little attention to either.

At last the house-physician arrived, and Thomson was taken away to the wards, without recovering consciousness, and I never saw him again.'

From Philip Bourke Marston to T.E. Clarke

June 2nd: 'A thousand thanks for all you did last night. Yesterday has rather shaken me. Sharp and I called upon Thomson to-day, and found him collected, but very ill. He asked for a shilling in case he should want to write any letters. What an awful revelation of things, is it not? I don't think he could have had sixpence in the world. We tried, but all in vain, to obtain any information about his recent residence.'

From Percy Holyoake to J.W. Barrs

June 3rd (telegram, 7.35 p.m.): 'He is dying at the University Hospital. Found him by accident. Very serious.'

From Resident Medical Officer, University Hospital to J.W. Barrs

June 4th (telegram, 1.08 a.m.): 'Regret to say James Thomson died this evening at 10.'

From Percy Holyoake to J.W. Barrs

June 4th: 'On going to the Hospital, I found Wright & Gibson waiting to see the doctor, to ascertain exactly the state of affairs. No inquest will be necessary, as they certify that poor B.V. died of broken blood-vessel, & it was from the bowels the great loss of blood came. A pitiable tale they tell; at the utmost he could have "lingered on a few days", his bowels being nearly non-existent. They make a post-mortem tomorrow. Bourke Marston did not know of the fatal ending, till I saw him this morning.

The nurse says he was conscious till within a few minutes of the end. About the funeral. We think on Thursday next at Highgate Cemetery, in my father's grave. See being a family grave, there would be a great saving of trouble by that arrangement. The suggestion came from Mrs W. – and unless any objection is raised by the brother, it strikes me as the best that can be done. On this I will make you more fully aware when an answer is received from him.

Poor Miss Scott is dreadfully cut up. Almost the first thing she said was that she would wish that a certain little purse & lock of hair, in her keeping, might be put with him in his last home.'

June 6th: 'The mss from Kegan Paul is here. He suggests a memorial volume, & wants to have the opportunity of considering it. See him damned first – that's my sentiments, ditto Chatto & Windus.

After you were gone, I went back to the Hospital & had a long chat with Miss Staynes, leaving with her poor old B.V.'s only treasure – the hair and purse – which she promised to see was placed with him. I just told her enough to enlist her sympathy & interest which was only too easily roused. I have asked her to come and see Mrs W. She seemed only too pleased feeling she said rather lonely at times. Besides I think it just as well to keep the doctor & nurses in sight, for of course some day we shall have the death-bed repentance business in all its details again. I am sending a copy of the "City" to the Dr.

I can't say I admire the way in which the funeral arrangements are being carried out. Economy is being studied a little too much. I had a bit of a tiff with Wright last night about it. Let's have the names up as soon as possible. Nothing from the brother pro or con. Am going to see Henry tonight.

11.30 p.m. Young Watts came asking up here last night for an article on this "sad event". He had nothing but the doormat.'

From T.R. Wright to Bertram Dobell

June 7th: 'In order to suit the conveniance of friends from Leicester it has been arranged for the funeral to leave 71 Euston Road (opposite St Pancras) at 12 exactly tomorrow.'

CHAPTER TWENTY-TWO:

POSTSCRIPTS

The fleeting accidents of a man's life, and its external shows, may indeed be irrelate and incongruous; but the organising principles which fuse into harmony, and gather about fixed predetermined centres, whatever heterogeneous elements life may have accumulated from without, will not permit the grandeur of human unity greatly to be violated, or its ultimate repose to be troubled, in the retrospect from dying moments, or from other great convulsions.

De Quincey: 'The Palimpsest' (*Suspiria de Profundis*)

So little do we know ourselves that when we begin a train of thought we never have any idea of where we shall end. Thus a sentence of Shelley's about sympathy and imagination has led to a series of reflections tending towards the doctrine that the conviction of personality is not a so-called 'Necessary Truth,' intuitive, axiomatic, above and inaccessible to logic, anterior to experience; that it is not simple but compound; and that a more extended and subtle analysis may reduce it to the rank into which the analysis of Hume reduced the idea of causation, the analysis of Berkeley the belief in the independent exterior existence of matter, the analysis of Kant the belief in the universal existence of space and time.

> We are such stuff
> As dreams are made on, and our little life
> Is rounded with a sleep.
> James Thomson: Conclusion to his essay 'Sympathy'

The remarriage of Austin Holyoake's widow had meant that there was space in the family lair, it being now unlikely she would be buried in the grave of her former husband. Thomson's coffin was thus able to be buried there on June 8th, and Austin Holyoake's own 'Secularist Burial Service' was again used at his own graveside. Theodore Wright added a farewell oration remembering Thomson as 'the pleasantest companion one could have': though the poetry showed gloom, 'those who knew him best must sometimes have been struck with the contrast between the tone of many of his poems and the merry mood which was habitual with him in society'. Thomson had found sadness easier to confide to the page than to people in the flesh; as for the cause of this sadness, he had had 'sorrows in early life which blighted his hopes and cast a gloom over his whole career, and which, though never spoken of, were, I believe, never forgotten. This consideration may well make us think gently of his failings, and they were not many, while his virtues would take long to recount.' The poet would have approved had he known it was to be in Austin Holyoake's grave that he would be buried: 'it would have given him pleasure to know that his ashes would mingle with those of his old friend and fellow-worker in the great cause of the redemption of humanity from the bondage of superstition.' Those present to hear this oration included the brother John Parker Thomson, Bertram Dobell, Percy Holyoake, Jack and Harriet Barrs, Harry Hood Barrs, Philip Bourke Marston, Mathilde Blind, Eleanor Marx, Gordon G. Flaws, and Thomson's former landlord, Mr Gibson.[1]

There was more than just Thomson's reputation at stake in the hope that people might 'think gently of his failings', for 'B.V.' had published over twenty years in secularist publications, and many would hold his memory as that of the movement's brightest if not only literary star. When Theodore Rich Wright's oration was printed in the *Secular Review*, it became only the first of many published deliberations that in the following years sought to protect Thomson's, and thereby Secularism's, reputation. It was feared that Christians reading the pessimistic poetry might charge that want of religious faith had made Thomson pessimistic: and that evangelical thunderers like Cumming might choose to see in Thomson's last weeks no more than further example of the miseries to be expected by any debauched infidel in his last awful hours before judgment. It became more than the duty of friendship to point up the cheery side of Thomson – which by numerous accounts certainly existed; and as for the gloomy side, which by other accounts also certainly existed, and which in the writing was indisputable, it became necessary to find exonerating cause for this beyond any supposed want of religious belief. The drinking and the final homelessness had to be made, if hardly respectable, then at least removed somehow from its place in the outer unspeakable limits of inexcusable scandal. The bowed-head 'veil of decency' ploy would only make some whispers more audible. In fact, just as before the life, so now after it: a bargain had to be struck between free will and determinism. As much as was praiseworthy should lie with volition, and all that was tarnished should lie with Fate. But it was not to be so easy.

The drinking, it was decided, was constitutional: his father drank, other members of the family drank, so therefore Thomson's drinking had been his 'miserable inheritance'.[2] Not surprisingly this was news that was not well received either with relatives north of the border or with Thomson's brother in Manchester. John Thomson saw no reason why his father's memory should be maligned in order that his late brother be made respectable for literary London; nor were other relatives glad to see themselves portrayed as a family with a weakness for producing children fated to terminal drinking.[3] Protests were made, but the 'inevitability' aspect was too tempting totally to be let go. A token placatory gesture was attempted: that though some said intemperance in Thomson's father had caused the family's 'fall in the social scale', there was no evidence for this – 'except that Thomson once told a friend, in after years, that intemperance ran in the family, and that "nearly all the members of it who 'had brains', especially a gifted aunt of his, fell victim to its power".'[4] There could be no argument, was the implication, with a quote from the dead man himself.

There was no argument either about the unhappiness caused Thomson by some circumstances of his life: the death of his young sister, his father's illness and change of mood, the boy's removal to an orphanage, his mother's death; his want of recognition as a writer, his isolation in lodgings, his penury in the last years of his life. These matters of circumstance could even be seen as predisposing factors towards a restrained adult unhappiness that the drinking if not the writing itself might have sought episodically to uninhibit. The question was whether such predisposing factors towards depression could cumulatively add up to the nature of a determinant. For some the answer was no insofar as this particular list of circumstances went, but yes in respect of a final Overshadowing Circumstance or Life-Event, which had tragically tipped the balance. Such memorialists, notably, were Bertram Dobell and Thomson's only major biographer, Henry Salt. For G.W. Foote though – 'that skunk' – no such Life-Event had even been necessary: what he called 'the secret of Thomson's life-tragedy' had been that he suffered from 'constitutional melancholia'. When this gathered strength Thomson, not a habitual drinker, would fight against it for weeks, then would succumb to fits of drinking 'like fits of madness'; in his last years these fits became more frequent. In other words, in twentieth-century language, Foote judged Thomson to have been a manic-depressive alcoholic of the bout-drinker type. 'Thomson's life does not require any defence or palliation,' wrote Foote, 'it only needs to be explained'.[5]

If people were inclined to look for 'the secret' or 'the key' to Thomson's life, this was understandable. Even beyond the desire to reduce the life to the behaviour, the behaviour to a type, the type to its precipitate – which would of course 'explain' everything – there was the mystery of the purse and locket of hair that Thomson had given Miss Scott and asked that she make sure was buried with him: 'poor old B.V.'s only treasure', as Percy Holyoake had called it. Could this not be taken as a valedictory statement by Thomson himself that what had been of value to him in his life had been centred on these objects – or that these were the only funerary objects he desired, like an ancient Egyptian, to sustain him in the afterlife? Again, there was the recurring motif of the poetry and the prose in pleas then visits from beyond the grave by a young girl to the solitary in his room: 'Mater Tenebrarum', the sonnets to the Barneses, 'A Lady of Sorrow', 'Vane's Story', 'I Had a Love', 'The Fair of Saint Sylvester', 'The Poet and His Muse'. Of course there was 'poetic convention', of course it was common enough for men to write of women as 'angels', 'divine' and so on – and leave the sexual repression, the prostitution, or men's fear of women for another book in another age. But why *this* use of the convention, why 'you adorable child', 'you good child', or the phrase 'who died so young' used again and again; each time with no filling-out or explanation, as if each different persona that Thomson presented in this way somehow referred to the same bereavement, and the same young girl? And what about the sonnet privately addressed to the Barneses (pp. 96-97) in which Thomson spoke of having had his life ruined by such a bereavement, the sonnet obviously having been written in the understanding that the Barneses knew exactly to whom he was referring?

In the sixth sonnet to the Barneses, wrote Bertram Dobell, was to be found as far as it is possible to find, that Overshadowing Circumstance, the Life-Event – the key: 'it is in the sixth sonnet that we find the key to Thomson's life-story – in so far at least as we can find in any one event the key to the complexities of the human soul. It was in the household of Mr and Mrs Barnes, as we are here informed, that Thomson first met his "Good Angel" – the young girl so much loved and afterwards so deeply regretted. She was the daughter of the armourer-sergeant of a regiment stationed in Ballincollig. Her name was Matilda Weller, and she was then about fourteen years of age.'[6]

Let us pause here for a moment, thank Theodore Wright for his careful speech – and now bury the poet properly. The free-will *versus* determinism debate that went on for decades over the poet's corpse could suggest that the life needed some apology; that exoneration was necessary in order that the Mr Bumble whose literary tastes Thomson had loathed, should now be persuaded that the poet and his work deserved a decent if retired seat in the 'private tragedy' room of Bloomsbury Hall. Here are fresh mourners at the graveside to pay their respects with other farewells – or whose occasional disrespect is useful in its self-revelation of the Bumble within.[7]

BERTRAM DOBELL

Though he will, I suppose, never be a 'popular poet' – which means no more, perhaps, than a poet whose works have an extensive sale, though it may be doubted if more than a few of those who buy them ever read them – his works, I think, should be known to a far larger number of readers and students than is now the case. If anyone chooses to say that, in this case, I am hardly an impartial judge, I shall not be particularly anxious to rebut the accusation. That I was of some use to the unfortunate poet in his lifetime is one of my most cherished memories; and it is now, as it always has been, my earnest desire to keep alive and extend the fame of 'B.V.' by all the means within my power . . .

Looking back upon what I have written, I feel how inadequately I have performed my task. I only attempted it because of my earnest desire to see some degree of justice done to the memory of one whom I admired indeed as an author, but whom, in even greater degree, I loved as a man. The world is strangely blind to its great men, and a Shelley, a Wordsworth, a Browning, or a George Meredith has to die, or at least to labour unnoticed for many years, before the great British public begins to discover that a splendid addition has been made to its glorious endowment. If I have done a little to hasten the coming of the time when Thomson's great gifts shall be appraised at their true value, my labour has not been in vain, and I shall not go unrewarded.

PHILIP BOURKE MARSTON

No tears of mine shall fall upon thy face;
  Whatever City thou hast gained, at last,
  Better it is than that where thy feet passed
So many times, such weary nights and days.
Those journeying feet knew all its inmost ways;
  Where shapes and shadows of dread things were cast,
  There moved thy soul, profoundly dark and vast,
There did thy voice its hymn of anguish raise.

Thou wouldst have left that City of great Night,
  Yet travelled its dark mazes, all in vain;
But one way leads from it, which, found aright,
  Who goes by it may not return again.
There didst thou grope thy way, through thy long pain;
Hast thou, outside, found any world of light?

HARRIET BARRS

. . . his extraordinary charm of manner, and great insight into character. His eyes read your thoughts.

GEORGE MEREDITH

I had a full admiration of his nature and his powers. Few men have been endowed with so brave a heart. He did me the honour to visit me twice, when I was unaware of the tragic affliction overshadowing him, but we could see that he was badly weighted. I have now the conviction that the taking away of poverty from his burdens would in all likelihood have saved him to enrich our literature. For his verse was a pure well.

He probably had, as most of us have had, his heavy suffering on the soft side. But he inherited the tendency to the thing that slew him. And it is my opinion that, in consideration of his high and singularly elective mind, he might have worked clear of it to throw it off, if circumstances had been smoother and brighter about him. For thus he would have been saved from drudgery, have had time to labour at conceptions that needed time for maturing and definition even before the evolvement of them. He would have had what was also much needed in his case, a more spacious home, a more companioned life, more than merely visiting friends, good and true to him though they were. A domestic centre of any gracious kind would have sheathed his over-active, sensational imaginativeness, to give it rest, and enabled him to feel the delight of drawing it forth bright and keen of edge.

We will hope for a better fate to befall men of genius. Nothing is to be said against the public in his case. But I could wish that there were some Fund for the endowing of our wide Literary University with the means of aid to young authors who have put forth flowers of promise, as Thomson did when he was yet to be rescued.

HELEN BIRKMYRE

I deeply regret now that we did not make him come to see us here, if we had done so it might have been so much better for him.

JULIA THOMSON

You see from his letters how genial & happy & funny he could be. I know he cheered me many a time – & I know too that my separation from his brother (who seems to have inherited his father's failing) caused him an additional pang which could well have been spared him.

ALGERNON SWINBURNE

. . . a writer whose ability is unquestionable, but who has left behind him, as well as some remarkable and creditable verses some of the silliest and most offensive rubbish whether regarded from the point of view of a poet, a critic, or a free thinker that ever discredited the memory of a man who might have left behind him a respectable and memorable name.

JOHN ADDINGTON SYMONDS

I cannot as yet construct him for myself as an actual person, or persuade myself that I have any grasp upon the central nature of the man. This is not strange. He has left the world too recently, and while he lived in it he was too far from the average Englishman (e.g. from the ordinary public schoolboy, Oxonian, and litterateur such as I am) to be approached familiarly.

KARL MARX

[*Of the Heine translations*] . . . no translation, but a reproduction of the original, such as Heine himself, if master of the English language, would have done.

HERMAN MELVILLE

The 'Weddah and Om-el-Bonain' gave me more pleasure than anything I have seen a long while. The fable and the verse are alike supremely beautiful. 'Sunday up the River', contrasting with 'The City of Dreadful Night', is like a Cuban humming-bird, beautiful in faery tints, flying against the tropic thundercloud. Your friend was a sterling poet, if ever one sang. As to pessimism, altho' neither pessimist nor optimist myself, nonetheless I relish it in the verse, if for nothing else than as a counterpoise to the exorbitant hopefulness, juvenile and shallow, that makes such a muster in these days – at least in some quarters.

'The City of Dreadful Night' – one can hardly overestimate it, massive and mighty as it is, – its gloom and its sublimity. The confronting Sphinx and Angel – where shall we go to match them?

It is long since I have been so interested in a volume as in that of the *Essays and Phantasies* . . . The motions of his mind in the best of the essays are utterly untrammelled and independent, and yet falling naturally into grace and poetry. It is good for me to think of such a mind – to know that such a brave intelligence has been, and may yet be for aught anyone can demonstrate to the contrary.

Perhaps it is not inappropriate after all that the most finished surviving manuscript of 'The City of Dreadful Night' should have ended up in America.[8] But what of this 'key' to Thomson's life? Let us, as we walk up Gower Street – noting that Number Twelve is now inhabited by the philosophy department of Birkbeck College – consider a summary of the main positions.

Both Dobell then Henry Salt in his 1889 biography *The Life of James Thomson (B.V.)*, made clear that Helen Gray had had place in Thomson's affections. Both quoted Agnes's memory of Thomson's admiration for Helen. Salt drew attention to the poem 'Meeting Again', wrote that perhaps Thomson's cessation of visits to the Grays was due to a revival of his earlier affections for her – Helen at the time of the last visit being engaged to be married – and mentioned that Thomson had 'treasured' in later years a purse that Helen had 'worked for him'. But in 1889 Salt only mentioned that 'a locket, with a tress of yellow hair – the one memento of his lost love' had been buried, though the later revised biography changed this to 'a small purse with a locket' – leaving alert sleuths to make their own speculations from the mention of Helen's purse earlier. Perhaps the married Helen Gray had no desire that biographers portray her as she in whose memory a broken-hearted poet had drank his way to the grave. Salt was likewise put firmly off the scent when he made enquiry about Thomson's rumoured attraction for Harriet Barrs at Forest Edge. There are obstacles as well as advantages for the biographer of the recently dead.

At any rate – shall we go round by Huntley Street? The house is no longer there, just flats that look as if they were built about sixty years ago – at any rate, it was Matilda Weller that both Bertram Dobell and Henry Salt settled on as the girl with whom Thomson had been in love, and whose death had been the great calamity in Thomson's life. Bradlaugh was not impressed, and Bradlaugh had been there. He may not have been pleased with Dobell's having written that the wonder was not that Bradlaugh and Thomson had split up, but that they had remained friends for so long. Bradlaugh said of the supposed tragic love story that in fact the girl had been only 'a little child, playing with children's toys', and that only in later years had Thomson 'built bit by bit a poetical romance around her memory'.[9] When Salt went to see him, Bradlaugh said Matilda had been 'about 13', and that any idea of a betrothal having occurred was 'purely imaginary – a poetical invention on Thomson's part'.[10] Still at least he seemed not to dispute that it was Matilda around whom a romance had been built, and that it was Thomson initially who had built it. Foote, with his 'constitutional melencholia' theory, said that if Matilda had not died, some other prime source of grief would equally have served as focus.[11] Hypatia said that from her own experience Thomson simply loved children, and children 'adored' him; if she or her sister had died young, he could easily have built the romance around the memory of one of them.[12] Of course it all came down to what this 'love' consisted of, given the sexual-border age at which Matilda had died.

Let us imagine we have walked the five-minute walk down to Museum Street, and the attendant has let us both in to the Reading Room at the Museum. Here is the 1889 *The Life of James Thomson ('B.V.')* by Henry Salt. What a readable book it is, both here and in its shorter later versions! Whatever the criticisms that have been made of Salt and of Bertram Dobell for their emphasis on the effect of Matilda Weller's death on Thomson, where is the scholar who has done their equal on Thomson's behalf? Nowhere. That is all that need be said, with respect, on that matter. Here is Salt's conclusion:

> There can be no doubt whatever not only that his sorrow was overwhelming at the time, but that it left its traces on his whole subsequent career. To what extent this early bereavement can be considered the *cause* of his later pessimism and unhappiness, is a more subtle question, which it is easier to raise than to decide . . . we are compelled to believe, at the same time, that it was the death of this young girl that, above all circumstances, fostered and developed that malady to which Thomson was perhaps predisposed, and that in this limited sense at least, it was a cause of his subsequent despondency . . . It would, I think, be as unfair to Thomson to assume that he was only lightly and transiently affected by the death of the girl he loved, as to make the contrary mistake of attributing to this the weakness of allowing his whole life to be wrecked by it.[13]

He has already mentioned that it was at Aldershot in 1854 that Thomson first started drinking. The coded message is that Matilda's death was the trigger setting off the alcoholism that destroyed him.

Salt writes that Matilda was 'about fourteen' at the time. When Salt was interviewing people for the book, Grant told him he understood Matilda had been about fifteen or sixteen. The Barneses apparently had told Grant of 'the love' between Thomson and Matilda, 'undoubtedly a sort of engagement'. Thomas Carson, in 1888 the headmaster at the Royal Military Asylum, seemed to confirm that the Barneses had spoken of this. Carson told Henry Salt (here we may briefly imagine ourselves in the lovely quiet beside the leaded windows in Duke Humfrey's Library, the Bodleian, Oxford) 'his engagement with Matilda Weller was mentioned often by Mr Barnes. She was one of the girls' class in the regimental school. And very beautiful.' Salt saw Matilda's surviving young brother William, who had been about ten at the time. William remembered nothing other than that he thought Matilda had been about fourteen or fifteen when she died. But he told Salt that his mother, now dead, did once mention to his wife that there had been 'a distinct engagement'. But this 'engagement' which Salt three times noted his separate interviewees as having mentioned: what did it really mean?[14] Let us look again at Salt's biography, and at Dobell's introductory memoir in *A Voice from the Nile*. We are still under the Rotunda of the British Museum Reading Room. It was only in our imagination that we had travelled to Oxford.

Dobell mentions the sole statement about Matilda Weller attributed to Mrs Barnes, writing that 'She was described by Mrs Barnes as resembling in character the Evangeline St Clair of *Uncle Tom's Cabin*.'[15] Both he and Henry Salt then expand on this by quoting a description of the young Eva as first introduced by Harriet Beecher Stowe in her novel:

> Her form was the perfection of childish beauty, without its usual chubbiness and squareness of outline. There was about it an undulating and aerial grace, such as one might dream of for some mythic and allegorical being. Her face was remarkable, less for its perfect beauty of feature than for a singular and dreamy earnestness of expression, which made the ideal start when they looked at her, and by which the dullest and most literal were impressed, without knowing why. The shape of her head and the turn of her neck and bust were peculiarly noble, and the long golden-brown hair that floated like a cloud around it, the deep spiritual gravity of her violet-blue eyes, shaded by heavy fringes of golden-brown, all marked her out from other children, and made every one turn and look after her, as she glided hither and thither . . . Always dressed in white, she seemed to move like a shadow through all sorts of places without contracting spot or stain.

Dobell writes that the portrait of Eva St Clair is of 'quite a young girl' but it needs only some adjustment to make it fit one 'much older'. Salt writes of the description of Eva that 'Such was Matilda Weller as she lived in Mrs Barnes's recollection.' When he had tried to contact Mrs Barnes, he had in fact received a letter from the tenant of her former house in the Isle of Man, saying that she had died four years before.[16]

A pity. It would have helped much to have had Mrs Barnes clear it up, once and for all. The eternal complaint of the biographer. But it is not impossible that this 'engagement' to which Salt found repeated hearsay mention, was the same one that Thomson in fact informed the Barneses about in 1862; that they in other words, though remembering Matilda and Thomson as friends, jumped to the same conclusion as Salt and Dobell – from the same material. The strength of this speculation is that it allows for everyone to be remembered as having been telling their own version of the truth. The 'error' of the two biographers would then have lain in their taking the autobiography in the sonnets at face value. But even 'autobiography' is not innocent, and not when addressed in homage to two former adoptive parents. Having praised Joseph and Alice as separate paragons of male and female virtue, Thomson as it were then exculpated his own avowed worthlessness by pointing to a might-have-been. Then, four days later, though not for the Barneses, he finished another love poem.

Let us have a look again at this Eva St Clair whose character Matilda so resembled, and whose portrait as painted by Harriet Beecher Stowe was apparently such as lived in the memory of Mrs Barnes. Here we have a copy of *Uncle Tom's Cabin*. There is the quoted portrait, in Chapter Fourteen. Restored to context, it can be seen, somewhat incongruously, to be the introductory portrait of a little girl 'aged between five and six' running about a steamboat on the Mississippi. If we look at where else in the book she is described – between Chapters Twenty-Two and Twenty-Six – we can see that this is an unusual character for Mrs Barnes to have mentioned. Eva does die young, but rather younger even than Matilda Weller; the novel has only moved on 'a little over two years' before she falls ill and dies.

But what is most striking about Eva St Clair is neither her looks nor the fact that like so many children of her time, she dies young; what is most striking about her is her religiosity. In fact this little child at the heart of *Uncle Tom's Cabin* has been pointedly portrayed by Harriet Beecher Stowe as a little female Christ-figure, whose love and example can convert the Black slaves to Christianity, and make the white slave-owners repent. The child's favourite Biblical texts apparently are *Revelation* and the Prophetic Books; she knows she is dying and looks forward to being with Jesus. 'No more than Christ-like' Eva lies on her deathbed under a carved wooden angel, with a statue of Jesus on the mantel and her fingers in a Bible. True she does not break bread and ask that this be done in remembrance of her. Instead she has her long hair cut, asks for the servants to be assembled, and tells the crowd round her deathbed: 'I want to give you something that, when you look at, you shall always remember me. I'm going to give all of you a curl of my hair; and when you look at it, think that I loved you and am gone to heaven, and that I want to see you all there.'

The portrait of Evangeline St Clair, in other words, is part of that literary tradition which would include the portrait of Isabella Campbell of Fernicarry as described in Storey's memoir *Peace in Believing*; and her sister Mary's experiences as described in the memoir of the MacDonalds of Port Glasgow. It would connect also with that letter written by Sarah Kennedy in 1831, the letter which she asked Ann Thomson to destroy. But Ann did not destroy that letter, for it found its way to John Parker Thomson in Manchester,[17] who let Charles Brodie of Port Glasgow copy it in 1895. Then W.F. MacArthur in his 1933 *History of Port Glasgow* mentioned a Charles Brodie who had 'done much valuable research' into Thomson;[18] and in 1976 the author of this book which you now hold in your hand, sent a photocopy enquiry to all the Brodies in Port Glasgow and Greenock whose names were in the telephone directory. Mr Brodie's surviving daughter and grandson very kindly responded from Surrey, to where one of the photocopies had been redirected. The research, and the letter, had survived.[19]

Shall we go and pay our respects at the grave of Ann Thomson, who lies in the same grave as two of her sisters in the cemetery on the hill overlooking Port Glasgow? No sooner said than done, in our imagination, and as you can see from here it is but a few yards' step to where we have a view over the whole Firth of Clyde, with the Rosneath peninsula on the left fronting the mouth of the Gareloch, and the town of Helensburgh straight ahead across the water.[20] Let us cross the Firth and travel the road up through Helensburgh, a mile up past Rhu where MacLeod Campbell used to preach, till we come to Garelochhead and follow the road as it swings left then left again onto Rosneath peninsula. We come to the house by the road called Fernicarry House, and turn up the lane that runs up by its right hand side. We push open the gate into the field at the top, and walk up the hill at the edge of the field, beside the burn. We come to a bend in the burn coming down the hill, where it makes a little waterfall over some large boulders at the point of its turning. As you can see people have levelled out an area with a wall around it at this spot, and put in a small iron gate. On the tablet on the wall in front of you are the barely legible words HERE ISABELLA CAMPBELL WAS WONT TO PRAY.[21]

Across to the left you can see the remains of the farmhouse built in the 1880s to replace the one that Isabella Campbell once knew. The present farmhouse has been bought a few years ago by the Ministry of Defence; but here we now are, standing in its courtyard, the buildings derelict around us. What a grand view we have again over the trees up the loch, Rosneath on the right. A pity, as the locals all complain, that the view is spoiled by the submarine base that takes up so much of the opposing shore. And over the hill at our back, the same hill that Isabella and Mary Campbell prayed and had their religious ecstasies on, down at the shore of Loch Long on the other side is the huge new base at Coulport, from where a new fleet of submarines will patrol the seas of the world.[22]

from VOLNEY: *Meditation on the Ruins of Empires* (1794)

I sat down on the base of a column; and there, my elbow on my knee, and my head resting on my hand, sometimes turning my eyes towards the desert, and sometimes fixing them on the ruins, I fell into a profound reverie.

Here, said I to myself, an opulent city once flourished; this was the seat of a powerful empire. Yes, these places, now so desert, a living multitude formerly animated, and an active crowd went here and there about streets which at present are so solitary . . . And now a mournful skeleton is all that subsists of this opulent city, and nothing remains of its powerful government but a vain and obscure remembrance! The silence of the tomb is substituted for the hum of the market place. The opulence of a commercial city is changed into hideous poverty. The palaces of kings are become the lair of wild beasts, and obscene reptiles inhabit the sanctuary of gods. What glory is here eclipsed, and how many labours are annihilated! Thus perish the works of men, and thus do nations and empires pass away! . . . Reflecting that if the places before me had once exhibited this animated picture; who, I said to myself, can assure me that their present desolation will not one day be the lot of our own country? Who knows but that hereafter some traveller like myself will sit down upon the banks of the Seine, the Thames, or the Zuyder sea, where now, in the tumult of enjoyment, the heart and the eyes are too slow to take in the multitude of sensations; who knows but he will sit down solitary amid silent ruins, and weep a people inurned, and their greatness changed into an empty name?

Unhappy man! said I in my grief, a blind fatality plays with my destiny! a fatal necessity rules by chance the lot of mortals! But, no: they are the decrees of celestial justice that are accomplishing! A mysterious God exercises his incomprehensible judgements! He has doubtless pronounced a secret malediction against the earth; he has struck with a curse the present race of men, in revenge of past generations. Oh, who shall dare to fathom the depths of the Divinity! . . .

THE APPARITION: *How long will man importune the heavens with unjust complaint? How long with vain clamours will he accuse Fate as the author of his calamities? . . . What is this blind fatality, that, without order or laws, sports with the lot of mortals? What is this unjust necessity, which confounds the issue of actions, be they those of prudence or those of folly? In what consists the maledictions of heavens upon these countries? Where is the divine curse that perpetuates this scene of desolation? Monuments of past ages! Say, have the heavens changed their laws, and the earth its course? . . . Falsely do you accuse Fate and the Divinity. Wrongly do you make God the cause of your evils. Tell me, perverse and hypocritical race, if these places are desolate, if powerful cities are reduced to solitude, is it he that has caused the ruin? Is it his hand that has thrown down these walls, sapped these temples, mutilated these pillars? or is it the hand of man? Is it the arm of God that has introduced the sword into the city and set fire to the country, murdered the people, burned the harvests, rooted up the trees, and ravaged the pastures? or is it the arm of man? And when, after this devastation, famine has started up, is it the vengeance of God that has sent it, or the mad fury of mortals? When, during the famine, the people are fed with unwholesome provisions, and pestilence ensues, is it inflicted by the anger of heaven, or brought about by human imprudence? When war, famine and pestilence united, have swept away the inhabitants, and the land has become a desert, is it God that has depopulated it? Is it his rapacity that plunders the labourer, ravages the productive fields, and lays waste the country; or the rapacity of those who govern? Is it his pride that creates murderous wars, or the pride of kings and their ministers? . . . And what is this* infidelity *which founded empires by prudence, defended them by courage, and strengthened them by justice; which raised magnificent cities, made deep harbours, drained pestilential marshes, covered the sea with ships, the earth with inhabitants, and like the creative spirit, diffused life and motion through the world? If such be impiety, what is true belief? Does holiness consist in destruction? Is then the God that peoples the air with birds, the earth with animals, and the waters with reptiles; the God that animates universal nature, a God that delights in ruins and sepulchres? Does he ask devastation for homage, and conflagration for sacrifice? Would he have groans for hymns, murderers to worship him, and a desert and a ravaged world for his temple? Yet such,* holy and faithful *generation, are your works! These are the fruits of your piety! You have massacred the people, reduced cities to ashes, destroyed all traces of cultivation, made the earth a solitude: and you demand the rewards of your labours! Without a doubt miracles must be worked for you! For you the peasant you have murdered should be revived; the walls you have thrown down should rise again; the harvests you have ravaged should flourish; the conduits that you have broken down should be rebuilt; the laws of heaven and earth, those laws which God had established for the display of his greatness and magnificence, those laws anterior to all revelations and to all prophets, those laws which passion cannot alter, and ignorance cannot pervert, should be superseded. Passion knows them not; ignorance, which observes no cause and foresees no effect, has said in the foolishness of her heart, 'Everything comes from chance; a blind fatality distributes good and evil upon the earth; success is not to the prudent, not felicity to the wise.' Or else, assuming the language of hypocrisy, she has said: 'Everything comes from God; and it is his sovereign pleasure to deceive the sage and to confound the judicious'. And she has contemplated the scene with complacency. 'Good!' she has exclaimed: 'I then am as well endowed as the science that despises me! The prudence which haunts and torments me, I will render useless.' Cupidity has joined the chorus: I too will opress the west; I will wring from him the fruits of his labour; for such is the decree of heaven; such the omnipotent will of fate.*

This is the *Ruins of Empires* which Shelley so admired,[23] and which was amongst the books found in Gunner Scott's possessions at Aldershot before his arrest then suicide in 1862. We can hand the book over at the desk now, be it not too tendentious an artifice that we are back in the Reading Room at the Museum. I want this book to finish in the room where Thomson spent so much of his life. Let us call up Thomson's own books that are held here now: *The City of Dreadful Night, Vane's Story, Essays and Phantasies*; the posthumous collections – *A Voice from the Nile, Satires and Profanities, Biographical and Critical Studies, Shelley, Whitman, Poems Essays and Fragments*, the *Collected Poems*. Look at them. What life needs exoneration for these?

But though neither to exonerate nor to blame, it might still be asked if Thomson himself ever gave reason for choosing this specific myth of the young girl who saved. Nobody now knows whose was the tress of hair that was buried with him; whether it be his mother's, his sister's, Agnes Gray's, Matilda Weller's, or 'somebody else''s. Even if it was Matilda Weller around whom he did build a myth in his work, what was the myth based on? To ask this is simply to ask if there might have been a personal reason that he *chose* this – not to suggest that this was an underlying 'key' that somehow chose him. Did he ever, for instance, even directly mention Matilda Weller's name?

The answer is that he is recorded only once as having done so, and further to that is recorded – nothing. The person who remembered his having mentioned the name was Harriet Barrs, who told Salt simply that Thomson mentioned Matilda Weller's death once when speaking to her of his childhood. He liked his mother more than his father, according to Harriet, and he had told her 'the death of his sister, who had been his playmate, was a great grief to him'.[24] The only other reference outside of the poems and fictions that has been taken to be a reference to Matilda, is that 'someone else' mentioned by Thomson in the letter to Julia written five months before his death. The letter is that reproduced on pages three to five of Salt's biography, and already quoted in this book. Referring to his mother's 'cloud of melancholy', Thomson wrote that this had been 'probably deepened by the death of my little sister, of whom I remember being devotedly fond, when she was about three and myself five, of measles caught from me. Had she or someone else lived, I might have been worth something'.

So on these two occasions that Thomson's name has been linked with Matilda, the one definite, the other speculative, in fact it is the little sister whose memory Thomson recalls with feeling. This is the sister whose name is not to be found in the parish records, who lived and died outside of literature. At least here though we have one fact that is not speculation: that up to the last months of his life, Thomson could remember his affection for this young person who was his family playmate in the days before he became, as he put it in that letter to Julia 'Ishmael in the desert from my childhood'.

Let us leave these works of Thomson lying here on this reading desk under the dome in the room he knew so well. You can see that his first collection, *The City of Dreadful Night*, ends with nineteen pages of his Heine translations, which he with customary modesty calls 'Attempts at Translations from Heine'. The second collection of his poetry, the last he saw published in his lifetime, ends with just one Heine translation, which this time he describes as 'After Heine'. It is another poem from the *Buch der Lieder*, a poem whose previous translators include Elizabeth Barrett Browning. You can see that Thomson quotes Heine's dedication. I will have *Vane's Story* lie open at this poem, and now we must leave this place where we have met, and return into our own lives.

CHILDHOOD

to his sister

My child, we both were children,
  And merry days we saw,
We used to creep into the fowl-house
  And hide there under the straw.

And then we sat up a crowing;
  The people who passed on the road –
Cock-a-doodle-doo! – they thought it
  Was really a cock that crowed.

The cases that lay in our courtyard,
  We fitted them up with care;
And made a magnificent mansion,
  And lived together there.

And the cat of our next-door neighbour
  Came to visit us too;
We gave our bows and courtseys,
  With compliments fine and new.

As to her health we asked her,
  With friendly and earnest air;
Many old cats have we since asked
  The like with the like deep care.

And often we sat discussing,
  As if we were old and grey;
Bemoaning how things were better,
  Better indeed, in our day.

How Love, Truth, Faith had vanished,
  And left the world all bad;
How the price of coffee was shameful,
  And money was not to be had! . . .

Past, past, are the sports of childhood,
  And all rolls past in sooth, –
The World, and Time, and Money,
  And Faith, and Love, and Truth.

APPENDICES

THE RESEARCH OF CHARLES BRODIE

The research of Charles Brodie has been drawn on at several points in this book, and acknowledged at each point in the notes beginning 'Brodie:'.

Charles L. Brodie was a Port Glasgow headmaster and poet, author of *The Outcast and other Poems*, Oliver and Boyd, 1919. He researched Thomson from the 1890s, interviewing surviving relatives in the town and giving occasional lectures to Burns Clubs and literary societies. He contributed three articles on Thomson for the *Port Glasgow Express and Observer* of March 13th 1896, April 24th 1903, and the *Port Glasgow Express* as it had become, of December 12th 1906. These articles both provide information and give a record of Mr Brodie's progress in trying to establish Thomson's birthplace. Two letters to Salt dated 26/2/95 and 26/10/97 are in the Salt Mss. He told Salt, 'I had a good deal of research and enquiry among old bed ridden men and women'.

Charles Brodie's surviving papers have been preserved by his grandson Mr Bruce Brodie Leeming of Chiddingfold in Surrey. The papers date from the early 1890s until sometime during the First World War. There are the typescripts of two lectures – 34 and 56 quarto pages respectively – the first dating from 1895, the second from 1916. There are also the notes made towards the three newspaper articles, with some marginal added information.

Brodie provided Salt with the verification of Thomson's parish registration of birth for the second edition of his *Life*. After Thomson's death a rumour had spread that he had been the illegitimate son of Lord Bulwer-Lytton, neatly linking the scandalously dead poet with the once scandalously-living literary fop. Thomson would indeed have turned in his grave: he thought Baron Lytton 'one of the most thorough and hollow humbugs of the age .. who, intellectually worthless as he is, now and then serves well as a straw to show how the wind blows among the higher and more educated classes.'

The most significant items in Brodie's research in addition to his location of the parish registration of birth, are:

1. The place of birth claimed in Church Street. Brodie was confident of this, as was his son E. Mortimer Brodie forty years later when he offered to show Henry Farmer the place of birth at the time of the poet's centenary. Farmer had written to the *Glasgow Herald* asking if anyone knew where Thomson was born. The correspondence is in Glasgow University Library Ms. Bi.22 – Z.30 (14). The evidence that Charles Brodie found to establish the birthplace has not survived in the papers.

2. A paternal family tree, with notes made from interviews. This has been

the trunk on which some branches have been added in Chapter Two of this book.

3. The facsimile made from a letter of Sarah Kennedy, the latter having been loaned Brodie by John Thomson in Manchester in 1895.

THE DATING OF 'THE CITY OF DREADFUL NIGHT'

The following is a guide to Thomson's manuscript dating of completed compo-
nents of 'The City of Dreadful Night', which dating is used as a structural device
in Chapters Twelve and Fourteen. It must be stressed that by several accounts
Thomson often worked on poems over years, not putting them to paper until
he had arrived almost at his completed version. There is for instance an undated
poem which seems to be a prior version of the 'Melencolia' description of Section
21. (Ridler pp 66–67). The manuscript dates here therefore do not at each point
– or at least not *necessarily* – represent 'the day he wrote it'; but can be taken
as that ascribed by Thomson for when a particular piece was completed though
there was a final tidy-up at the beginning of 1874, and the entry for 12/6/70 is
noted 'wants careful rewriting'.

Under 'Section' is given the section number as finally decided by Thomson.
On the far right where appropriate is the number given at the time of first dating
the manuscript. From 13/6/73 this (Pierpont) manuscript number concurs with
that published. 'f' after a verse number means final verse of a section.

CHAPTER TWELVE – 1870

Section

Sunday	January 16	2 – First two verses	
Tuesday	January 20	2 – verses 3–5	} Noted as two
Sunday	March 6	2 – " 6–8f	
Sunday	May 22	18 – First four verses	
Monday	May 23	18 – verses 5–7	
Tuesday	May 24	18 – " 8–12	} Noted as 4
Thursday	May 26	18 " 13f	
Sunday	June 12	20 – First three verses	
Thursday	July 7	20 – " 4–5	} Noted as 6
Saturday	July 9	20 – " 6–8f	
Sunday	July 10	1 – First three verses	
Monday	July 11	1 – fourth verse	
Friday	July 15	1 – verses 5–8	} Noted as 1
Saturday	July 16	1 – " 9–11	
Tuesday	July 19	1 – " 12f	
Friday	August 26	5 – First two verses	
Saturday	August 27	5 – verses 3–4f	} Noted as 3
Saturday	August 27	11 – First two verses	
Sunday	August 28	11 – verses 3–4f	} Noted as 5
Sunday	August 28	7 – verses 1–3f	} Noted as 7
Sunday	August 28	4 – First 2 verses	
Wednesday	October 5	4 – verses 3,5,7,8;	
		9–12 (verse 5	} Noted as 8
		Sunday August 13 1871)	
Thursday	October 6	10 – First three verses	} Noted as 10
Thursday	October 13	10 – verses 4–8	
Friday	October 14	6 – First two verses	} Noted as 12
	October 20	6 – verses 3–19f	
Sunday	October 23	3– verses 1–4f	} Noted as 9, (3 or 4) 11

CHAPTER FOURTEEN – 1873

		Section	
	May	8 – verses 1–5	
Monday	June 2	8 – verses 6–13f	} Noted as 14–8
Friday	" 6	19 – verses 1–4	} Noted as 13
Saturday	" 7	9 – verses 1–3f	} Noted as 9
Wednesday	" 11	Proem – verses 1–6f	} Noted as 15
Friday	June 13	21 – verse 1	
Thursday	July 3	12 – verses 1–13f	
Thu-Sat	" 3–5	14 – verses 1–15f	
Wednesday	Oct 1–2	17 – verses 1–4f	
Saturday	" 4	15 – verses 1–3f	
Saturday	" 4	13 – verse 1	
Monday	" 6	16 – verse 1	
Saturday	" 11	16 – verses 2–11f	
Friday	" 24	21 – verse 2	
Sunday	" 26	21 – verse 3	
Tuesday	" 28	21 – verse 4	
Wednesday	" 29	13–2–6f	
Wednesday	" 29	21–5-12f	

B.M. Ms 38532 has two dated drafts, in pencil and ink. The manuscript which Flaws sold in America found its way in 1911 to the Pierpont Morgan Library, New York. It was located there by Anne Ridler, whose substantial *Poems and Some Letters of James Thomson* (Centaur/Southern Illinois UP, 1963) has been of great help, in its annotation of manuscript sources, variants and datings as above, in the compilation of this book. (It is referred to throughout the notes as 'Ridler'.) Anne Ridler notes (p. 270) that a microfilm of the Pierpont Morgan Ms was made for her by the library, and a copy of this is in the Bodleian.

MANUSCRIPT SOURCES QUOTED

BODLEIAN LIBRARY, OXFORD: The Thomson manuscripts gathered by Bertram Dobell and sold to the library by his son. A reference number beginning Ms. Don. signifies that the manuscript is in the Bodleian collection; the numbers are Bodleian Mss. Don. c.73, d.104–110, e. 36–50, f.8–24, and g.1–7. Those most quoted here include Ms. Don. d.108, a substantial volume including pasted-in manuscripts of a collection written out by Thomson for John Grant; Thomson's transcription of C.B. Cayley's Dante translations, and the unfinished 1858 poem beginning 'The dice to play this dubious game of life'. Ms. Don. e.37 holds dated manuscripts of early poems, and translations of Heine. Ms. Don. e.48 includes Dobell's transcript of Thomson's translation of Novalis's *Hymns to the Night*.

For biographical material, Ms. Don. d.109/1 has been often quoted as it contains the letters between Thomson, Dobell, Rossetti, and J.W. Barrs. Ms. Don. d.109/2 includes material connected with persons in Thomson's last years and beyond.

Direct autobiographical information is in the fragmentary and fading small notebooks in pencil from the 1860s, Mss. Don. g.5, g.6, and f.8; the small notebook that includes jottings on the move travelling to and from America, Ms. Don. g.7; the business diary kept there in 1872, Ms. Don. e.47, and the personal diary Ms. Don. e.46; the notebook diary in Spain, Ms. Don. f.16; and in the pocket diaries that Thomson kept which have survived for 1874 and 1876 to 1881. As mentioned within, a solitary date given from Chapter 15 Notes onwards, refers to a diary entry: the references are as follows:

1874 Ms. Don. f.18	1878 Ms. Don. f.21	
1876 Ms. Don. f.19	1879 Ms. Don. f.22	
1877 Ms. Don. f.20	1880 Ms. Don. f.23	1881 Ms. Don. f.24.

SALT MSS. Recently donated to the Bodleian Library has been the collection of manuscripts relating to the gathering of information by Henry Salt for his biography of Thomson. This includes 47 letters addressed to Salt including letters from Thomson's brother John, sister-in-law Julia Thomson, Helen Birkmyre, John Grant, and three letters from J.W. Barrs. These have been given the classification Ms. Eng. c.2383.

Also there are notes on interviews, and transcriptions: notes on seven interviews undertaken in 1888, with Bradlaugh, Matilda Weller's brother William, Harriet Barrs, John Grant, A.A. Thomson (no relation), Mrs Duncan – widow of George Duncan, and Thomas Carson; and the notes of an interview with J.W. Barrs in 1898 regarding Thomson's final days at Forest Edge.

Other material includes transcripts of two letters to Potterton about 'Sunday up the River' and twenty-three occasional verses sent to him on army life, original no longer extant. The material outwith the letters to Salt has been given the number Ms. Eng. c.2384.

Throughout these notes the material is referred to as 'Salt Mss.', with description.

BRITISH LIBRARY: Add. Mss. 38532–38535.

Mss. 38532 contains two draft versions of fifteen of the sections of 'The City of Dreadful Night', with datings of verses.

Mss. 38533 has proofs of 'Sunday up the River' with Froude comments.

Mss. 38434 and 38435 include jottings and fragmentary notes from the 1860s, together with a draft of 'In the Room'.

PIERPONT MORGAN LIBRARY, NEW YORK

The library holds the most complete manuscript of 'The City of Dreadful Night', the poem largely as published though lacking one verse, with parts 13 and 15 interchanged, and with what became the opening 'Proem' put last after Section 21.

Mr Robert E. Parks, Robert H. Taylor Curator of Autograph Manuscripts, kindly sent a complete photocopy.

GLASGOW UNIVERSITY LIBRARY

As pointed out by Robert Crawford in *Notes and Queries* of August 1983, the run of *Cope's Tobacco Plant* 1875–1880 held here has corrections at Thomson's contributions and isolated marginalia in Thomson's own handwriting.

NOTES

LIST OF ABBREVIATIONS

Bonner
: Bonner, Hypatia Bradlaugh: *Charles Bradlaugh: A Record of his Life and Work (with an account of his Parliamentary Struggle, Politics and Teaching by John M. Robertson)*, 2 vols, Fisher Unwin, London, 1898.

Dobell (1884)
: Memoir prefacing James Thomson's *A Voice from the Nile and Other Poems*, Reeves and Turner, London, 1884.

Dobell (1895)
: Memoir prefacing *The Poetical Works of James Thomson*, Reeves, Turner and Dobell, 2 vols, London, 1895.

Dobell (1910)
: *The Laureate of Pessimism: A Sketch of the Life and Character of James Thomson ('B.V.')*, Bertram Dobell, London 1910.

Ridler
: *Poems and Some Letters of James Thomson*, edited with a biographical and critical introduction and textual notes, by Anne Ridler, Southern Illinois University Press, Carbondale, 1963.

Salt
: Salt, Henry S., *The Life of James Thomson ('B.V.')*, Reeves, Turner & Dobell, London, 1889.

Salt (1914)
: 3rd edition, Watts & Co., London, 1914.

Schaefer
: *The Speedy Extinction of Evil and Misery: Selected Prose of James Thomson (B.V.)*, University of California Press, Berkeley and Los Angeles, 1967.

Tribe
: Tribe, David: *President Charles Bradlaugh MP*, Elek Books, London, 1971.

B.C.S.
: *Biographical and Critical Studies*, ed. Dobell, B., Reeves and Turner, London, 1884.

B.I.
: Bishopsgate Institute. The library holds the Bradlaugh Collection of letters and other material once held by the National Secular Society. It includes letters from John Grant, and a manuscript copy of Thomson's Six Sonnets to Joseph and Alice Barnes. The collection has been indexed by Edward Royle.

C.D.N.
: *The City of Dreadful Night and Other Poems*, Reeves and Turner, London, 1880.

E.P.
: *Essays and Phantasies*, Reeves and Turner, London, 1881.

P.E.F.
: *Poems, Essays, and Fragments*, ed. J.M. Robertson, A. & H.B. Bonner, London, 1892.

R.C.S.
: Royal Caledonian School, Bushey, near Watford Junction. The school holds guardbooks and record books going back to

	Thomson's period. All relevant material has been mentioned in the notes to Chapters Two and Three.
S.P.	*Satires and Profanities*, ed. G.W. Foote, Progressive Publishing Co., London, 1884.
V.N.	*A Voice from the Nile and other Poems*, Reeves and Turner, London, 1884.
V.S.	*Vane's Story, Weddah and Om-el-Bonain and Other Poems*, Reeves and Turner, London, dated 1881.

NOTES TO CHAPTER ONE

1 Frequently bound together as in *The Confession of Faith; the Larger and Shorter Catechisms, with the Scripture Proofs at Large: together with The Sum of Saving Knowledge; Covenants, National and Solemn League; Acknowledgment of Sins, and Engagement to Duties; Directories for Public and Family Worship; Form of Public Authority in the Church of Scotland, with Acts of Assembly and Parliament Relative to, and approbative of, the same,* Hunter Blair & Bruce, Edinburgh 1831.

2 *The Confession of Faith,* Chapter 3 Section 6.

3 Campbell, Rev. John MacLeod (ed. Campbell, D.), *Reminiscences and Reflections Referring to his Early Ministry in the Parish of Row 1825–31,* Macmillan, London 1873, p. 25.

4 Ibid., p. 18.

5 Ibid., p. 24.

6 A weaver James Grubb in 1827, mentioned in Norton, Dr R., *Memoirs of George and James MacDonald of Port Glasgow,* Shaw, London 1840, p. 64; a local poor man called John Chalmers in 1828, mentioned in Story, R.H., *Memoir of the Life of the Rev. Robert Story, Late Minister of Rosneath, by his son,* MacMillan & Co. London 1862, p. 86. Their heralding a 'new dawn' was mentioned by Edward Irving in his 'Facts Connected with Recent Manifestations of Spiritual Gifts' in *Fraser's Magazine,* Jan. 1832.

7 Story, Rev. Robert, *Peace in Believing. A Memoir of Isabella Campbell of Fernicarry,* Rosneath, R. Lusk, Greenock 1829.

8 Ibid., p. 471.

9 Ibid., p. 475.

10 Quoted in Dallimore, Arnold. *The Life of Edward Irving,* The Banner of Truth Trust, Edinburgh 1983, p. 35.

11 This was the praise that followed the dispraise 'I have no faith in his prophesyings; small sympathy with his fulminations; and in certain peculiarities of his *theological* system, as distinct from his religious principles, I cannot see my way. But I hold withal, and not the less firmly for these discrepancies in our moods and judgments, that Edward Irving possesses' etc. Coleridge, S.T., 'On the Church Neither National nor Universal', *Collected Works,* vol. 10, ed. J. Colmer, Routledge & Kegan Paul, Princeton U.P., 1976, p. 143.

12 Irving, Edward. *The Nature and Use of the Gift of Tongues,* Robert Lusk, Greenock 1829.

13 The fullest biography of Irving remains that by Margaret Oliphant (*Life of Edward Irving,* Hurst & Blackett, 2 vols 1862); the clearest guide to his beliefs on the human nature of Christ, the power of the Holy Spirit and the charismatic events in Port Glasgow and London is contained in Strachan, C.G., *The Pentecostal Theology of Edward Irving,* Danton, Longman &

Todd, London 1973. Irving's 1826 interpretation of the prophecies in the Book of Daniel and Revelation was revised in 1828 as *Babylon and Infidelity Foredoomed of God: A Discourse on the Prophecies of Daniel and the Apocalypse*, Collins, Glasgow 1828.

14 *Fraser's Magazine,* ibid., p. 754.

15 Mary Campbell was finally influenced in this by MacLeod Campbell's probationer assistant A.J. Scott, who visited her. Scott – who subsequently joined Irving at Regent Square – persuaded Irving that one shouldn't have to wait for the Second Coming for the restoration of miraculous gifts, one should pray for them now. MacLeod Campbell's preaching on the universal nature of the Atonement was also a crucial factor at this point with Irving, who began preaching it himself after meeting MacLeod Campbell at Rosneath. In a way the cognition of an infinite love was thus set up against the background of the coming end of the world, as precedent to an inspiration indefinable and uncontrollable.

16 Irving: *Fraser's Magazine*, ibid., p. 757.

17 Ibid., pp. 759–60.

18 Norton, Dr. R., ibid. p. 108.

19 Ibid., p. 110.

20 Ibid., p. 125.

21 Robertson, Rev. A., *A Vindication of 'The Religion of the Land' from Misrepresentation; and an exposure of the Absurd Pretensions of the Gareloch Enthusiasts in a letter to Thomas Erskine Esq. Advocate,* W. Whyte & Co., Edinburgh 1830, p. 250.

22 Ibid., p. 256.

23 Drummond, A.L., *Edward Irving and His Circle*, Clarke & Co., London 1936, p. 146.

24 McVickar, John: Letter to the *Churchman* of 1832, quoted in the essay by Beer, J., 'Transatlantic and Scottish Connections: Uncollected Records'; in Gravil, R. & Lefebue M. (eds): *The Coleridge Connection: Essays for Thomas McFarland*, Macmillan 1990, pp. 321–322. McVickar was an episcopalian minister at Columbia University.

25 Oliphant, M., ibid., p. 323.

26 Cameron, G.G. *The Scots Kirk in London*, Becket, Oxford 1979, p. 109.

27 *The Times*, November 29th 1831.

28 *The Trial of the Rev. Edward Irving Before the London Presbytery*, London 1832, p. 88.

29 Oliphant, Mary. ibid., p. 301, 316.

30 *The Trial of the Rev. Edward Irving Before the London Presbytery,* London 1832; quoted in Norton, Rev. R., *The Restoration of Prophets and Apostles in the Catholic Apostolic Church*, Bosworth & Harrison, London 1862, p. 58: 'I solemnly declare my belief that the Protestant churches are as truly in Babylon as the Roman church; and I do separate myself from that Babylonish confederacy, and stand in the Holy Ghost under the great Head of the Church, waiting for His appearing.'

31 Irving, E.: Preface to *The Confessions of Faith* and the *Books of Discipline*

of the Church of Scotland, Baldwin & Cradock, London 1831, p. cix.

32 Irving: *Fraser's Magazine*, ibid., p. 758.

33 The driving force behind the group that met annually from 1826 at his estate in Albury, Surrey to share views on prophecy, was the wealthy banker Henry Drummond. Robert Story had with Irving attended the first Albury Group 'conference', though only Irving continued the association, contributing to the group's *Morning Watch*. The lawyer Henry Cardale along with Drummond effectively led (with the co-operation of 'the Holy Spirit') the direction of the new church that developed at Newman Street, the Catholic Apostolic Church; whose effective headquarters became the chapel at Albury, where Mary Campbell and her husband went after leaving Scotland. The sequence of events at Newman Street is described in Norton, Rev. R., ibid., p. 65 et seq.

34 Norton, Rev. R., ibid., pp. 118–20.

35 Campbell, Rev. J. MacLeod. Letter of May 14th 1834, in Campbell, D. (ed.). *Memorials of John MacLeod Campbell*, MacMillan, London 1877, Vol. I p. 119.

36 Quoted in the *Paisley Advertiser*, September 6th 1834.

37 Ibid., October 25th 1834.

38 Quoted in Ker, David. *Observations on Mrs Oliphant's 'Life of Edward Irving'*, T. Laurie, Edinburgh 1863, p. xvii.

39 See 'The Research of Charles Brodie' p. 323. In an article on Thomson for the *Port Glasgow Express and Observer* of April 24th 1903 Charles Brodie says of Sarah Kennedy 'She was a very pious woman, as a letter of hers in my possession testifies.' The letter was one that he had obtained from the poet's brother John, and he made a facsimile copy before returning it. This facsimile is still in the possession of the Brodie family.

Brodie wrote at the beginning of the facsimile: 'Copy of letter from Miss Sarah Kennedy to her sister-in-law Miss Ann Thomson. Sarah Kennedy became subsequently the wife of James Thomson shipmaster and mother of James Thomson (B.V.) the poet, author of "The City of Dreadful Night", "Vane's Story" etc. etc. The original of this letter is in the possession of Mr John P. Thomson, brother of the poet, presently (14-3-95) Cashier Goods Department Manchester Sheffield and Lincolnshire Railway, Sheffield. Concerning the letter: the date is to be noted – it was just in the full blaze of the Irvingite dream. Miss Kennedy was a zealous Irvingite. Neither address nor town mentioned. The capitals spelling and other principal characteristics are kept as in the original.'

Brodie encloses a sketch to show that the letter was in a single folded sheet of paper, a sealing mark in one top-left corner on one outside, the words 'Miss Thomson' on the other. Brodie appended a note: 'This letter has not evidently been enclosed in an envelope, but only folded up in note form and sealed with sealing wax at two corners. It looks as if she was in the town, other side see front and back of this note. Evidently a stamp or seal at left side of back.'

The letter itself contains echoes of the following Bible verses: Heb. xi

37, 38; Mat. vi 20, xix 27, xii 34; Isaiah lxvi 13; Job xxix 23; Psalms lxxii 6, lxviii 9, cxxxviii 7; John viii 12.

NOTES TO CHAPTER TWO

1 Galbraith, V.M.: letter to Henry Farmer of November 20th 1934. Miss V.M. Galbraith was the granddaughter of Margaret Kennedy, her mother having been brought up in Port Glasgow with Thomson's brother John. Farmer Collection, Glasgow University Library, *Correspondence Regarding the Birthplace of James Thomson ('B.V.')* – Ms. Bi22-Z30(14).
   Also *Fowler's Directory for the Lower Ward of Renfrewshire* 11th ed. 1834/35, p. 161.
2 Galbraith, V.M.: ibid.
3 Ibid. Also Grant, F.J.: *Register of Marriages of the City of Edinburgh*, Scottish Record Society, 1922, p. 417.
4 Glasgow 16/9/1803.
5 OPR 624/1 Blantyre.
6 Greater London Record Office Archives, P93/ANN. Entry no. 171.
7 OPR/376/2 Logierait.
8 Ibid. 14/11/08.
9 OPR/574 Census 1861.
10 Charles b. Logierait 3/6/04. Ann b.2/2/02.OPR 376/2.
11 Brodie. See note 39 Chapter 1.
12 Brodie: Note on back of paternal family tree: 'Old Mr Thomson was in the customs service – was a "tide waiter".'
13 Brodie: Note as preceding entry. A Mrs Hagart told him the story in 1895, she having been told it by a sailor.
14 The 1861 census for Clune Park notes Ann and Mary Thomson now living with Helen, the last-mentioned described as 'head of house/widow – sailmaker employing 6 men and 4 boys'. The white marble tombstone on a grave near the summit of Port Glasgow cemetery – a few yards from where one can have a view of the Firth and across to Rosneath – lists Malcolm McLarty manufacturer and shipowner, d. 1847, Helen Gow Thomson d. Clune Park 13/6/70; their five children; Mary Thomson's husband John Keith, shipwrecked; Mary Thomson d. 29/5/84 and Ann Thomson d. 1/1/84.
15 OPR 574. She married Malcolm White, ship's carpenter, before the local minister David Inglis of the United Secession Church on February 3rd 1834.
16 The daughters were Agnes b. 28/12/34; Margaret b. 28/5/36; Mary b. 7/3/38.
17 Galbraith V.M.: ibid.
18 OPR 574. Charles Thomson married Mary Rogerson 27/9/1830. Son James b. 27/9/32; Helen 4/8/35. Helen Gow McLarty b. 10/7/34. Susan b. 30/4/38.

19 Brodie: 'Old Mr Thomson lived at Church Street above Mr Spence's shop' (paternal family tree). *Fowler's Directory*, ibid. (Mrs Kennedy).

20 Brodie: In the *Port Glasgow Express and Observer* for April 29th 1903 Brodie wrote: 'It seems impossible to identify the place of the poet's birth, and if anyone can throw light on that point it will be a matter for great satisfaction. I, for one, have made a diligent search, and interviewed many people, but all to little purpose.'

Another article 'James Thomson (B.V.) His Birthplace in Port Glasgow' appeared on December 7th 1906. It stated that it was prompted by the speech of a retiring town bailie who mentioned Thomson as having been from Black Bull, one of the town's poorest parts. Brodie wrote: 'The Baillie said, in striking phrase, that Thomson was "the product of a Black Bull slum". This needs amplification rather than correction. As one who took ten years to satisfy myself as to the identity of the exact locus of Thomson's birth, I may be permitted to say that while B.V. was not born in Black Bull Close, his early infancy was passed there . . . Unfortunately, the Parish Church registers which I examined in the Register House gave no clue, nor was the brother John, who still lives and holds an important position in England, able to give the information. All the other relatives were equally ignorant of the exact birthplace. Old residents suggested one place after another, but none of them stood examination. I had almost given up in despair, when certain circumstances and certain evidences came to my knowledge – circumstances with many elements of romance which would require much larger space to detail than can be afforded in this article – which at last satisfied me . . . It will be enough to say meantime that James Thomson (B.V.) of great and growing and enduring fame, was born at the head of Church Street in the house removed to make room for the heightening of the roof of Mr John Gibb's shop. The babe was almost immediately removed to a house in Black Bull Close, and was there for nearly a year.'

The draft in Brodie's papers of a lecture given sometime during the First World War says 'in Port Glasgow in a house at the west end of Church Street (I took ten years to locate the spot) the subject of our sketch was born.'

Amongst the surviving papers there are sketches concerned with locations being checked in the 1890s, but no substantiating remarks about the birthplace finally settled on.

The building in Church Street was demolished about the middle of the twentieth century.

21 OPR 574/8. The entry is made in sequence on May 19th 1848, p. 365, but also vertically in the margin for November 1834 p. 258, with a horizontal abbreviated entry squeezed in with the added words 'Vide 19th May 1848'. The ink used on the p. 258 entry is from the later date and obviously different from the other entries there.

22 'James Thompson of this parish Bachelor and Sarah Kennedy of this parish spinster were married in this church by licence with consent of —

this twelfth day of January by James Williams curate. This marriage was solemnised, [signed] James Thompson Sarah Kennedy. In the presence of [signed] John Morley [?illeg.] Mary Smith.' Greater London Record Office Archives, P93/ANN.

23 She signed 'Sarah Thompson' to the application form requesting in August 1842 admission for James to the Royal Caledonian Asylum (Royal Caledonian School archives); 'Sarah Thompson' is the name given her on her death certificate.

24 PRO BT 98/5728.

25 Thomson, J.: Letter of January 1882 (undated) to his sister-in-law Julia Thomson. Quoted in Salt, pp. 3–5.

26 Ibid.

27 Salt Mss. Letter from Helen Birkmyre of 21/7/1888. Mrs Helen Birkmyre was the daughter b. 10/7/34 of Mrs Helen McLarty, Thomson's father's sister.
   Also Brodie: 'James Thomson (B.V)' in *Port Glasgow Express and Observer* 24/4/1903: 'In justice to the kith and kin they are indignant at the biographer's representing the Captain as a dipsomaniac. One of them writes me – "It is quite an untruth. He was a thoroughly good and true man with strong religious views and feelings; a bright, sanguine and cheerful nature which endeared him to all who knew him.".' Salt's biography had suggested Thomson's drinking was a tendency inherited from his father.

28 Barr, Rev. J.: 'Port Glasgow' in *The New Statistical Account of Scotland* Vol. 7, Blackwood, Edinburgh 1845. The next 5 quotes are from this.

29 Norton R.: *Neglected and Controverted Scripture Truths*, Shaw, London 1839, p. 404.

30 Ibid., pp. 375–376.

31 Miller, E.: *The History and Doctrines of Irvingism*, Kegan & Paul, London 1878, Vol. 1, p. 180.

32 Ibid., pp. 223, 235.

33 *The New Statistical Account of Scotland*, ibid., 'Greenock' p. 463.

34 Campbell, Rev. J. Macleod: Letter of March 3rd 1836 to his father; in Campbell, Rev. D. (ed.): *Memorials of John MacLeod Campbell*, MacMillan, London 1877, Vol. 1, p. 135.

35 Ibid., p. 127.

36 As 25.

37 Miller, E.: ibid., pp. 59–60. She married in 1831 and first went south supposedly on her way abroad with her new gift of tongues to spread missionary work. She and her husband settled at Albury Park with the church there established by Henry Drummond. In a letter to Robert Story Irving called her 'a saint of God' (Oliphant, ibid., Vol. 2., p. 236).

38 Story, R.H.: *Memoir of the Life of Robert Story* ibid., p. 217.

39 Thomson, J.: ibid.

40 Ibid.

41 Galbraith V.M.: ibid. There is some contradiction in the available evidence. V.M. Galbraith in her letter of 1934 says that her grandmother's sister went

to London and learnt court dressmaking with Margaret Lawson's money after James Thompson's stroke, i.e. after September 1840. Charles Brodie in his manuscript of a lecture dated April 1895 says that Sarah Kennedy was one of those who left Regent Square Church with Irving: 'She was a Port Glasgow woman but was engaged in a London court dressmakers' – i.e. in 1832. In the *Port Glasgow Express and Observer* of April 24th 1903 he again wrote that Thomson's father in London 'met and married Sarah Kennedy who was engaged at the time in the establishment of a Court dressmaker.'

In another note on the back of the Thomson paternal tree Brodie writes 'Sarah Kennedy is supposed to have gone to London to be married to James Thomson father of BV when he arrived home from a voyage.'

It is not possible from the foregoing to say definitely whether or not Sarah Kennedy was already a member of Irving's congregation in Regent Square and a court dressmaker at that time. Central to the problem is the ambiguity in a phrase used by Thomson when writing of his mother in the 1882 letter to his sister-in-law Julia. He refers to Sarah Kennedy as 'following Irving from the Kirk when he was driven out'. The ambiguity resides both in the word 'following' – whether it means literally following Irving's footsteps or continuing to follow his beliefs, perhaps from Scotland; and whether by 'the Kirk' is meant Regent Square Church or the Church of Scotland as a whole, from which Irving was officially expelled after trial at his parish of Annan in Dumfriesshire in 1833.

42 Thomson, Julia: Letter of 23/1/1882 to James Thomson. Ms. Don. c. 73.

43 Thomson, James: ibid.

44 Ibid.

45 'Report to the Council of the SSL from a Committee of its Fellows appointed to Make an Investigation into the State of the Poorer Classes in St Georges-in-the-East', *Journal of the Statistical Society of London*, Vol. XI (1848) pp. 139–249. All the details succeeding are from this report, some of which details are from comparative tables.

46 Gavin, H.: *The Unhealthiness of London and the Necessity of Remedial Measures*, J. Churchill, London 1847, p. 30. The inadequacy of surface drains and thrice weekly water is discussed pp. 20–45. Gavin concluded (p. 63) 'Mortality in towns is referrable to the inadequate supplies of water by Company Monopolists'.

These private monopolists were at the root of it according to another report made to the Statistical Society of London in 1845: 'A copious supply of water to the poor can, in my opinion, *be given by a public body only*'. Until the beginning of the seventeenth century the supply of water in London had been a municipal undertaking. Private companies had taken over, and 'such companies ought never to have been allowed a separate municipal existence'; they had acted 'with every private interest which could lead them to oppose that of the public and neglect the poor consumer', whilst 'making mutual treaties to levy a monopoly price on these consumers, whom they assume to make over to each other's mercy.'

(Fletcher, J.: 'Historical and Statistical Account of the Present System of Supplying the Metropolis with Water', Journal of the R.S.S.L., Vol. VIII, pp. 149, 180–181.)

47 *Statistical Society of London.* Vol. XI (1848) ibid.

48 Ibid.

49 Quoted in Neff, W.F.: *Victorian Working Women: An Historical and Literary Study of Women in British Industries and Professions 1832–1850,* Allen & Unwin, London 1929, p. 122.

50 Dickens: *Nicholas Nickleby*, Chapter 17, Paragraph 2. Neff, ibid. p. 123, uses this quote as illustration.

51 Thomson obtained the details and made note of them prior to his brother's wedding in 1867, Ms. Don. f. 8.

52 *The Times*, Report on 25th Anniversary Festival 29/5/43.

53 *The Times*, 14/6/42.

54 *General Regulations* listed on rear of official form of application to enter a child in the Royal Caledonian Asylum. R.C.S., bound volume of applications.

55 Boyd signed the application form 'The petitioner is personally known to me.' His company is listed in the London Trade Directory. Salt was sent a copy of Thomson's registration by the asylum secretary Thomas Inglis in 1881, but he misread 'Burgess Hill' for 'Breezers Hill'.

56 Sarah Thompson did not take the oath printed to be sworn before the magistrate. 'I do hereby make oath' was altered to 'I do hereby solemnly and sincerely dictate' (That the circumstances stated in the foregoing petition and testimonials are true). 'So help me God' was also scored out and replaced with 'and I make this declaration conscientiously believing the same to be declared and subscribed'. R.C.S. ibid.

57 Ibid. At the time of the declaration Sarah was actually two days short of her 44th birthday and her husband was four days past his 36th. Excepting Caroline and Satelite, all the ships were overseas traders out of Port Glasgow or Greenock. (*Fowler's Renfrewshire Directories*).

58 He also put a cross instead of a signature when registering his son John Parker's birth earlier in the year. Thomson (see n. 51) commented 'Couldn't write, being paralysed in all the right side'. Ms. Don. f. 8.

59 R.C.S. Bound Quarterly General Reports: 1/12/42 He received 384 votes.

60 Galbraith, V.M.: ibid.

61 A fourth child Malcolm was born in 1842. After Sarah Kennedy's death Margaret White named her next child, born in 1844, Sarah Kennedy White. (OPR 574/8)

62 The death certificate shows that she died on May 4th, 1843 at 24 Mary Ann Street, the cause being given as 'dropsy'. The registration informant made a cross, 'the mark of Susannah Stevens, present at the death, 6 Well Street Wellclose Square'.

63 Registration Book R.C.S. The entry gives details from the birth certificate, parents' names, the date of admission (1/12/42) date due to be discharged (23/11/48), number of votes cast for him, and the place and date of the parents' marriage. Immediately after the last is entered

'Residence 19 Upper East Smithfield E'.

64 Hair, J.: *Regent Square: Eighty Years of a London Congregation*, Nisbet & Co., London 1898, p. 159.

NOTES TO CHAPTER THREE

1 Turnbull, W.B.: *Memoranda of the State of the Parochial Registers of Scotland*. Turnbull published this as part of the campaign to have registration made compulsory by statute. He wrote to 174 of the Scottish parishes: 'in nearly all the reports complaints are made of the refusal or reluctance to register on the part of Dissenters' (p. xii). Also *Sketch of the Imperfect Condition of the Parochial Records of Births Deaths and Marriages in Scotland*, Seton George Constable & Co., Edinburgh 1854. 'Another very irregular practice consists in the entries being made at a different period from the occurrence of the events recorded, in consequence of which, great inconvenience is not infrequently experienced in the consultation of parish registers.' (p. 27) Regarding the number of missing entries 'by far the most frequent cause is the reluctance or refusal, on the part of Dissenters, to make use of any of the registers.' (p. 46) '. . . in the year 1850 considerably less than a third of the probable births in the whole of Scotland were inserted in the register.'

2 R.C.S. bound record book.

3 Aberdein, J.W.: *John Galt*, Oxford U.P. 1936, p. 87; Cameron, J.: *The Scots Kirk in London*, Becket Publications, Oxford 1979, p. 105.

4 Maclean, Norman, D.D.: *The Life of James Cameron Lees*, Maclehose, Jackson & Co., Glasgow 1922, pp. 7–8.

5 Ibid.

6 Ibid. p. 6.

7 Galbraith V.M.: ibid.

8 Dobell (1895).

9 Ibid. pp. xiii–xiv.

10 Agnes Robertson Gray was born on the 27th February 1842 at 19 Wellclose Square – 3 weeks after John Parker Thompson was born in Mary Ann Street a short distance away. In the Charles Brodie papers there are galley proofs to his *Port Glasgow Express* article on Thomson of April 25th 1903. In the margin besides the sentence 'in 1840 the family removed to London' he pencilled 'They lived in Well Close near St Katherine's Dock.'

11 William Gray is described as a plumber on Agnes's birth certificate. The Tower Hamlets public library local archives contain a number of card-indexed documents concerning William Gray, plumber: these show that in 1859 he took a lease on a house and premises at 12 Archer Terrace, Limehouse (TH 6862, 6619). He was in business at 6 Jamaica Terrace – at 28 West India Dock Road – and was featured in the London Trades Directory in the 1850s. His business prospered sufficiently for him to have become by 1870 a trustee of the Ocean Permanent Building Society, settled in Snaresbrook by 1874 (TH 4860, 5480) – from where Agnes Gray (now

married as Mrs Grieg) wrote to Thomson's biographer Henry Salt in 1888.

The 1861 census for Archer Street describes William Gray (then 51) as 'master painter employing 16 men and 4 boys'. His wife Margaret was 49.

12 They had 4 children with a gap of about a year between each of them: the oldest Helen born in 1839 (left home by 1861), Margaret, Agnes, and David.

13 Maclean, Norman, D.D.: ibid. p. 16.

14 His scepticism on hearing 'the tongues' is described in his sermon on *Corinthians* in Cumming, J.: *Sabbath Evening Readings on the New Testament*, Hall, Virtue & Co., London 1858, p. 225. His admiration for Irving's oratory is in Cumming J.: *Music in its Relation to Religion – A lecture delivered before the Y.M.C.A. in Exeter Hall 29th January 1850*, Nisbet & Co., London 1850, p. 9.

15 Irving, E.: *The Confessions of Faith*, etc ibid. Note 31 Chapter 1. Irving preferred a Confession drawn up at Geneva in 1560 as nearer in spirit to the Reformation and 'purely a Confession of Faith, containing neither matters of church government nor discipline' (pp. xcv-xcvi); that Confession also seemed to approve belief in the visible return of Christ: 'I, who am a millenarian, ask no other confession of my creed' (p. ci). He also preferred Craig's 1592 Catechism to the Shorter (p. cxxv). Irving said the Westminster Confession had been maligned and misinterpreted by those who said it taught that Christ had died only for the Elect; but 'we do exceedingly blame the Westminster Divines for being silent on the great head of orthodox doctrine, the redemption of all mankind and of all the material creation' (p. cliii).

16 Ibid., p. cxxv.

17 Dobell, ibid., p. xxvi.

18 Cameron, G.: ibid., pp. 133–134; p. 241.

19 Hair, J.: ibid., pp. 159, 157. Hamilton shortly before the Disruption itself summarised the case for the Seceders in *The Harp on the Willows or The Captivity of the Church in Scotland*. The edition in Glasgow University Library has '25th thousand' on the title page.

20 Arnot, W.: *The Life of James Hamilton D.D.*, Nisbet & Co., London 1870, pp. 228–233.

21 Cumming, J.: *The Present State of the Church of Scotland*, Shaw, London, 2nd ed. 1843, p. 22.

22 August 6th, 1844. Also in letter to the secretary of the asylum dated July 15th 1844 (R.C.S. letter book).

23 *The Times*, ibid.

24 Ibid. There was a steady turnover of schoolmasters in the next few years: 1846 Schoolmaster Alexander Lightbody; 1847 R.A. McDougal; 1848 Andrew Crawford, assistant John Pearson Watson; 1849–1850 Simon Kerr.

There was also a schoolmistress after an annexe added 25 girls to the school roll in 1845. Details in annual *Edinburgh Almanack*.

25 *The Times*, 6/9/44.

26 Ibid. 11/6/45. After the march of the children at the 'anniversary festival' a fortnight earlier on May 28th *The Times* had reported that 'more handsome healthy lads could not be found anywhere, their appearance and bearing doing great honour to those having the care of them.' At the festival the following year the march round the room was of 72 boys and 34 girls (ibid., July 23rd 1846).

27 Ibid., 23/7/46.

28 Brown, John Tod: *Moral Murder*, W. Freeman, London 1865. p. 7. His account of his coming to the Caledonian Church was written after he had left, become an Anglican minister, then been imprisoned for misappropriation of church property. He had been landed with a debt in his new parish, the former minister having gone to the Continent. Tod Brown had sold some of the church property to meet the debt, and wrote *Moral Murder* as an entreaty for royal pardon after his imprisonment.

When Tod Brown was appointed and the children stopped attending Regent Square, asylum secretary John Burnie conveyed to Hamilton and his elders 'the very best thanks of the court for the past accommodation, kindness and attention' (R.C.S. letter book Feb. 10th 1847).

In 1846 Regent Square donated £105 subscription to the asylum. In 1847 the same amount was donated by Crown Court.

29 Brown, John Tod: *The Union of Christians*, London 1846, p. 72, 75.

30 R.C.S. School Record Book.

31 R.C.S. Record book regarding band fees and performances.

32 Letter from secretary John Burnie to Lord Buccleuch 1/7/46. R.C.S. letter book.

33 Ibid. Letter from Burnie to Rev. F.C. Cook 15/9/47; letter to Buccleuch, 10/10/48.

34 R.C.S. Quarterly Court Meeting records: 8/10/49.

35 Salt, p. 7.

36 Thomson, J.: Review of R.H. Hutton's *Walter Scott* in C.T.P. September, 1879.

37 Salt, p. 7.

38 Brown, J.T.: *Moral Murder*, ibid., p. 7.

39 Letter from John Burnie to Tod Brown of 10/10/48 (R.C.S. Letter Book).

40 Church of Scotland *Fasti.*, ed. H. Scott, Vol. 7. Oliver & Boyd, Edinburgh 1928, p. 446.

41 Edinburgh PRO CH2/852. Scotch Church Crown Court Session Minutes. Minutes for 31/1/50 show a decision was made to add £60 to £3 already paid the Caledonian Church from the Home Mission Fund. In July 1851 a new grant was made to Magill from Crown Court of £60 per annum; this was cut the following year to £40 when it was reported he had earned £200 in the year succeeding the new grant.

42 Cumming, J.: 'Our Queen's Responsibilities and Reward' in *Occasional Discourses*, Hall Virtue & Co., 2 vols, London 1852, Vol. 1 pp. 146–147.

43 Cumming J.: *God in History*, Shaw, London 1849, pp. 134–135.

44 Ibid., p. 144.
45 Cumming J.: *Is Christianity from God?* Hall & Co., London 1847 pp. 191, 193.
46 Ibid., pp. 200–201.
47 Ingersoll, R.G.: 'Some Mistakes of Moses' in *Lectures and Essays* (2nd Series), Watts & Co., London 1929, pp. 44, 47. The essay was first published in 1879.
48 Cumming, J.: *The Age We Live In,* n.d. n.p. pp. 329–330.
49 Thackeray, W.M.: Letter 22/4/55 to Mrs Carmichael-Smyth: in *The Letters and Private Papers of W.M. Thackeray* (ed. Ray, G.N.) 4 vols, Oxford U.P., 1946. Vol. 3, p. 439: 'Take Cumming whom you like. I think him a bigot, a blasphemer.'
50 *Alfred Lord Tennyson: a Memoir by His Son,* 2 vols, Macmillan, London 1897. A letter to the poet's son by Dr Ker is quoted Vol. 1 p. 265, describing the poet's relationship with his mother: 'He often jested with her about Dr Cumming and his "bottles", the bottles being the seven vials of St John's Revelation. You have heard, I dare say, that your grandmother confined her reading at that time to two books, the Bible and Dr Cumming's work on Prophecy.' Critics have taken the millenarian 'heated pulpiteer' in Tennyson's 1860 poem 'Sea Dreams' to be a portrait of Cumming.
51 Eliot, George: 'Evangelical Preaching: Dr Cumming': in *Impressions of Theophrastus Such: Essays, and Leaves from a Note-Book,* Blackwood & Sons, Edinburgh & London 1901, pp. 419–421. The essay first appeared in the *Westminster Review* in 1855.
52 See pp. 203–4.
53 *In Memoriam John Cumming.* Privately printed, pp. 38–39. Neither author nor date mentioned. Cumming died in 1881.
54 Elliott, Rev. E.B.: *Horae Apocalypticae, or a Commentary on Apocalypse, Critical and Historical* Seeley, Burnside & Seeley, 4 vols, London 1844. This had reached its third edition by 1847.
55 Cumming, J.: *Apocalyptic Sketches,* 2nd Series: Hall & Co., London 1849, p. 576. Also Cameron G.G.: ibid., p. 144. The extended quote is from the 1st series of *Apocalyptic Sketches* ibid., 1848, footnote pp. 461–2.
56 Ibid. 1st Series p. 82.
57 Ibid. p. 106.
58 Ibid. 2nd Series. pp. 34, 35, 47.
59 Ibid. pp. 46, 44, 45.
60 Ibid. pp. 63–64.
61 Ibid. pp. 48, 173, 175–176.

NOTES TO CHAPTER FOUR

1 R.C.S. Registry Book: entered at end of entry for James Thompson: 'Thompson left August 1850 for approval as a Monitor Royal Asylum Chelsea S.W.'
2 Dobell (1895) p. xiv.

3 House of Commons Parliamentary Papers 1850 (662) X.1. *Select Committee on Army & Ordinance Expenditure* Answers 660; 1528 et seq; Appendix A Nos. 106, 108. The 16 monitors at Chelsea were paid 4 guineas a year, an increase for Thomson of 4 shillings.

4 P.P. ibid., Answer 520.

5 Ibid., Answers 552, 554.

6 Parliamentary Papers 1862 XXXII. 389–577. *First Report by the Council of Military Education on Army Schools*, p. 5.

7 White, Col. A.T.C.: *The Story of Army Education 1643–1963*, Harrap, London 1963, p. 256.

8 'National Education' in *Edinburgh Review*, April 1852, p. 325.

9 Ibid., p. 326.

10 Education Commission: *Communications from Edwin Chadwick respecting Half-time and Military and Naval Drill and on the Time and Cost of Popular Education on a Large and on a Small Scale* (The Lord Monteigle of Brandon). Ordered to be printed July 2nd, 1861. pp. 70–77. 'On the Results of Reduced School Time Training', Mr Walter McLeod Head Master of the Royal Military Asylum. Reprinted in P.P. 1862 XLIII, p. 35.

McLeod also says there under questioning that in his 13 years at Chelsea 200 trained masters had passed through his hands 'more than through the hands of any other master in England'.

11 P.P. 1850 ibid., Answer 521: 'There was one especially, a sergeant of the dragoons, of the name of Barnes. He came there and he showed so good an example in point of discipline to those who were not yet soldiers, and proved himself so capable of acquiring all that was taught in school, and at the same time so ready in acquiring the art of teaching under the new system, that he was amongst the first who went back again to their duty with a certificate of being a perfect teacher. He went back to a dragoon regiment. It fell into garrison, I think at Cork, and his school was overrun with scholars seeking information.'

There were just over 400 non-commissioned officers and men at Ballincollig. (P.P. 1850 ibid., Answer 659.) The number of adults attending the school increased to 108 on Barnes's appointment. Ibid. *Appendix to Second Report of Select Committee on Army & Ordinance Expenditure*, p. 941.

12 Statistical tables for the incidence of illiteracy in the Cork area as a result of what the author calls 'mass illiteracy and ignorance produced by a century of deliberate English suppression of Catholic education at all levels' are in Donnelly, James, Jnr.: *The Land and the People of Nineteenth Century Cork*, Routledge & Kegan Paul, London 1975, p. 248.

13 *Edinburgh Review*, ibid., p. 332. Orphaned or destitute Catholic children of servicemen were not taught at Chelsea but at the Royal Hibernian School in Dublin. (P.P. 1850 (662) X.I., Answer 1528.) Hence the basis for army education of children and soldiers was culturally a Protestant bible-based education, though its teachers might see it as basic Christianity. Archbishop

Cullen, Primate of All Ireland, complained that there was no provision for Catholic children in the schools of the British Army. (*Cork Examiner*, January 30th, 1852.)

14 P.P. 1850. (662) X.I., Appendix A, No. 47: 'Books and Apparatus Supplied for the use of Garrison and Regimental Schools.' Also *Edinburgh Review*, ibid., p. 333.

15 McLeod, W.: *The Second Poetical Reading Book: Compiled for the use of Families and Schools*, Longman, Brown, Green, and Longman, London 1850.

16 McLeod, W.: *The Geography of Palestine, or The Holy Land including Phoenicia and Philistia; with a description of the towns and places in Asia Minor visited by the Apostles. Specially adapted to the Purposes of Tuition, with introductory remarks on the method of teaching Geography and Questions for Examination appended to each section.* Longman, Brown, Green, and Longman, London 1847.

17 Cody, Bryan A.: *The River Lee, Cork and the Corkonians 1853*, Charles Mitchell, London, W.B. Kelly, Dublin 1859, p. 42. Lewis, Samuel: *A Topographical Dictionary of Ireland*, S. Lewis & Co., London 1837.

18 Hair, J.: ibid., p. 122. *The Times*, May 5th, 1832.

19 Harrison, J.F.C.: *Robert Owen and the Owenites in Britain and America: the Quest for a New Moral World*, Routledge & Kegan Paul, London 1969, pp. 96–97, 204–205. Irving and his congregation moved on to a chapel in Newman Street, off Oxford Street, in October. (*The Times*, October 22nd, 1832.)

20 Carlyle, Thomas: Letter of July 2nd, 1832, to his brother John. Quoted in Froude, J.A.: *Carlyle*, Longmans, Green, London 1882, Vol. 2, p. 298.

21 Harrison, J.F.C.: ibid., pp. 205–208.

22 McCabe, Joseph: *George Jacob Holyoake*, Watts & Co., London 1922, chapters 2–4, pp. 11–45. Holyoake, George Jacob: *Sixty Years of an Agitator's Life*, London, T. Fisher Unwin, 6th impression 1906, chapters 22–24 pp. 115–125; chapter 26 pp. 133–140 et seq. Royle, Edward: *Victorian Infidels: The Origins of the British Secularist Movement 1791–1866*, Manchester University Press 1974, p. 72 et seq.

23 Royle, E.: ibid., pp. 31–43 (Carlile); pp. 43–53 (Owen). Shelley wrote at the time of Carlile's first trial that it filled him 'with an indignation that will not and ought not to be suppressed . . . In persecuting Carlile they have used the superstition of the jury in crushing a political enemy'. (Shelley: letter of November 3rd, 1819 to Leigh Hunt in *Complete Prose Works*, ed. Forman H.B., Vol. 1, pp. 291, 299.)

After his release Carlile carried on as before, founding a company which published reissues of 'blasphemous' works such as Shelley's own 'Queen Mab'.

24 Royle, E.: ibid., p. 40. She founded a weekly called *Isis* dedicated to 'the young women of England for generations to come or until superstition is extinct'.

25 Bonner, Vol. 1, pp. 8–23.

26 Bradlaugh, Charles: *A Few Words on the Christians' Creed*, Charles Bradlaugh Jnr., London 1850. Quoted in *Champion of Liberty: Charles Bradlaugh* (issued for the Bradlaugh Centenary Committee, gen. editor Gilmour, J.P.) C.A. Watts & Co.; The Pioneer Press (G.W. Foote & Co) London 1933 p. 108.

27 Headingley, A.S.: *The Biography of Charles Bradlaugh*, London 1880. Quoted in Bonner, Vol. 1 pp. 26–27.

28 Ibid., p. 40.

29 The *Cork Examiner*, January 30th, 1852.

30 Benn-Walsh, Sir John (ed. Donnelly, James Jnr.): *The Journals of Sir John Benn-Walsh Relating to the Management of his Irish Estates 1823–64*; in the *Journal of the Cork Historical and Archaeological Society*, Vol. LXXXI, 1975. Introduction, p. 87.

31 Ibid., p. 117. This and the quotes in the succeeding 4 sentences are from the journal entry for Tuesday, September 2nd, 1851.

32 Ibid., p. 119, Monday, October 11th, 1852.

33 Ibid., p. 121. Monday, October 18th, 1852.

34 *Cork Examiner*, March 5th, 1852.

35 *General Orders for the Guidance of the Troops in Affording Aid to the Civil Power and to the Revenue Department in Ireland*, A. Thom, Dublin 1847, 1865, pp. 14–15.

36 Bradlaugh, C.: 'English Misrule in Ireland and the Remedy: Passages from a lecture delivered at Steinway Hall, New York, on October 6th 1873'. Quoted in *Champion of Liberty: Charles Bradlaugh* ibid., p. 243.

37 'Indeed you set me in a happy place': opening line of last of 6 commemorative private sonnets addressed by Thomson to Joseph and Alice Barnes in 1862.

38 Thomson: Review of R.H. Hutton's *Walter Scott*, ibid.

39 Bodleian Ms. Don. d.108. 'Love's Dawn' shows traces of Keats, Byron, Shelley ('her awe-inspiring gaze,/ Whose beams anatomise me nerve by nerve/ And lay me bare, and make me blush to see/ My hidden thoughts' – *The Cenci*, Act 1, Scene 2, 11. 83–86). The conjunction of 'unbelief', 'weakness' and 'lack of charity' is a kind of reversal of *Corinthians* 1 Chapter 13: 'And now abideth faith, hope, charity, these three; but the greatest of these *is* charity.' This type of reversal – and this echo of *Corinthians* – was to stay with Thomson throughout his writing career, notably to the 'Dead faith dead love dead hope' theme of 'The City of Dreadful Night'. *Corinthians* 1 was a key text for the Irvingites, especially Chapter 14 – which immediately follows the text quoted here – as that chapter was claimed as validation for the reclaiming of the gift of tongues and prophecy. It was this which Irving quoted when the outbreak first occurred at Regent Square Church in 1831. The phrase 'my heart's caged lusts' can bring to mind *Matthew* V, 28: 'But I say unto you, That whosoever looketh on a woman to lust after her, hath already committed adultery with her in his heart.' This is one of the 'proofs from Scripture' given to substantiate Answer 72 of the Shorter Catechism,

'The seventh commandment forbiddeth all unchaste thoughts, words and actions.'

'Love's Dawn' was first published in *Tait's Edinburgh Magazine* in October 1858. It appeared as the first of a four-sectioned sequence called 'Four Stages of a Life'. Thomson later revised the poem and intended to include it in the third collection of his poetry that was not in fact published until 1884, 2 years after his death.

40   Ms. Don. e.37. Dated Friday 15/10/52.

41   Matilda Weller's birth certificate says that she was born of Mary Ann (formerly Bennett) and Henry Weller, soldier, on August 21st 1839 in Barrack Street, Leeds.

42   Salt, p. 17, quoting a former fellow student, A.A. Thomson.

43   Salt Mss. Notes of an interview with Mr Thomas Carson Headmaster Duke of York School Chelsea, August 31st 1888.

44   Salt Mss. Letter from Thomas Inglis, secretary, Royal Caledonian Asylum, June 1st, 1888: 'You should communicate with Mr Gray Esq. Inverkip Cottage Snaresbrook Essex. Mr Thompson was a weekly visitor at his house when in Royal Asylum Chelsea.'

45   Ibid. Letter from Julia Thomson, October 1st, 1888.

46   Ibid. Notes of an interview with John Grant, July 24th, 1888.

47   The graveyard in Cahir is disused and overgrown, the church a roofless ruin. After an unsuccessful afternoon search by the author of this book the grave was located by Mr Timothy Looney of Pearse Street, Cahir, who sent a transcription of the tombstone, photographs and a map indicating the precise site.

48   Tribe, p. 43.

49   This is the second verse of five in an untitled poem dated 1853 in Bodleian, Ms. Don. e.37. Bradlaugh was given this and another verse in 1854. (Bradlaugh Index, Bishopsgate Institute, 1854 no. 33.)

NOTES TO CHAPTER 5

1   Warrant of 1854. Quoted in Lefroy, Col. J.: *Report on the Regimental and Garrison Schools of the Army and on Military Libraries and Reading Rooms* Eyre & Spottiswoode, London 1859, p. 474; P.P. 1870 (2nd Report of the Council of Military Education on Army Schools and Libraries) Appendix I, p. 102.

2   P.P. 1862 ibid., p. 474.

3   Foublanque, Eward Barrington de: *Treatise on the Administration and Organisation of the British Army*, Longman, Brown, Green, Longman and Roberts, London 1858, pp. 185, 265–267.

4   Lefroy: ibid., p. 237.

5   Kemshead, W. M.: Letter of March 12th, 1861, in P.P. 1862 ibid., p. 484. Kemshead was a 1st class schoolmaster at Aberdeen, due shortly to retire.

6   White, A.T.C.: ibid., p. 263.

7   Ibid.

8   Kemshead: ibid., p. 485.

9   Salt Mss. Grant interview, ibid.

10 The *Reasoner* was edited weekly by G.J. Holyoake from June 3rd, 1846, to June 30th, 1861. A full list of nineteenth-century freethought papers and magazines with dates of publication and editors is in Royle, E.: ibid. pp. 320–323; and in his succeeding volume *Radicals, Secularists, and Republicans: Popular Freethought in Britain, 1866–1915*, Manchester University Press, Rowman and Littlefield, London 1980, pp. 345–348.

11 Tribe, p. 39. Royle: *Victorian Infidels* ibid., pp. 174–175.

12 The word 'agnostic' did not appear in print until used by Huxley in the *Spectator* in January 1869. Before that the word 'atheist' would be applied to some for whom 'agnostic' later more precisely defined their position. The word 'secularist' was also open to disagreement, some secularists maintaining that only the belief in a personal God was what they opposed.

13 McCabe, J.: *George Jacob Holyoake*, Watts & Co., London 1922, p. 32.

14 Bonner, Vol. 1, pp. 90–91.

15 'Suggested by Matthew Arnold's "Stanzas from the Grand Chartreuse" ', Ms. Don. d.108. Dated July, 1855. (V.N.)

16 'The Approach to St Paul's' Ms. Don. e.37. dated 1855. (Ridler).

17 Salt, p. 8.

18 'Parting', Ms. Don. d.108., dated 10.1.57. *Tait's*, Oct. '58.

19 Ms. Don. e.37. Unpublished, 48 lines. Dated 1855. The address 'Sister' appears twice in the poem. On the ink manuscript the quotes round the word have been added in pencil.

20 Salt Mss. Grant interview.

21 Salt, p. 8.

22 'Tasso to Leonore', *Tait's Edinburgh Magazine*, May 1859. (V.N.)

23 'Bertram to the Most Noble and Beautiful Lady Geraldine', *Tait's Edinburgh Magazine*, November 1859. (V.S.)

24 'The Dreamer', Dated 1855. V.N.

25 'Marriage', Ms. Don. d.108. Dated June 1854, *Tait's Edinburgh Magazine*, October 1858.

26 Jackson, Pilkington, Capt.: 'Report to the Secretary of State for War on Soldier's Institutes at Aldershot and Plymouth.' in P.P. 1862 XXXII ibid., Appendix p. 707.

27 Ibid., p. 717.

28 Ibid., p. 709.

29 Ibid.

30 Jordan, T.: 'The Present State of the Dwellings of the Poor, Chiefly in Dublin', in *Journal of the Royal Statistical Society* January, 1857, p. 18. Paper delivered before the Society, December 15th, 1856.

31 Ibid., p. 17.

32 Salt Mss, transcription. On May 24th 1858 Thomson sent his friend James Potterton occasional stanzas about army life, written as he was preparing

to leave Ship Street Barracks 'once more to Richmond' Barracks, also in Dublin. Thomson referred to 'this purgatorial Ship Street – curse the stifling skyless hole'.

33 'The Doom of a City', Ms. Don. e.38 and Don. d.108, the latter a copy for Grant. First published V.N., minus first 310 lines, the poem grouped as in three parts, not four. First printed in full in Ridler.

34 The monster (I. II. 245–289) with 'coil on coil' and eyes like lamps coming through the dark was of a type feared by some travellers of the time. The *Illustrated London News* of October 28th, 1848 (pp. 264–268) gives drawings with accounts of alleged encounters with the 'Great American Sea Serpent' (*Scol Ophus Atlanticus*) a hundred feet long, with huge eyes kept four feet above the water. There is more on this in the same magazine on April 14th and May 19th, 1849.

35 IV. 4, 11. 121–132.

36 III. 16, 11. 497–504; 521–528.

37 Quoted by Dobell in notes to V.N. p. 260.

38 Lane, E.W. (ed.): *The Arabian Nights*.

39 II. 6, 11. 143–144.

40 Stephens: 'Account of visit to Petra' in Laborde, L. de: *Journey to Arabia, Petriae to Mount Sinai and the Excavated City of Petra, the Edom of the Prophecies*, 2nd ed. John Murray, London 1838, pp. 179–182.

41 Meredith: Sonnet: 'Fame' – To Alexander Smith.

42 The discussion here about the sphinx reminds the author of this book of D.W. Winnicott's words when describing mother-infant facial interplay, and the problems that can occur when these do not work well: 'some babies, tantalised by this type of relative failure, study the variable maternal visage in an attempt to predict the mother's mood, just exactly as we all study the weather. The baby quickly learns to make a forecast: "Just now it is safe to be spontaneous, but any minute the mother's face will become fixed or her mood will dominate, and my own personal needs must then be withdrawn otherwise my central self may suffer insult." ' (Winnicott D.W.: *Playing and Reality*, Tavistock, London 1971, p. 113.) Those wanting a Freudian analysis of Thomson's work might link the petrified city of 'The Doom of a City' with castration anxiety and unresolved Oedipal conflict. That in both 'Sarpolus of Mardon' and 'The City of Dreadful Night' the narrator sees in the presence of the Sphinx 'an angel leaning on his naked sword' will not go unnoticed by those following this line. But it should be borne in mind that 'the' sphinx in its different cultural guises was not always female. The Theban sphinx of Greek mythology is female and winged, but those of Ancient Egypt are wingless and usually though not always male. Yet reference to a female cannot simply be taken to exclude the sphinx of archaeology. Meredith's poem seems to have a monumental sphinx in mind when describing her 'stony immortality'; and Heine makes no mention of wings when describing a female sphinx in the prologue to the *Buch der Lieder*, which Thomson translated (Ms. Don.e.37) thus:

Before the gate there lay a Sphinx,
  Hybrid of joy and dread;
A lion's body, lion's claws,
  A woman's breasts and head.

The description of the Egyptian monumental sphinx which Thomson noted when at work on 'The City of Dreadful Night' was also female (see close of Chapter 18, note 82); but Fate the Sphinx in his Burns essay of 1859 (quoted p. 95) is seen as a male jailor; whilst the Sphinx which appears in Section 20 of 'The City of Dreadful Night' is simply 'it'.

NOTES TO CHAPTER SIX

1 Bodleian Ms. Don. d.108. See photograph for final page of script.
2 'Sarpolus of Mardon', *Progress*, February, 1887. The 10,000-word unfinished fragment was published in G.W. Foote's monthly *Progress* by instalments from February until June 1887.
3 Ms. Don d.108. The untranslated postcript, marked 'from Novalis', is from the opening of Section 4 of 'Hymns to the Night'. In Thomson's complete translation of this (Ms. Don. e.48) the opening reads 'Now know I when the last morning shall be; when Light shall never more invade Night and Love; when Slumber shall be eternal, and solely an inexhaustible vision.'
4 The *Investigator*, November 1st, 1858: editorial statement 'Our Policy', published in Bradlaugh's first issue as editor. The paper had been first launched as the *London Investigator* in April 1854 under Robert Cooper; then in April 1857 it had become the *Investigator* under 'Anthony Collins' (W.H. Johnson). The *Investigator* ran under Bradlaugh until its demise in August 1859.
5 *Investigator*, February '58.
6 V.N., 1884. (Though not completely until Ridler, 1963.) See n. 33 Chapter 5.
7 P.P. 1862 ibid., p. 457.
8 Ibid., pp. 457–458.
9 Ibid., pp. 401–403. Lefroy: ibid., p. 37.
10 Salt, p. 7.
11 1862 p. xiii.
12 Ibid., Appendix I.
13 Ibid., pp. 419–420.
14 Lefroy, ibid., pp. 171–172, quotes letter from Barnes (garrison master at Royal Barracks Dublin) claiming that 18–20 year olds could be taught to read a newspaper & write an intelligible letter if they attended regularly for four hours a week. Of sixteen wholly illiterate at Ballincollig, in fifteen months, three reached the 1st class, seven the 2nd, and one the 3rd, while five remained in the 4th. A schoolmaster J. Newson based at the Curragh reported in February, 1861 – while Thomson was there – that out of two

battalions 780 had attended in the previous twelve months, of whom 252 'who previously knew nothing, had learned to read and write'. (P.P. 1862 ibid., p. 512.)

15 Salt, pp. 25–26.

16 Salt Mss. (transcription). The full verse letter was in 3 parts, the first (May 24th 1858) from Ship Street, the next 2 (May 31st, June 11th) from Richmond Barracks. Potterton had evidently been complaining about his lot, and Thomson in breezy joking fashion told him to be stoical, expect nothing from Fate, and accept the compensations such as the week of spree that went on at the annual change-round, as at present, even if 'uncompanioned – I've no moneys and the damned girls have no heart'. He addressed Potterton as '*Mein leiber freund*' and signed off:

> Health & peace & blessings to you; may frail Fortune ever woo you;
> May your flesh-pots cede abundance to your lemans who succeed:
> So imploreth from his quarter drench'd in whiskey, verse, & porter,
> Your half-blind life-mulcted Jimmy – faithful friend for friend in need.

Potterton and Duncan left R.M.A. January 1855. – W.O. 143/47.

17 Ibid. Grant interview.

18 P.P. 1862, ibid., p. 433.

19 Ibid.

20 21/11/60, Salt, p. 43.

21 Ibid.

22 P.P. 1870 (c.214) XXIV. 701. *Second Report of the Council of Military Education on Army Schools and Libraries* p. 91.

23 War Office circular of May 31st 1858. Mentioned in P.P. 1862, ibid., Appendix II, No. 2 Section 26.

24 Letter as 16 above.

25 *Tait's Edinburgh Magazine* ran from 1831 until November 1861. Troup had bought it (for a second time) in 1855. He wrote many of the articles himself along with an Irish journalist called James Withers who died in 1860. Troup was interested in the pioneering social work in Glasgow of the minister Thomas Chalmers, and after the demise of *Tait's* Troup was given the editorship in December 1861 of the *Beehive*, a paper closely connected with the incipient trade union organisation of London building workers. Thomson contributed to twelve issues of *Tait's* between July 1858 and June 1860. Despite Troup's moving to the *Beehive* it should not be thought that *Tait's* under him was at all radical. It was directed at a readership that it presumed would be interested in the 'problem' of getting decent female domestic staff, as an article of August 1858 indicated: 'The reformation of the female serving classes is pre-eminently women's work. Men have little to do with it. A man has no business in his kitchen, ordering, and meddling with his female servants; and a good servant will tell him so. The master may have to take a recreant vixen to task, but, as a general rule, a master has nothing to do with his female servants – that is the wife's province, and hers alone . . . we hope that the class of female servants will

in time be improved, and they will prove, as they should be, a blessing to their employers among mankind.'

For a history of *Tait's Edinburgh Magazine* and a summary of contents up to 1855, see Houghton W.E. (ed.) *The Wellesley Index to Victorian Periodicals*, Vol. IV, University of Toronto, Routledge & Kegan Paul, 1987, pp. 475–587.

26 'Tasso' May '59; 'Bertram' November '59.

27 Verse thirty of thirty-two.

28 The fourth poem was 'At Death's Door'.

29 Ms. Don. e.36 dated 5.8.58 'Composed in Spring Dublin; Arbour Hill behind Royal Barracks'. N.R. 22/11/62 as 'Heresy', given title 'A Recusant' in C.D.N., 1880.

30 Tribe, p. 26.

31 *Investigator* December 1st, 1859. (P.E.F.)

32 His reading of the essay is referred to in his *Journals*, ed. Gilman, W.H. & Ferguson, A.R., Cambridge Mass., 1960, Vol. 2, pp. 348–351. See Wellek, R.: *Confrontations*, Princeton U.P. 1965, Chapter 6, 'Emerson and German Philosophy'.

33 Carlyle, Thomas: 'Novalis' in *Critical and Miscellaneous Essays*, Vol. 2. The edition used for this work is the *Chelsea Edition* of Carlyle's works, Chapman and Hall n.d., 4 vols.

34 René Wellek in his *Immanuel Kant in England 1793–1838* (Princeton U.P., 1931) discusses this fully pp. 183–202, including specific attention to the 'Novalis' essay. On the one hand 'Thomas Carlyle has done probably more than any one else to make England receptible for the type of mind expressed in German idealism.' However, argues Wellek, Carlyle not only wrote as if Kant and Fichte and Schelling were all saying the same thing, but he misunderstood and misrepresented fundamental Kantian statements. 'Like many others, Carlyle confused the term 'phenomenon' with 'illusion' and even 'delusion' and 'lie'. He expressed this un-Kantian sense of the dreamlikeness of life in many different ways . . . While in Kant man is free and creating, in Carlyle he is a light-sparkle floating in the aether of Deity . . . In Kant he had found a few appealing thoughts (or possibly mostly in second-hand reports of Kant): the general idealism and immaterialism, the ideality of space and time, the difference between Reason and Understanding, the Moral Law within us. But he gave a twist to all, which makes them Carlyle instead of Kant . . . Carlyle is simply in the very depth of his being a Christian, and not only a Christian, but also a Puritan, who seeks to reconcile his faith by new formulas to a new time.'

35 Carlyle: ibid.

36 Ibid.

37 'The Over Soul' was first published in 1840. Thomson wrote another article on Emerson in 1861 when he reviewed *The Conduct of Life* (N.R. 3/9/60) and detected Spinoza behind some of Emerson's ideas. Quoting the essay 'Worship', Thomson added comments in brackets: ' "In our definitions we grope after the spiritual by describing it as invisible. The true definition of

spiritual is *real* [good Platonism this]; that law which executes itself, which works without means, and which cannot be conceived as not existing [good Spinozism] . . ." '

38 Ms. Don. e.48. Thomson's complete translation, never published, has survived in a transcription by Dobell from a notebook of Thomson's that was in the possession of G.W. Foote. The final ms. is dated 14/6/65; and Dobell has a prefatory note expressing the view that the translation 'should be published I think some day with a note stating that the translations never received the author's final revisions.'

39 The compendium *Half Hours with the Free Thinkers* was issued at the end of 1857 and had reached its third edition ten years later. It contained all twenty-four of the original pamphlets issued fortnightly in 1856 and 1857, bound as one. Each number originally cost a penny, was edited either by 'Iconoclast', 'Anthony Collins', or John Watts, and those besides Shelley included Descartes, Spinoza, Hume, D'Holbach, Paine, Epicurus, and Volney.

40 The atheism quote is from the preface to the April 1857 *Investigator* by 'Anthony Collins'. The Novalis is Thomson's translation of 'Hymns to the Night' Section 5. (Ms. Don. e.48.)

NOTES TO CHAPTER SEVEN

1 Novalis: 'The reason why people are so attached to Nature is probably that, being spoilt children, they are afraid of the father and take refuge with the mother.'(*Schriften,* 1923, vol. 2. p. 186; trans. M. Hamburger, *Reason and Energy*, Weidenfeld & Nicolson, 1970, p. 81.)

2 II. 19, 11. 459–466.

3 'The Happy Poet' begun November 1857, finished on April 3rd 1859. First published in *Tait's Edinburgh Magazine*, December 1859, where it was headed 'Inscribed to Alexander Smith, author of "A Life Drama" etc'. The Kilmarnock poet's 1854 verse drama had caused a literary stir and had quickly gone into several editions. Smith is remembered in Scotland now mostly for one of his 'city poems' – 'Glasgow'.

4 Salt Mss. As note 16, Ch. 6.

5 *Tait's*, March '59.

6 Section translated by Carlyle, ibid.

7 Letter to Potterton p. 80 (Salt p. 43). A contemporary translation of Schiller read:

> 'But the same
> Unerring voice, hath it not likewise said,
> "Whoso dares raise the veil, shall Truth behold;"
> Be what there may behind, I dare to lift it!' –
> (With louder voice he cries) – 'I will behold her!'
> 'Behold her!' –

In lengthen'd accents echo mocking cries.
No sooner spoke, he hath the veil uprais'd.
   And now you ask, what there did he behold:
Thither the priests, who pale and senseless found him
Stretch'd out on Isis pedestal. What there
He saw, or what experienc'd, hath no tongue
Ever disclos'd. But all his Light of Life
Thenceforth was vanish'd, and deep-rooted sorrow
Hurried him fast to an untimely grave.
'Woe to the man,' – these were his warning words
To eager questioners, when urg'd to tell –
'Woe to the man who Truth would reach through sin.
He never shall enjoy her beauteous face.'
        "The Veiled Statue at Saïs", G. H. Merrivale, 1844.

8   Berkeley: *Principles of Human Knowledge*, Section 6.

9   Carlyle, ibid.

10 Lefroy, ibid., p. 19.

11 Salt, p. 21. Grant had 'heard anecdotes from Mr Barnes of Thomson's intellectual prowess and originality of character, so that his interest was already awakened before they actually met'.

12 Ibid., p. 23.

13 Letter from Grant to Charles Bradlaugh of March 25th 1859 from Richmond Barracks Dublin. Bishopsgate Institute, Bradlaugh Collection Index no. 72a.

14 Letter of April 8th 1859: Salt, p. 29.

15 After the Duncans went abroad in 1860 Thomson still kept in touch by letter. Mrs Duncan wrote 'A correspondence was kept up, and the friendship also, after we went out to India; and if we wanted anything done in England, "Jimmy" was always the one to do it.' The Duncans returned to England for a short while in the 1870s. Thomson and Grant said farewell to him 'for last time' on April 11th 1874, 2 days before he set out again for Madras.

16 Letter of May 14th, 1859 from Richmond Barracks. Salt, p. 30.

17 Ibid., pp. 31–32.

18 Letter of June 27th from Curragh Camp. Salt, p. 35.

19 Lugard, Lt. Col. H.W.: *Narrative of Operations in the Arrangement and Formation of a Camp for 10,000 Infantry in the Curragh of Kildare.* Thom & Sons, Dublin 1858, pp. 12–13.

20 As note 18, pp. 33–34.

21 Letter of January 6th 1860 from Curragh Camp. Salt, p. 37.

22 Ms. Don. e.36 dated 5/8/58. Ms. Don. d.108, with note 'Written in an access of fierce emotion, one evening while waiting for Waters to go to a dance.'

    In De Quincey's *Suspiria de Profundis* the chapter 'Levana and Our Ladies of Sorrow' presents the 3 goddesses Mater Lachrymorum

(Madonna), Our Lady of Tears; *Mater Suspiriorum*, Our Lady of Sighs. And the third: 'But the third sister, who is also the youngest – ! Hush! Whisper whilst we talk of *her*!. . . She is the defier of God. She is also the mother of lunacies, and the suggestress of suicides. Deep lie the roots of her power; but narrow is the nation that she rules. For she can approach only those in whom a profound nature has been upheaved by central convulsions; in whom the heart trembles and the brain rocks under conspiracies of tempest from without and tempest from within. Madonna moves with uncertain steps, fast or slow, but still with tragic grace. Our Lady of Sighs creeps timidly and stealthily. But this youngest sister moves with incalculable motions, bounding, and with tiger's leaps. She carries no key; for, though coming rarely amongst men, she storms at all doors at which she is permitted to enter at all. And *her* name is *Mater Tenebrarum*, – Our Lady of Darkness.'

23 Cumming, J.: *The Great Tribulation, or the Things Coming on the Earth* Bentley, London 1859.

24 Review, pp. 655–664.

25 Tribe, pp. 57–58.

26 Quoted in Bonner Vol. 1, note p. 120.

27 Holyoake, G.J.: *Sixty Years of an Agitator's Life*, T. Fisher Unwin, London, 6th impression, 1906, Vol. 2 p. 99. (The full account is given in Vol. 2 Chapter 75, 'Bequest of a Suicide' pp. 97–101.)

28 Salt, p. 40. In the mid-1870s a former minister of Mrs Gray's in Greenock, William Maccall, came to know Thomson and mentioned him to the Gray family. Agnes concluded her description of Thomson's 1860 visit: 'He went out from us with the intention of again going to Aldershot; but from that day until Mr Maccall mentioned him to us, we never once heard of him. Ever since we have felt greatly puzzled to account for his singular conduct.'

29 Ms. Don. e.37 noted as Aldershot 24/9/60. Monday. 'Love and Sin' scored out; above ink 'Meeting Again', pencil 'A Parting V Meeting' with 'Together' scored out.

30 Salt, p. 41: 'It is known that he still treasured many years afterwards a purse which she had worked and given to him.' The burial instructions which Thomson gave to his housekeeper Sarah Scott are discussed in Chapter 22.

31 'A Letter Addressed to the Editor, on Shelley's Religious Opinions', N.R. 25/8/60. (B.C.S.)

NOTES TO CHAPTER EIGHT

1 Note to 'Queen Mab' Part IV, ll. 178–79. The notes follow on the lines 'These are the hired bravos who defend/ The tyrant's throne.' Elsewhere Shelley notes of the statement 'There is no god' (Part VII, l. 13): 'This negation must be understood solely to affect a creative Deity. The hypothesis of the pervading Spirit co-eternal with the universe remains unshaken.'

2 Thomson's quotation – from Shelley's 'Essay on Life' – together with the succeeding series of quotes are all from his letter to the editor, N.R. 25/8/60.

3 Wordsworth: 'Elegiac Stanzas'.

4 'Scrap-book Leaves – 1' N.R. 1/9/60.

5 Poem 'Shelley' written 1861, unpublished until *Shelley* anthology 1884.

6 The opening of essay 'Shelley', N.R. 22/12/60. (B.C.S.) The succeeding quotes are from this.

7 *The Prose Works of Shelley* ed. Forman, H.B., Reeves & Turner, London 1880, Vol. 2, p. 268.

8 Ibid., Vol. 4. Plato's *The Banquet* pp. 219–221.

9 'Shelley' as n. 6 above. The succeeding quotes are again from this.

10 'Scrap-book Leaves – 2' N.R. 22/9/60. Secularist readers might not have been too happy at being admonished with a Biblical quote which restored to its context of II *Peter* 1. 10, 11 reads: 'Wherefore thee rather, brethren, give diligence to make your calling and election sure: for if ye do these things, ye shall never fail: For so an entrance shall be ministered unto you abundantly into the everlasting kingdom of our Lord and Saviour Jesus Christ.'

11 Ms. Don. d.108.

12 See notes to the collected *Shelley's Prose*, ed. D. L. Clark, New Mexico Univ., 1954.

13 In essay note to the line 'Necessity – thou Mother of the World': 'Queen Mab', Part 6, l. 198.

14 Ibid.

15 Carlyle, T.: *Sartor Resartus* Book 2, Chapter 7, 'The Everlasting No'.

16 Novalis: *Christianity or Europe* (trans. Dutton, Rev. J.) Chapman & Hall, 1854. Carlyle himself also translated this section near the end of his 1830 'Voltaire' essay.

17 'The Mask of Anarchy', written in response to the Peterloo massacre, advocates a large assembly to gather peacefully and, if the military attack, no resistance should be offered: the soldiers would be shamed by their actions. Shelley's attitude of a kind of assertive forgiveness echoes Spinoza's *Ethics* 4.46: 'He who lives according to the guidance of reason strives as much as possible to repay the hatred, anger, or contempt of others towards himself with love or generosity.'

18 Prometheus started the process of his release and the overthrow of Jupiter through abandoning the desire for vengeance. In the concluding verses of 'Prometheus Unbound', Demogorgon – Necessity – says that Love 'springs/ And folds over the world its healing wings.' . . .

> To suffer woes which Hope thinks infinite;
> To forgive wrongs darker than death or night;
>   To defy Power, which seems omnipotent;
> To love, and bear; to hope till Hope creates
> From its own wreck the thing it contemplates;
>   Neither to change, nor falter, nor repent;

This, like thy glory, Titan, is to be
Good, great and joyous, beautiful and free;
This is alone Life, Joy, Empire, and Victory.

19 In a letter to W.M. Rossetti of April 2nd 1873, Thomson wrote of 'Epipsychidion': 'It has always seemed to me that Shelley never soared higher than in this poem, which I find full of supreme inspiration.'

20 See opening of Chapter 6, p. 63.

21 'A Few Words about Burns', *Investigator*, April '59.

22 Ms. Don. e.36; Don. d.108. The first half of the 32-verse poem was completed by the time Thomson left the Curragh at the end of May 1860. The full poem was completed in Aldershot on December 6th. See Chapter 9, note 11.

23 See n. 22, Chapter 7.

24 Letter from Aldershot 11/10/60. Salt, p. 42.

25 Letter of 22/2/61. Salt, p. 43.

26 The 55th Foot was split between barracks at Fort Regent, at St Peter's in the west and at Grève de Lecq in the north of the island. Fragments in Ms. Don. g.5. suggest that Thomson sometimes (Aug. 21st, Sep. 29th) stayed overnight at St Peter's.

27 Letter from Fort Regent Jersey 24/7/61, Salt, p. 44.

28 Ms. Don. g.5. Other scraps in the notebook indicate a visit to Mont Orgeil, and to Princes Tower; watching the St Catherine's Bay regatta on August 13th 1861; and a visit the previous month to Jersey Races on July 17th and 18th. The races were held annually on Gorey Common, on land near the shore now occupied by a golfcourse.

29 Ms. Don. e.37, dated Tuesday 14/1/62. The first of two songs; the second dated the following day.

30 See n. 25, Chapter 7.

31 Salt Mss. Letter from Harney of 21/8/88. Harney told Salt that he knew Thomson 'but did not meet him very frequently'. Harney's translation of the Manifesto had been in his *Red Republican*. In Jersey he loaned Thomson some books, including *Sartor Resartus*.

32 *Jersey Independent* 7/3/62. There were six poems from the *Buch der Lieder*: one from the 'Lyrical Intermezzo' and five, including the following, from 'The Return Home':

We travelled alone in the mail coach,
  In darkness the whole of the night;
We cosily nestled together,
  We jested and laughed with delight.

But, oh, in the dawn of the morning,
  My child, how frightened we were!
For who sat with us but Amor,
  The sightless passenger!

The translations were attributed as having been done for the paper by 'T.J.'. A preface read: 'Although the sentiment of Heine's songs is often extravagant, often scornfully and bitterly heterodox, they are true lyrics which we cannot but admire and prize for their spontaneity, subtle melody and rare suggestiveness.

'It may be worth while to remark that German love-songs are peculiarly difficult to translate into pure English, because abounding in naive diminutives of endearment for which we have no synonymes: hence the best of our dialects in which to render them is that 'Doric Scotch' made classical by the glorious genius of Robert Burns. This hint may be of use to others.'

In modern times Heine has been translated into Scots by Edwin Morgan and by Donald Goodbrand Saunders.

33 'Robert Browning's *Men and Women*', *Jersey Independent* 20/2/60. (Schaefer 1967).

34 The six sonnets to Joseph and Alice Barnes were begun on March 25th 1862 and finished on April 10th. They were first published in full in Dobell's 1895 memoir. Bodleian Ms. Don. e.36; also a manuscript copy in the Bradlaugh Collection, Bishopsgate Institute, Index No. 1855 45F.

35 Bodleian Ms. Don. d.104. Dated Tuesday 15/4/62. Later published as the tenth section of the poem-sequence 'Sunday Up the River' which appeared in *Fraser's Magazine* in October, 1869.

36 Salt Mss. Notes of an interview with Charles Bradlaugh, June 5th, 1888.

37 Bonner, Vol. 1 p. 109: 'When my father quitted the service they kept up a close correspondence, and many a time have I heard my mother remark that Mr Thomson's "Beautiful letters" had been destroyed.' See Concluding Appendix.

38 Salt, p. 47. Also Grant interview, ibid.

39 Ms. Don. g.5 'From Portsmouth to Aldershot for C.M.' Thomson's charge is listed in P.R.O. Kew, WO 8612. Bowen was charged with being disobedient, drunk, and using abusive language.

40 Salt noted Bradlaugh in his interview as saying that the cause of his dismissal was 'connected with drink, T. having been under arrest more than once'.

41 Ms. Don. g.5.

42 Ibid. (P.E.F.)

43 *Dante's Divine Comedy; The Paradise* Translated in the Original Ternary Rhyme by C.B. Cayley. Longman, Brown, Green and Longman, London 1854. This was the third in the 4-volume set: *Hell* 1851, *Purgatory* 1853, and a supplementary volume of notes in 1855.

Thomson's unascribed transcriptions from the translation are in Bodleian Ms. Don. d.108. All the quotations that follow are from sections copied out by him.

The first four lines here are from Canto 18, 11. 19–21 (p. 132).

44 Ibid., Canto 23, 11. 70–75 (p. 172).

45 Ibid., Canto 31, 11. 71–84 (pp. 232–253).

46 Ibid., Canto 33, 11. 4–9 (p. 244).

47 Ibid., 11. 100–114, p. 249.

48 Ibid., I. 117.
49 Ibid., II. 124–132. (p. 250).
50 P.R.O. Kew, WO 25.3871. Thomson's character was noted as 'Good'. Cause of discharge was given as 'Conviction by court martial'. Bowen was reduced to the rank of private and discharged on 20th November.
51 Salt Mss. Undated letter from a Mr Boulton at the War Office to a Mr Creighton who had requested information on Salt's behalf; Creighton's letter had been passed to Boulton via another department. Creighton replied that the documents should now be sought at the P.R.O.: 'Our records give no more information than that contained in Mr Salt's letter (herewith returned) viz: that Schoolmaster Thomson was discharged with disgrace on 30/10/62.'

NOTES TO CHAPTER NINE

1   Agreed 17/1/62. Tribe, p. 80; stamped in June. Bonner, p. 99.
2   Tribe, p. 79.
3   Bonner, Chapter 20, pp. 203–206.
4   Tribe, p. 56.
5   Bonner, p. 204.
6   Ms. Don. g.5.
7   Refused May 1862. Bonner, p. 130.
8   Bradlaugh had at first shared the editorship with Joseph Barker, but the two men took to disagreeing from separate halves of the paper before Barker left at the end of August, 1861. Bradlaugh was then voted sole editor with effect from the issue of 7/9/60. George Jacob Holyoake became a 'special contributor' at the beginning of 1862, receiving £2 of Bradlaugh's £5 editorial salary. However he too took issue with Bradlaugh's Malthusian views and his use of the word 'atheist' to describe the paper's editorial line. So Holyoake also moved on, the result being a messy court dispute about money he claimed for contracted payments in anticipation of his remaining. Tribe, pp. 74–77, 80–82. Bonner, pp. 121–130.
    The *National Reformer* was to stay in publication until 1893.
9   Heine, N.R. 6, 20, 27/12/61. 'E.B.B.' N.R. 29/11/61. After Elizabeth Barrett Browning's death Thomson noted in his Jersey notebook 29/10/61: 'A remarkable dream. Mrs Browning appeared in the place where I was. She had in her hand a book written by herself – a book (in my dream) wonderfully fascinating. Her face was adorable – sweet, suave, benignant, wise. I passed her on the shore; she was reading.' Ms. Don. g.5.
    Thomson copied out 18 of her 'Sonnets from the Portuguese' and made copies in whole or part of another 22 poems. These are as transcribed after Thomson's death by John Grant in Ms. Don. d.108.
10 N.R. 15/11/62.
11 N.R. 28/2/63. Prefaced 'My dear Iconoclast – I transcribed this piece for you, intending to introduce it with a few remarks upon the doctrine of the

immortality of the human soul; but I have not been able to catch the few right words, and the rhyme itself is so lengthy, that I must not also inflict upon the patient reader a long preface of reason, or unreason. Suffice it, then, for me to affirm that in my calmest and purest hours of contemplation, my own verdict upon my own life attests this poem (which was written more than a year since) to be genuine as the utterance of my individual self; whether it is true or not for others, themselves must decide. It may be worth while to remark that the Three Ladies were suggested by the sublime sisterhood of "Our Ladies of Sorrow" in the "Suspiria de Profundis", and that the stanza was moulded under the influence of the "Guardian Angel" in "Men and Women." So, if any good reader finds no good in this poem, let me humbly suggest that he or she may most easily and profitably forget it in the study of those noble works of Thomas De Quincey and Robert Browning. Fraternally yours, B.V.'

The poem was later titled simply 'To Our Ladies of Death' in C.D.N.

12   N.R. 3/1/63.
13   N.R. 24/1/63 Quoted in Schaefer p. 235.
14   Notably when readers complained after the appearance of 'The City of Dreadful Night' in 1874. Other contributors sometimes caused complaint, as when a regular contributor Edward Guillame expressed the viewpoint something on the line of Thomson's late 1850s poems to the effect that as he 'stood beside the grave' of one dearly loved, only the thought of a future reunion could support him, and that the 'passion of Love' could not die: only on this 'the important doctrine of the immortality of the soul is at all tenable'. N.R. 16/7/64, 'The existence of a Future Life'.

An editorial comment noted, 'We need scarcely say that we entirely dissent from the statements contained in the above article', and it was followed a fortnight later by further tart comments about this theory mixing emotion with reason; if the theory were true it would cause confusion in the afterlife of those who had remarried after bereavement. 'The Hope of Immortality'. N.R. 23/7/64.

15   3/2/63 Bradlaugh Papers No. 104(a).
16   Adams, W.E.: *Memoirs of a Social Atom*, Hutchinson, London 1903, p. 499.
17   Ibid., pp. 440–441.
18   Ibid., p. 448, 443 et seq.
19   Ibid., pp. 443–444.
20   Adams, W.E.: *Recollections of Charles Bradlaugh* quoted in Bonner, p. 109, footnote.
21   Bonner, p. 110.
22   Ibid.
23   As note 16, p. 449.
24   Ms. Don. g.5. '25/8/63. Cease connection with Polish Committee commenced 23/4/63 – Four months and ten days – £11 once end of July.'
25   As note 20 above: ibid.
26   Salt Mss. Bradlaugh interview, 'Purity of Thomson's nature. Love for

children'; Letter from J.W. Barrs of July 5th, 1886: 'Thomson was naturally very loving with children and children invariably returned his affection'; H.B. Bonner, 'Childish Recollections of James Thomson' in *Our Corner* August 1886: 'Mr Thomson was very fond of children . . . and in return children adored him'.

27 *Our Corner*, ibid.

28 Ms. 38534 dated 7/8/64.

29 Ibid., dated Friday 12/2/63.

30 Ibid., dated Thursday 24/3/64.

31 Salt Mss. Transcription. 'Sunday 2/9/66'.

32 Bonner, p. 111.

33 N.R. 4/6/64.

34 N.R. 24/6/64.

35 The *National Reformer* though continued to bait Cumming, as when an editorial of September 10th, 1865 wrote: 'Is Dr Cumming's prophecy in reference to the end of the world about to be fulfilled? Signs and wonders are certainly coming to pass; and an important question is, what do they portend? Whoever would have thought a few years since of Edinburgh and Glasgow indulging in the madness of Sunday trains?' As late as August 9th, 1874, a correspondent in the N.R. drew attention to the fact that when the same kind of Greek numerical calculations were applied to the name 'Cumming' as Cumming had himself applied to show that Pope = Antichrist ('Latinus' = 666) his own tally was 667: – 'but one poor figure difference between the two of them. Such is the vanity of earthly things!'

The freethought movement was not the only source of ridicule, especially after 1867 had come and gone. Lord Frederic Hamilton, whose family attended Cumming's sermons, recalled that 'His influence with his flock rather diminished when it was found that Dr Cumming had renewed the lease of his house for twenty-one years, only two months before the date he had fixed with absolute certainty as being the end of all things.' (*My Yesterdays*, Hodder & Stoughton.) Thomson also had cause to mention this (see pp. 203–204).

Cumming continued to preach the coming end, and a description of two visits to his church can be found in the chapters 'Dr Cumming in Crown Court' and 'Dr Cumming on the Present and Future of Europe' in Davies, C.M.: *Unorthodox London: Phases of Religious Life in the Metropolis*, Tinsley, London 1873, pp. 201–217.

36 De Béranger's 'The Good God' N.R. 11/7/64; review of Peacock's *Poems and Songs*, N.R. 19/11/64.

37 N.R. 14–28/7; 4–25/8; 1/9/67. Quotes E.P. pp. 1–2; 17–18.

38 The Spenser is *Faerie Queene* Book 1 Canto 9 Stanza 40. The following is the full sequence as it originally appeared in N.R. Asterisks indicate the sections removed by Thomson when he printed a shortened sequence in E.P.

Chaucer: 'The Pardoner's Tale', ll. 727–738; *stanzas from ballad 'The Marchioness of Douglass' and 'Marie Hamilton'; Spenser: *The Faerie*

Queene Book 1 Canto 9 Stanza 40; Shakespeare: *Macbeth* V 5. 19–28; *The Tempest* IV 1. 156–158; *ibid., 152–156; Beaumont and Fletcher(?): *Thierry and Theodoret* IV 1.; *Webster: *The Duchess of Malfi* IV 2. 184–191; *Chidiock Tichborne: 'Elegy' Stanzas 1, 3; James Thomson (1700–48) 'The Castle of Indolence' Canto 1, Verse 12; *Byron: 'Euthanasia' Stanza 9; 'Cain' I, 1. 287–289; Shelley: 'Invocation to Misery' Stanza 9; *ibid Stanza 10; 'Julian and Maddalo 11. 505–510; **'Adonais' Stanza 52; Keats: 'Ode to a Nightingale' Stanza 3; *Ebenezer Elliot: 'Lyrics for my Daughter' Stanzas 3, 4, 5; *James Montgomery: 'The Grave' Stanzas 1, 3, 5; *Poe: 'For Annie' Stanzas 5, 6, 8; Emily Brontë: 'The Philosopher' 11. 7–10, 53–56; Anna Brownell Jameson: 'Take me, Mother Earth' Stanza 3; *ibid., Stanza 2; Elizabeth Barrett Browning: 'De Profundis' Stanzas 6, 7, 12; *Tennyson 'The Lotus Eaters' 11. 88–98; Arnold: 'Requiescat' Stanza 18; *ibid., Stanzas 3, 4; Robert Browning: 'Paracelsus' 363–365; *Job* iii, 13–15,17–22; *vii, 9, *x.18–20; x.21–22; xvii.14; *Ecclesiastes* ii.17; iii.19–21; iv.2; *ix.5, 6; ix.10; xii.8; *Jeremiah* xx.14–18; Plato: *Apology of Socrates* paragraphs 13, 17; Raleigh: *History of the World* Book 5 Chapter 6 penultimate paragraph; Mornay: 'A Discourse of Life and Death' trans. Mary Sidney, Countess of Pembroke, paragraph 1; 'An Essay on Death' paragraphs 1, 2, 3 in *The Remaines of the Right Honorable Francis, Lord Verulam* (spuriously ascribed to Bacon); John Eliot: ms of *Monarchy of Man*; Sir Thomas Browne: *Hydriotaphia** opening paragraph Chapter 5; ibid., paragraph 2; *ibid., paragraph 9; *ibid., paragraph 10; spurious passage attributed to Browne; De Quincey: *Suspiria de Profundis* 'Levana and Our Ladies of Sorrow' from last paragraph; G.W. Curtis: *Nile Notes of a Howadji* Chapter 19 (from) paragraphs 3, 14, 15; Carlyle: *French Revolution* Book 1 Chapter 2 (from) paragraph 5; ibid., Book 5 Chapter 5 (from) paragraph 12.

Most of this is listed in Schaefer p. 323.

39 N.R.13/5, 27/5, 3/6, 10/6/66. Ms. Don e.36 is severally dated from 16/3/64 to 9/11/64 (Prologue); also 5/7, 5/8/65. The poem is in three sections: 'Prologue' 33 lines; 'The Story' 1205 lines; 'Epilogue' 30 lines.

40 From 'The Romantic School' (trans. Fleishman) in Ellis, H.: *The Prose Writings of Heinrich Heine*, Walter Scott Pub., London and New York, n.d., p. 124.

41 'Heinrich Heine' (4) *Secularist* 29/1/76, Schaefer p. 258.

42 'Hammonia': Caput xxv. of 'A Winter's Tale': *The Poems of Heine; completely translated into the original metres with a sketch of his Life*, ed. Bowring, E.A., Bell & Sons, 1916, p. 374. (*Bonn's Classics*, orig. pub. 1860.)

43 As 41: part 6, 12/2/76. Schaefer p. 269.

44 The opening chapter of Novalis's *Heinrich von Ofterdingen* describes a poet who falls asleep on his couch and dreams of travelling to a land where his sensations are transformed and he is profoundly drawn to 'a lovely blue flower' which, 'As he rose to examine it more closely, it seemed to move and change; the glossy leaves hung down by the stalk, and the blossom bent

towards him; the petals slowly opened, and he saw a lovely, tender face.' At this point he wakes up on his couch again.

Having set out on his quest to Augsburg, he meets there Klingsöhr's daughter Matilda. They dance, and 'Heinrich wished the dance would never end.' When they part he reflects: 'I feel just as I did when I saw the magic blue flower . . . The face which I saw in that calyx was Matilda's . . . For Matilda I will live, and a changeless faith shall unite our souls. Dawn rises for me – the darkness of night is at an end for ever.' (Complete translation of *Heinrich von Ofterdingen* in *Novalis: His Life, Thoughts and Works* (ed. Hope, M.J.) Stott, London 1891. (Quotes here pp. 55; 116; 120–121.) The Blue Flower episode and another section describing Heinrich and Matilda are translated in Carlyle's 'Novalis' essay.

45   The poems quoted are: Four verses beginning '*Ich bin die Prinsessin Ilse*' from *The Hartz Journey*; the 'Epilogue' to *Lazarus* which Thomson translates as an epilogue to his own poem; and an untranslated section from 'Babylonian Sorrows' which is given as a footnote to ll. 919–920. A contemporary translation renders the section:

> Believe me, my child, Matilda, my wife,
> That the angry sea, in its wildest strife,
> And the cruel forest less dangers give
> Than the city where now we're fated to live.
> Though fearful the wolf and the vulture may be,
> The shark, and the monsters dread of the sea,
> Far fiercer, more furious beasts have their birth
> In Paris, the proud capital of the earth.
> That hell to the angels, that heaven to devils, –
> That thee I must leave in this dungeon sad,
> This drives me crazy, that drives me mad.
>   (*Bohn* Classics, Trans. E.A. Bowring)

46   ll. 391–394. Dated 7/7/65 in Ms. e.36; N.R. had footnote to this passage: 'This was written before Mr J.S. Mill published a similar declaration. It will be noticed, however, that while the philosopher treated the matter with his habitual lofty earnestness, the flippant rhymester but makes it a subject for mockery and laughter.'

47   ll. 603–618.

48   ll. 663–675. The concluding lines refer to Spenser's *Faerie Queene*, Book 1, Canto 3.

49   'Epilogue' as n. 45.

50   Tribe, p. 339 n. 5.

51   Tribe, p. 340 n. 26. P.R.O. BT 31 1182, 2594C.

52   Adams: *Memoirs of a Social Atom*, p. 450.

53   As 51.

NOTES TO CHAPTER TEN

1 Mss. 38534. Verses rejected for the poem 'Sunday up the River'.
2 R.C.S. notebook detailing band performances and fees.
3 Ms. Don. e.41, 'Star and Garter – II' dated Monday 10/4/65.
4 Ms. Don. e.41, 'Star and Garter – I' dated Thursday 25/5/65 (Thomson numbered as first the one he dated second).
5 Ms. Don. d.108. Initially written as 'Two up the River: A Midsummer Day Dream', fifteen sections totalling 343 lines. Became 'Sunday up the River', twenty sections totalling 413 lines. *Fraser's Magazine* November, 1869.
6 Section 14. Trans. of '*Mit deinen blauen Augen*' from *Neue Gedichte*.
7 Section 16.
8 Undated letter, with notes on poem enclosed, together with letter enclosing additional sections of poem, dated Friday 16/6/65. Both letters addressed 'My Dear Potterton'. Salt Mss. Transcription.
9 N.R. 14/10/66. King Polycrates was advised to throw away his most valued possession to placate the gods for his having enjoyed too much success. His favourite ring was thrown in the sea, but there it was swallowed by a large fish which was caught and innocently given the king as a gift. (Herodotus: *Histories* III 40–41.)
10 N.R. 17/12/65.
11 First published in memoir by Dobell (1884).
12 Sections 1–3, and what became the final twelfth section; dated 2/8, 5/8, 10/8 and 6/10/63. Ms. Don. e.37, Ms. Don. e.40. Ridler p. 264 lists full datings and variants.
13 In sections 5 to 9, a member of the company tells how 'Ten thousand years ago' there had been Indians and Squaws on the site of their present meeting, and at equal 10,000 intervals into the past, there had been nomadic tribespeople; a palace with 'goddesses'; mermaids under the sea, and before that – a group of four couples, with one telling a story about the past: 'The ring is round, Life naught, the World an O,/ This night is fifty thousand years ago!'
14 Section 1: verses 1–5. The Sunday campaigns are discussed in Royle, E.: *Victorian Infidels*, ibid.
15 Salt Mss. As 8 above.
16 P.R.O. WO.25 3863. He left October 15th.
17 Tribe, pp. 90, 340 n. 30. Naples Co. P.R.O. BT 31 1220/2810 C. Potterton was living in Oakley Street, Chelsea.
18 Bonner, p. 100.
19 Ms. Don. f.8. '9/10/65. Began the Italian'. '23/8/66. Began the Italian for the second time – having forgotten the little I learned last year.' 'Sunday 9/6/66. Must begin the shorthand – Pitman's phonographic system.'
20 *The Diaries of W.M. Rossetti 1870–1873* (ed. Bernard, O.) Oxford University Press, 1977, p. 266.
21 Foote, G.W.: 'James Thomson – I: The Man', *Progress*, April 1884.

22 He was based at Windsor in 1865, where his son Kenneth was born, and at the Tower of London in 1868, where his daughter Alice was born.

23 Ms. 38534 13/5/65; Ms. Don. f.8: July, 66; 22/4/67 'To Kew and Richmond with Grant & Potterton'; Ms. Don. g.5 '10/11/69 Windsor (Grant's) Virginia Water.'

24 Ms. Don. f.8; Ms. 38534.

25 Letter to Agnes 14/5/59. Salt, p. 32.

26 List Ms. 38534. 'Cousin Helen' could have been one of three: two in Port Glasgow (see note 18 Chap. 2); or Miss Helen Birkmyre, 20-year-old daughter of Thomson's Aunt Susan.

27 Ms. Don. f.8: *Giovanni* 8/6/66 (with Potterton), *Barber* 11/6/66.

28 Letter to Mrs Bradlaugh, Salt, p. 92.

29 Adams, W.E.: ibid., p. 450.

30 A list of the references made in fourteen of the articles Thomson contributed to the *National Reformer* between September 1865 and December 1867 shows the width of his reading. To make such a list comprehensible, the references are here loosely categorised as E = Essay, F = favourable, D = derogatory, P = passim, or neutral passing mention, and Q = quote:

Charles Kingsley (E, D); Newman's *Apologia Pro Vita Sua* (D); Melville's *Mardi* (P); Gibbon (P); *The Heimskringla* (F); Arnold's Essay on Heine (F); Hogg's *Life of Shelley* (F); Thackeray (D); Thomas à Kempis (P); Dryden's 'Mackflecknoe' (F); Pope's 'Dunciad' (F); Shelley's 'Peter Bell the Third' (Q); Cowper (D); Balzac (F); Heine (F); Carlyle's 'Oxen of the Gods' (P); Keats's 'Hyperion' (Q); Aristophanes, Lucian, Rabelais, Montaigne, Shakespeare, Swift, Voltaire, Lessing, Goethe, Leopardi, Burns, Carlyle (P, F); Shakespeare (Q); Balzac's *Prince de la Bohème* (P); Murger's *Scenes de la Vie de Bohème* (F); Emerson, Shelley (P, F); Bulwer-Lyton (D); Hook (D); *Ingoldsby Legends* (D); Browning (F); Carlyle (F); Garth Wilkinson (F); Carlyle's *French Revolution* (F); Ruskin (F); Pope's 'Essay on Man' (F); Swift's *Tale of a Tub* (F); E.B. Browning's 'The Great God Pan' and 'Aurora Leigh' (F); Dante (P); Milton (P); Novalis (P); More, Raleigh, Bacon, Selden, Sidney, Bunyan, Swift, De Foe, Jonson, Scott (P, F); Benvenuto Cellini's *Autobiography* (P); Raleigh's *History of the World* (P); Cervantes's *Don Quixote* (F); Bunyan's *Pilgrims' Progress* (P); Coleridge (P); Swift (P); Browning's 'Bishop Blougram's Apology' (F); Byron's 'Prophecy of Dante' (Q); Spenser's *The Faerie Queene* (E, F); Hebrews (Q); Leviticus (Q); Plato's *Phaedo, Phaedrus, Timaeus* (P); Herbert's 'Faith' (Q); Macaulay's essay on Bunyan (D); Drayton's *Polyolbion* (F); Blake (E, F); Cowper (D); Poe's 'Adventures of Hans Pfael' (F); Wordsworth (D); Coleridge's 'Ancient Mariner' (F), 'Lay Sermons' (D); Scott (P); Byron (D); Keats (F); Shelley (F); Novalis's *Die Kinder sind Anliken* (Q); Tennyson (D except 'The Lotus Eaters'); Byron's 'The Dream' (F); Browning's 'Epistle of Karshish' (F); E.B. Browning's 'Sonnets from the Portuguese' (F); Emerson's poems 'Compensation', 'Art', 'History', 'Heroism' (F); Plato, Spinoza, Bacon, Berkeley, Fichte, Schelling (P, F); Herbert's 'The Elixir' (Q); Plato's *Phaedrus* (Q);

Shelley's *A Defence of Poetry* (F); William Jones's *Dissertation on the Mystical Poetry of the Persians and Hindus* (F, Q); Shelley's 'Epipsychidion' (F); Luke (Q); Milton's 'Paradise Lost' (Q); Hume, Berkeley (P); Bentham, Mill (P); Burns (Q); Plato's *Apology of Socrates* (Q), *Phaedrus* (Q); George Eliot (F); Thackeray (D); Ecclesiastes (Q); Goldsmith (P); Pascal (F); Burns (F); Shelley's 'Julian and Maddalo' (F); Cowley (Q); Arnold's *La Grande Chartreuse* (D); Emerson on Montaigne (F); Herbert's 'Giddiness' (Q); Addison's *Vision of Mirza* (P, F); Goethe's *Dichtung und Warheit*, Rousseau's *Confessions*, De Quincey's *Confessions of an English Opium-Eater* (P); *The Arabian Nights* (P); Shakespeare's *The Taming of the Shrew* (P); Swinburne (E, F); Chaucer, Spenser, Dryden, Pope, Swift, Fielding, Sterne, Smollett, Burns, Byron, Shelley (P, F); De Musset, Sand, Hugo, Ovid (P, F); Charlotte Brontë (F); Thackeray's *Pendennis* (D); Balzac's *Un Grand Homme de Province à Paris* (F).

31 Ms. 38534: 'Ronald and Helen' rej. *Blackwoods, Cornhill, English Domestic Woman's Magazine*; Ms. Don. f.8: 'Sunday up the River' rej. *Fortnightly Review, Blackwoods*. Prose pieces including 'Sympathy' and 'William Blake' were rejected by the *Saturday Review* and the *Fortnightly*.

32 Tribe, p. 91.

33 'The Story of a Famous Old Jewish Firm', N.R. 24, 31/12/65. Quotes S.P., pp. 43–44, 46.

34 Ibid., p. 51.

35 N.R. 18/3/66. Quote S.P., p. 96.

36 Ibid., p.91.

37 Ibid., p. 93.

38 'The One Thing Needful', N.R. 5/8/66. Quote S.P., p. 96.

39 Ibid., p. 94.

40 N.R. 29/10, 5/11/65. Quote E.P., pp. 186–188.

41 Letter to Harriet Barrs 15/9/81, Salt, p. 166. Borrow 'an old special favourite of mine'. The diaries show Thomson read some Borrow works several times.

42 Review of J.C. Morrison's *Gibbon*, T.P. 6/79. Also in review of Foster's *Swift*, T.P. 4/76: 'As for the general English public, with its soft-hearted and soft-headed sentimental optimism, a genius of such stern and unblenching insight is damned at once and for ever by being denounced as a cynic. It loves to blubber till tear-dry over its Dickens and Farjeon.'

43 'William Blake', N.R. 14/1/66 – 4/2/66. Quote P.E.F., pp. 142–143.

44 'An Evening with Spenser', N.R. 26/11/65. Quote E.P., pp. 186–188.

45 Spenser's original intentions were indicated in the letter that he wrote to Raleigh, that is usually prefaced to the poem in the manner it was prefaced to the first three books when they were published in 1590. Spenser was settled by Queen Elizabeth at Kilcolman which is in northern County Cork between Cork and Limerick. His lands were sacked in 1598 the year before his death.

As he mentioned in a later review of a Spenser biography (T.P.

1/80) Thomson read Spenser three times in his life, besides dipping into his favourite sections. Here in the N.R. essay he singled out from amongst these Book One Canto Ten, stanzas 53–54, 57–59, and 60–76; Book Three, Canto Six, stanzas 30–38, 42; the *Mutabilitie* Cantos, Canto Seven stanzas 5, 6, 7; 41, 46, 58; and the two stanzas of Canto Eight.

46 As 43.
47 N.R. 18, 25/2, 4/3/66. Quote E.P., p. 196.
48 'Sayings of Sigvat', 30/9, 14/10/66. Quote E.P., pp. 214–215.
49 As 47, Quote E.P., p. 211.
50 'Per Contra: The Poet, High Art, Genius', N.R. 12, 19/11/65. Quote E.P., pp. 214–215.
51 The verses are from Section 3 of 'Art', N.R. 17/2/67.
52 N.R. 13, 27/5; 3, 10/6/66.
53 Tribe, p. 94; elected September '66. A Reform League statement of aims appeared on the same page as the first instalment of 'Vane's Story'.
54 Printed in the *Secularist Manual of Songs & Services*, ed. Holyoake, A. & Watts, C.
55 Quoted in Bonner, p. 225.
56 'The Hyde Park Meeting', N.R. 29/7/66.
57 Bonner, p. 263.
58 Tribe, p. 91.
59 Ibid.
60 Tribe, p. 116.
61 Bonner, pp. 110–111.
62 Bonner, pp. 103–107.
63 Bonner, p. 30.
64 Bonner, pp. 50–51. Hypatia writes that she began to show 'absolute and confirmed intemperance'. Mrs Bradlaugh died 'very unexpectedly from heart disease engendered by alcoholism' in May 1877.
65 Ms. Don. f.8.
66 Ibid.
67 N.R. 14/10/66.

NOTES TO CHAPTER ELEVEN

1 Ms. Don. g.6.
2 Ms. Don. f.8.
3 Ms. Don. f.8. A laundry list noted of 20/10/66 lists '11 shirts + 4 (15/12/66) 3 night shirts 4 pairs drawers, 2 merino undershirts 10 prs socks – 6 pr socks 16/3/67 20 collars 13 pocket h/chief (1 silk) 2 white waistcoats'.
4 'The *Saturday Review* on Mr Bright' N.R. 3/2/67. Quoted S.P. p. 104. Retitled in S.P. 'The Swinburne Controversy'.
5 'Sympathy' N.R. 28/10, 18, 25/11/66. Quote E.P. p. 229.
6 Quoted Salt, p. 54.

7   As note 5. E.P., p. 231.
8   As n. 48 Chapter 10. Quote E.P., pp. 213–214.
9   'In Praise of Indolence', published S. 22/7, 5/8/76. Dated 1867 in E.P.
10 Ms. Don. f.8 dated 17/7/76.
11 Ms. Don. f.8, Don. e.41 N.R. 6/6/67. The poem is subtitled with 3 untranslated lines quoted from Leopardi's '*Alla Primavera o Delle favole antiche*' ('To Spring, or, Concerning the Ancient Myths'):

> In mysterious dance
> Immortal feet shook the wild ridged fells
> And tangled woods (which now the winds have made
> Their desolate den);

(G. L. Bickersteth, 1923)

12 Ms. 38535.
13 Ibid.
14 Ibid. Mss. Don f.8, Don e.41. N.R. 19/5/72, with this footnote: 'This room is believed to have been situated in Grub Street, concerning the name of which street the following curious note from Johnson's Contradictionary may come home to here and there a reader: – "Some assert that this renowned street is so named on the well-known ironical principle, because its inhabitants have never much and often nothing to eat. Others because these inhabitants drag out a crawling existence on leaves, differing from most other *larvae* in this, that it is only as by a miracle that any one of the swarm develop into the brilliant and wined condition of the *imago* or butterfly; the bulk perishing of atrophy in their grub state, probably through lack of succulence in the leaves on which they desperately try to subsist. But, whatever the etymology of the name, which perhaps no amount of grubbing industry could now settle, it is certain that in our own days, this Grub Street is the street not of grub but of grubs."'
15 'Dialogue of Plotinus and Porphyry', N.R. 5, 12/4/68.
16 'Copernicus: a Dialogue', N.R. 3, 10/11/67.
17 'Dialogue between a Natural Philosopher and a Metaphysician', N.R. 1/12/67.
18 'Dialogue of Timander and Eleander', N.R, 8, 15/12/67.
19 'Dialogue between Nature and the Soul', N.R. 29/12/67.
20 'Dialogue of Christopher Columbus and Peter Gutierrez', N.R. 5/1/68.
21 'Dialogue between Frederick Ruysch and his Mummies', N.R. 26/1/68.
22 'Dialogue between Tristan and a Friend', N.R. 9, 16/2/68.
23 'Dialogue between a Vendor of Almanacks and a Passer By', N.R. 15/3/68.
24 'In Praise of Birds', N.R. 22/3/68.
25 'Comparison of the Last Words of Brutus the Younger and Theophrastus', N.R. 3, 17/5/68.
26 Bonner, Chapter 26.
27 Tribe, p. 110.
28 Bonner, pp. 264–265.

29 Letter to Mrs Bradlaugh 3/1/72. Salt, p. 62.

30 Salt, p. 50.

31 Barnes's death on Oct. 29th 1868 is noted twice in Ms. Don. g.6.

32 'Priory Villa, Priory Road Wandsworth Road', Ms. Don. g.5. Potterton is listed as a 'merchant's clerk' in the Naples Colour Co. list of shareholders in Oct. '67; as a 'schoolmaster' in Oct. '68. (P.R.O. BT 31 1182, 2594C.)

33 Tribe, p. 112.

34 N.R.19/11, 3/12, 24/12/71; 21/1 28/1/72. Quote Part 4 verses 16–17.

35 Salt, p. 156.

36 Ms. 38535.

37 Ms. Don. g.5. Sunday 19/4/69. Landlady Mrs Reeve, board 7/6d.

38 Ms. Don. g.5. 'Potterton died Monday 21st June 1869. I got a letter Wedy. afternoon. Buried Tuesday 29/6/69 Brompton Cemetery.' The death certificate gives the cause as pthisis. He was aged 35, and died at Priory Villa. The October Naples Colour Co. list of shareholders gives 'Elizabeth Ann Potterton, Widow'.

39 Ms. Don. g.5.

40 Ibid. 'Aunt Helen 26 Cambridge Street Hyde Park'.

41 Letter 21/7/88 Salt Mss. She died on June 13th 1870 of a heart disease. New Register House 1870.574.131.

42 Alongside one of the two Miss Sherley college addresses Thomson added '2 Hyde Villas, Albert Road, Teddington'. Helen Birkmyre is listed there in the 1871 census as a 'governess', with three children staying in the house as 'scholars'. Her widowed mother is described as an 'annuitant'. See Concluding Appendix 'Of Miss Barnes and Miss Birkmyre'.

43 The essay was published in sixteen parts in the *National Reformer* between 3/10/69 and 6/2/70. The quote here is from a letter by Leopardi to his friend the writer Giordani in March 1820. N.R. 7/11/69.

44 N.R. 21/11/69.

45 *Fraser's Magazine*, October 1869. 'Sunday up the River' Section 17.

46 Tribe, p. 115. Charles Jnr. died unexpectedly of kidney disease in 1870.

47 16/12/69, Salt, p. 59.

48 19/11/59, Salt, p. 58.

49 Letter to W.M. Rossetti, 8/2/72. See pp. 163–164.

50 Salt Mss. Grant interview.

51 Tribe, p. 115.

52 Salt, p. 58.

53 These were sections highlighted by Thomson in his 1865 Spenser essay. Arlo Hill is Galtymore Mountain to the east of Spenser's estate.

NOTES TO CHAPTER TWELVE

1 See 'The dating of "The City of Dreadful Night",' pp. 324–326.

2 Extraordinary meeting 30/3/70. P.R.O. BT 31 11282, 2594C.

3 Company address, November '71, 39 Lombard Street; in January 1872

Thomson signed as secretary, the new address being 20, Great Winchester St, Old Broad Street; by October the office was 9, Dowgate Hill, Cannon St. BT 31 1659. 5816.

4   Bonner, H.B.: 'Childhood Recollections of James Thomson', ibid.

5   Ms. Don. g.5.

6   Ms. 38535.

7   Salt Mss. Letter from John Grant dated 14/8/88.

8   Salt, p. 62.

9   Austin & Co., 17 Johnson's Court, n.d.

10   *Thoughts on Atheism*, p. 7.

11   In Holyoake, A. and Watts, C.: *The Secularist Handbook of Songs & Ceremonies*, Austin & Co., n.d. (pub. 1871).

12   Ibid., pp. 67–69 'Essentials of Elocution'. G.J. Holyoake quoted p. 69.

13   Ibid.

14   Tribe, p. 58.

15   'Paul Louis Courier' N.R. 24/7, 7, 14/8/70. Paul-Louis Courier '. . . on the Land Question', N.R. 9/10/70; '. . . on the Character of the People', N.R. 16/10/70.

16   'How Heine Forewarned France' (from *D'Allemagne*) N.R. 11/9/70.

17   'Prometheus' N.R. 31/7/70. Eight poems from the 'West-ostlicher Divan' (with introductory essay), N.R. 22/1/71.

18   Thomson's Leopardi translations were gathered, edited and introduced by Bertram Dobell as *Poems Essays and Dialogues*, Routledge, London 1905. They are in draft form in Ms. Don. c.73, copied in Ms. Don. d.104. Separate works are dated as follows: 'The Story of the Human Race' 6/10/70; 'Dialogue Between Hercules & Atlas' 7/10/70; 'Dialogue of Fashion & Death', 7/10/70; 'Prizes Proposed by the Academy of Sillographs', 10/10/70; 'Dialogue Between a Sprite & a Gnome', 13/10/70; '. . . Malambruno & Farfarello', 14/10/70; '. . . Earth & the Moon', 21/10/70.

'Memorable Sayings of Filippo Ottonieri', 15/11/73; 'Pensieri' last dated 15/11/73 (as elsewhere, much underlining of words, Thomson's indication of to-be-revised); The Wager of Prometheus 2/12/73.

'Dialogue Between Tasso & his Familiar Spirit', 22/6/74; '. . . Nature & an Icelander', 24/6/74; 'Parini's Discourse on Glory' (Chapters 1–8), 26/10/74.

Completion of biography partially published N.R., dated 25/10/75.

'Parini's Discourse . . .', (Chapters 9–12) 3/10/77; 'Preface to Isocrates', 19/11/77; 'Apocryphal Fragment of Strato of Lampsacus', 15 / 11/77.

Dobell says in his introduction that since much of the material was what Thomson himself had termed 'rough draft', he decided that it 'required to be largely, if not entirely, rewritten.' The material published in Thomson's lifetime though he had considered differently: 'I did not indeed consider myself at liberty to deal as freely with the printed as with the unprinted matter, therefore I have made but few and slight alterations in the former.' However when one actually compares for example 'Pensieri No. 27' between Dobell and its version in the *National Reformer*, one has: 'There is no greater sign of being poor in philosophy and wisdom, than to want the whole of life wise and philosophical' – N.R. 31/5/68; 'Nothing indicates more clearly that one has little wisdom and little philosophy than to desire that everything in life shall be wise and philosophical' (Dobell, p. 344). Or 'Pensieri' No. 57: 'Men are ashamed not of the injuries they do, but of those they receive. Therefore there is no other manner of making those who injure ashamed, than to give them tit for tat.' – N.R. 31/5/68; 'Men are ashamed, not of the injuries they inflict, but of those they receive. Therefore the only way to shame wrongdoers is to pay them back in their own coin.' – Dobell, p. 362.

In other words the 1905 *Essays Dialogues and Thoughts* owe their finished form throughout as much to Dobell as to Thomson. They cannot be taken at any point as definite example of Thomson's untouched translation, but rather the book can serve as indication of works that Thomson did in draft form translate. To mention this is not to belittle Dobell: as late as 1967 John Heath-Stubbs could still mention the book as the 'most noteworthy' of the three English translations of the *Operette Morali* then extant, 1905 having been the last year such had appeared. (*Leopardi: Selected Prose & Poetry* Oxford University Press, 1966, Signet, 1967, p. 299.)

19 N.R. 27/8–24/9, 8/10, 22/10, 5/11, 12/11/71. Schaefer, pp. 15–33.

20 Salt, p. 63.

21 Diaries show: 1872 – letters to Julia (from America) 4; 1873 (from Spain) – 1; 1874 – to Julia 5, from 2; 76 – to, 1; 77 – to 4, from 3; 78 – to 4, from 1; 79 – from 2; 80 – to 3; 81 – to 3; 82 – to 1 from 1. Letters may have not been noted, especially given the many gaps in the diaries.

22 1/1/72, Salt, pp. 66–67.

23 13/3/72, Salt, p. 68.

24 N.R. 19/11, 3/12, 24/12/71; 21/1, 28/1/72.

25 Rossetti's edition first appeared in 1868.

26 'Moxon's Cheap Edition of Shelley', N.R. Mar. 12 1871.

27 8/2/72, Salt, p. 72.

28 10/4/72, Salt, p. 76.

29 Though at the British Museum Thomson could read what was available in print by and about Shelley, he had no access to the manuscripts themselves, therefore his questioning of Rossetti's edition was not based on original texts. But as no definitive scholarly text had been accepted let alone published it was Thomson's eye for incorrect grammar, solecisms and illogicality – evident sometimes in his correspondence but especially in his later *English Men of Letters* reviews for *Cope's Tobacco Plant* – that he used to raise with Rossetti a thoroughgoing series of questions. These Rossetti found useful enough to acknowledge Thomson's help when his 3-volume edition of Shelley appeared in 1878.

Before he went to America for instance Thomson questioned, in Rossetti's text of 'Alastor', lines 530–532:

> And nought but gnarled roots of ancient pines
> Branchless and blasted, clenched with grasping roots
> The unwilling soil.

Thomson wrote 'Here are gnarled *roots* clenching the soil with grasping roots. Should it not be gnarled *trunks* in the first instance?' Oxford Standard Authors Shelley (ed. Hutchinson, T. 'corrected' by G.M. Matthews, 2nd ed. 1971, latest paper reprint 1989) still prints both 'roots', though in its brief notes states 'a palpable misprint. Rossetti conjectures *trunks*, but *stumps* or *stems* may have been Shelley's word.' (p. 886).

Ms. Don. c.73 has the notes Thomson subsequently sent Rossetti in 1873 on 'Epipsychidion', 'Hellas', 'The Triumph of Life', 'Adonais', 'The Cenci', 'Julian and Maddalo', 'The Witch of Atlas' and 'minor poems and fragments'. His twenty-three pages of notes on 'Prometheus Unbound' he later edited for the *Gentleman's Magazine* in 1881, and this 'Notes on the Structure of Shelley's "Prometheus Unbound"' is included in the material gathered by Dobell in 1884 for the limited edition volume of Thomson's work, *Shelley*.

30 Ms. Don. g.7.

NOTES TO CHAPTER THIRTEEN

[P] = Personal Diary, Ms. Don. e.46. [B] = Business Diary, Ms. Don. e.47.

1 Letter 5/8/72, Salt, pp. 83–85.
2 [B] 10/6, 13/6 22/7/72.
3 [P] 28/7, 16/8/72.
4 Lowe and Thatcher – the banker with whom Thomson had to deal – shared information that Thomson only later discovered. Engines at mines were sold ([B] 9/4) and Thomson wrote on November 7th 'Thatcher has probably had money from L[owe] paying for collusion with permission to take the $1300 salary & probably to sell engine'. ([B] 7/11/72).
5 [B] 22/5/72. It had been agreed between Thomson and Thatcher on May 20th. Thomson hoped the directors of Champion would accept 'since Thatcher will give us no better'.
6 [B] 22/7/72.
7 Ibid.
8 [B] 27/7/72.
9 'Got money at last per Wells Fargo', [P] 5/6/72.
10 A.E. Walton, arrived [B] 29/8; More money [B] 11/10/72.
11 [B] 9/12/72.
12 [P] 27/6; other visits [B] 21/8, 17/9, 16/11/72.
13 [B] 21/8/72, 400 ft of water in 'California' mine shaft.
14 Four sent to Grant, and to Julia; three each to Mrs Bradlaugh, Chaplin, Hollett; two to Jacques and to Bradlaugh.
15 Salt, pp. 80–81.

16 [P] 31/7/72. Also described in letter to Mrs Bradlaugh 7/8/72, Salt, p. 69: '. . . first dance since "Old City Road Hall of Science days".'

17 [P] 20/7/72, 'Down with short but sharp attack of "Mountain Fever" complicated with overdose of Hydrate of Chloral. Felt at death's door.' The doctor's attendance cost $35. 'Illness very expensive here, besides the lonesomeness, every little common service & thing having to be paid for.'

18 Salt, pp. 91–92.

19 [P] 26/8/72.

20 [P] 31/8/72.

21 Ibid.

22 Moved [P] 7/11/72. Freezing noted 29/10, 40 degrees below 15/11, noted 17/11.

23 [P] 17/11/72.

24 [P] 7/8/72.

25 [P] 1/12/72. Also at church Thanksgiving Day 28/11, 22/9 and twice on 15/9/72. ('Mr Turner's last day').

26 A letter to Dobell, 20/4/74, enclosed the 'third and concluding part of the Rocky Mountain letter, which was found too wicked for publication. The stories I really heard from one who had been on the other side of the range in Nevada. They seem to me pleasant and profitable, and rather moral than otherwise.' Ms. Don. d.109/1.

27 'Religion in the Rocky Mountains', N.R. 20/3, 13/4/73. Full text S.P., quote p.34.

28 Ms. Don. g.7. All subsequent quotes about the journey home are from this.

29 Ibid. Published with manuscript comment S., 29/1/76.

30 Ms. Don. g.7.

31 Salt, p. 95. Letter pub S.R., 15/7/82.

32 Ms. Don. d.109/2.

33 Letter 28/2/73, Salt, pp. 95–96.

34 Ms. Don. c.73.

35 Letter 2/4/73, Salt, p. 96.

36 Letter 18/4/73, Ms. Don. d.109/1.

37 Letter 21/4/73, ibid.

38 Letter 22/4/73, Salt, p. 97.

39 As n. 20, chap. 10, pp. 266–267.

40 Salt, p. 71. But Henry Farmer's comments in a letter published at the time of Thomson's centenary should be noted: 'G.W. Foote, his friend, told me that Thomson's speech frequently revealed his Scottish origin or upbringing. This was particularly noticeable when in the company of Scots. Foote's reply to the remark of W.M. Rossetti, that Thomson's h's were insufficiently aspirated, was "Nonsense".' *Glasgow Herald*, 17/11/1934.

41 P.E.F., p. 262, '15th May 1873'.

NOTES TO CHAPTER FOURTEEN

1 See 'The Dating of "The City of Dreadful Night"' pp. 325–326.
2 Dobell noted 25/7/82 (Ms. Don. e.49) that the landlady at Tachbrooke St. (where Thomson stayed 13/4/74–12/12/75) had been owed £5 when Thomson left, and a Vauxhall Bridge Road landlady was owed about £30. Ms. Don. g.7 has a calculation made by Thomson just before he left 230 Vauxhall Bridge Road in April 1874 which deducts 7s. 8d. (evidently the rent) from £36 10s. 6d. leaving £36 2s. 10d. Weekly board at 7s. 8d. works out at £19 8s. 8d. annually.
3 Ferdinand VII was overthrown in 1820, and restored by the French before he died in 1833. His brother Don Carlos, in the First Carlist War, unsuccessfully contested the succession of Ferdinand's niece. His son, calling himself Don Carlos VII, in 1873 launched the Second Carlist War against the newly declared Spanish republic.
4 Details of the Spanish trip are all, unless otherwise noted, from the dated journal Ms. Don. f.16 which runs from July 22nd 1873 with prior lists of provisions taken, as quoted. After September 8th the diary stops apart from a few scattered names of people, and places travelled through on the road home. There is also a sketch of what looks like a room's balcony window with scrawled writing on the facing page (not conclusively Thomson's): 'My Dear Colonel – This is a good friend of mine who has campaigned with me. He will tell you all about your humble servant, who at the moment is being touched up by a chemist, for sunburn, Thine – [Initials illeg. could be J]'.
5 *New York World*, 12/8/73. Quote Schaefer p. 180.
6 Ibid.
7 'Carlist Reminiscences – 1', S., 11/3/76. The three remaining instalments followed on successive weeks.
8 Ibid., 18/3/76.
9 Ibid.
10 Ibid., 1/4/76.
11 Bonner, pp. 112–113.
12 Letter to Rossetti 12/11/73, Salt, p. 105.
13 24/9/73, Salt, p. 103.
14 24/11/73, Salt, p. 104. See also letter of 9/10/80, p. 243.
15 Salt (1914), p. 71: 'During this prostration [three days at Alsasua, ten at Santestaban] as he afterwards told a friend, he worked out in his mind a portion of "The City of Dreadful Night" '. For October datings, see 'The Dating of "The City of Dreadful Night" ', pp. 325–326.
16 Letter 30/1/74, Salt, pp. 107–108.
17 Ms. 38532 has at 11/6/73 (marked as Section 15) 'Commence with the "Melencolia" statue' in pencil above the verses, with below them 'The above for Proem?' Another pencilled note says 'For, The City of Night': above 'of' and 'Night' is pencilled 'dreadful?'
18 The three untranslated prefatory quotes are:

373

1) Dante – *Inferno*, Canto 3, line 1: ('Through me you pass into the city of woe'.)

2) Leopardi: '*Canto Notturno di un Pastore errante dell'Asia*', lines 93–98: ('In so much using then, so much movement of every celestial and earthly thing, circling without rest to return whence they were moved, I can see neither use nor profit.' Trans. Ridler).

3) Leopardi: Chorus of the Dead in the Laboratory of Frederic Ruysch in the 'Dialogue Between Frederic Ruysch and his Mummies' lines 1–6, 31–32. Thomson himself translated this chorus (N.R. 26/1/68), prefacing it, as he prefaced a number of his translations, with an apology: 'This chorus in the Italian is one of the marvels of literature. Unable to translate it into anything like poetry, and feeling that it could not be left out altogether, I have been reduced to give the baldest literal version; a version even less like the original than a mummy of Ruysch like a living man; for the mummy preserved form with substance, while the version preserves substance only, and both are lifeless.

> In the world alone eternal, unto whom revolveth
> Every thing created,
> In thee, Death, reposes
> Our naked nature;
> Joyous no, but secure
> From the ancient suffering. Profound night
> In the confused mind
> Obscures grave thought;
> For hope, for desire, the arid spirit
> Feels itself void of strength;
> And thus from affliction and fear is free,
> And the blank slow ages
> Consumes without tedium.
> We lived: and as confused remembrance
> Of terrible phantom
> And sweating dream
> Wanders in the soul of the suckling child;
> Such memory remains to us
> Of our life; but far from fear
> Is our remembrance. What were we?
> What was that sharp point
> Which had the name of life?
> A thing mysterious and stupendous
> Now is life to our thought, and such
> As to the thought of the living
> Unknown death appears. As from death
> Living it drew back, so now draws back
> From the vital flame
> Our naked nature;
> Joyous no, but secure;
> For to be blest
> Fate denies to mortals and denies to the dead.

The Pierpont Morgan Library Ms. includes: *Job* X. 22.: 'A land of darkness itself, and of the shadow of death; without any order, and where the light is as of darkness'; John Marston *Antonio and Mellida* Part I, i, 5–6: 'Can man by no means creep out of himself/ And leave the slough of viperous grief behind?'; Aeschylus, *Prometheus Bound*, 26–27, 'And evermore shall the burthen of the agony of thy present evil wear thee down; for he that shall deliver thee exists not in nature'.

Ms. 38532 contains Shelley: 'The Triumph of Life', lines 58–59: 'And others mournful within the gloom/ Of their own shadows walked, and called it death.'

Textual variants of the poem in its several mss. are in Ridler pp. 271–274. That used in this book is as published in C.D.N.

NOTES TO CHAPTER FIFTEEN

From here on a date given singly refers to a diary entry.

1   As n. 11, chap. 12. The quote represents the opening quarter of the suggested peroration in which there was a place for the insertion of 'any personal matters relating to the deceased'.
2   'Funeral of Mr Austin Holyoake', N.R. 26/4/74. Thomson signed it 'X'.
3   'Austin's all week', 7/2, 14/2, 21/2, 28/2/74.
4   18/4/74.
5   As 2 above.
6   Letter 9/4/74, Salt, p. 116.
7   As note 2, chap. 14.
8   Salt Mss. Letter from Grant.
9   Letter 18/4/74, Salt, p. 119.
10 17/5/74.
11 Salt, p. 111.
12 Salt, pp. 112.
13 Ibid., p. 113.
14 Letter 24/6/74, Ms. Don. d.109/1.
15 Mentioned in letter to Dobell 11/11/74. Congratulated W.M.R. on 'excellent Blake' 16/11/74 (Both Ms. Don. d.109/1).
16 Ibid. Letter to Rossetti 24/6/74.
17 Mentioned in letter to Dobell 24/6/74, Salt, p. 117.
18 To Rossetti 27/7/74, Ms. Don. d.109/1.
19 He apologised without explanation 5 months later in a letter of Nov. 22nd. (Ms. Don. d. 109/1). Dobell noted on Oct. 13th 1882 a story circulating that Thomson had been invited to Rossetti's once but failing to appear, had been 'found in the street extremely drunk and eating whelks at a fish stall!' (Ms. Don. e.49.)
20 Watts, C., 'Some Reminiscences of No. 17 Johnson's Court': 'In my apprentice days James Thomson . . . was press-reader to the firm, and I

was his reading boy. Reputedly "the melancholy poet" he was really the most joyous soul in the building. I recall one Christmas week spent at my father's house when he was the life of the party.' *The Literary Guide*, January 1924. His father was the younger brother of editor John Watts who died in 1866.

21 Watts, C.: 'About Personal Matters', ibid., June 1918.

22 Ms. Don. d.109/1.

23 He had been contacted on April 23rd; on 1/5/74 'with WDB getting ready & sending off prospectuses & circulars'; 5/5/74 'sent some *Mining Worlds* to clergymen & brokers'.

24 N.R. 19/7/74.

25 Ibid.

26 N.R. 2/8/74; ibid.; 23/8/74; ibid.; 6/9/74; 20/9/74; 15/11/74.

27 N.R. 6/12/74. The *Syllabus of Errors* had been issued in 1864.

28 N.R. 25/4/75.

29 N.R. 27/9/74.

30 Ibid.

31 N.R. 26/7/74.

32 A rewrite of an article published firstly as 'A Commission of Enquiry upon Royalty', N.R., Sept. 18 1870; reissued as a twopenny pamphlet by the *Secularist* in April 1876.

33 N.R. 16/8/74.

34 N.R. 14/3/75.

35 N.R. 15/11/74.

36 Letter to Dobell 16/11/74, Salt, p. 124.

37 *Kreutzer*, 23/3/74; 4,5,7/12/74 (weekend); 28/3/74 (boat race).

38 Letter to Mrs Bradlaugh, 29/11/74, Salt, p. 122.

39 13/4/74.

40 Regents Park 8/3, 12/4/74; Cribbage, Hampstead with Mrs J. 26/4, Kew 21/6, Richmond 5/7/74.

41 15/2/74.

42 19/7/74.

43 Jacques 3/4/74; family 12–17/7/74; fête 2/7/74.

44 'Walt Whitman', N.R. 26/7/74–6/9/74. Keats was 25. Thomson was probably following the Preface to 'Adonais' – Keats 'in his twenty-fourth year'.

45 'Mill on Religion', N.R. 8/11/74–27/12/74. He reiterated in the Nov. 15th instalment his own pessimism regarding progress, saying that Schopenhauer and Leopardi had shown Mill to be wrong in assuming that good will prevail in the world. Man will become extinct like other species. In the second last instalment of December 20th he wrote that he had thought evolution of the species the likeliest answer twenty years previously, before it had been popularly promulgated by Darwin.

46 23/11/74. He was at the B.M. in the morning and at a concert of 'Schumann & Mendelssohn pieces' in the evening for which he 'didn't care'.

47 Tribe, p. 170.

48 Quoted in Manvell, R: *The Trial of Annie Besant and Charles Bradlaugh*, Elek/Pemberton, London 1976, p. 18.

49 Tribe, p. 159.

50 12/11/74.

51 Salt, p. 125.

52 Letter of 18/5/75. Salt, p. 126.

53 'May Meeting Speeches', N.R. 6/6/74. Thomson continued: 'It was all very well for a poet, and one of the wisest of poets, in Elizabeth's time to have such ideas [see *Faerie Queene*, Prologue Book, V and 'Mutabilitiee', Canto VII] but we doubt whether a single man of science or statesman, unless perhaps deeply deluded by the contemptible humbug of Spiritualism, can be 'mystic' enough to cherish such dreams now'.

54 'Henri Beyle', N.R. 31/1/75–14/2/75.

55 Bonner, p. 113.

56 Letter to Dobell 12/11/82. Ms. Don. d.109/2.

57 Letter of G.G. Flaws to T. Mosher, 8/2/93. Ms. Don. d.107. Flaws, who sold the most finished of the three manuscripts of 'The City of Dreadful Night', claimed to this American publisher that he had frequently been in Thomson's company in the last weeks of his life and that Thomson gave Flaws 'one little scrap of paper in Bradlaugh's hand, stating that he had discharged him for drunkenness. I was to avenge his memory on that'.

58 N.R. 6/9/74.

59 In fact Maccall and Margaret Hatrick had fallen in love with each other (Maccall to Thomson 20/2/82, Ms. d.109/2). Maccall left the ministry he held at Greenock between 1833 and 1834 to stay in Geneva for two years before he settled in England. He translated Spinoza's *Theological-Political Treatise*, became known as a pantheist, and was for a time associated with a pantheistic 'Brotherhood of the Religious Life'. He wrote for a range of freethought journals – though this is not mentioned in his *Dictionary of National Biography* entry – including the *National Reformer*, the *Secular Review* and the *Investigator*. The first number of the *Investigator* in 1854 advertised him in public debate on the topic 'God is Nature and Nature God', and in the *National Reformer* on June 17th, 1866 he remarked 'Instinctively a Pantheist, a Pantheist I must live and die'. But it was for his views on his theory of 'individualism' that he became best known, and after a lecture he gave in 1866 the *National Reformer* report on April 29th noted that he had 'introduced his pet theory of the individuality of the individual'. Thomson had been at that lecture, but the poem he wrote about it, 'Mr Maccall at Cleveden Hall', indicated that he had found the profile of a woman sitting in front of him as interesting as the words of the speaker.

Maccall's 1847 *Elements of Individualism* listed, amongst its 'Articles of Faith': 'I believe that I am an Individual Man . . . that my mission is to develop my Individuality . . . that the grandest attribute of every man is his individuality, and that the Mission of every Man consists in the Whole and Harmonious Development of his Individual nature . . .

377

that the more human an Individual, the diviner he is, in opposition to all previous doctrines, which have invariably taught that the Divine could only be comprehended and exemplified by being opposed to the Human . . . that every individual best helps all other Individuals to develop their Individuality, by most perfectly developing his own; and that Morality is thus simply that fidelity to our Nature in action which Religion is in consciousness . . . that the Revelations of God are perpetual, and that every Individual, while a fresh revelation of God and the Universe, is the highest of all Revelations to himself . . . I believe that every man is good in proportion as he manifests the Spirit of Love, and great in proportion as he manifests the Spirit of Sacrifice.' Maccall added that he had been inclined towards these beliefs from his Scottish upbringing since 'Scotland has the advantage over England in that the institutions that operate most directly and potently on the people, such as the Church, the Schools, the Universities, are more democratic. This of course encourages Individuality.'

Thomson and Maccall met briefly by chance once at the *National Reformer* office, but they never saw each other again despite the correspondence they maintained. Maccall died in 1888.

60 See note 28, chap. 7.
61 Maccall, William: *A Nirvana Trilogy: Three Essays on the Career and the Literary Labours of James Thomson*, n.p. London 1886, p. 7.
62 N.R. 25/4/75.

NOTES TO CHAPTER SIXTEEN

Sole dates refer to diary entries

1 'Baudelaire on Hasheesh', T.P., Oct. '75.
2 'Gautier as Hasheesh Eater', T.P., Nov. '75.
3 'The Fair of Saint Sylvester', T.P., Jan. '76. Quote E.P., p. 269.
4 Salt, p. 131: Letter to Dobell 15/12/75. He had moved 13/12.
5 Ibid.
6 [Wright, T.R.] *Practical Politics for Plain People*, C. Watts, E. Truelove, London 1874. Reviewed N.R., 10/8/74.
7 'Short Secular Sermons on Scripture Texts: The foxes have holes, and the birds of the air have nests but the Son of Man hath not where to lay his head'. N.R. 19/4/74.
8 'Secular Principles and Policy', S., 1/1/76.
9 'Heinrich Heine', S., 8/1/76–12/2/76. Review of Stigand W.: *The Life, Work and Opinions of Heinrich Heine*, Longmans, London 1875.
10 'The Mountain Echo', (trans. of *'Die Bergstimme'*).
11 His resignation was announced on Feb. 26th.
12 Carried as an editorial for three weeks from 18/3/76.
13 3/3/76: 'A few pounds will oblige, as I have been short this month.'
14 6/4/76: 'Keen says 400 Famous Old Firm gone'. Keen published for the Secularist at Bookseller's Row, Strand. 6/11/76: 'Shop (10s. from Keen)'.

15 Gaps in the diaries make the course of the tuition impossible to chart exactly. Mentions occur 13/9/76, 'Resumed Italian reading with Adeline'; 30/4/77 'Aftn. – Adeline (Italian again)'; the arrangement is mentioned further in 1877 6, 9–11/7, 18–19/9, 15/11/77. The 1878 diary has 25/11 'Arithmetic with Adeline' then 29/11 'Adeline for French some afternoons'; then daily Dec. 4th–14th, evidently cramming for an exam due Dec. 17th. Then 16/2/79, 'Adeline – Tuesday & Friday afternoons Italian'. Then a gap in the diary 8/3/79–22/6/79, before 29/6/79: 'Adeline henceforth Monday and Thursday afternoons.' October 29th, 30th 'Adeline, French'; then throughout November 1879 twice weekly into December until 12th, an exam the following Tuesday to Thursday. On January 16th, 1880, 'Arranged for Monday and Thursday afternoons with Adeline, she to Drawing Class Tuesdays, Wedys. & Satys.' The lessons were again Italian, but a diary gap follows Jan. 24–March 3rd. Visits in March and April are mentioned though sometimes Adeline had an excuse to avoid the lesson.

16 5/6/76; 24/6, 13/9/77; 14/4, 5/5, 14/5/78; 19/6/79.

17 He was in Flaw's company with Foote 1/3/74, and the three went to a Woman's Suffrage lecture 13/5/76; Flaws at Gower Street weekend of 21/10–23/10/76.

18 7/5, 4/8/76.

19 This seems to have been an isolated visit 28/6/79.

20 9/4, 16/4/76; 7/5, 14/5, 21/5/77; 'Both Hembers' 16/9/77. Sometimes Hember visited for the evening as 25/2/76 'stopped till half past one'; 21/6/76 'stopped till one'. Hember lived at 24 Noel St Islington.

21 S., 8/4/76.

22 S., 22/4/76 (Bradlaugh's attack 16th).

23 S., 13/5/76.

24 An attack on the N.S.S. principles was printed in S., 4/3/76. Foote's suggested amendments appeared 27/5/76.

25 'The Leeds Conference', S., 10/6/76.

26 Ibid., 17/6/76.

27 Letter to Maccall, pub S.R., 14/3/85; in Ms. Don. e.49.

28 'To Charles Bradlaugh', S., 17/6/66.

29 S., 13/5/76 'Mr G.J. Holyoake on Party Unity', quoting Holyoake in N.R. 7/5/76.

30 Ibid. Thomson derided the Bradlaugh-Holyoake alliance, quoting at length a public row they had had in 1864 when Bradlaugh had replied to Holyoake's accusation that some of his works were 'disgraceful' by saying 'They were never so disgraceful to the reputation of Freethought as is the endeavour to cajole the sporting public into buying your *English Leader* by promising to tell them who shall win the next Derby.'

31 T.P., April '76.

32 'Saint-Amant', T.P., Feb. – April 76; 'Rabelais', Jun. – Aug., Oct. '76. Quote B.C.S. p. 30.

33 'Beauchamp's Career', T.P., Jun. '76; 'Ben Jonson', Nov. '76 – Mar. '77; May – June, Aug. '77 – Feb. '78. (B.C.S.)

34 'The Devil in the Church of England', S., 26/2, 4/3/76. Quote S.P. pp. 15–16.
35 S., 12, 19/8/76.
36 Quoted in Foote 'The Christian World and the Secularist', S., 2/9/76.
37 'The Christian World and the *Secularist* Again', S., 9/9/76. Quote S.P. pp. 130–132.
38 'Our Obstructions', S., 6/1/77. Quote S.P. pp. 139–140.
39 'The Primate on the Church and the World', S., 7/10/76. Quote S.P. pp. 160–161.
40 As 38. Quote S.P. pp. 144–145.
41 Salt, p. 127; 21/1/76, 'first time of seeing the girls I could not speak'.
42 Salt, pp. 113–114; 120. Hypatia and Alice had been sent to school in Paris by Bradlaugh.
43 Cherubini 14/9/76. Also Auber's *Fra Diavolo* 18/9/77; with the Wright family to *The Magic Flute* 16/11/77; got times mixed up for Weber's *Oberon*, didn't get in 18/12/78; Wagner's *Rienzi* with the Wrights 24/2/79, Bizet's *Carmen* 28/11/79.

   Wagner with Foote: 19/10/76 (he had already seen it 3/10) and Wagner prom. 26/10.
44 S., 30/9/76.
45 They visited Michael Wright's factory on Friday 22nd, and were shown round the area including the local racecourse. It was raining the next two days; Thomson 'wrote a little' on Saturday morning before going out, played cards in the evenings at Gimson's. He went to two of Foote's three lectures on the Sunday. On the Monday it was a bit brighter and they were taken around again, driven to Josiah Gimson's new factory in a trap. They returned at night to London. Michael Wright stayed in Regent St, Gimson at 'Albion Villas', Leicester.
46 31/1/76, 'Noticed passing blood again'; 1/2 'Still passing blood'; 2/2 'Still blood'.
47 28/12/76 lists some present at 'Miss Mathilde Blind's, 52 Torrington Sq'; 29/12 lists her amongst those at Gower St for birthday party for a Miss Heimann.
48 Salt Mss. (Transcription). 'Extract from Memoranda by W.M. Rossetti (Omitted from *Life*)'.

NOTES TO CHAPTER SEVENTEEN

1 Tribe, p. 173.
2 Manvell R.: ibid., describes and quotes the book Chapter 4 pp. 57–60.
3 Ibid., p. 61.
4 Ibid., pp. 44–45; Tribe, p. 172.
5 Ibid., p. 51.
6 Bonner, Vol. 2, p. 27.
7 S.R. & S., 7/7/77.

8   For example, S.R. & S., 6/4/78. George Millar, Glasgow: 'Attempts have been made to place very peculiar views as to marriage and the population questions before us in lieu of Secularism.'

9   Reproduced S.R., 14/3/85.

10 Royle, E., *Radicals, Secularists, and Republicans*, ibid., pp. 18–19. The B.S.U. maintained the position outlined by Foote in the first issue of the *Secularist* that theists and pantheists were welcome. 'Secularism intrinsically does not contend against the evidence of Deity, but against dishonouring conceptions thereof.' S.R. & S., 15/9/77.

11 S.R. & S., 7/7/77 (concluded 14/7/77).

12 12/4, 20/4, 2/5, 12/6, 13/6/77.

13 Account sent 21/6/77; 'long letter' 27/6; £5 for Flaubert review 5/7; request for £2 2s. od. outstanding 9/8/77; 'Stupid note' from Watts 10/8; cheque 'at last' 22/8 – though made out to 'Jas Thomas'.

14 Letter to Dobell 28/5/75: had called on Chapman and Hall to pick up ms. as they hadn't bothered to acknowledge it. 'I suppose they were too busy to attend to my little matter, and would therefore call for my packet of verse in a day or two.' (Ms. Don. e.49) To Dobell 9/7/75: Chapman not prepared to risk (Ms. Don. d.109/1); to Dobell 24/8/75: King's say 'volume could not possibly pay its expenses if it were published' (ibid.).

    26/10/76. 'Left poems at King & Co.'s for Mr Paul.'

    22/2/77. Kegan Paul withdrew. 'This is bad treatment. Four months lost.' 27/2/77. Left Ms. with Chatto & Windus.

15 Henry King & Co. 'We may presume they funked': Letter to Dobell 7/3/77, in Dobell (1910).

16 Salt, p. 136. As note 14.

17 Letter of 17/12/77 'to one of the editors'. Facsimile reproduced in C.P.

18 14/6, 5/7/77.

19 Called with Blind. Letter to Dobell 18/5/75, Ms. Don. e.49.

20 Letter to Dobell 22/6/77, Mrs Foote seriously ill 2 months 'only married about three'. Ms. Don. e.49. 1/11/77. 'Saw GWF for first time since Mrs F.'s death'.

21 Complained of this 6/11/79.

22 25/6/77.

23 As n. 17.

24 The eighth instalment began 'Having sketched the life of Rare Ben and spoken generally of his works, it remains to speak of them particularly in connection with the subject wherein the *Tobacco Plant* is most profoundly interested.' The tone is ironic, almost self-mocking, but in fact Thomson ranges extensively through *Every Man in his Humour, Every Man out of his Humour* – 'Coming to the play itself we find almost every act oderous with those rich fumes that cheer but do not inebriate' – *Epicoene, Volpone, The Alchemist* – 'the culmination of Jonson's genius . . . not least admirable for its construction' – *Bartholomew Fair*; giving plot summaries and sometimes extensive quotes from the plays in a way that would have acted as a decent introduction without their being reduced to the status of jocular vehicles

for smoking references. He had to perform a balancing act with his writing register in these and other articles. He was earning his living in a way that would have stretched those who only publish about Literature within the 'professional' literary circles. The complete 'Ben Jonson' is in B.C.S.

25 T.P., Nov. '78. It had run since May.
26 Quoted P.E.F. p. 266.
27 Quoted Ridler pp. xxxiii–xxxiv.
28 19, 20, 24/8; returned diary 9/9/78.
29 Ms. Don. e.49. Also 16/9/78 'Actually got writing verses again! *I had a Love* – but hard & gloomy. (7 six-line stanzas)' 17/9: ' "I had a Love" 9 stanzas more, but hard & harsh; more truth than poetry,' 18/9: 'Finished "I had a Love". 9 stanzas more. 25 in all in this first draft.'
30 Saw Hollett 29/8, 12/9/77, wrote to 31/10/77; sent him *Tobacco Plants* 5/10/78, saw him 19/11, 24/12/78. With his wife Annie 'First time I've seen her since their marriage', 3/3/79.
       Wrote to Grant 13/9, 15/9/77 – 'Appt. next Saty. or Sunday?' – also 31/10.
       Letter from, 15/9/77.
       Salt Mss. Notes of Grant interview: 'After 1874 Grant did not see him (much) till 1880' [Salt put a question mark over 'much']. In 1880 contact was renewed with the publication of Thomson's book.
31 The series opened 6/10/78 with Theodore in the chair. (S.R., 12/10/78). 15/11/78, 'TRW £40 out of pocket South Place'.
32 It became the *Secular Review* again from March 23rd.
33 S.R., 11/10/79.
34 Ibid., also 12/10/78, 16/11/78.
35 S.R., 8/11/79.
36 S.R., 2/11/78.
37 21/6/78.
38 22/11, 29/11, 13/12/78.
39 S.R., 30/9/78.
40 S.R. & S., 8/9/77; 2/2/78; S.R., 16/2/79.
41 *The Collected Letters of George Meredith*, ed. Cline, C.L.: 3 vols, Oxford, 1970. Letter to Foote 19/8/78, Vol. 2 pp. 561–562.
42 2/12/78.
43 30/11/78, 'Dinner & tea out Chop with tea at Collegiate'; 13/12 'Tea Collegiate'. Usually where he ate is not mentioned.
44 Letter of 23/12/78, Salt, p. 136.
45 'In the Valley of Humiliation', *Liberal*, Jan. '79. Schaefer.
46 4/1/79.
47 20/1, 23/1/79.
48 'Professor Huxley on Hume', *Liberal*, March '79.
49 'Tobacco Smuggling in the Last Generation', T.P., May – Nov. '78; 'The Tobacco Duties', Dec. '78: Jan., March '79; 'Tobacco Legislation in the Three Kingdoms', March – April, Sep. – Dec. '79; Jan, March – June, Aug., Sep., Nov. '80.

50 'Tobacco at the Opera', T.P., Feb. '79

51 'John Wilson and the *Noctes Ambrosianae*' T.P., April '78, May '79.

52 'An Old New Book' T.P., May '79.

53 Letter to Foote 30/5/79. As 41 ibid., p. 572.

54 24/6/79.

55 5/7/79; letter of 4/7/79 to Thomson as 41 ibid., pp. 575–576. The seven letters from Meredith are in Ms. Don. d.109/1.

56 'T.H. Huxley's *Hume*', June '79; 'Principal Shairp's *Robert Burns*', 'R.H. Hutton's *Walter Scott*', both Sep. '79.

57 'James Hogg the Ettrick Shepherd', Aug. – Oct. '79. B.C.S.

58 T.P., Sep. '79; Schaefer, pp. 289–290.

59 27/1, 29/1/79.

60 17/2/79.

61 28/2/79.

62 14/8/79.

63 14/11/79.

64 Hawkes: Mentioned 11/3, 1/11, 18/11/77; 'Hawkes room' 7/7; walk before dinner 1/9/77; 24/5/78, 'long chat'; 9/7/78 'chat with Hawkes in his room. Bed 1.'

   Hopkirk: 5/7/77, 'Returned from Rossetti's 12.30. Bed 4.15 after chat with Hopkirk.' 2/5/78, with Trousselle; 19/8/80 Hopkirk 'back after 2 years 3 mos.', working as teacher; 21/8/80 'smoking & chatting till nearly 4 a.m.', 27/8 'till 1.30 a.m. . . . Drank too much beer'.

65 10/10/79.

66 28/10/79.

67 6/11/79.

68 3/12/79; 9/1/80.

69 In his lifelong admiration for the writings of the Swedenborgian homoeopath doctor James John Garth Wilkinson, Thomson was following Emerson, who said of Wilkinson's introductions to his Swedenborg translations that they 'throw all the contemporary philosophy of England into shade'. Wilkinson's own magnum opus, and a favourite of Thomson's, was his 1851 *The Human Body and its Connexion with Man*. In the introduction to that book Wilkinson wrote: 'The human body, as an object of science, has hitherto been the property of one profession; it has been studied only after death, when it is the reverse of human, to afford light to medicine, which takes no cognisance of it but when diseased. Death has slyly proffered *his* torch to the art of healing. A different study, not superseding yet subjugating the former, is needed to connect the body with life, health, and business; a study that brings the plain to illustrate the obscure, and the common to interpret the extraordinary. To further such a study is the object of the present work, in which we hope to show by examples that the anatomy of man is other than that of the dissecting room, and that the knife is the feeblest although the first instrument for opening the mysteries of the human being.'

Wilkinson believed that 'the body is the form of the soul, according to the order of the universe', and that 'the ratio of the brain to the body is that of man to the planet'. He advocated homoeopathy because, he wrote, 'it tends to make us think more worthily of our bodies'. Of surgeons' having refused to countenance mesmerism being used in place of anaesthesia for surgery, he wrote 'It was like them to believe in bottles, and to disbelieve in man'. He summed his position thus: 'we have the position, that *the human body is a living, moving, substantial, enduring, inviolable subject* . . . that *the human body is alive* . . . and that *the living body is a man, with nothing in him but humanity.*'

Thomson's admiration for Wilkinson can be set beside his welcoming, in the work of Burns and Whitman, a rejection of that shame of the body which 'The Naked Goddess' also attacked. The Swedenborgian side of Wilkinson's work, setting the human in image of the universal, can perhaps be seen as lending another aspect in which to view 'The City of Dreadful Night'; an aspect put by the poet William Carlos Williams when he wrote in his preface to *Paterson*: 'a man in himself is a city, beginning, seeking, achieving and concluding his life in ways which the various aspects of a city may embody – if imaginatively conceived – any city, all the details of which may be made to voice his innermost convictions'.

70 'A Strange Book', *Liberal*, Sep. – Dec. '79. B.C.S.
71 'Cope's Mixture', T.P., Dec. '79 – Feb. '80; April – May '80.
72 6/12/79.
73 13/12/79.
74 The etiquette rules appeared in the 1880 and 1881 editions of *T.J. & J. Smith's Pocket Diary and Almanack No. 2*. They cost 1s. 6d.
75 The entries follow the sequence throughout December 1st – 31st 1879; January 1st – 23rd, 1880.

NOTES TO CHAPTER EIGHTEEN

1   Letter, 7/4/74. Salt, pp. 151–152.
2   9/4/80.
3   Salt, pp. 153–154.
4   'George Meredith's New Work: *The Egoist*' T.P., Jan. '80.
5   Ibid.
6   1/1/80.
7   'Walt Whitman' T.P., May – Oct. '80.
8   J.A. Symonds' *Shelley*, John Morley's *Burke*, Trollope's *Thackeray*, Mark Pattison's *Milton*: reviewed Feb., June, July, Aug. '80.
9   In a review of W. Black's *Goldsmith* T.P., Jul. '79.
10 1/1, 9/3/80.
11 10/3/80: wh. = which; crs. = creditors.
12 8/3/80; Ms. Don. d.109/1.

13 Grant's address this school in 1880 diary, changed during the year to '48 Cambridge Buildings Vauxhall Bridge Road'. He visited Thomson on June 30th.

14 9, Victoria Rd., South Lambeth (1880 diary).

15 5/10/78.

16 18/6/80.

17 24/3, 20/6/80.

18 23/4/80.

19 Letter 14/5/80. Ms. Don. d.109/2.

20 15/6/80. Eleanor Marx was sometimes amongst guests at the Wrights' in Gower Street. She attended Thomson's funeral.

21 17/6/80. Mrs Wright at Gower St gave Thomson a letter from Karl Marx enclosed in a letter to herself from Eleanor. Thomson wrote to Marx on June 18th, then 'answered Karl Marx' ten days later. No letters survive – though a quote by Marx on Thomson's Heine translations is in Salt, (1914) p. 161., and is reproduced in Chapter 22 here. Third of the 10 addresses listed in Thomson's 1880 diary is 'Marx, Karl, Ph.D. – 41, Maitland Rd., N.W.'.

22 16/1, 23/1/80.

23 'Crowded Table', N.R. 18/4/80.

24 13/6, 17/8/80.

25 Reeves: 27/6/80, 'church evening; floral service'; 19/12/80, 'To go there any Sunday I like; they always at home'; 6/2, 20/3/81.

26 Bound in V.S. at rear of volume.

27 Tribe, pp. 192, 194.

28 24/6/80.

29 22/6/80.

30 17/8/80.

31 20/8/80.

32 Ibid. Appointment had been for July 8th.

33 Aug. 30th – Oct. 3rd.

34 7/10/80. On June 28th he had written '£10 on a/c from Fraser; another if I want it (yes!)'.

35 Salt, pp. 155–156.

36 13/10/80.

37 Oct. 16th – Dec. 13th.

38 Letter 25/10/80, Ms. Don. d.109/1.

39 8/3/80.

40 Salt, p. 156.

41 Ibid., pp. 156–157.

42 The reviews were enclosed at end of E.P. as 'Opinions of the Press' pp. 1–8.

43 16/6, 23/6/80. He had tried W.M. Rossetti and Garnett. She had recently moved after marriage.

44 29/12/80. Also letter to Dobell 5/1/81, Salt, p. 158: 'It was wretched tramping through the slush, and then standing in the rain for about

three-quarters of an hour, with nothing to see but dripping umbrellas. I was disappointed by there being any chapel service at all.'

45 29/12/80.

46 1/1/81.

47 7/1/81.

48 13/1/81. 'Christians' abbreviated as original.

49 6/1/81. He sent Fraser the 14th instalment of 'Tobacco Legislation' and told him he had for reviews '4 vols in hand besides 3 already done'. He began work on Instalment 15 on 15th, and was reading H.A. Page's *De Quincey* in the B.M. on January 16th. 'Letter from Fraser' that day.

50 11/1/81.

51 21/1/81.

52 2/2, 17/2/81.

53 5/3/81. 'Address on the Opening of the New Hall of Leicester Secular Society' privately printed.

54 4/3/81. Diary comment having been sent the programme in advance. Events 5/3/81.

55 9/3/81.

56 Ms. Don. c.73.

57 14/3/81. 'aftn.' He had last seen Blind on February 7th. On March 12th she had written asking for advice about approaching Reeves with a view to publishing her own work.

58 30/3/81 dinner, 'long friendly chat'; 2/4, tea: Furnivall seems to have had some idea about work for Thomson but 'gave up scheme as to me'. Sent tickets June 6th.

59 24/3/81.

60 From April 10th – September 2nd there are only two entries each in April, June, and July; six in August.

61 Ms. Don. e.49.

62 4/6/81.

63 23/7/81.

64 9/9/81.

65 'Browning's *The Ring and the Book*', *Gentleman's Magazine*, Dec. '81.

66 'Notes on the Structure of Shelley's "Prometheus Unbound" ', *Athenaeum*, 17, 24/9; 8/10; 5, 19/11/81.

67 Letter 15/9/81. Salt, pp. 166–167.

68 8/3/81. 'Bradlaugh's attempt on House of Commons. Grand field day for J.W.B. Percy and I.'

At the evening visit to the Hall of Science, where Bradlaugh made a subsequent appearance, Jack Barrs later recalled Thomson had to be restrained from going to speak to Hypatia and Alice: 'it took Holyoake and myself all our time to prevent BV forcing his way through the crowded meeting to the platform in order that he might speak to Alice and Hypatia who were there by the side of their father.' Salt Mss. Letter from J.W. Barrs of 18/6/98.

69 10/9/81. *De L'Allemagne* 'loose & incomplete & Leland's trans. Reise-bilder for another week'.

70 17/9/81. Hood Barrs lived at 51 Great Percy Street Finsbury. In November '81 he moved to 27 Disraeli St Putney. (Letters Ms. Don. d.109/2) His practice was at Cliffords Inn.

71 Diary cash account section at back, March '81.

72 Letter, 18/10/81. Salt, pp. 168–169.

73 Ms. Don. d.109/1; 11/10, 15/10/81.

74 17/10/81.

75 21/10/81.

76 Letter 21/10/81. Ms. Don. d.109/1.

77 26/10, 28/10/81.

78 Letter from Harry to Jack Barrs 18/10/81. Ms. Don. d.109/2.

79 10/10/81.

80 28/10/81: 'Theatre well filled; many ladies. Kirkman on Browning Made Easy'. Furnivall, M.D. Conway, Bourke Marston amongst those present. 'Miss Marx, (who wanted to see me, but whom I missed, speaking to Marston)'.

81 29/10/81; itemised Ms. Don. c.73.

82 Ms. Don. c.73. Of this Jack Barrs told Salt 'It may interest you to know that the Voice from the Nile was projected *ten* years before it was written. I have the Ms. notes for it.' Salt Mss. Letter from J.W. Barrs 5/7/86.

NOTES TO CHAPTER TWENTY

1 Letter 21/6/80. Salt. p. 160.

2 25/6/80. ibid., pp. 161–162.

3 Sat. 2nd – Mon. 4th July '81. (Letter to Percy 6/7/81: ibid., p. 163.)

4 Letter 6/7/80. ibid.

5 Ibid., pp. 171–172. A photo marked 'about 1881' is in Ms. Don.c.73. The face is faded; not reproduced herein.

6 'To H.A.B. on my 47th birthday' ibid., pp. 176–178.

7 Letter 31/12/81, ibid., p. 173.

8 Salt Mss. Letter from J.W. Barrs 18/6/98.

9 Ibid.

10 Ms. Don. d.109/2. Letter from Harry to Jack Barrs 5/1/82. (Parr was at Kirby Muxloe at the time of the 1881 census, and his occupation is given there.)

11 Ibid.

12 First published V.N.

13 Ms. Don. d.109/2. Letter 28/1/82 to J.W. Barrs.

14 *Cornhill Magazine*, March '82.

15 Transcribed in Ms. Don. d.108, dated January 1882, V.N.

16 Published V.N.

17 Ibid.

18 Letter of 3/3/82. Ms. Don. d.109/1.

19 Salt Mss. Letter from J.W. Barrs 5/7/86.

20 Ms. Don. d.109/2. Letter 21/1/82 to J.W. Barrs.

21 Ms. Don. c.73. Letter from Fern Villa Stretford. John and Julia had now split up. 'Aunt Mary' is possibly Mary Keith, Thomson's father's sister.

22 Undated. Salt, pp. 3–5.

23 Ms. d.109/2. Letters 6/1/82, 31/1/82, 31/1/82 to Thomson from Furnivall.

24 'Notes on the Genius of Robert Browning', Quote B.C.S. p. 453.

25 Ms. Don. d. 109/2. Letter to J.W. Barrs 26/1/82.

26 Ms. Don. d.109/2. Percy to J.W. Barrs 30/1/82. A 'head in chancery' is a boxing or wrestling term meaning a head pinned underarm by a fighter's opponent.

27 Ms. Don. d.109/2. Letter from Percy to J.W. Barrs 4/2/82.

28 Ms. Don. e.49, Dobell diary note 2/2; ibid. as 27.

29 Salt, p. 172.

30 Maccall, W.: ibid., p. 175.

31 Ms. Don. d.109/2. Letter 26/2/82, the day after Maccall's 70th birthday.

32 Ms. Don. d.108, dated Feb. '82. V.N.

33 Ms. Don. d.108. VN. The sections here follow the dating on the ms. However that marked here March 7th–8th is more precisely:

ll. 230–250 [He closed his eyes . . . unmoving hours] '7/3/82
(Tues morning)'
251–270 [He paused . . . planted waiting there] '(Tues evening)'
271–300 [As phantom . . . maze of dreams] '8/3/82'

A quotation from De Quincey's *Confessions of an English Opium Eater* seems appropriate: 'For this, and all other changes in my dreams, were accompanied by deep-seated anxiety and melancholy, such as are wholly incommunicable by words. I seemed every night to descend, not metaphorically but literally to descend, into chasms and sunless abysses, depths below depths, from which it seemed hopeless that I could ever reascend. Nor did I, by waking, feel that I *had* reascended.'

It is not clear just how far Thomson went in his identification with De Quincey. Salt when interviewing Bradlaugh noted when Thomson was living in Bradlaugh's home he 'used to talk of De Quincey . . . and make experiment with opium; but no evidence that he took it habitually'.

Hypatia Bradlaugh however in her 1886 remembrance of Thomson complained about the attitude of memorialists who only knew Thomson in the last eight or nine years of his life 'when the craving for alcohol-drinking and opium-eating had so grown upon him that he had lost the power to resist it, and from an occasional vice it had become a chronic disease'. It is difficult to say just how precise she was being in her language here, whether the opium-eating part was thrown in because she knew he had sometimes taken it before, and speaking as she is of the period when he was no longer friend of the Bradlaugh family.

34 Letter 28/3/82. Salt, p. 174.

35 'Law v Gospel', *Weekly Dispatch*, March '26.

36 Ms. Don. e.49; Salt Mss.

37 At Withers & Fowler. Ms. Don. c.73.

38   Salt Mss. As 8 above.

NOTES TO CHAPTER TWENTY-ONE

1   J.W. Barrs held letters received from Harry Hood Barrs and from Percy
Holyoake when they were both trying to keep him informed, evidently
under instruction, of Thomson's progress as they could follow it, between
March and June 1882. Barrs sent the letters and telegrams to Salt on 9/6/98;
Salt then sent transcriptions to Dobell, who himself made copies under the
heading 'Thomson's last days' (Ms. Don. e.49). Salt's copies are in Mss.
Eng. c.2384. The letters themselves are amongst the material in Ms. Don.
d.109/2.

The sequence reproduced here is substantially as transcribed, with occasional minor differences in relation to material missed out or restored.
There has been added some material not in the letters, mostly to be found
in Salt (1914):

   Thomson's morning letter of April 22nd to Dobell (pp. 137–138). It
and the afternoon one also given here in Ms. Don. e.49, as is Thomson's
last letter dated May 4th.

   The description given by W. Stewart Ross (pen name 'Saladin') is from
the *Agnostic Journal* of April 6th 1889, 'A Last Interview with a Man of
Genius'. The article is pasted into Ms. Don d.105, and a slightly different
quote is taken from it in Salt (1914) pp. 138–139.

   The account T.E. Clarke sent Salt is in (1914) pp. 140–141. This account
quotes the letter of June 2nd from Philip Bourke Marston, here quoted
separately. T.R. Wright to Dobell of June 7th is in Ms. Don. d.109/2.

NOTES TO CHAPTER TWENTY-TWO: POSTSCRIPTS

1   S.R., 17/6/82, 'The Burial of James Thomson' (unsigned); Salt, pp.
182–184.
2   Bonner, H.B.: *Our Corner*, August 1886. Salt, Bradlaugh, Foote all said
likewise. Dobell suggested 'love of drink' and a religious fervour was in the
blood over generations in Scotland. Dobell, 1910, p. 60.
3   Charles Brodie in a lecture manuscript dated April 13th 1895 quoted
'one who ought to know if anyone does' (in the margin 'Mrs B.') state that
with respect to Thomson's father 'That he was a dipsomaniac is quite an
untruth'. Brodie added 'and the poet's brother has recently written denying
the aspersion cast on the father'.
4   Foote, G.W.: 'James Thomson 1: The Man', *Progress*, April 1884.
5   Ibid.
6   Dobell, 1895.
7   The quotes are as follows: Dobell: Memoir, 1884; Bourke Marston: second

of two sonnets from *Word-Voices*: in *The Collected Poems of Philip Bourke Marston*, ed. Marston, L.C., Ward, Lock, Bowden & Co., London 1892, p. 332; Harriet Barrs: Salt Mss. Notes of interview with Harriet Barrs (now Mrs Pelluet) 1/9/88; Meredith: letters to Salt 1/6/88 (1st para), 5/6/88, *Collected Letters* Vol. 2, pp. 917, 919; (Mrs.) Helen Birkmyre: Salt Mss. Letter to Salt, 31/7/88; Julia Thomson: ibid., letter of 1/10/88; Swinburne: letter to Dobell 31/7/88, Ms. Don. d.109/2; Symonds: letter to Dobell 13/12/84, Ms. Don. d.109/2; Marx: quoted in Salt (1914) p. 161 (See chapter 18 n. 24); Melville: letters (Salt Mss. transcriptions) from Melville to James Billson 1/12/84; 'March 85'; 20/12/85; 31/12/88.

Symonds did praise Thomson's work in print, and in another letter to Dobell of 17/1/85 spoke of it as 'remarkable' and 'inadequately recognised'. (Ms. Don. d.109/2) Swinburne was reacting to a request from Dobell to quote his praise of 'Weddah and Om-el-Bonain'; he had already been annoyed when a publisher had quoted the letter to Rossetti containing this praise, without anyone's permission, on the cover of a pamphlet by Col. Ingersoll. (Letter from Thomson to Rossetti 29/1/81. Ms. Don. d.109/1.)

An example of a contemporary Scottish estimate of Thomson, which it was thought better to confine to the annexe of footnotes at the back of this book, was given by D.H. Brechin in his *Modern Scottish Poets*, Volume 7, (1884): 'The voice of the typical Scottish poet is the voice of courage. He has little love for the night-side of Nature, and rises above despair into the calmness of hope. It is to be regretted that an exception should be found in a man of great genius, of lofty thought, of pre-eminent ability, and a man possessed, too, of an exceptionally fine nature. He seems to have been capable of high affection, gratitude, friendship, love . . . He had a true poet's favourites among the poets, Leopardi, Heine, Shelley, Browning; but there is the essence that perfumes and the essence that poisons, and it was the latter that he extracted from the flowers of poesy.'

'It is a curious and melancholy fact that his gradual separation from orthodoxy kept pace with the increase of his poetic power . . . He soared among the problems of life and death, and cowered before phantoms. He lacked the courage of true and steadfast manliness based upon the faith that, in submitting to that Power which brought us here, and has infused into human life so much beauty and joy, all must needs be well.'

James Billson, recipient of the Melville letters that Salt transcribed from J.W. Barr's material, is listed as a visitor at the Barrs' house at Forest Edge on the night of the 1881 census. His age then was twenty-two, his occupation given as 'coal merchant, florist'.

8 G.G. Flaws in a letter of 10/1/93 to the American publisher Thomas Mosher told him he had a copy of Thomson's 'carefully revised copy of the poem as completed for publication'. He claimed to have been given this by Thomson, together with other manuscripts and letters, during the last weeks of Thomson's life. He also claimed to have been offered $125 for the manuscript, but would wish $300 dollars monthly advance for a novel on Thomson, 'the history of the minds and bodies of himself, of Poe, and

of my own self'. Dobell wrote to Mosher on 19/2/93 saying that he didn't trust Flaws or know how he got the manuscript: 'I fear not honestly'. (Ms. Don. d.107.) The manuscript was bought by W.C. Stedman and 'acquired by the Pierpont Morgan library in 1911' (Ridler p. 270).

9 Review of memoir in V.N., N.R. 9/11/84.

10 Salt Mss. Bradlaugh interview.

11 As n. 4.

12 As n. 2.

13 pp. 14, 16.

14 Salt Mss. Notes of interviews with John Grant 24/7/88; Thomas Carson 31/8/88; W. Weller, 3/8/88.

15 Dobell (1884).

16 Letter to Dobell 3/7/88. Ms. Don. d.109.2.

17 See note 39 chap. 1.

18 MacCarthur, W.F.: *History of Port Glasgow*, Jackson & Co., Glasgow 1933, p. 184.

19 Mr Brodie's daughter Mrs A. Enid Leeming first wrote from London, and indicated that her son Mr Bruce Brodie Leeming of Surrey had care of his grandfather's research. Mr Leeming offered to meet and hand over the research, which was taken back to Scotland for examination.

20 The site of the marble tombstone can be located by consulting Mitchell, John F., & Sheila: *Monumental Inscriptions (pre-1855) in Renfrewshire* produced for the Scottish Genealogical Association 1969; where it is listed on p. 350 as no. 37, in the section dealing with Port Glasgow Cemetery, and where its position is indicated on the cemetery map p. 347.

   It is situated a few yards from a perimeter cemetery path on the side of the hill on which the cemetery stands. Ironically (in the light of the local millenialist movement of the 1830s) this is the hill which Stanley Spencer chose to depict as the *Hill of Zion* with the Resurrection and Last Judgment in his Port Glasgow Resurrection series of paintings 1940–1945.

21 Story in the 1829 *Peace in Believing* wrote (pp. 34–35) that Isabella's brother 'made a little garden for her in a sequestered spot, overhanging one of the waterfalls, formed by the rivulet flowing down the hill at the foot of which Fernicarry stands. . . It continued for years her favourite spot, and so long as she was able to walk, she spent in it a portion of almost every day, – a secluded oratory, well fitted for meditation and prayer'. The memorial is mentioned in Maughan's *Rosneath Past and Present*, 1893.

22 This is the new nuclear submarine fleet of four ships each with the capacity to fire one hundred and fifty-six warheads. The *Sunday Mail* of July 12th 1992 reported that on the previous Friday the first four nuclear warheads had been conveyed by lorry from Berkshire to Coulport, passing across the Kingston bridge in the centre of the city of Glasgow. A spokesman for the Scottish Campaign for Nuclear Disarmament complained that 'Over the next few years, about 500 Trident warheads will be brought through Scotland in this way'.

23 Volney was one of the writers in the *Half Hours with the Freethinkers* series

produced by the *Investigator*. It has been taken as a source for *Queen Mab*, and its influence on 'The Revolt of Islam' is discussed in Cameron, K.M.: 'A Major Source of The Revolt of Islam', PMLA Vol. 19, pp. 175–206.

24 Salt Mss. Harriet Barrs, as n. 7.

CONCLUDING APPENDIX

OF MISS BARNES AND MISS BIRKMYRE

Two references to women have caused speculation about their possible romantic involvement in Thomson's life. The following has been kept from the main text so that research could be carried on, which it was, until the book was in proof, which it now is. I thank Jonathan Cape for their patience.

When interviewing Bradlaugh and asking about the letters Thomson had written to him, Salt noted that Bradlaugh 'gave them to a Miss Barnes who was in love with Thomson'. A month later on July 3rd, 1888, Salt wrote to Dobell: 'The attempt to trace the letters to Bradlaugh has failed, as I hear from the brother of the girl to whom they were given that her papers have been lately (only *lately* – the more provoking!) destroyed. He promises, if any shd. have survived and shd. turn up, to send them to me, but I fear there is no hope of this.'

This was not the same Barnes family as that of the army schoolmaster Joseph and his wife Alice. Salt told Dobell that when he wrote to 'Mrs Barnes (of Ballincollig)' he discovered she had died four years before at her last home in Douglas, Isle of Man. Her surviving son was Rev. Charles Marston Barnes, who then wrote from Hull telling Salt that he could not help him, having been too young: 'My mother and brother who knew him well are both dead.' 'Fancy B.V. being godfather to a parson!' wrote Salt to Dobell.

The brother of the 'Miss Barnes' in question wrote from 422 Mile End Road on June 22nd 1888 signing himself T.J. Barnes Jnr. The address was that of the photographers Thomas John Barnes and Son. Tracing this to the 1861 census, it shows Thomas John then aged 20 and at that time still resident alone with his parents, having been born in St Matthew's Bethnal Green. The parish records in the Greater London Record Office give his place of birth in 1840 as West Street, and indicate a Sarah Barnes born there two years later in 1842. The 1841 census for West Street reveals another sister Mary Barnes then aged four, three years older than Thomas John Jnr. I have not located the Barneses in the 1851 census. A Sarah Barnes was married in St Matthew's Bethnal Green in 1861. In the 1841 census and in his children's birth registrations, the elder Thomas John Barnes is described, before he began his photographic business, as a 'brace maker'. Bonner (Vol. 1 p. 19), when describing the young Bradlaugh's attempts to earn a living after being expelled from the family home and before he joined the army, writes: 'For a little while he tried selling buckskin braces on commission for Thomas J. Barnes.' Tribe describes this Barnes as 'an admirer'.

In his 1888 letter to Salt, T.J. Barnes Jnr wrote: 'I remember the time though knew little of the circumstances – being younger and only occasionally a visitor at Mr. Bradlaugh's house where I met Mr Jas. Thomson several times.' This would suggest the relevant 'Miss Barnes' period as being when Thomson stayed

393

with Bradlaugh between November 1862 and October 1866. In a very arch and cryptic (without its context) letter to Mrs Bradlaugh, written in 1863 during the months that Thomson had temporarily left Bradlaugh's home to live in Queens Square, John Grant makes fun of Thomson's 'having attempted to convince thee that I – I, Grant, regard unfavourably any passive acquiescence of his in the blandishments of a taller Sal. . . than she in the sunshine of whose favours the scoundrel lazzario at present basks.' (Bradlaugh Collection, B.I. no. 112a). Possibly this letter has no romantic significance, just as Bradlaugh's statement that a Miss Barnes was in love with Thomson does not mean he thought Thomson was ever in love with her. All that Bradlaugh said in his interview with Salt was, 'Thomson idealised several women, especially one in Jersey.' The studio imprints on Thomson's portraits, it should be added, are not those of Thomas Barnes and Son.

The 'Miss Birkmyre' business is another generator of speculation. Julia Thomson wrote to Salt on September 23rd 1888: 'I may say that should a copy of Mr Thomson's answer to a letter from Miss Birkmyre ever come into your hand I am sure James would not wish it made public in any way. Her letters and his answer were in my possession for a year or two, for the purpose of silencing any gossip and sensation which might and did arise, but I gave them to him and wished him to secure them and visit at their house again thinking it might brighten his life a little having some of his own kin to go to occasionally. The mother never knew anything of the affair at all – and always made him welcome.'

Firstly it is important to distinguish between 'Miss' and 'Mrs' Helen Birkmyre, the first being the daughter of Thomson's father's sister Mrs Susan Birkmyre. Miss Helen with her widowed mother appears in the 1871 census for 6 Albert Road Teddington, Helen being then aged twenty-six, and described as a governess born in 'St James, London'. The other Helen is the daughter of Susan's twin sister Mrs Helen McLarty, whose daughter Helen married a John Birkmyre in Port Glasgow in 1855. Both Helen Birkmyres were therefore first cousins of James Thomson, the Port Glasgow Helen being the same age as Thomson, ten years older than the London Miss Helen. It was the London Miss Helen about whom Julia wrote to Salt; the Port Glasgow Mrs Helen on the other hand wrote to Salt herself, saying amongst other things that she only met her cousin as an adult in London once and that very briefly.

The word 'affair' in Julia's letter need not be understood in a sexual sense about Miss Helen Birkmyre, and there are aspects of Thomson's life which could have been meat for gossip in replies to one cousin questioning another who had been a young boy in an asylum in the city when she was a baby. Dobell may well have been pointing the finger at the Birkmyres when in his 1884 memoir he wrote, 'He had, it is true, well-to-do relatives in London, but they gave him no assistance.' Neither Dobell nor Salt repeated in print this fairly scandalous remark. Julia in another letter to Salt written eight days after the letter quoted above, implied her own criticism of relatives, albeit by default. She was worried that Salt, whom she did not know, would not be a sympathetic biographer. She listed Thomson's misfortunes including his father's stroke and the loss of his mother, and 'his going to the Caledonia School a lonely little mite'. She then began a new paragraph, 'His relations at Port Glasgow, but I will say nothing of that –'; and changed the subject.

In relation to romance, it may be appropriate here to mention another cited admirer of Thomson's, name unknown. Charles Brodie in his article on Thomson in the *Port Glasgow Express and Observer* of April 24th 1903 wrote: 'A local lady, one who loved literature, and whose death I shall always regret, knew poor "B.V." when she lived in London. Her reminiscences of him were extremely interesting. He was then a solitary but in his writings uttering his grand, majestic language of gloom, anguish, despair and unalterable pessimism. He went out from her house into the darkness one strange night and, for reasons of his own, never came back. Perhaps they have met. There is so much to be learned – Somewhere.' In the margin of his proof copy for this article Brodie wrote beside the above 'It was an affair of the heart on the lady's part.'

INDEX

Notes

T. is James Thomson
A number in brackets refers to a page in
the diaries chapter, Chapter Nineteen
(Stone on Stone)
5/32 means Chapter Five, Note 32
* under Thomson's entry means that the work
is quoted in the text
P2 means Preface, page 2